In Their Time

In Their Time

The Greatest Business Leaders
of the Twentieth Century

Anthony J. Mayo
Nitin Nohria

Harvard Business School Press
Boston, Massachusetts

Printed in the United States of America

09 08 07   5 4 3

978-1-59139-345-0 (ISBN 13)

Library of Congress Cataloging-in-Publication Data

Mayo, Anthony J.
      In their time : the greatest business leaders of the twentieth century / Anthony J. Mayo,
Nitin Nohria.
          p. cm.
      Includes bibiliographical references and index.
      ISBN 1-59139-345-0
          1. Executives—United States—History—20th century. 2. Leadership—United States—
History—20th century. 3. Success in business—United States—History—20th century.
I. Nohria, Nitin. II. Title.
      HD38.25.U6M34 2005
      338.092 '273—dc22

                                                                    2005002391

The paper used in this publication meets the minimum requirements of the American National
Standard for Information Sciences—Permanence of Paper for Printed Library Materials, ANSI
Z39.48-1992.

[CONTENTS]

Contents

It seems absurd even to have to point this out, but techniques don't change the world, nor do theories. People change the world. And this book has much to teach us about the manner of people who were able to serve as some of the greatest change agents in human annals.

In Their Time is one of the most significant business books in this new century so far, in that it single-handedly can remedy the ahistorical nature of modern studies of management and organization. In most business schools and executive training seminars today, the very concept of management is preserved and presented in small, tidy packages and case studies. Here in this volume, it bursts forth, unrestrained and exhilarating in the lessons that it teaches and the questions it provokes.

Tony Mayo and Nitin Nohria have prepared an exhaustive study of the great business executives who built the world in which we now live. Yet the book is remarkably accessible; the reader can breeze through the decades, which come wonderfully alive, as do the men and women described therein.

Any serious entrepreneur, manager, or leader will want to learn from the example of the giants detailed in these pages. There is still another compelling reason to dig deep here. This is not merely a history of great businesspersons; it is a history of the great American *consumer*, in a sense the same man or woman whom today's business executives still strive to woo and serve.

I should add that, as Mayo and Nohria point out, business has impacted our twenty-first-century world more than perhaps any other sector has. As a result, *In Their Time* is not simply for those actively engaged in business but for anyone who seeks to have a deeper understanding of the forces that shape us.

I cannot overestimate a modern business executive's need to understand the past relationship of a Robert Woodruff of Coca-Cola or a Ray Kroc of McDonald's with the American consumer. After all, one must know what the object of one's affections did and cared about yesterday in order to grasp what he or she may do or care about tomorrow.

To study the masters of the recent past is to step back and cultivate a sense of wonder for how they could stay nimble and stay aware of inflection points that heralded opportunity or crisis. These executives understood and acted on creative possibilities implicit within their own particular moment.

Mayo and Nohria illustrate applicable lessons, such as how the single-minded genius that lifted Henry Ford to the top later calcified into a stubborn deafness to the heartbeat of the consumer, or how Alfred P. Sloan Jr.'s attention to that same heartbeat drove his General Motors Corporation past the Ford empire by the end of the 1920s. This pattern was echoed recently, when Levi Strauss grew complacent about target demographics and allowed Old Navy and Gap to redefine the cool factor for youthful American casual wear.

Some years ago I wrote in *On Becoming a Leader* about how the leaders I studied and interviewed had all "mastered their context." Here, Mayo and Nohria have taken that idea further, displaying how *contextual intelligence* helped CEOs and founders and their organizations overcome the most mountainous of obstacles or chart new economic frontiers.

Emotional intelligence—"getting" other people and enabling them to "get" you—is crucial to leadership, as Daniel Goleman has shown us, but contextual intelligence goes beyond this to grasping and handling all the social, economic, and environmental factors that influence the direction an organization takes.

Howard Gardner, in *Leading Minds*, explored the notion of leader as storyteller. A good leader can capture followers' longings in words, can inspire narratives, and can even embody those narratives. The persons surveyed throughout *In Their Time* embody some of the most powerful leadership narratives conceivable: these are stories of gifted and ambitious persons grinding against fate, cajoling fortune, and prodding destiny. Accordingly, reading this book is something like sitting at a campfire, hearing legends and parables that ignite our own imaginations.

It is a shame only that we must wait several years before we receive the gift of Mayo and Nohria's sequel on another decade of business history.

—WARREN BENNIS

Distinguished Professor of Business
Administration and University Professor,
University of Southern California

[ACKNOWLEDGMENTS]

Like the paths taken by many of the individuals profiled in this book, our journey was not a linear one. It was filled with many interesting twists and turns, a few disappointments and frustrations, many difficult yet exciting challenges, and some incredible "aha!" moments. When we began our journey to create a canon of great business leaders in the summer of 2001, we had only a vague notion of the task that lay ahead. Our guides were the one thousand business executives we studied. Some were true heroes who inspired us, some were legends who awed us, and some could even be considered villains (especially looking back with a twenty-first-century lens), but most were simply individuals who made the best of their times. It is through their legacies that we were able to see the power and influence of context on leadership, and as such, it is their lives that we must first acknowledge.

The work of many individuals helped to shape and mold our research. We were particularly inspired by Professor Richard Tedlow's study "The Chief Executive Officer of the Large American Industrial Corporation in 1917." Intrigued by his comparison of CEOs from two distinct points in history, we sought to better understand CEO profiles across all decades of the twentieth century. We also drew inspiration from the seminal works of Joseph Schumpeter, Alfred Chandler, and Warren Bennis. Their groundbreaking analyses of business leadership in the twentieth century helped us crystallize our own research and especially our understanding of how context influences leadership.

In researching and writing *In Their Time*, we received generous support throughout our journey from Harvard Business School's Leadership Initiative, and the Division of Research, under the leadership of Professors Teresa Amabile and Krishna Palepu. We feel fortunate to be a part of an institution that demonstrates such a high level of commitment to its research teams. To that end, we are grateful to Kim Clark, Dean of Harvard Business School, for his support and encouragement. We are especially indebted to Professor Linda Hill, faculty chair of the Leadership Initiative, for her ongoing enthusiasm and endorsement.

At various stages in the writing process, we received guidance and advice from many individuals who graciously reviewed portions of the manuscript. We are grateful for the feedback and insights we received from Professors Warren Bennis, Monica Higgins, Linda Hill, Rakesh Khurana, John Kotter, Joseph Nye, and Scott Snook. Our gratitude also extends to Maria Farkas, Tom Gaffny, Bridget Gurtler, Sarah Kauss, Eva Maynard, Lisa Pode, Mark Rennella, and Jennifer Suesse, who provided helpful advice on various chapters. We are particularly appreciative of the contributions made by Mark Rennella; Mark was instrumental in verifying references, supporting the laborious fact-checking process, and providing important historical perspectives and connections. In addition, we are thankful for the editorial feedback provided by Lucy McCauley on chapters 5 and 6. Finally, we benefited considerably from the advice and support of Carol Franco and Melinda Merino, our editors at HBS Press. In the early stages of our research, Carol gently encouraged us to be bolder in scope and depth, while Melinda's thoughtful feedback and creative insights constantly challenged and stretched our thinking.

The arduous process of researching a thousand business executives across the twentieth century would not have been possible without the support and assistance of a number of individuals. Bridget Gurtler, in particular, deserves our thanks for her tireless efforts to find archival information in the dusty halls of Harvard's libraries. In addition, we are grateful to Chris Allen, Lindsay Greene, KC Hazarika, Albert Jiménez Howell, Kyle Klopcic, Joan McDonald, Eva Maynard, Agata Mazurowska-Rozdeiczer, Lisa Pode, Nicolay Siclunov, Laura Singleton, Monica Mullick Stallings, Jennifer Suesse, Emily Thompson, Sarah Woolverton, and James Zeitler, who provided assistance in various research-related tasks. Harvard Business School's Multimedia Department, including Laurence Bouthillier, David Habeeb, Doug Heath, and Jeffrey Martini, was incredibly helpful in the design and development of the Web-based survey. We also wish to thank Christine Fairchild and the HBS Alumni Relations team for their support in providing access to our alumni. Finally, we are deeply grateful to the staff of Baker Library, especially the Historical Collections Department, for their patience and assistance with our myriad archival requests.

The photos that accompany this book were selected based on the research efforts conducted by Alison Comings and Lisa Pode. We are particularly appreciative of Lisa's ability and willingness to take on this monumental task and complete it with efficiency, grace, and dedication. Lisa also deserves special recognition for her thoughtful proofreading of the entire manuscript.

———————

I (Tony Mayo) wish to thank my coauthor Nitin Nohria for his brilliant insights, his collaborative spirit, his infectious energy and passion, and mostly, his friendship. On a final note, I am truly grateful to my family (my wife Denise and our three children Hannah, Alexander, and Jacob) for their love and support throughout this project. Their spirited enthusiasm, unwavering faith, and constant encouragement were enormous sources of strength for me.

This book has reinforced my (Nitin Nohria's) belief in the extraordinary power of collaboration. Working with Tony Mayo has been a true privilege. Tony is not only a great student of leadership, but a great leader himself. But for his courage to plunge into the unknown and his tireless stamina to keep at it when the end was unseen, we would never have been able to take on and complete a project of this scale and scope. I have learned a great deal from him and feel fortunate that he is my colleague and friend.

This book is about leadership in context—not leadership that emerges solely from the qualities of the human character, but leadership that springs forth from an appreciation and understanding of one's situation in the world. Economic, social, and political conditions change over time, and these changes require distinct leadership styles and approaches for success. Would Walt Disney be a success in today's hypermedia environment? What about Henry Ford—would his steadfast and uncompromising focus on productivity through mass production resonate with today's automobile industry? It is hard to even imagine that someone as recently heralded as Jack Welch could lead today in the manner and approach that gave him and his company such prominence just a few years ago.

Context is vitally important because it shapes the opportunity structure of any time. The demography, technology, regulations, geopolitics, labor conditions, and social mores of any given time powerfully influence the business opportunities available. Different contexts can spawn either brand-new opportunities or opportunities to dramatically grow and expand existing businesses. In other cases, opportunities lie in restructuring declining businesses for their survival and future prosperity. Individuals as agents of will and action are equally important in this equation because they not only seize the opportunities of any specific age, but also create opportunities that define that age. Understanding how to make sense of one's time and to seize the opportunities it presents is at the heart of this book. We have come to see this sensing capability as *contextual intelligence*—the profound sensitivity to macro-level contextual factors in the creation, growth, or transformation of businesses.[1] *In Their Time* is about business legends who possessed this contextual intelligence; they had a nose for sensing opportunities and avoiding threats. Certainly, many of these legends also had distinct personal characteristics (a propensity for risk, a clear vision, a thirst for innovation, an infectious charisma, etc.), but we found that the success of these people was derived not by the mere possession of these characteristics but by the application of them within unique contextual settings. It is these legends' stories in their own times that we tell.

Our Starting Point: A Canon of Business Legends

Like many research endeavors, however, our path to this point and this book was not a linear one. When we embarked on this project in 2001, we had one goal in mind—to begin to develop a canon of business leaders. The lack of such a canon seemed to us to be a void in our field. It is inconceivable that a student of literature would not be required to study and embrace the historical classics of Homer, Shakespeare, or Whitman. It is equally inconceivable that a student of art would not study the great masters—Renoir, Monet, and Picasso. An appreciation for the history of a field and its great masters is at the core of most liberal-arts programs. History and biography provide the foundation upon which progress in these fields rests. Most fields of human knowledge seem to imbibe Pearl S. Buck's view that "knowledge of history as detailed as possible is essential if we are to comprehend the past and be prepared for the future."[2]

This appreciation of history is generally not very strong in business, though we believe that it should be. Did great business executives and enterprises not forge modern industry? Has business not been central to the progress of civilization and the rise and fall of nations? Indeed, it is hard to imagine any sphere of activity that has had a greater influence than business has on the evolution of society in the twentieth century. The day-to-day existence of Americans (and, increasingly, people around the world) bears the name of great business executives and the companies they created. The impact that these executives and their companies have on our lives is so pervasive that we rarely appreciate it; we go about our lives taking it for granted. Yet, we need only consider a typical day in our lives to see the overwhelming impact of business.

After awakening in the morning, we stumble to the bathroom and brush our teeth with Colgate or Crest toothpaste, shave with Gillette or Schick products, and shower with Ivory or Dial soap. Invigorated from our morning cleansing routine, we will probably eat a Kellogg breakfast before jumping into our GM, Ford, or Chrysler automobile to head to the office. On our way there, we often stop for a latte or tall cappuccino from Starbucks. At work, we sit in front of an Apple, an IBM, or a Dell computer running software by Microsoft, Lotus, or Oracle. At lunch, we often indulge our impulses for a Big Mac from McDonald's, pizza from Domino's, a sandwich from Subway, or a bucket of chicken from the Colonel. A cool, refreshing Coke or Pepsi hits the spot in midafternoon. On our way home, we talk on our Motorola cell phones, which are powered by AT&T and paid for by our Visa or American Express cards. Once at home, we sit in front of our Sony televisions watching shows on CNN or Disney's ABC. As dusk approaches, we turn on lights, not thinking about the work of Edison and successive generations of great General Electric CEOs who have kept their promise to "bring good things to life." By using these products and services, we are in a small way honoring the legacy of these companies and the individuals who founded or sustained them. But why are we brushing with Colgate, driving a Ford, or using an IBM computer when we could have easily used so many other products? What makes these brands enduring and others not?

Beyond recognizing their influence on our daily lives, a historical canon of business can help us better understand the origins of organizational practices we now take for granted—from the creation of organizational structures to the institutionalization of benefits to the design and implementation of the factory floor processes to the marketing launch of products to the participation of employees in profit sharing. Many aspects of business that are seemingly commonplace today were, in fact, the pathbreaking inventions of pioneering executives. Individuals who broke new ground in business policies and procedures left a broader legacy than the work of their companies or brands; these men and women often changed how we worked. For instance, the almost ubiquitous practice of product sampling today was sparked by the imagination and persistence of C. W. Post, one of the great business executives we studied. Trying to build a market for his caffeine-free coffee substitute, Postum, he brewed the caramel-flavored concoction and offered free samples to customers of local general stores throughout the upper Midwest. Though there were numerous coffee substitutes on the market, Post broke through the competition by reaching directly to the end consumer, through a practice completely unheard-of at the turn of the twentieth century. His pioneering sampling process not only made Postum a success, but also set the stage for a new business practice in the retail sector—one that has evolved over the past century.

A review of history also enables us to see the undeniable impact that business executives have had on the course of world affairs. This role was prevalent in many areas and at many times, but never more so than during times of war. Throughout the twentieth century, businesses have been important partners in U.S. defense, often converting commercial operations to defense production with unprecedented speed and efficiency. Though sometimes reluctant at first, business executives have demonstrated an uncanny ability to harness vast resources and lead monumental spikes in productivity to aid the war effort. Some of these executives should rightly be counted as members of the title group in Tom Brokaw's *Greatest Generation*, a testament to the contributions of World War II veterans.

In a speech one month before the attack on Pearl Harbor, Carle C. Conway, chairman of Continental Can Company (also in our study), noted almost prophetically: "It is American businessmen and the businesses they conduct which are performing and will increasingly perform miracles of prodigious production in our nation's emergency."[3] Time and again, business executives heeded the call of war, and their efforts, especially during World War II, helped reverse an almost unfathomable outcome. Conway concluded his speech by invoking a sense of national pride and duty: "We have the opportunity, the responsibility, yes, the sacred duty of proving for all time that under the American system of free enterprise, American businessmen, doing things the American way, can accomplish more than any other system on earth."[4] Yes, businesses benefited tremendously from war mobilization efforts, but the productive capacity that the firms unleashed had long-standing repercussions for the world as we know it today.

In addition to their abilities to penetrate all aspects of our daily lives, influence business practices, and shape global affairs, some executives need to be recognized simply for their prosaic ability to create economic value. Our own empirical research confirmed prior findings that after controlling for economic conditions, industry factors, and unique company attributes, the impact of a CEO on company performance appears to be roughly 15 percent.[5] Simply put, a change of a CEO has roughly the same impact on company performance as the industry in which the company operates (figure I-1). Imagine the implications if you are a board member. Your choice of a new CEO can be as significant as the choice to change the industry in which your company operates.

Despite the extraordinary impact of business executives, why do we not have a canon of business leadership? Perhaps it's because we believe that the primary preoccupation of an executive must be to tackle the immediate challenges at hand and to drive, as Warren Buffett has famously said, by looking through the windshield rather than the rear-view mirror.[6] No doubt, they

FIGURE I-1

Variance in company performance explained by different factors

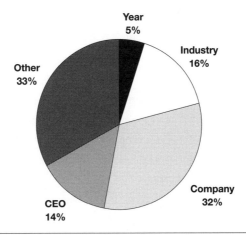

must look ahead. Yet, we contend that business executives could better address the task at hand, forge a brighter future, and leave a more lasting legacy if they understood the history of their forebears who struggled and mastered similar problems before them.

But who should be included in a canon of the most influential American business executives of the twentieth century? Which individuals were vital to the economic progress of our nation? These are the questions that we sought to address when we embarked on a path to identify the candidates for a canon—those individuals who have shaped the way we live, work, and interact. We began by identifying one thousand great CEOs and founders of American companies during the twentieth century.* We focused on this group not because we think that the only people who make a significant difference in business are the CEOs or founders, who sit at the apex of an organization. It is simply much harder (and, arguably, almost impossible) to produce even a systematic list, let alone detailed biographical information, of

---

*The methodology that we used to identify these one thousand business executives is included in the appendix of this book. For purposes of this study, all business executives were founders, chairmen, presidents, or CEOs of their respective companies. We use the terms *CEOs* and *founders* throughout this text to represent our pool of business executives.

executives in other organizational roles. Many executives who never became CEOs deserve to be recognized for their individual achievements and their contributions as members of the team that enabled the accomplishments of the CEOs and founders we do recognize. Alas, these other executives must remain the unsung heroes in our celebration of great business legends.

Our original plan was to narrow this list of a thousand down to a smaller representative group.[7] In essence, we believed that this subset would form the foundation for the canon. To that end, we surveyed seven thousand business executives, asking them to evaluate and rank our data set of one thousand CEOs and founders. From this exercise, we planned to create a "top one hundred" ranking of great American executives. The survey asked the respondents to rate candidates for inclusion in a canon of business leadership and to provide some basis for their choice. Specifically, we were interested in how the respondents interpreted what it meant to be a great business leader (figure I-2). Almost one-quarter of the respondents based their selection on a business executive's ability to articulate and harness a vision for a company. This response was followed closely by respondents who valued innovation and then by respondents who valued an executive's contribution to advancing an entire industry. Somewhat surprisingly, an executive's ability to produce stellar financial performance was the fourth most cited reason for greatness, followed by

FIGURE I-2

Survey results: Why individual executives should be considered great

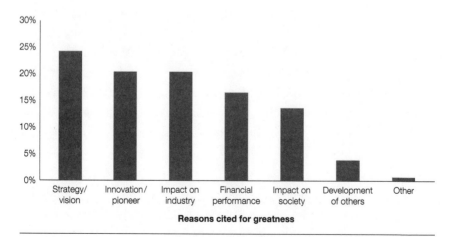

an individual's impact on society. Very few respondents attributed greatness to the executive's ability to develop others.

Though we were intrigued by the respondents' notions of greatness and did produce a top one hundred list, we realized that the analysis of the full data set of one thousand was likely to generate insights that would be lost if we simply focused on the top hundred. From the results of the survey and the rich biographical data that we had amassed, we recognized an interesting parallel between our data and the preeminent historical classifications of business executives. Specifically, when asked who should be included in a canon of business leadership, survey respondents often cited one of three prototypical executive types—the *entrepreneur*, the *manager*, and the *leader*. Our respondents' notions of greatness seemed to be aligned with one of these executive types. As we delved deeper into the lives of our one thousand business executives, our path evolved from a celebration of one hundred great business leaders and the development of a business canon to an understanding of the emergence of specific leadership archetypes over time. *In Their Time* is a direct product of this expanded scope. The book is now more than a canon of business legends. It also provides insight into how context creates different kinds of business opportunities, and how business legends can be defined by the types of opportunities they pursued. The book offers a deeper appreciation of the importance of entrepreneurs, managers, and leaders as dynamos of the capitalist system. It also highlights the importance of contextual intelligence in business.

Entrepreneurs, Managers, and Leaders

Entrepreneurs

By far, most survey respondents gravitated to the classic *entrepreneurs* of the twentieth century: those rogue individuals who broke down barriers to create something new and exciting. The celebrated rags-to-riches stories of the bootstrap entrepreneur have captured the imagination of Americans almost since the inception of the country, and it was evident from our survey that the entrepreneur's story has become woven into the fabric of the American dream. For many people, these entrepreneurs represented the quintessential values of American ingenuity, perseverance, and determination. Entrepreneurs broke molds, took risks, and stretched the imagination. Our survey

TABLE I-1

Survey results: Top one hundred business leaders

Rank	Name	Rank	Name
1	Samuel M. Walton	51	Adolph S. Ochs
2	Walter E. Disney	52	Katharine M. Graham
3	William H. Gates III	53	Elisabeth Claiborne
4	Henry Ford	54	Richard W. Sears
5	John P. Morgan	55	Paul V. Galvin
6	Alfred P. Sloan Jr.	56	Lido (Lee) A. Iacocca
7	John (Jack) F. Welch Jr.	57	Leo Burnett
8	Raymond A. Kroc	58	Edward C. Johnson III
9	William R. Hewlett	59	Howard D. Johnson
10	David Packard	60	Robert W. Johnson
11	Andrew S. Grove	61	Bernard Marcus
12	Milton S. Hershey	62	Charles E. Merrill
13	John D. Rockefeller Sr.	63	Margaret F. Rudkin
14	Thomas J. Watson Jr.	64	Leslie Wexner
15	Henry R. Luce	65	Dee Ward Hock
16	Will K. Kellogg	66	Cyrus H. McCormick Jr.
17	Warren E. Buffett	67	Stephen D. Bechtel
18	Harland Sanders	68	King C. Gillette
19	William C. Procter	69	Bernard H. Kroger
20	Thomas J. Watson Sr.	70	Edwin H. Land
21	Asa G. Candler	71	Sanford I. Weill
22	Estée Lauder	72	Franklin P. Perdue
23	Henry J. Heinz	73	Thomas S. Monaghan
24	Daniel F. Gerber Jr.	74	John G. Smale
25	James L. Kraft	75	Stanley C. Gault
26	Steven P. Jobs	76	Lammot du Pont
27	John T. Dorrance	77	Berry Gordy Jr.
28	Leon L. Bean	78	William Randolph Hearst
29	William Levitt	79	Charles Lazarus
30	Howard Schultz	80	John W. Marriott
31	Michael Dell	81	Harvey S. Firestone
32	Robert W. Johnson Jr.	82	Louis V. Gerstner Jr.
33	James E. Casey	83	David D. Glass
34	Herbert D. Kelleher	84	William L. Mellon
35	George Eastman	85	Edmund T. Pratt Jr.
36	Philip H. Knight	86	John S. Reed
37	James O. McKinsey	87	William S. Paley
38	Charles R. Schwab	88	R. David Thomas
39	Frederick W. Smith	89	William Steere Jr.
40	William Wrigley Jr.	90	Henry Ford II
41	Gordon E. Moore	91	Juan T. Trippe
42	Robert (Ted) E. Turner	92	Eli Lilly II
43	J. Willard Marriott Jr.	93	Conrad N. Hilton
44	James Burke	94	Edward C. Johnson II
45	David Sarnoff	95	Harry M. Warner
46	William E. Boeing	96	Samuel Sachs
47	Walter A. Haas	97	Jean Riboud
48	Henry J. Kaiser	98	Jean Paul Getty
49	Walter A. Haas Jr.	99	Mary Kay Ash
50	Clarence Birdseye	100	Roberto C. Goizueta

respondents heralded the accomplishments of Sam Walton, Walt Disney, Ray Kroc, Henry Ford, and Bill Gates.

The study of the entrepreneur was at the core of Joseph A. Schumpeter's work in the 1920s and 1930s. In his seminal book, *The Theory of Economic Development*, Schumpeter provided an early definition of an entrepreneur: "the carrying out of new combinations we call 'enterprise,' the individuals whose function it is to carry them out we call 'entrepreneurs.'"[8] He saw an entrepreneur as "more self-centered than other types [presumably traditional managers], because he relies less than they do on traditions and connection and because his characteristic task—theoretically as well as historically—consists precisely in breaking up old, and creating new, tradition."[9] Schumpeter studied the entrepreneur just when the industrialization of America was reaching new peaks. Individuals who capitalized on the expanding marketplace and the possibilities for new products and services were at the forefront of technological innovation, and this innovation fueled the burgeoning economy. In his follow-up work, *Capitalism, Socialism and Democracy*, which he wrote in the 1940s, Schumpeter further described the entrepreneurs: "We have seen the function of entrepreneurs is to reform or revolutionize the pattern of production by exploiting an invention, or more generally, an untried technological possibility for producing a new commodity or producing an old one in a new way, by opening up a new source of supply of materials or a new outlet for products, by reorganizing an industry and so on."[10] Schumpeter noted that the ability to overcome resistance and persevere in the creation of new entities was present in only a small fraction of the population.[11] Though this group is admittedly small, the stories of successful entrepreneurs have become a part of American folklore, and as evidenced in our survey, these business executives are often the first to be associated with greatness.

Managers

Other survey respondents were less enamored with the innovation of entrepreneurs. They heralded the steady-state, classic *managers* who thrived through discipline, structure, and organization. For these respondents, the prototypical CEO focused on proper allocation of resources, alignment of organizational elements, efficiencies of scale and scope, and predictability of superior business results. The business heroes for this group of respondents understood the zeitgeist of their times and harnessed it to create successful and efficient organizations. Managers, more than entrepreneurs, often helped an organization grow to reach its maximum potential. Classic managers like Alfred P. Sloan, J. P. Morgan, John D. Rockefeller, and James Burke represented the epitome of success.

Whereas Schumpeter emphasized the role of the entrepreneur in the early decades of the twentieth century, Alfred Chandler lionized the role of the manager in his equally seminal work, *The Visible Hand.* Although he looked at essentially the same time frames that Schumpeter did, Chandler's focus was not necessarily on the creators of new enterprises. Instead, he considered the standardization and efficient management of large-scale businesses, those formed organically and those formed through massive consolidations and mergers. The invisible forces of the market that had shaped the nature of commerce for decades were being counterbalanced by what Chandler called the visible hand of management. Chandler highlighted this visible role of management: "Whereas the activities of single-unit traditional enterprises were monitored and coordinated by market mechanisms, the producing and distributing units within a modern business enterprise are monitored and coordinated by middle managers. Top managers, in addition to evaluating and coordinating the work of middle managers, took the place of the market in allocating resources for future production and distribution. In order to carry out these functions, the managers had to invent new practices and procedures which in time became standard operating methods in managing American production and distribution."[12]

As industrialization marched forward and as technological innovations became more productive (i.e., commercialized), Chandler believed that the top manager in a business enterprise would assume control and command of the American economy.[13] As businesses matured in the middle decades of the twentieth century, Chandler saw the increasingly important role of the top manager in extracting value through standardization, organization, and structure. The actions of these managers, in turn, helped shape the economic infrastructure of the United States and, in many cases, the world.

Leaders

The third type of executive cited by still other respondents was the change agent: the *leaders* who embraced and thrived in seemingly impossible situations. These individuals saw possibilities and opportunities in businesses that others had abandoned. Breathing new life into declining companies was the modus operandi of this type of executive. Where others saw failure and demise, this breed of executive saw kernels of possibility and hope. The executives reinvented, reinvigorated, and reengineered organizations, often giving them a new purpose. For many survey respondents, Jack Welch was the hallmark of this leadership archetype. His ability to transform General Electric from a faltering industrial conglomerate into a financial, product, and services powerhouse was the essence of great leadership.[14]

The work of Warren Bennis has focused on the business executive not as an entrepreneur or as a classic manager, but as a leader. Though the words *leader* and *leadership* have become ubiquitous in American society and are often used interchangeably with *manager* and *management*, Bennis views leadership as a process of change and transformation. In *Leaders: The Strategies for Taking Charge*, Bennis and coauthor Burt Nanus note: "Effective leadership can move organizations from current to future states, create visions of potential opportunities for organizations, instill within employees commitment to change and instill new cultures and strategies in organizations that mobilize and focus energy and resources. These leaders are not born. They emerge when organizations face new problems and complexities that cannot be solved by unguided evolution. They assume responsibilities for reshaping organizational practices to adapt to environmental changes. They direct organizational changes that build confidence and empower their employees to seek new ways of doing things. They overcome resistance to change by creating visions of the future that evoke confidence in and mastery of new organizational practices."[15] For Bennis and Nanus, the leader is fundamentally an architect of change.

Leadership in Context

Though certain periods of the last century seem most aligned for the emergence and dominance of a particular type of executive (e.g., the entrepreneur in the early twentieth century, the "organization man" or manager in the post–World War II 1950s, and the change agent in the tumultuous 1980s), we found that all three types coexist and are pervasive through every decade. Beyond being present in each decade, all three archetypes were vital to sustaining the vibrancy of the capitalist system. Entrepreneurs create new businesses, managers grow and optimize them, and leaders transform them at critical inflection points. Over and over, the cycle of the American capitalist system has borne witness to this business life cycle, whose ongoing regeneration ultimately sustains development and progress.

To better understand the connection between the individual and his or her context, we sorted our one thousand business executives into the decade in which they became CEO or founded their company. Sorting our entire pool of one thousand candidates into these archetypes and their corresponding contexts provided a unique opportunity to assess the changing historical landscape of business and brought into focus the lives of individuals who influenced and were influenced by their times.[16] While there are many contextual factors at play within any era or time frame, we found that six factors—government intervention, global events, demography, social mores, technology, and labor—are especially influential in shaping business. These six factors are not exhaustive; they merely open a window into a specific era and show how different circumstances influenced the opportunity structure that the entrepreneurs, managers, and leaders of that era exploited.

Though contextual factors ebb and flow at different rates, we have organized our discussion of context by the decades of the twentieth century. Decades, we found, are a good temporal proxy for an era or a specific combination of contextual factors. Decades also have the benefit of being natural markers in how we characterize the passage of time—there is a commonsense understanding, for example, of how the 1950s were different from the 1970s. As the reader will see, the intensity of one contextual factor may be the same from one decade to the next. In other cases, one contextual factor can have a disproportionate impact on the zeitgeist of the times. But the degree, impact, and interaction of all six factors typically create a unique configuration that allows us to characterize each decade and understand the opportunities it created for entrepreneurs, managers, and leaders to make their mark. We present a brief overview of each contextual factor in this introduction. A more complete review of how these factors unfolded in each decade is presented in the subsequent chapters.

Over the course of the twentieth century, major business trends included a shifting power and influence of business in governmental policies, a fluctuating emphasis on employee rights, a rhythmic advancement of technology and the importance of innovation, a growth in consumer activism, and an intensification of competition domestically and abroad.[17] Though we spend considerable time discussing the implications of six macro-level contextual factors on

TABLE I-2

Brief overview of the six contextual factors considered in this book

Government intervention: The extent to which the U.S. government intervened in the business world influenced the degree of autonomy that a CEO or founder could exert. At times, intervention was severe—specifically during the Depression of the 1930s and the war mobilization of the 1940s—and at other times, government policies were considered laissez-faire. As the intervention ebbed and flowed, business executives needed to adapt to the changing environment; sometimes the changes provided opportunities for new businesses and unfettered competition, and other times they forced divestiture, retrenchment, and compliance.

Global affairs: Did the business executives retrench from international competition, or did they face it head-on? Were global events treated as threats or opportunities? Did the executives become ruled by arrogance, or did they seize new opportunities? The ability of individuals to adapt to and optimize global events in the twentieth century had significant consequences for their perceived and lasting greatness.

Demography: How the business executives dealt with the waves of immigration in the early and later decades of the twentieth century and the greatest internal population explosion in the United States after World War II (the baby boom) revealed these executives' ability to capitalize on the opportunities of the times. Similarly, how today's executives either embrace or reject the inherent diversity of both the population and the workforce will impact their legacy. Demography has implications for both the management of the workforce and the marketing of products and services.

Social mores: Not only did the social mores of the times significantly influence how businesses went to market with their products and services, but these social factors also played a pivotal role in determining which new businesses flourished. Of all the factors, social mores were the most cyclical. The interpretation of this contextual factor often required the greatest amount of adaptability and flexibility on the part of business executives. For some individuals, this adaptability opened doors to new opportunities; others found the requirement to adapt constricting.

Technology: The role of technology is arguably one of the strongest, if not the strongest, contextual factors to shape business in the twentieth century. The contributions that businesses have made to advancing technology and the benefits that businesses have derived from technology are immense. Technology has shaped industries, created new businesses, and spawned innumerable opportunities, yet its impact was not always immediate. It often took a visionary business executive to understand and then fulfill the potential of a specific technology.

Labor: Much like government intervention, the labor movement experienced cycles of progress and retrenchment tied to the country's overall levels of economic prosperity and opportunity. Though relatively few business executives stand out for their treatment of their workforces in the twentieth century, the ones who do are a breed apart—not just for their concern for employees, but also because, in many cases, there was no mandate or other pressure to pursue this course of action. These executives chose to manage this contextual factor before it managed them.

business creation, growth, and transformation during each decade, it is also important to understand the role of the consumer in the contextual landscape. In fact, we have placed the consumer at the center of the context-based leadership model in figure I-3. The consumer was often the key target of government regulation and protection. Fickle and demanding, the increasingly

FIGURE I-3

Context-based leadership

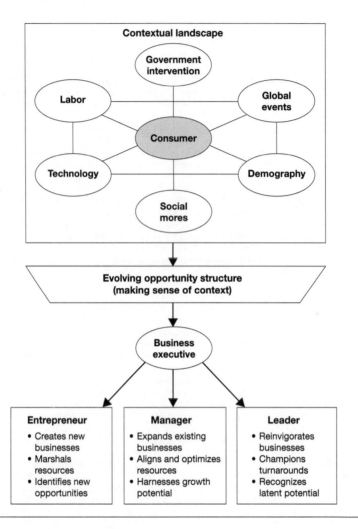

sophisticated consumer was also pivotal to the ultimate acceptance or rejection of new forms of technology. Demographic changes influenced the creation of target consumer segments, while consumers shaped and were shaped by the social mores of their times. Most important, complex consumers defined which products and services would become enduring successes and which ones would become flash-in-the-pan fads.

The ability of some business executives to sense and capitalize on new consumer opportunities was often a major component of their greatness. For other business executives, it was their ability to reinvent themselves and their businesses to revitalize product and service offerings. Some executives actually set consumer trends, while others were merely successful followers or interpreters of the trends. To be successful, business executives must be keenly attuned to the context of the times.[18] As sociologist Orrin E. Klapp once noted: "The same act performed too soon or too late or in the wrong scene may make a person a fool rather than a hero."[19] As we have noted in figure 3, there was no single path to success, and no exclusive approach to seizing opportunities created by the context of the times. Some of our great executives were like Schumpeter's entrepreneur, individuals who broke through the context of their time to forge something new. Others were like Chandler's manager, who optimized and capitalized on the opportunities of the present. And still others were like Bennis's leader, individuals who infused new life into business through the monumental impact of transformation. Table I-3 summarizes the archetypal entrepreneur, manager, and leader and their approaches to context.

By reviewing the contextual landscape and the individuals who shaped and molded it, we hope to demonstrate the critical role that understanding context can play in building and shaping lasting legacies. Through the interconnections and intersections described in each chapter, we believe that the reader will begin to develop his or her own sense of contextual intelligence.

TABLE I-3

Business executive archetypes and their approaches to context

Entrepreneur: Entrepreneurs were not necessarily bound by the context or era in which they lived. They revolutionized processes, businesses, or even whole industries. To do so, entrepreneurs often overcame seemingly insurmountable obstacles and challenges to persevere in finding or launching something new.

Manager: Managers were skilled at reading and optimizing the context of their times. They deeply understood the landscape in which they operated and took advantage of the contextual factors at play to shape and grow businesses.

Leader: Leaders fundamentally reinvigorated businesses or industries that were often at a crossroads. They consolidated businesses, reformulated product and service offerings, and restructured organizational processes to extend the life of an enterprise.

While each chapter stands on its own and could be read independently, we recommend a full reading of the book. A comprehensive review is the best way to develop a strong appreciation of the role of context in shaping business legends. If time does not permit a full reading, however, we urge the reader to explore the three chapters that exemplify the changing contextual landscape of the twentieth century. These chapters focus on the business landscape at three pivotal moments: (1) the emergence of government intervention in business affairs during the 1910s; (2) the explosion of business growth and prosperity in the post–World War II 1950s; and (3) the information-technology revolution and irrationality of the 1990s.

In the words of Martin Luther King Jr., "we are not makers of history. We are made by history."[20] By appreciating the significance of our historical landscape and contextual frameworks, we can better understand where we have been, who we are, and where we are going. Although many of the stories in this book are inspirational, they are not stories in a vacuum; the individuals profiled made the most of their times. They embraced opportunities, they maximized potential, and they confronted challenges. Who will be the business legends of the twenty-first century? What will be needed for success? What will the times bring? By understanding the history and biography of our predecessors and their approach to context, we can gain greater self-confidence in our own ability to read the times. Beyond this understanding, we hope that this book motivates or inspires our readers to make the most of their own times.

In Their Time

ONE

1900–1909

Land of Business Opportunity

"There she lies, the great Melting Pot—listen! Can't you hear the roaring and the bubbling? There gapes her mouth—the harbour where a thousand mammoth feeders come from the ends of the world to pour in their human freight. Ah, what a stirring and a seething! Celt and Latin, Slav and Teuton, Greek and Syrian, black and yellow, Jew and Gentile . . .

"Yes, East and West, and North and South, the palm and the pine, the pole and the equator, the crescent and the cross—how the great Alchemist melts and fuses them with his purging flame! Here shall they all unite to build the Republic of Man and the Kingdom of God. Ah, Vera, what is the glory of Rome and Jerusalem where all nations and races come to worship and look back, compared with the glory of America, where all races and nations come to Labor and look forward! Peace, peace, to all ye unborn millions, fated to fill this giant continent—the God of our children give you Peace."

—David, in Israel Zangwill's *The Melting-Pot*

THIS 1908 VERSION of the Romeo and Juliet saga tells the tale of a young, poor Jewish composer (David) who falls in love with the Christian daughter (Vera) of an anti-Semitic Russian nobleman. What might have been cause for ruin and despair can now be a rightful and joyous celebration, for the couple no longer resides in the closed world of Europe, but in the openness of America at the turn of the twentieth century. And in the America of the new century, it was possible for love to transcend religion, nationality, and class—or so it seemed for David and Vera in Israel Zangwill's play, *The*

Melting-Pot. Zangwill's version of America was a land of opportunity, a land of hope, and a land of freedom. The nation was on the precipice of a new world order—one that fused the cultures, traditions, and races of the globe into one great melting pot.

Zangwill's play opened to rave reviews at its 1908 debut and ran for over six months to sold-out audiences. More than its early commercial and critical success, however, the play popularized the notion of America as a melting pot—a metaphor timelessly used and examined by historians, social scientists, and demographers. Successive generations of immigrants experienced both major triumphs and heart-wrenching tragedies in trying to achieve the elusive promise of the American dream. For some, there have been tremendous opportunities and fortune, and for others only misery and poverty, but for most, the promise has resonated. While Zangwill's version of America is, in many respects, overly generous and eminently hopeful, his character David was correct when he told his betrothed Vera that America was where the world would come "to Labor and look forward." And labor they did.

America at the end of the nineteenth century and beginning of the twentieth was in the midst of a major transformation—from a rural, agrarian-based economy to an urban, industrial-based economy; from a diffuse collection of mom-and-pop establishments to big, consolidated corporations; from a Western European–infused demography to a global melting pot of multiple nationalities; and from a scattered, disconnected population to an interconnected nation. In many ways, the first decade of the twentieth century foreshadowed the continuous power struggles between business and government, between business and labor, and between business and consumers. Businesses often exerted an uneven balance of power during this decade, but that power would no longer remain unchecked. America was changing and reevaluating its perception of itself and its institutions.

Changing Landscape

The most significant factor shaping America at the dawn of the new century was its burgeoning population and changing demography. More immigrants came to the United States during this decade than any other decade, save the 1990s. The allure of the melting pot was particularly powerful, as immigrants contributed to more than half the population growth. Almost 9 million im-

TABLE 1-1

Social and demographic facts about the 1900s

- 76 million Americans in 45 states in 1900; grows to 92 million in 46 states by 1909
- Police arrest women for smoking in public
- 8,000 cars; 10 miles of paved roads
- New York enacts speed limit law: 10 mph in city, 15 mph in small towns, 20 mph in country
- W. E. B. DuBois establishes the National Association for the Advancement of Colored People
- 96 auto deaths and 115 lynchings in 1900
- 20 percent of labor force is composed of children, ages 10 to 15
- Fads: bobbed hair, nickelodeons, barbershop quartets
- Games: Ping Pong, baseball
- New words: *teddy bear, muckraker, melting pot, pork barrel*
- Average annual earnings (1900): $375
- Life expectancy (1900): 48.3 years for females, 46.3 years for males

Sources: The sources for this table and all subsequent tables on social and demographic facts for each decade are as follows: "The Basics of Business History: Top 100 Events in Chronological Order," TheStreet.Com Web site, http://www.thestreet.com/basics/countdown/747950.html (accessed 5 December 2002); George Thomas Kurian, *Datapedia of the United States: American History in Numbers*, 3rd ed. (Lanham, MD: Bernan Press, 2004); S. Mintz, "A Chronology of American History," Digital History Web site, http://www.digitalhistory.uh.edu/historyonline/chron20.cfm (accessed 15 July 2004); Allan Metcalf and David K. Barnhart, *America in So Many Words: Words That Have Shaped America* (Boston: Houghton Mifflin, 1997); Floyd Norris and Christine Bockelmann, *The New York Times Century of Business* (New York: McGraw-Hill, 2000); "One Hundred Most Important Women of the Twentieth Century," *Ladies Home Journal*, 1999; Public Broadcasting Service, "The American Experience: Technology Timeline, 1752–1990," http://www.pbs.org/wgbh/telephone/timeline/timeline_text.html (accessed 6 February 2003); Richard Robinson, *U.S. Business History: A Chronology, 1602–1988* (Westport, CT: Greenwood Publishing, 1990); "Twentieth Century Inventions 1900–1999," http://www.inventors.about.com/library/weekly/aa121599a.html (accessed 3 December 2002); "Twentieth Century Inventions 1926–1950," http://www.inventors.about.com/library/weekly/aa122299a.htm (accessed 6 February 2003); "Twentieth Century Inventions 1951–1975," http://www.inventors.about.com/library/weekly/aa122299a.htm (accessed 30 July 2003); "Twentieth Century Inventions 1976–1999," http://www.inventors.about.com/library/weekly/aa010500a.htm (accessed 30 July 2003); U.S. Bureau of the Census, *Historical Statistics of the United States, Colonial Times to 1970*, bicentennial ed. (Washington, DC: U.S. Bureau of the Census, 1975); U.S. Bureau of the Census, *Statistical Abstract of the United States: 2004–2005* (124th Edition) (Washington, DC: U.S. Bureau of Census, 2004); and Yale University, "The Formation of Modern American Culture Since 1920: Timeline," http://www.yale.edu/amstud/formac/amst191b/timeline.htm (accessed 23 June 2004).

migrants came to America's shores from 1900 to 1909, approximately three times the number that arrived in the preceding decade.[1] In one year alone, 1907, the number of immigrants peaked at 1.2 million.[2] Overall, during the first decade, the U.S. population grew from 76 million to 92 million, or by 21 percent, by far the largest rate of growth in the twentieth century.[3]

The swelling ranks of immigrants strained America's perception of itself as a tolerant and open land of opportunity and freedom. For many immigrants, there was very little in the way of a welcome. Earlier generations and their offspring saw the new wave of Asian and Eastern European immigrants as a

Immigrants waiting to take the ferry to New York from Ellis Island in 1900; 9 million immigrants came to America during the first decade of the twentieth century. (Source: Bettmann/CORBIS)

threat to their employment opportunities. The animosity between newly arrived immigrants and current residents was always simmering below the surface. The brewing antagonism was mitigated only by the abundant employment opportunities created by the exploding industrial base of the country. Individuals were often employed in dangerous or unsanitary conditions, or both, but despite these circumstances, there was strong antiunion sentiment—if you didn't like your job, there was a line of immigrants ready and willing to take it from you.

The massive influx of immigrants played an important role in transforming not only the literal face of America and its workforce but also the concentration of its population. In particular, immigrants contributed to the already rapid growth of the country's urban population. Between 1870 and 1900, American cities grew at a phenomenal rate in every section of the country. In the West, Seattle's population increased from 1,107 to 80,000, Los Angeles from 5,700 to 102,000, and Denver from 4,700 to 133,000. Further east, Chicago's population expanded from 298,000 to 1.7 million, and New York from 942,000 to 3.4 million. And in the South, Birmingham, which was only founded in 1871, leaped to a population of 132,000 in less than thirty years.[4]

This concentration of individuals in growing cities led to an enormous number of opportunities for businesses, including the creation and expansion of a variety of food-based enterprises. Prepared foods became more important, as city dwellers tended to work very long hours and had little time or space to grow their own food or prepare their own meals. With the average worker in America logging sixty hours per week, there was less time to address the myriad number of household chores.[5] For many immigrant families, it was also not unusual for an entire family to work long hours—which created an even greater need for convenience and accessibility to prepared goods. This decade also saw a number of advances in technology aimed at making the home or apartment more efficient and tolerable; the improvements included indoor plumbing and centralized heating.

While the city landscape changed dramatically, its rural counterpart experienced its own transformation. In 1893, through a ten thousand dollar Congressional appropriation, rural free delivery (RFD) routes were adopted by the Post Office Department. The routes provided mail service to a whole new constituency. For the first time, rural residents had access to frequent mail deliveries. In prior years, mail delivery required a sometimes day-long excursion into town to visit the local general store. This new rural access was tapped by a number of enterprising businessmen, including Richard Sears and Aaron Montgomery Ward, both of whose catalogs became so popular that they were the second most widely read books in the country (second only to the Bible) for several decades. Through the efforts of these businessmen, products became more affordable across the country, and the masses could now purchase and enjoy items that were previously available only to elite urban dwellers.

Beyond tapping into a new market, RFD routes played a significant role in continuing the development of roads, bridges, and rail lines throughout the country. The growing interconnections of the nation provided a means to level and accelerate the flow of information, enabling newspapers and magazines to reach a much broader audience in a timely fashion.

The Sears, Roebuck and Co. catalog brought a host of new products to rural America. (Source: Bettmann/CORBIS)

This opportunity was not lost on the early newspaper executives, including William Randolph Hearst of American Newspapers, Harrison Otis of the *Los Angeles Times*, Adolph Ochs of the *New York Times*, and Robert Abbott of the *Chicago Defender*. With this growing and increasingly accessible audience, public opinion became more important. When cultivated and nurtured, it could influence a community, a region, or an entire nation. An influential group of social and political activists who became known as Progressives capitalized on this emerging opportunity to reach far and wide with their messages.

Progressivism Takes Root in Society

Broadly described, Progressivism was a movement of America's new and evolving middle class to eradicate corruption in government and especially in big business. Progressives believed that businesses wielded too much power— power that controlled the labor force as well as the output and distribution of goods and services. Progressives also believed that the government was overly lenient in its treatment of corporations, which were essentially allowed to define and set their own rules of operation.[6] For many people, especially those within the lower socioeconomic strata, these concerns were not new; poorer people had been fighting, however unsuccessfully, to be heard for many decades. In many ways, their movement gained popularity and traction only when, as many historians have noted, their cause was co-opted by the emerging middle class in America and plastered in the nation's newspapers.

The first decade of the twentieth century saw a number of important investigative works aimed at exposing alleged corruption. They included Henry Demarest Lloyd's *Wealth Against Commonwealth*, which exposed the overly influential role of monopolies in controlling government policies; Ida M. Tarbell's controversial *History of Standard Oil Company*, which documented the questionable practices of John D. Rockefeller's oil giant; and Lincoln Steffens's *Shame of the Cities*, which detailed municipal scandals. It was President Theodore Roosevelt who labeled these investigative journalists and others like them "muckrakers" after a character in John Bunyan's *Pilgrim's Progress*. The character could look no way but downward with a muckrake in his hands. "The 'muckrakers' are often indispensable to . . . society," Roosevelt said, "but only if they know when to stop raking the muck."[7] And in Roosevelt's view, many of the muckrakers did not know when to stop.

As important as the work of the muckrakers was in exposing corruption and calling for change in business and government relations, it was only a first step. The concrete change in the Progressive movement actually came through the actions of Roosevelt. Though *delicate* would not be the first characteristic to come to mind if one were describing Roosevelt, he did, in fact, walk a very delicate line between enforcing dramatic change without fully alienating the business community. Roosevelt did so by championing some of the less controversial causes of the Progressives—namely, the fair treatment and employment of women and children. Although there was still some resistance to any form of labor progress, a stance against women and children was hardly a winnable position (anymore). On the business front, Roosevelt staunchly defended the rights of big business and worked for controls and regulations that enabled greater efficiency and progress in manufacturing, not dismemberment of the organization: "The mechanism of modern business is so delicate that extreme care must be taken not to interfere with it in a spirit of rashness or ignorance."[8] He sought not to eliminate business combinations but to supervise them.

Government Flexes Its Muscle

Though he advocated caution, Roosevelt greatly accelerated the pace of government intervention in business by enforcing the Sherman Antitrust Act, which had been adopted in 1890 to regulate and control monopolies. Prior to Roosevelt's administration, the Sherman Antitrust Act was rarely utilized to contain business expansion. Roosevelt initiated over twenty-five antitrust suits during his seven years in office, starting with the fight to control the nation's railroads.[9] Railroad ownership in the late nineteenth and early twentieth century epitomized the height of corporate success. Two of the preeminent railroad barons, James J. Hill, who controlled the Great Northern Railroad, and Edward H. Harriman, who controlled the Union Pacific Railroad, fought to gain control of the Northern Pacific Railroad—a line that flowed through the important city of Chicago and served the growing northern Midwest region. Their fight for the Northern Pacific line created rampant speculation in the stock market as Hill and Harriman attempted to buy up all possible shares in the railroad. The *New York Times* reported on the scheme: "In the stock market, it is possible to sell stock that you do not own—that is, to sell short. A substantial number of investors did just that as the price of Northern Pacific soared to levels completely unjustified by the railroad's profits. Those investors thought that they would profit [sell short] when the share price fell back. Between them, [J. P.] Morgan [who was backing Hill] and Harriman's camps had bought more shares of Northern Pacific than existed. That meant they could force the short-sellers to pay them any price they wanted to close out the short positions. The realization that that had happened produced panic on Wall Street."[10]

Speculators who bet that the Northern Pacific stock price would fall to a more reasonable level were unprepared for its continued rise. The escalating stock price created a very unstable and untenable situation on Wall Street, thereby eliciting panic and ruin for many speculators. Hill's and Harriman's warring efforts eventually pushed the railroad's stock price to the unrealistic and unsustainable level of one thousand dollars per share (before the power struggle, the stock had been trading for roughly 10 percent of this amount). Being unable to outbid each other and hoping to avert even more widespread panic, Hill and Harriman, with the assistance of financier J. P. Morgan, de-

Railroads connected the expanding American landscape, providing an efficient means for distribution as well as travel. (Source: Bettmann/CORBIS)

cided to cease their independent battles for Northern Pacific. Instead, they joined forces through the creation of Northern Securities Company—a holding company that essentially controlled the vast majority of the nation's midwestern and western rail lines. At the time of the combination in 1901, Northern Securities was the largest holding company in the nation.

With pressure from speculators who were ruined from the fight and subsequent collusion of the railroad titans, Roosevelt enacted the provisions of the Sherman Antitrust Act and filed suit against Northern Securities Company in 1902. The suit eventually made its way to the U.S. Supreme Court, which ruled against the Northern Securities Company, forcing it to dissolve. The government's intervention in dissolving the monopoly power of these railroad barons inspired confidence in the Progressive movement that championed the next major antitrust lawsuit against the beef trust. In 1902, Gustavus F. Swift, John Ogden Armour, and four other business executives were accused of colluding to control the price and distribution of beef.[11] With injunctions leveled against them, the meat packers attempted to consolidate their operations into one large beef trust, and it was this trust that caught the ire of federal regulators. Like Northern Securities, the beef trust was eventually forced to disband. This was only the first defeat suffered by the meat packers. The second one was much more costly, both politically and socially.

For years, various splintered groups tried to organize a set of laws and other regulations to protect consumers from the potential hazards of prepared foods and drugs. In fact, over the course of the preceding two decades, "at least 190 bills concerning food and drug regulation were considered [by Congress] and defeated."[12] Even the popular support of several muckrakers could not break the logjam. It took a socialist sympathizer, Upton Sinclair, to bring about significant change. Through his publication of *The Jungle* in article form in 1905 and later in book form in 1906, Sinclair exposed the inner workings and corruption of the meatpacking industry. His vivid and detailed descriptions of the unsanitary and unsafe working conditions within the meatpacking factories caused such a stir in America that Roosevelt was compelled to authorize a government investigation. Through his publication, Sinclair had hoped to spark interest in the fair treatment of employees and garner support for socialism, but his detailed account of rat-infested meat being processed into sausages and other beef products caused outrage and alarm. Instead of a concerted socialist movement, Sinclair secured a different type of movement. On the heels of his exposé and the confirming Roosevelt investigation, the Pure Food and Drug Act and the Meat Inspection Act were passed in 1906. These acts placed new restrictions and operating standards on manufacturers, and though they were considered unprecedented at the time, they were only precursors to tougher food and drug regulations passed in the 1930s.

Even though Roosevelt exerted pressure to control large businesses, he was not above asking for a handout when the country was in dire straits. This situation was dramatically illustrated during the Wall Street panic of 1907, when an international liquidity crisis forced many U.S.-based trusts to call in speculative loans that further reduced the global money supply. Lacking a central federal banking entity to manage the crisis, Roosevelt's government turned to financiers such as J. P. Morgan and James Stillman (National City Bank) to provide liquidity to the trusts affected. The group of financiers essentially functioned as a quasi-central banking syndicate. Their power, through their access to capital, was stronger than that of the government, and Morgan and Stillman's actions were regarded with both praise and disdain. Though heralded as heroes in averting a far more dangerous financial crisis, Morgan and Stillman were viewed as too powerful. The panic of 1907 set the stage for the eventual creation of a central bank through the adoption of the Federal Reserve Act in 1913.[13] Here we see how business executives were influenced by, and in turn, have influenced important regulations that have had an enduring impact on American business.

Though Roosevelt and his legal team secured several regulatory "busts" and Roosevelt's personal reputation as a trustbuster became legendary, his presidency was fraught with contradictions on this score. Roosevelt was a strong proponent of size; he believed that larger businesses were more efficient and more productive than smaller entities, and he often fought to protect corporate rights. His efforts to rein in large companies were not centered on their inherent bigness, but rather on how they exercised control in dealing with their constituents.[14] Despite Roosevelt's reputation as a bona fide trustbuster, his handpicked successor, William Howard Taft, initiated more antitrust suits and did more to increase the government's control over the nation's businesses. In the four years of his administration, Taft pursued ninety antitrust suits, which was far more than Roosevelt pursued in seven years.[15]

Though he is less known for his far-reaching policies than Roosevelt, Taft's push to secure the passage of the Tariff Act of 1909 did much to change the relationship between government and business. The Tariff Act imposed an excise tax on corporations and authorized the Internal Revenue Service to audit corporate records to ensure compliance with the new law.[16] This seemingly simple provision to allow the IRS to examine and audit a corporation's financial records had significant implications. It forced businesses to shed the veil of secrecy that had so long protected personal and private interests, and the need for efficient inspection also contributed to the growing standardization of accounting principles, practices, and procedures. Roosevelt and Taft did much to redefine the role of business and government relations in the first decade of the twentieth century, though they did far less to recalibrate relationships between business and labor.

Labor Organizes

At the turn of the century, 11 million (or 42 percent) of the 26 million employed Americans worked in agriculture, and of the 15 million nonfarm workers, only 500,000 were union members.[17] Labor's first major opportunity in the new century came with the celebrated strike of the anthracite coal miners in 1902. The coal miners sought an increase in wages, safer and otherwise better working conditions, and recognition as a bargaining unit. Their concerns, though not unique, were given public prominence during the strike, as the coal that these miners extracted was used as a primary heating source for several communities and states. The emerging national media played a role in fueling the public outcry.

Fearing a critical shortage during the winter months, the public pressured the government to step into the contentious fray between the mine owners and coal workers. Bowing to public pressure, Roosevelt intervened. He invited the principal representatives of both the company and the employees to the White House to orchestrate a reconciliation. Though the hoped-for reconciliation did not materialize at this meeting, what did occur was far more important. This was the first time that the government gave labor a seat at the table, and the symbolic meaning of this gesture reverberated throughout the country. Government had always been seen as an impartial friend of business, and with this invitation, that perception began to change. The strike was eventually settled, with the workers receiving a 10 percent raise in wages and some minor working condition concessions. Though the workers lost the larger battle for formal representation, their efforts galvanized the overall union movement in the country.[18] Within one year of the strike, the number of workers with union representation increased to over 2 million.[19]

The recognition of the union concerns by government in the anthracite coal miners strike was followed by another symbolic act by Roosevelt—the creation of the Department of Commerce and Labor. Roosevelt made this a cabinet-level entity that included oversight of the Bureau of Labor and the Bureau of Corporations. Its charter was to "investigate and provide information on corporations, industrial working conditions, and labor management disputes."[20] Though the department initially concentrated on the collection, analysis, and dissemination of market and labor statistics for the benefit of new and existing corporations, the mere fact that a cabinet-level group had been created to focus on labor issues was viewed as a success. By 1913, the organization split into the Department of Commerce (focusing on business and market information and statistics) and the Department of Labor (focusing on industrial labor-management issues).

Though these two events—the coal miners strike and the creation of the Department of Commerce and Labor—gave hope and encouragement to the labor movement, the working conditions and pay for most laborers were nevertheless appalling and repressive. During this decade, the Supreme Court even overturned a New York State law limiting the hours of bakers to ten hours a day—"the court ruled that the law violated the right of the workers to enter into a contract to work longer hours."[21] Essentially, businesses were granted the freedom to contract with workers in any manner they saw fit, with little threat of state or federal intervention. State and federal minimum wage and maximum working hours were years away from adoption.

While there was a concerted effort to reach out to certain immigrant groups in the labor movement, black Americans were virtually ignored. Of the 9 million African Americans in America, almost 90 percent lived in the South and the vast majority were employed in agriculture. Apart from their legal freedom, very little had changed for black people at the turn of the century. In fact, in 1896 the landmark *Plessy v. Ferguson* case was decided by the U.S. Supreme Court, which established the concept and practice of "separate but equal" as constitutionally protected. This ruling did much to seal the fate of African Americans for more than half the century. Separate but equal was also often the only path for black business executives, who faced some of the stiffest challenges during the twentieth century. They often had to break through far more difficult barriers to achieve success than did their white counterparts. The work of Madam C. J. Walker (born Sarah Breedlove) is a case in point.

Over the course of thirteen years, Walker went from a washerwoman in St. Louis earning $1.50 per day to the owner and president of the largest black-owned business in the United States. Walker was orphaned at age eight, married at fourteen, a mother at eighteen, and a widow by twenty. As a single mother of a two-year-old, Walker was forced to support her daughter in one of the few jobs that were open to African American women at the turn of the century, a laundress, or washerwoman. Walker toiled as a laundress for eighteen years, during which time she was constantly subjected to harsh chemicals produced by the steaming process in the laundry preparation. The constant exposure to these steaming vapors and the stress of her occupation caused Walker to lose some of her hair, and it was this personal hardship that set her on a quest to develop a remedy.

The invention of what became known as the Walker Hair Growing System is shrouded in mystery. Was it dream-induced divine inspiration as Walker recounted or a simple case of corporate espionage as claimed by an early competitor? Regardless of the source, Walker created a breakthrough product and system of distribution that became the precursor to future personal-care consultants. In 1907, Walker began selling her "Hair Grower" product door to door. She soon developed a networked model of sales agents across the southern and eastern United States. Though David McConnell of Avon Products had established the door-to-door selling of personal care products in the late 1880s, Walker was the first to specifically target African American women as both agents and clients.

Just eight years after leaving her job as a laundress, Madam Walker held a national convention for two hundred Walker agents in Philadelphia, which established a precedent for managing and inspiring direct-sales organizations. Agents were recognized equally for their personal sales accomplishments and their philanthropic activities within their home communities. Within a few years, the number of Walker agents expanded to over twenty thousand, and Walker became the first self-made female millionaire in U.S. history.[22] Walker stands out among business executives because she was able to break through not only her destitute beginnings but also the formidable barriers to success for all women and minorities in business.

Walker's early employment experience as a laundress, however, was clearly more representative of the times, and though working conditions were unsafe and pay was extremely low, what workers wanted most of all was a sense of job security. It was this lack of security that made working unbearably long hours palatable, for one never knew when the job might end. In many ways, the plight of the worker was akin to the survival of the fittest. Those who could persevere through the tough conditions were often given opportunities to secure a solid future for their families and themselves. The success of some brought at least a little validity to the melting-pot dream.

A Global Debut

While the melting pot continued to stir within America's own borders, the country took some tentative steps to expand its presence on the world stage. Roosevelt, who had earned a large part of his national reputation and stature through his efforts to exert American military prowess in the waning years of the nineteenth century, was all too willing to explore global possibilities. Though Roosevelt worked to guard against the imperialistic tendencies of Europe, he had few misgivings about expanding U.S. influence outside its borders, which was especially evident in the aftermath of the Spanish American War.

The Spanish American War evolved out of Cuba's fight for independence from Spain; it was a struggle that Cuba had endured for almost half a century and that the United States had politely ignored for many years. The U.S. ability to stay neutral in Cuba's relationship with Spain was put to the test when the American battleship *Maine* exploded in Havana harbor in 1898 killing 266 men. At the time, there was wide speculation that Spain had precipitated the attack on the *Maine*. Subsequent evidence demonstrated that the explosion was caused not by military action but by an internal accident in the ship's coal bunker. The lack of irrefutable evidence, however, did not stop the "yellow press" from reporting the explosion as military aggression, and Roosevelt, as assistant secretary of the navy, did little to squelch these rumors.

Roosevelt's constant urgings and public grandstanding, combined with the full weight of the nation's newspapers, placed incredible pressure on President William McKinley to exert military control in the Caribbean. McKinley succumbed to the pressure, and with the backing of the U.S. Congress, he demanded the independence of Cuba and declared war against Spain. The war was fought on two fronts and lasted only four months, but its implications were dramatic and far-reaching. With Roosevelt's authorization, a U.S. Navy fleet, under Commodore George Dewey, took control of the Spanish-controlled Philippine Islands with minimal resistance. Though the Philippines were not directly involved in Cuba's plight, Roosevelt sought to distract the Spanish forces with a bold pan-oceanic attack. Roosevelt himself led a team of Rough Riders (cavalry on horseback) into Cuba to liberate the island. The battles were swift and one-sided.[23] The United States did not stop with the Philippines and Cuba, but went on to take possession of Spanish-controlled Puerto Rico, also with minimal resistance. The peace treaty that ended the war was signed in August 1898. It gave Cuba its freedom, albeit with many concessions, including the permanent installation of a U.S. military base on Guantánamo Bay. In the aftermath of the war, the United States acquired three new territories—the Philippines, Puerto Rico, and Guam. Spain's defeat simultaneously marked the end of its empire and the ascendance of the United States as one of the world's major powers.[24]

Following the Spanish American War, Roosevelt believed that America should take the lead in overseeing developments in its own hemisphere, a sentiment shared by many business executives who saw vast opportunity beyond the boundaries of the United States, both as sources of raw material and as potential new markets. Roosevelt's primary effort to exert control of the region and the transportation of goods was centered on the design and development of a water route between the Atlantic and the Pacific oceans. Having failed to reach an agreement with the Colombian government, which controlled the Panama territory at the turn of the century, Roosevelt helped support an independence movement in 1903. Deploying American ships as a deterrent to the Colombian army, Roosevelt was successful in helping Panama achieve its independence. He used his influence to secure the rights to a canal at terms very favorable to the United States. Roosevelt's trip to oversee the progress of the Panama Canal in 1906 marked the first international trip for a sitting U.S. president.[25] Although the Panama Canal became an important

Early construction of the Gatan Locks in the Panama Canal. (Source: Underwood & Underwood/ CORBIS)

trade route after it opened in 1914, its initial purpose was to showcase the military and technological prowess of the United States.

Technology Foundation

From the ocean-bridging waterways of the Panama Canal to the continent-spanning rails of the American West, the early innovators of the twentieth century attempted to shape and control their environment. The development of the steam engine and advances in the design and use of dynamite and other explosives are but two significant innovations that fundamentally altered the American landscape. Both contributed to the golden age of the railroad. Another key component to the expanding rail system was the newfound efficiency in the fast-growing steel industry. The open-hearth furnace, perfected in 1900, was a pivotal breakthrough in the manufacture of more efficient and cost-effective steel. The new production efficiency increased supply and made steel more readily accessible for railway expansion.

Arguably, the most important innovation of the first decade (and possibly of any other decade) was the horseless carriage, or automobile. This single invention spawned numerous businesses and did much to further connect the lives of Americans through new roadways, jobs, and status symbols. Like many other innovations, though, the automobile would not gain significant market coverage until productivity and design innovations made the personal vehicle both affordable and accessible.

Beyond transforming the American frontier in this decade and in subsequent ones, technical innovations became a primary path to business success, especially when they could be easily commercialized. For instance, the advances in electricity championed by George Westinghouse and Thomas Edison fundamentally changed the lives of Americans everywhere. One of the first to recognize the commercial significance of this technology was Edison's colleague Charles Coffin, the first president of General Electric Company. Coffin commissioned and funded an internal research and development department within GE. In doing so, he redefined the role of technology in business expansion and growth. Following on this same path, Earl Richardson and George Hughes invented the electric iron and electric range, respectively, and did much to create demand for the burgeoning electric utility industry in the country. Other notable innovators were Leo Baekeland, who was credited with creating the first substances made of plastic; Walter Kohler, who made indoor plumbing a viable option for the masses; and John Underwood, who perfected the design of the first "visible typewriter," enabling typists to see their words while they typed. The first decade was replete with pioneers and inventors like these, whose discoveries fundamentally redefined the American way of life.

Managers: Size Matters . . . Bigger Is Better

As the industrial revolution marched forward, several businesses capitalized on the country's interconnected and newly opened railway systems and access to cheap and abundant raw materials. More important, managers understood the power that businesses could wield and the advantages of size and scale to service the growing nation. This decade bore witness to the first massive wave of consolidation and the first efforts to achieve economies through vertical integration. Financiers like J. P. Morgan, Andrew W. Mellon, Philip Lehman,

TABLE 1-2

Business events that shaped the 1900s

Date	Event
1900	Hawaii and Puerto Rico become U.S. territories
1901	Consolidation of U.S. Steel Corporation, first billion-dollar corporation
1901	Oil discovered in Texas (Spindletop)
1902	Willis Carrier invents the air conditioner
1902	President Theodore Roosevelt mediates Pennsylvania coal strike
1902	United States creates Bureau of Census
1903	Wright brothers invent the first gas-powered and manned airplane
1903	Congress creates Department of Commerce and Labor
1903	Panama declares independence, signs canal pact with United States
1904	First nickelodeon theater opens, in Pittsburgh
1904	Supreme Court dissolves Northern Securities
1904	Work begins on Panama Canal
1905	Supreme Court indicts beef trust
1905	Sears opens Chicago mail-order plant
1905	First drive-in gas station opens, in St. Louis
1906	Upton Sinclair publishes *The Jungle*, exposing unsafe working conditions in meatpacking industry
1906	Congress passes Pure Food and Drug Act
1907	U.S. immigration peaks
1907	Wall Street panic prompts a run on banks; J. P. Morgan and other financiers intervene
1908	First Ford Model T sold
1909	Bakelite (first synthetic plastic) introduced by Leo Baekeland
1909	Congress passes corporate income tax

Sources: The sources used for this table and all subsequent tables on business events for each decade are as follows: "The Basics of Business History: Top 100 Events in Chronological Order," TheStreet.Com Web site, http://www.thestreet.com/basics/countdown/747950.html (accessed 5 December 2002); S. Mintz, "A Chronology of American History," Digital History Web site, http://www.digitalhistory.uh.edu/historyonline/chron20.cfm (accessed 15 July 2004); Allan Metcalf and David K. Barnhart, *America in So Many Words: Words That Have Shaped America* (Boston: Houghton Mifflin, 1997); Floyd Norris and Christine Bockelmann, *The New York Times Century of Business* (New York: McGraw-Hill, 2000); "100 Most Important Women of the 20th Century," *Ladies Home Journal*, 1999; Public Broadcasting Service, "The American Experience: Technology Timeline, 1752–1990," http://www.pbs.org/wgbh/telephone/timeline/timeline_text.html (accessed 6 February 2003); Richard Robinson, *U.S. Business History: A Chronology, 1602–1988* (Westport, CT: Greenwood Publishing, 1990); "Twentieth Century Inventions 1900–1999," http://www.inventors.about.com/library/weekly/aa121599a.html (accessed 3 December 2002); "Twentieth Century Inventions 1926–1950," http://www.inventors.about.com/library/weekly/aa122299a.htm (accessed 6 February 2003); "Twentieth Century Inventions 1951–1975," http://www.inventors.about.com/library/weekly/aa122299a.htm (accessed 30 July 2003); "Twentieth Century Inventions 1976–1999," http://www.inventors.about.com/library/weekly/aa010500a.htm (accessed 30 July 2003); and Yale University, "The Formation of Modern American Culture Since 1920: Timeline," http://www.yale.edu/amstud/formac/amst191b/timeline.htm (accessed 23 June 2004).

and Samuel Sachs were extremely influential in providing financing mechanisms to create business consolidations like U.S. Steel Corporation, which was formed in 1901 through the merger of ten steel companies. Its formation created the first billion-dollar corporation in the United States.[26]

Others who saw the potential for early industry consolidation included Charles F. Brooker, who controlled the U.S. brass industry for sixty-five years by buying up his competitors; Eldridge A. Stuart, who controlled the country's supply of evaporated milk; and Thomas C. du Pont, who consolidated the nation's gunpowder supplies. Two individuals whose consolidations provoked antitrust suits were Cyrus H. McCormack Jr. and James B. Duke. McCormack's combination of several farm machinery providers into International Harvester Corporation in 1902 controlled over 85 percent of the harvester and reaper business in the country, and Duke's American Tobacco Company, which resulted from the merger of five major cigarette makers, controlled 90 percent of the nation's cigarette business in the early 1900s.[27] Although International Harvester eventually withstood the antitrust suits, American Tobacco became a victim of government intervention. In the end, however, both companies reaped enormous financial, political, and social clout.

Notwithstanding the risks of government intervention, business executives who saw the consolidation opportunity early were often the most successful. They were not necessarily the first to start a new business, but they were among the first to seize upon the opportunities of concentration especially as businesses and whole industries matured. An optimum business in 1900 was a big one that could absorb unskilled labor, operate essentially unscathed from growing consumer or political actions, and reach a vast array of customers. Clarence M. Woolley, who played a pivotal role in modernizing the new American home, saw the vast potential, in his time, for consolidation, standardization, and operational efficiency.

Clarence M. Woolley (1863–1956), American Radiator Company

The odds are that you see the American Standard name or logo every day, and most likely several times a day. The name is associated with some of our most personal and private moments, yet it is probably only vaguely familiar to most of us. The last time you washed your hands, cleaned the dishes, or flushed the toilet, it is likely that you used an American Standard product; its logo is in more than 60 percent of the bathrooms in the world.[28] This company name was the shortened version of the American Radiator & Standard Sanitary Company, which was derived from the merger of the American Radiator Company and the Standard Sanitary Manufacturing Company in 1929—a merger championed by Woolley. This was not his first merger. In fact, the merger with the Standard Sanitary Manufacturing Company culminated a series of mergers and acquisitions that transformed the American Radiator Company into a worldwide provider of building and home supplies.

Woolley hailed from Michigan and spent his entire career in the manufacturing world—first as a consummate salesman and later as a skillful organizer and manager of a global network of manufacturing and distribution facilities. He left the public schools of Detroit in 1878, at the age of fifteen, to work as an office clerk with Fisk & Company, a wholesale crockery firm, where over the next eight years he advanced to the position of general manager. Though doing quite well with Fisk & Company, Woolley opted to leave the firm in 1887 to pursue an exciting new venture—the production and sale of an indoor heating device, the radiator.[29]

During the 1800s, the open fireplace gave way to the iron stove as the principal heating source for many American homes. Iron stoves fueled by wood or coal were also the principal heating source of most businesses throughout the first half of the nineteenth century. Things began to change after the Civil War with the advent of the modern office building and apartment complex; these new building designs demanded a more feasible and practical source for heating. The building owners' desires to avoid the practical limitations of multiple heating sources within a multilevel facility became the impetus for the advancement of central-heating technology.

Businesses were drawn to central heating less out of altruism and concern for their employees but more for what it meant for increased productivity. Out of this desire for greater productivity, the demand for new and more efficient heating mechanisms grew, and with it, a concentrated effort at perfecting the technology. Once central heating was adopted by businesses and wealthy Americans, who could initially afford the costly heating system, demand grew in other sectors of society, especially in the burgeoning urban centers in the country. The growing demand created further impetus to improve the efficiency of the design and reduce the operational price. As historian

Daniel Boorstin has asserted, the development of the radiator was another example of "democratizing luxuries for Americans"—essentially taking a premium, exclusive product and, through demand creation and greater production efficiencies, leveling the access to it.[30] The development of the practical radiator in 1874 by William Baldwin was the natural result and extension of leveling the playing field. Baldwin's radiator functioned as an efficient and relatively space-conscious advancement in the distribution of steam or hot water from a central-heating plant (for businesses) or furnace (for homes). The original radiator designs were made of expensive custom-designed steel components, but over the next fifteen years, the steel frame gave way to a less expensive and easily standardized cast-iron version.

Michigan Radiator and Iron Company, which Woolley joined in 1887, sought to capitalize on the standardization of the radiator. Woolley, more than most executives at the firm, personally benefited from this convergence of technology and market growth. As the principal salesperson for the firm, Woolley achieved tremendous success; by the 1890s, he was making in excess of $150,000 a year.[31] Five years after joining the firm, Woolley helped organize its first major consolidation effort, bringing together Michigan Radiator and Iron Company with the Detroit Radiator Company and the Pierce Steam Heating Company to form the American Radiator Company in 1892. The new consolidation enabled American Radiator to gain an early leadership role in capturing domestic market share and the manufacturing wherewithal to enter the European marketplace. Woolley was instrumental in helping American Radiator establish distribution centers and, later, manufacturing concerns throughout Europe by capitalizing on the firm's ability to offer a standardized product in an efficient and cost effective manner. He entered Europe in 1893 principally as a means to weather an economic downturn in the United States, and American Radiator was very successful in penetrating the market. Under Woolley's direction, the firm responded with products and services that were sensitive to European tastes, styles, and specifications.[32]

Woolley's success in the United States and Europe garnered the attention of financier J. P. Morgan, who helped Woolley consolidate virtually all radiator manufacturers in the United States in 1899. Woolley and Morgan were quick to capitalize on the development of a consolidated business trust to serve even broader market segments with greater manufacturing efficiencies and capabilities. Though their consolidation efforts did not provoke the government's antitrust sentiments, one historian of the heating and ventilation industry has referred to American Radiator as the "Microsoft of its time." One of the first companies to use advertising in the central-heating industry, American Radiator boasted in its ads: "the largest makers of radiators in the world."[33]

Though Woolley was officially elected president of American Radiator Company in 1902, he had served as the firm's principal leadership figure during the waves of consolidations that he orchestrated with Morgan. Early on, Woolley recognized the benefits of leveraging scale and scope to capture market share. He worked to further standardize the radiator design to achieve greater volume efficiencies and economies, and he supplemented this internal investment with an ongoing acquisition effort. By buying his competitors, he reasoned that he was in a stronger position to continue to optimize his operation. In a sense, he could dictate standard designs and processes by buying up the competition. Woolley's 1929 acquisition of the Standard Sanitary Manufacturing Company enabled the firm to dramatically expand its own line of plumbing and steam heating systems and become an integrated supplier of a multitude of home and building supply components.[34]

Entrepreneurs: Feeding America's New Table

While Woolley and other managers profited from the consolidation of established entities, entrepreneurs saw promise in the changing composition of the country. With the nation's railways connecting its population centers, businesses could now think and act on a national scale instead of a local one. During the first decade of the twentieth century, a number of consumer-oriented companies were spawned. They had begun as mere speculative ventures, yet became legendary household names, such as Kellogg, Kraft, H. J. Heinz, Carnation, and Hershey. There was certainly no precedent for creating brands on a national scale, but these entrepreneurs understood that the fundamental shifts in the population were changing the nature of what was considered important to Americans. Not only did these entrepreneurs foresee the shifts (e.g., a greater focus on convenience and a greater willingness to purchase ready-made food), but their products and services contributed to the acceleration of these changes. A few entrepreneurs, like Hershey, Kellogg, and Cannon, even built company towns (Hershey, Pennsylvania; Battle Creek, Michigan; and Kannapolis, North Carolina) to produce their revolutionary products while providing a stable and affordable existence for workers. This approach had the added benefit of accelerating the growth of urban areas, which, in turn, relied on these companies' very products.

The nation was in one sense becoming larger with the expansion to its outermost frontiers. Yet at the same time, it was becoming smaller. The smallness came as newspapers reached farther afield, as postal routes opened, and as advances in technology became commercialized products. Some of the early proponents of national reach included Henry Crowell, who made oatmeal a national breakfast option through the mass advertising of Quaker Oats; William Wrigley Jr., who funded eccentric marketing approaches to enhance the popularity of chewing gum; and King C. Gillette, who invented the safety razor and extensively invested in advertising to drive volume and thus achieve tremendous economies of scale.

Entrepreneurs like Will Kellogg, Henry Heinz, and C. W. Post were also exceptionally adept at marketing their products as conveniences for the newly industrializing nation. As more family members entered the workforce and more Americans flocked to the cities, there was a growing need for products that were easy to obtain and prepare. For the first time, business considered the consumer's time valuable, and products that afforded convenience like prepared pickles, instant oatmeal, premade breakfast cereal, or processed milk reinforced this importance. It was also a time when some bold companies decided to offer money-back guarantees, further reinforcing the growing value of the consumer. The vehicles that were most often used to spread the word of these products and services were newspapers and magazines, and no one did more to create the new rules of publishing than Cyrus H. K. Curtis.

Cyrus H. K. Curtis (1850–1933), Curtis Publishing Company

More than most business executives in the late nineteenth and early twentieth century, Cyrus H. K. Curtis embodied, through his personal and professional life, the transformational nature of America. His publications, notably, the *Ladies' Home Journal* and the *Saturday Evening Post*, were both contributors to and reflections of the changing nature of America. They celebrated the emerging middle class, espoused beliefs in the promises of the melting pot, targeted specific consumers (mostly female—contributing to the growing importance of women as significant purchasers and decision makers), and adopted break-through advertising and marketing techniques. One historian noted, "The *Post* profoundly influenced the shape and direction of an American national consciousness."[35] Curtis's personal transformation from his humble and inaus-picious beginnings in Maine to the recognized pioneer of the modern maga-zine industry is reminiscent of many entrepreneurs throughout the century. These individuals were capable of overcoming both personal and professional obstacles to achieve greatness.

Curtis was born in 1850 and was raised in Portland, Maine, by supportive yet poor parents. To supplement the family's income, Curtis pursued a num-ber of jobs while trying to finish his schooling. At fifteen, he started his own small newspaper, *Young America*, which quickly sold over four hundred copies in the Portland area. His success with *Young America* was short-lived, as his printing operation was lost in a fire the next year. The fire also took most of the family's possessions and resulted in the end of Curtis's formal education. He quit school at age sixteen to provide for his family, taking a series of clerk-ship opportunities. Intrigued by his early newspaper efforts, Curtis left the Portland homestead when he was nineteen to pursue publishing opportuni-ties in the larger city of Boston, where he found positions as an advertising salesman for the *Traveler's Guide*, the *Boston Times*, and the *Independent*.

With capital borrowed from a partner, Curtis soon established his own weekly newspaper, the *People's Ledger*, a publication that featured full reprints of stories that were sometimes several decades old. Curtis's publication of the full story in one edition was considered radical by his competitors, but satisfy-ing for readers. At the time, the trend in weekly publications was to serialize a story for successive editions. Through this practice, the publisher hoped to se-cure longer-term interest and therefore ensure subsequent newspaper sales. The early success of the *Ledger* enabled Curtis to buy out his partner in one year. Curtis continued to prosper with the *Ledger*, even moving it to Philadel-phia in 1876 to take advantage of lower printing costs and eventually selling it in 1878 to pursue larger opportunities. With its abundant printing resources and low costs, Philadelphia had become a newspaper boomtown and compe-tition was very stiff. Curtis struggled after the sale of the *Ledger*, but soon found a new vehicle.

With two thousand dollars borrowed from his brother-in-law, Curtis established in 1879 the *Tribune and Farmer*, a four-page weekly providing information and other resources for the rural farming community and with a subscription rate of fifty cents per year. Serendipity struck when, running short of copy for an edition in 1883, Curtis decided to cobble together several reprints on subjects of importance to women. He titled the column "Women and Home." The new column was surrounded by advertisements for products or services geared to women and described in the editorial material. This was one of the first times that advertisements had been placed alongside synergistic editorial content. The typical scenario involved placing advertisements together in a supplemental section at the end of a publication. The combination of useful household tips and targeted advertisements was an early hit with readers. The column was so popular that Curtis decided to publish a *Tribune and Farmer* monthly supplement that featured more news and information for women. With his wife, Louisa Knapp Curtis, as its first editor, the *Ladies' Home Journal and Practical Housekeeper* was introduced in December 1883.

Cyrus H. K. Curtis (1850–1933), publisher of Ladies Home Journal *and* Saturday Evening Post. *Cover of 1906 Easter edition of the* Saturday Evening Post. (Sources: left, CORBIS; right, Bettmann/ CORBIS)

The supplement to the *Tribune and Farmer* became an instant success, and Curtis decided to abandon his original publication. Instead, he chose to publish the supplement (shortened to *Ladies' Home Journal*) as an independent magazine for middle-class women. He recognized the monumental shifts in the responsibilities and attitudes of women in America at the end of the nineteenth century and sought to cater to their needs. As a result of his efforts, the *Ladies' Home Journal* became the first magazine of any kind to boast a circulation of over a million copies (it did so in February 1904).[36]

Curtis did not achieve this phenomenal feat by chance, but through a concerted effort to make every aspect of the magazine a success. According to a study by the *Business History Review*, "it is estimated that 7,500 magazines were founded between 1885 and 1905, and that about half of them failed."[37] Curtis hired top-notch editors like Edward W. Bok, who replaced Louisa Knapp Curtis in 1899, and attracted popular authors like Mark Twain, Louisa May Alcott, and others to contribute articles. Curtis also employed an extensive army of customer service representatives to address the write-in concerns and questions of readers, expanded the size and scope of the publication, and spent massive amounts of money to advertise. In one year alone, Curtis borrowed over $300,000 from the N. W. Ayer and Son advertising agency to increase the circulation of the *Ladies' Home Journal*. His practice of lowering the price of the magazine (even below the cost to produce it) to expand the subscriber base became an industry standard. The increased circulation generated through the lower subscription price increased the attractiveness of the publication for advertisers and more than offset the initial financial shortfall.

In addition to ground-breaking advertising and circulation innovations, Curtis was also a pioneer in the use of the latest printing technology. In 1901, a trade journal noted that "the Curtis Company owned a printing plant that included forty-nine presses and twenty-one binding and cutting machines with a daily capacity of 25,000 copies . . . The *Ladies' Home Journal* was the first magazine to use color printing and also innovated in the use of two-, three-, and four-color printing."[38] Curtis's strategies simultaneously boosted both circulation and advertising revenues, which culminated in the publication of the most successful magazine in the country.

Curtis was by no means the publisher of a one-magazine wonder. In 1897, he bought the rights to the fledgling *Saturday Evening Post*, a publication with only two thousand subscribers and a negative cash flow. Employing many of the same strategies that made the *Journal* a success, Curtis built the *Post* into one of the most popular and successful magazines of the first half of the twentieth century. While the *Journal* celebrated middle-class women, the *Post* celebrated both men and women. Curtis tapped into the growing fascination with business that was capturing the imaginations of the new industrialized economy, and he used the *Post* to convey his support.[39] Under Curtis's stewardship, the *Saturday Evening Post* became a reflection of the country itself. It was a view that offered unbounded possibilities and promises not too different from the America portrayed in *The Melting-Pot*, with all its inherent contradictions.

For almost four decades, the *Ladies' Home Journal* and the *Saturday Evening Post* set the standard in magazine publishing. At one time, they carried more than 40 percent of advertising expenditures for all U.S. magazines.[40] The success of the magazines, however, did not significantly outlast Curtis, who resigned as president of Curtis Publishing in 1932 and died the following year. The *Post* was eclipsed by *Life* magazine in the 1940s, and the *Ladies' Home Journal* was overtaken by a host of more targeted women's magazines in the 1950s. Despite their lack of individual enduring success, the Curtis publications left a far broader legacy. Curtis's combination of gender-based articles and advertisements was revolutionary at the turn of the century, and it played a vital role in establishing the "genderization of commerce" as an advertising norm.[41] His magazines essentially set the tone for target marketing, and he contributed to the emergence of the consumer as an important and viable participant in the affairs of business.[42]

Leaders: Reinventing Business

While managers were creating bigger and bigger businesses and entrepreneurs were catering to a new consumer consciousness, leaders were reinventing businesses and looking for extended or enhanced commercial applications of their product lines. Many leaders headed companies that had risen to prominence in the late nineteenth century, and by breathing new life into these entities, they often guaranteed the entities' continuance and, in some cases, the legacy of the founder. They were able to imagine new possibilities and options for their businesses when others would have sold out or retreated.

To be successful required an all-too-simple yet all-too-elusive capability to recognize in a timely fashion when a business strategy or approach was no longer sustainable. That capability is what enabled Ira C. Copley to achieve tremendous acclaim. Taking over his father's fledgling business of supplying gas for street lamps, Copley recognized the limited long-term potential of such an endeavor. He embarked on a business conversion strategy by using his supply of and access to gas as a fuel, not just as a source of light. The success of this conversion led to the consolidation of other utility providers to form Western Utility Company.[43] Leaders like Copley recognized new opportunities for what appeared to be mature businesses, and their ability to seize on a new use of a product or service often set them apart. In other cases, they were able to discover untapped potential in a seemingly mundane or discarded product. That was the case for Frank C. Ball, who made the glass jar more than a simple container; he made it a household necessity.

Frank C. Ball (1857–1943), Ball Brothers Company

Chances are that the beverage you recently consumed was enclosed in one of the 33 billion cans or bottles produced by the Ball Corporation.[44] The lightweight durability of these aluminum cans and plastic bottles is a far cry from the firm's first product produced in 1880: a wood-jacketed tin can to house not beverages, but kerosene or paint. This early tin-based storage unit became the foundation on which the Ball brothers built a canning and bottling empire. Although there were five Ball brothers involved in the family business at some level, Frank Ball, the fifth of eight siblings, was for sixty-three years the rightful leader of the organization. He secured the future growth and development of the company by recognizing and exploiting a fortuitous opportunity—the end of a very important and business-altering patent, the Mason fruit jar.

Frank and his brothers were born in Ohio and spent the majority of their youth on the farm—first in Greensberg, Ohio, and later in Canadaigua, New York, where the family moved at the conclusion of the Civil War. Except for one brother, who became a physician, none of the boys pursued formal education beyond the local school academy. Their education was on the farm, training that served them well throughout their business careers as they catered to the needs of the farming family. When the patriarch of the Ball family died in 1878, his brother, George Ball, took it upon himself to help his nephews secure a future in business. With two hundred dollars borrowed from their Uncle George and after several unsuccessful starts, Frank and Edmund Ball established the Wooden Jacket Can Company in Buffalo.

The year was 1880, and there was a growing demand for sturdy and reliable containers to house varnish, paint, and kerosene. The early success of the Wooden Jacket Can Company encouraged the brothers to expand into other types of storage containers. They eventually replaced the tin lining of the wooden jacket with glass. Their new glass jars were so popular that the Balls quickly expanded their operation and looked for new or extended product opportunities, which included glass-based fruit jars. The future of the Ball brothers was essentially secured in 1885, when they discovered that the patent for the "Mason Improved Fruit Jar" had expired. This glass container, which was used for canning and preserving fruits and vegetables, included a patented rubber ring locking mechanism to effectively seal the contents in the jar. The previous iterations of the home canning container did not have the special seal, which did a far better job of retaining the flavor and freshness of the contents.

Though the "Mason Improved Fruit Jar" had been around for decades, the company that perfected the sealing process did not extensively expand its operations or attempt to sell them on a national scale. Frank Ball and his brothers, as typical of many leaders, recognized the untapped potential for the Mason jar. They seized on the expiration of the patent to dramatically expand their glass operations and incorporated their business in 1886 as Ball Brothers Glass Manufacturing Company. To further accelerate the expansion of the glass manufacturing operation, the Ball brothers searched for an easily accessible and abundant supply of natural gas, which was a key ingredient in the production of glass. Their search brought them to Muncie, Indiana, a town that enticed them with five thousand dollars toward their relocation expenses and access to free natural gas reserves.

Ball's mass-produced canning jars were extremely popular with both individual families and large farming operations that used the jars for the resale and distribution of their fruit and vegetable preserves. In 1894, Ball introduced the famous (and patented) wooden boxes that carried a dozen Ball fruit jars. According to Ball's corporate history, the wooden box of Ball jars was the first time a dozen of anything was shipped to grocers in the United States. Over the years, the Ball brothers expanded their operations to accommodate new designs and greater efficiencies. They vertically integrated their operations by producing the aluminum caps for the jars, rubber jar rings, and cardboard shipping cartons. In 1900, the Ball brothers invented the first automatic glass machine, and their facility became a fully automated operation eight years later. As his business outgrew the resources of Muncie, Frank Ball acquired several other operations throughout the country (eleven companies in ten years). Acquisitions included the original Mason Fruit Jar & Bottle Company in Coffeyville, Kansas, in 1909.

Though they expanded their operations throughout the country, the Balls became the royal family of Muncie, providing employment opportunities for many in the town. Muncie's infrastructure and population were examined in the 1920s Middletown study, which explored the sociological and anthropological underpinnings of a typical American town. Though the Ball names were disguised in the study, the observers noted: "In and out of the picture of Middletown [Muncie] in 1925 wove the influence of this family of brothers who had come to the city with the gas boom, begun with modest capital and became millionaires, and had ever since held an unostentatious but increasingly influential place in the city's life."[45] Frank and his brothers used their power and influence in Muncie to essentially underwrite its infrastructure, including the creation of a university (what became Ball State University), a hospital, a YMCA and YWCA, and several banks, retail establishments, and other institutions.

As their business expanded, the brothers bought or built factories to provide the supplies and raw materials they needed in the production of their glass jars. The Balls' influence throughout the area was pervasive and extremely powerful. Despite their municipal generosity, they were typical of most business leaders of the time in their treatment of employees. The Balls paid a very low wage for very long hours, and they consistently and successfully opposed any form of organized labor. Being one of the only viable employers in the area, the company held an undisputed position of power. As noted by the Middletown observers: "In their conscientious and utterly unhypocritical combination of high profits, great philanthropy, and low wage scale, they embody the hard-headed *ethos* of Protestant capitalism."[46]

The company's prominence and its advantageous position were strengthened further during the Depression of the 1930s. The Great Depression necessitated self-sufficiency, and the Ball fruit jar provided an inexpensive means of enabling even those with small urban gardens to preserve their much-needed produce. Not being one to miss an opportunity, Frank Ball was one of the few businessmen to dramatically expand his company during this time. In fact, the company generated some of its strongest profits during an otherwise bleak period in the country's history. Ball demonstrated his prowess as a shrewd and wise opportunist throughout his six-decade leadership of the company. He secured patent rights and raw material sources, acquired competitors, and established a national distribution network to expand the opportunities of his business. While others saw only small-scale regional business prospects, Ball saw an opportunity with national proportions.[47] He is an example of several business executives that we studied who demonstrated the ability to transition from a leader to an entrepreneur to a manager. For some like Ball, enduring success depended on an ability to modify their leadership style and approach based on the changing contextual landscape.

Leveraging Scale

The business executives of the first decade were driven, opportunistic, and innovative. They operated on a large scale and constantly expanded their base of power. They built businesses that often had far-reaching impact on the way society lived, but they were, for the most part, less concerned about the way people worked; there was generally little regard for progressive employment practices. The focus was not on the quality of work life or necessarily on the quality of the product; it was often the quantity of the output. For many, there was no better way to secure quantity in the 1900s than through consolidation, and the move toward consolidation subsequently spawned another fundamental shift in business—a focus on productivity and efficiency. Consolidators who wanted to capitalize on the sought-after economies of scale from combinations found assistance in the "scientific management" theory and practice that permeated business culture in the next decade. The focus on scientific management would also have a monumental impact on taming the last vestiges of the American frontier.

TABLE 1-3

Entrepreneurs, managers, and leaders of the 1900s

Entrepreneurs

Thomas Adams Jr., American Chicle Company
Leo H. Baekeland, Bakelite Corporation
Elizabeth E. Boit, Winship, Boit, & Company
Milton Bradley, Milton Bradley Company
Washington A. Burpee, W. A. Burpee Company
Asa G. Candler, Coca-Cola Company
James W. Cannon, Cannon Mills Company
Hattie Carnegie, Hattie Carnegie
James E. Casey, United Parcel Service
Roy D. Chapin, Hudson Motor Company
Adolph Coors, Adolph Coors Brewing
  Company
Richard T. Crane, Crane Company
Henry P. Crowell, Quaker Oats Company
Joseph S. Cullinan, Texaco
Cyrus H. K. Curtis, Curtis Publishing Company
William H. Danforth, Ralston Purina Company
Alfred B. Dick, A. B. Dick and Company
Frank N. Doubleday, Doubleday and Company
Herbert H. Dow, The Dow Chemical Company
John F. Dryden, Prudential Insurance
  Company
George Eastman, Eastman Kodak Company
Marshall Field, Marshall Field and Company
Edward A. Filene, Filene's
Harvey S. Firestone, Firestone Tire and Rubber
Frederick J. Fisher, Fisher Body Company
Henry Ford, Ford Motor Company
Alfred C. Fuller, Fuller Brush Company
King C. Gillette, Gillette Company
William T. Grant, W. T. Grant Company
Otto Haas, Rohm and Haas
George H. Hartford, Great Atlantic & Pacific
  Tea Company
Henry J. Heinz, H. J. Heinz Company
Alonzo F. Herndon, Atlanta Life Insurance
  Company
Milton S. Hershey, Hershey Chocolate
  Company
Charles E. Hires, Charles E. Hires Company
Elon H. Hooker, Hooker Chemical
Joseph L. Hudson, Hudson (J. L.) Company
George A. Hughes, Hughes Electric Heating
Eldridge R. Johnson, Victor Talking Machine
Robert W. Johnson, Johnson & Johnson
  Company
Will K. Kellogg, Kellogg Company
Arthur A. Kent, Atwater Kent Company
John A. Kimberly, Kimberly-Clark
  Corporation
Rose M. Knox, Knox Gelatin Company
Walter J. Kohler, Kohler Company

James L. Kraft, Kraft (J. L.) Brothers and
  Company
Sebastian S. Kresge, S. S. Kresge Company
Samuel H. Kress, S. H. Kress Company
Bernard H. Kroger, The Kroger Co.
Edmund D. Libbey, Owens Bottle Company
Louis K. Liggett, United Drug Company
Josiah K. Lilly, Eli Lilly and Company
Arthur D. Little, Arthur D. Little
Marcus Loew, Loew's
Glenn L. Martin, Glenn L. Martin Company
Frederick L. Maytag, Maytag Corporation
David H. McConnell, Avon Products
William L. Mellon, Gulf Oil Corporation
John Merrick, North Carolina Mutual Life
  Insurance
Joy Morton, Morton Salt Company
Frank A. Munsey, Munsey Publishing House
Conde M. Nast, Conde Nast Publications
Ransom E. Olds, Reo Motor Car Company
Anthony Overton, Hygienic Manufacturing
George S. Parker, Parker Brothers
James C. Penney, JC Penney
Joseph N. Pew, Sun Oil Company
Abe Plough, Plough, Inc.
Charles W. Post, Postum Cereal Company,
  Limited
John F. Queeny, Monsanto Company
Earl H. Richardson, Hotpoint Electric Heating
Charles Ringling, Ringling Brothers, Barnum &
  Bailey Circus
John D. Rockefeller Sr., Standard Oil of New
  Jersey
Edward I. Scott, Scott Paper
Edward W. Scripps, Scripps/United Press
  International
Richard W. Sears, Sears, Roebuck and Co.
Frank A. Seiberling, Goodyear Tire & Rubber
Lee Shubert, Shubert Theater Corporation
Ellsworth M. Statler, Statler Hotels
James W. Thompson, JWT Advertising
  Agency
Charles R. Walgreen, Walgreen Company
Sarah B. (Madam C. J.) Walker, Walker
  Manufacturing
Maggie L. Walker, St. Luke Penny Savings
  Bank
John Wanamaker, John Wanamaker and
  Company
George Westinghouse, Westinghouse
Frank W. Woolworth, Woolworth and
  Company
William Wrigley Jr., William Wrigley Jr.
  Company

TABLE 1-3 *(continued)*

Managers

Robert S. Abbott, Chicago Defender
J. Ogden Armour, Armour and Company
Jules S. Bache, J. S. Bache & Company
Ohio C. Barber, Diamond Match Company
Enos M. Barton, Western Electric
Bernard M. Baruch, Baruch Brothers
Edward T. Bedford, Corn Products Refining
James S. Bell, Washburn, Crosby Milling
  Company
Henry H. Benedict, Remington Typewriter
Edward J. Berwind, Berwind-White Coal Mining
Joseph Boyer, Burroughs Adding Machine
Charles F. Brooker, American Brass Company
Morgan G. Bulkeley, Aetna Life Insurance
Adolphus Busch, Anheuser-Busch Brewery
Hugh J. Chisholm, International Paper
William L. Clayton, Anderson, Clayton &
  Company
Charles A. Coffin, General Electric Company
Samuel P. Colt, United States Rubber Company
William E. Corey, United States Steel
  Corporation
James B. Duke, American Tobacco Company
Thomas C. du Pont, DuPont Corporation
Lothar W. Faber, Eberhard-Faber Company
Henry M. Flagler, Florida East Coast Railway
Frank E. Gannett, Gannett Company
Amadeo Peter Giannini, Bank of America
Isaac Gimbel, Gimbel Brothers Department
  Stores
Adolphus W. Green, National Biscuit Company
Daniel Guggenheim, American Smelting &
  Refining
William R. Hearst, American Newspapers
John R. Hegeman, Metropolitan Life Insurance
Alonzo B. Hepburn, Chase National Bank
James J. Hill, Great Northern Railroad
Louis W. Hill, Great Northern Railroad
George A. Hormel, Hormel
Henry B. Joy, Packard Motor Car Company
Darwin P. Kingsley, New York Life Insurance
Robert J. Kleberg Sr., King Ranch
Joseph P. Knapp, Knapp & Company
Philip Lehman, Lehman Brothers
Henry R. Mallory, Atlantic, Gulf & West Indies
  Lines
Thomas F. Manville, Johns-Manville Corporation
Charles D. Marshall, McClintic and Marshall
William G. Mather, Cleveland-Cliffs Iron
  Company
Oscar F. Mayer, Oscar Mayer
Howard H. McClintic, McClintic and Marshall

Cyrus H. McCormick Jr., International
  Harvester
James H. McGraw, McGraw-Hill
Andrew W. Mellon, Mellon National Bank
Ambrose Monell, International Nickel
  Corporation
John P. Morgan, J. P. Morgan & Company
William H. Nichols, General Chemical
  Corporation
Harrison G. Otis, Los Angeles Times
William G. Park, Crucible Steel Company
John H. Patterson, National Cash Register
  Company
Rufus L. Patterson, American Machine and
  Foundry
Christopher J. Perry, Philadelphia Tribune
John Pitcairn, Pittsburgh Plate Glass Company
Andrew W. Preston, United Fruit Company
William C. Procter, Procter & Gamble
John D. Ryan, Anaconda Copper Company
Samuel Sachs, Goldman Sachs
Jacob H. Schiff, Kuhn, Loeb and Company
Clarence W. Seamans, Union Typewriter
  Company
Dennis Sheedy, Globe Smelting and Refining
Samuel Spencer, Southern Railway System
Charles H. Steinway, Steinway and Sons
Lyman Stewart, Union Oil Company
James Stillman, National City Bank
Elbridge A. Stuart, Carnation Company
Louis F. Swift, Swift and Company
Theodore N. Vail, American Telephone &
  Telegraph
Frank A. Vanderlip, National City Bank
Sidney W. Winslow, United Shoe Machinery
William M. Wood, American Woolen Mills
Clarence M. Woolley, American Radiator
  Company

Leaders

Frank C. Ball, Ball Brothers Company
Robert A. Chesebrough, Chesebrough
  Manufacturing
Ira C. Copley, Western Utility Company
Charles S. Mott, Weston-Mott Company
Adolph S. Ochs, New York Times
Charles M. Schwab, Bethlehem Steel
  Corporation
Edward R. Stettinius, Diamond Match Company
Henry R. Towne, Yale and Towne Manufacturing
Frederick D. Underwood, Erie Railroad
John T. Underwood, Underwood Typewriter
James C. Wallace, American Ship Building

TWO

1910–1919

Breaking Frontiers

In the past the man has been first; in the future the system must be first.
This in no sense, however, implies that great men are not needed. On
the contrary, the first object of any good system must be that of developing
first-class men; and under systematic management the best man rises
to the top more certainly and more rapidly than ever before.

—Frederick Winslow Taylor

THE FREEWHEELING, unfettered business expansion so characteristic of the first decade continued with earnest in the 1910s. As companies grappled with the size and scale of their organizations, they benefited from the advice of the "father of scientific management," Frederick Winslow Taylor. From his early studies of coal shoveling techniques at the Bethlehem Steel Company, where he determined that a worker was most productive when he gathered exactly twenty-one pounds of coal with each scoop, Taylor went on to develop an efficiency model that has influenced business for decades.[1] Taylor believed that true efficiency could only be achieved through the creation of systematic processes that controlled individual behavior; he put little stock in the idea that workers could be motivated through anything but rational economic opportunity. He asserted that given the proper financial incentives, individuals would naturally exhibit appropriate behavior. Though his ideas were not universally accepted at the time, Taylor's principles (efficient management of time, the proper routing and scheduling of work, and the standardization of tools and equipment) became cornerstones of American manufacturing.[2]

In many respects, Taylor provided businesses with the tools and approaches to reach new heights and explore untapped frontiers. During the 1910s, frontiers were breached in such diverse areas as architecture, transportation, retailing, and construction. Railroads, automobiles, and airplanes pushed transportation boundaries ever outward. Even in geographically confined spaces like Manhattan, new frontiers were reached not horizontally but vertically. For seventeen years after its 1912 completion, the awe-inspiring sixty-story Woolworth Building in New York stood as the tallest building in the world.

Portrait of Frederick Winslow Taylor (1856–1915), author of The Principles of Scientific Management *(1911). Taylor's time and motion studies revolutionized manufacturing operations around the world.* (Source: Bettmann/CORBIS)

No product provided greater opportunities for new fortunes or broke more barriers than the automobile. Though he was arguably more of an entrepreneur than a manager, Henry Ford strongly believed that he was a beneficiary of being in the right place at the right time, as he explained in 1909: "I invented nothing new. I simply assembled into a car the discoveries of other men . . . Had I worked 50 or 10 or even five years before, I would have failed."[3] The automobile's position as a permanent fixture on America's landscape was further reinforced in 1916, when Congress passed the Highway Act, providing federal grants to states engaged in the development of their roads and bridges. As the automobile gained widespread popularity, it created a whole host of new competitors like General Motors Corporation and Nash Motors Company. It also spawned accessory businesses, including Edward G. Budd's auto parts operation, and created service providers such as the John D. Hertz's Driv-Ur-Self rental car station that opened in 1918 with twelve Ford Model T cars on the lot.

The Rise of the New Oil Baron

In lockstep with the monumental advances in the automobile business, the oil industry blossomed. Along the way, it received a significant boost when the government championed the high-profile breakup of the Standard Oil Company. While the government's divestiture of Standard Oil was successful in ending John D. Rockefeller's near monopoly of the oil business in the United States, it created untold wealth for Rockefeller and spawned a new era of oilmen who capitalized on the expanding American landscape. Buying un-developed tracts of land in remote parts of America's western frontier, these would-be oil barons built new communities, created jobs, and explored the nation's vast resources. Where Rockefeller built a tightly grouped affiliation of oil producers, refiners, and distributors, the new oil barons specialized in dif-ferent segments of the production process and often grew from a strong re-gional base.

Seizing the opportunity were James C. Donnell, who expanded the re-gional Ohio Oil Company into sixteen states and Mexico; John W. Van Dyke, who took part of the financially strapped, debt-ridden spin-off of Standard Oil and built one of the nation's largest oil distribution companies under the Atlantic Richfield name; and regional giant Joshua S. Cosden, known as the "prince of petroleum" for his role in making Oklahoma an oil-producing state.[4] They were joined by the likes of Ross S. Sterling, who created Humble Oil; Walter C. Teagle, who built Standard Oil of New Jersey (which became Exxon) into one of the largest oil companies in the world; and John and Joseph Pew, who transformed their father's small oil operation into the pre-cursor of Sunoco. Like many of his contemporaries, Frank Phillips, a staunch

No piece of land could escape the oil rush. Oil prospectors drilled wells on the property of this rural church in Tokawa, Oklahoma (1923). (Source: Bettmann/CORBIS)

individualist, had the homespun character of this new breed of oilmen; he was a free spirit who was prone to adventure yet was very disciplined.

Frank Phillips (1873–1950), Phillips Petroleum Company

Though Phillips left an indelible legacy as a pioneer in the refinement and use of natural gas and the development of one of the first service station networks across the country (Phillips 66), he was not always associated with the oil business. Growing up in the wide-open spaces of Iowa and Nebraska, Phillips, the oldest of ten children, left school at the age of fourteen to become a ranch hand. In his spare time, he learned the barbering trade, and over the course of the next eight years, he traveled throughout the Western territories as part-time barber, part-time rancher, and full-time explorer. He returned to his hometown in 1895 to own and operate the Climax Shaving Parlor. His quick wit, affable sales skills, and tales of the West, along with his improved barbering skills, soon earned him a thriving business in Creston, Iowa.

Before becoming a baron of the oil fields, Phillips was considered a "baron of baldness" as he marketed and distributed his own rainwater-based cure for baldness under the name Phillips Mountain Sage. His inspiration for the hair tonic came from his observations of hogs; these animals never lost their hair and were generally only exposed to one element, natural rainwater. Believing that there must be something to this pig's tale, Phillips concocted his own remedy for baldness by using rainwater and other natural ingredients. Given his own fast-receding hairline, the unbelievable success of Phillips Mountain Sage is a true testament to his sales ability. Phillips had visions of a career as a country barber, opening new shops throughout the surrounding communities, but his path was interrupted when he caught the eye of Jane Gibson, the daughter of one of Creston's most prominent bankers, John Gibson.

Mr. Gibson was also a customer of the Climax Shaving Parlor, and though he admired the sales and business acumen of the young barber, a man like Phillips was not what he had envisioned for a son-in-law. As a successful businessman, however, Gibson was not averse to structuring a deal with Phillips. If Phillips sold his barbershop business and pursued a more "respectable" career, Gibson would not stand in the way of the marriage of Frank and Jane. Phillips accepted the deal. After marrying in 1897, Phillips sold his three barbershops and became a traveling bond salesman for his father-in-law's banking operation. The sales skills and potential that Gibson thought he had seen in the young barber materialized. Within a few years, Phillips had become an extremely successful bond salesman, able to sell not only in his familiar Midwest, but also in the old-line banking worlds of New York and New England. Within five years, the ambitious and successful Phillips was earning more than $75,000 in commissions each year and was itching to explore new opportunities.

Having attended a preview exhibition of the St. Louis World's Fair in 1903, Phillips was intrigued by the stories being told about oil discoveries in the Indian Territory of Oklahoma. Phillips lined up a series of investors, including his father-in-law, and headed to Bartlesville, Oklahoma (prior to its declaration of statehood in 1907, Oklahoma was part of the western U.S. Indian Territory), where he bought land and secured drilling lease rights from the Osage Nation. He established his operation with one of his brothers (L. E. Phillips) as the Anchor Oil and Gas Company in 1903, and so began a transformation for Phillips, from barber to bond salesman to wildcatter. Wildcatters were considered bold risk takers who were willing to wager their entire fortunes in the hopes of finding oil. Phillips's love of the West and his sense of adventure, combined with his shrewd business instincts, made him a natural candidate for this speculative enterprise.

Although his first forays were not successful, he continued to look for oil-producing land in the new territory, and within a few years, he found his first gusher. Unable to secure enough financing to expand their investments in the speculative oil industry, Frank and L. E. Phillips, again with the help of Gibson, opened their own banking operation in 1905, Citizens Bank and Trust Company. What was expected to be a relatively short-term source of financing became a second career for the Phillips brothers. The banking operation was almost immediately successful and thrived as the town of Bartlesville and its surroundings grew. The growth of the banking operation was not insignificantly attributed to Phillips's open lending policies to both Indians and outlaws.[5] Over the course of the next ten years, Phillips was both a wildcatter in search of new oil and a country banker in search of more capital. The success of Phillips and others in discovering oil in Oklahoma quickly transformed the territory into a haven for speculators. With the speculators came new money and an increased capital infrastructure in the region. The Citizens Bank and Trust Company benefited tremendously from both the influx of funds and the need for financing.

As the level of competition in the region intensified, Phillips wondered if there were too many oil producers. Frank and his brother decided that the time was right to exit the oil business before excess competition made it completely untenable. As he was wading through the decision in 1915, Frank remarked to his brother, "Hell L. E., we're not oil men, we're bankers."[6] The Phillips brothers began to sell off their land rights and oil production operations, but were unable to transfer the lease rights to several hundred acres of land that they had obtained through deliberations with the Osage Nation.

While they were selling their properties and making plans for a banker's life, a war was escalating in Europe and the automobile was fast becoming a national phenomenon. Banking on America's need for oil to support both the war effort and intense domestic production, Phillips decided to try to find oil on the Osage-leased land that he could not sell. The decision paid off. Though they initially hit some modestly producing wells, Phillips's team of oilmen eventually hit a gusher that was, by far, the largest and most productive since the company had begun exploration in Oklahoma fourteen years earlier.

Phillips quickly abandoned his vision of a banker's life, though he did retain control of the banking operation for the next twenty-five years. Citizens became, through additional acquisitions, the largest bank in northeastern Oklahoma. He rededicated himself to the oil business and decided that the time had come for the company to seek public financial support outside the region. In 1917, he formed Phillips Petroleum Company with twenty-seven employees by pooling together the disparate wildcat ventures that his brother and he had created. He took the company public on a base of $3 million in assets, and remarkably, in just three years, he grew that asset base tenfold, to over $34 million. From this point forward, Phillips invested heavily in the business, allocating significant sums of money to research and development.

Over the next twenty years, Phillips bought back more land than he had sold in Oklahoma and, through his research endeavors, created one of the most progressive and diverse new oil exploration companies in the United States. His company perfected a technique to extract and convert waste gas produced at oil wells into usable gasoline that could be sold at the company's roadside service stations. Phillips was also an early proponent and pioneer of both natural gas and aviation fuel. He purchased the Oklahoma Natural Gas Company and began producing "Philgas" in storage tanks as a natural-gas alternative for rural communities that were not served by main gas lines. As his

*One of the early Phillips
Petroleum Service stations
in Kansas.* (Source:
Wichita-Sedgwick County
Historical Museum)

fascination with exploration overflowed into a fascination with airplanes, he strongly encouraged the company's research and development activities in the discovery of efficient aviation fuel. Though the company's breakthrough developments in this area would provide a new source of revenue for the company, Phillips's interest ran deeper. His love of adventure played a major role in the company's sponsorship of many distance flights.

Though he did much to build the oil business that allowed the automobile to prosper, he never learned to drive, preferring instead to be chauffeured around his oil estate. As a testament to his legacy, Phillips Petroleum remains the only major turn-of-the-century oil company that is still named after its founder. Fiercely independent like its founder, Phillips Petroleum survived much of the acquisition mania in the oil industry for almost eight decades, finally succumbing to a merger with Conoco in March 2002.[7]

Government Sometimes Intervenes

The deployment of the Sherman Antitrust Act against the oil industry opened the door for many wildcatters like Phillips and enabled the government to test its growing powers. These powers were tested again in the government's antitrust action against the American Tobacco Company. According to the U.S. Supreme Court ruling in 1911, American Tobacco demonstrated unreasonable business practices by "buying out rivals [over 250 in 10 years], excluding rivals from access to wholesalers [the dominant distribution arm for cigarettes], and

TABLE 2-1

Business events that shaped the 1910s

Date	Event
1910	First mail carried by plane flown from Albany to New York City in Glenn Curtiss airplane
1910	Henry Ford starts manufacturing plant at Highland Park, Michigan
1911	Triangle Shirtwaist Company fire kills 146 and sparks worker safety movement
1911	Standard Oil Company required by U.S. Supreme Court to divest its holdings
1911	American Tobacco Company required by U.S. Supreme Court to divest its holdings
1911	Frederick W. Taylor publishes *The Principles of Scientific Management*
1913	Congress passes tariff reform bill
1913	Congress creates national banking structure—Federal Reserve Act
1913	U.S. federal income tax introduced by Sixteenth Amendment
1913	Ford deploys modern assembly line in automobile production
1914	Congress passes Clayton Antitrust Act and establishes Federal Trade Commission
1914	Ford establishes minimum $5-per-day wage for 8-hour workday
1914	Panama Canal opens
1915	Delaware liberalizes incorporation laws
1916	Radio tuners invented
1916	War Industries Board created to oversee mobilization for war effort
1916	Congress passes Highway Act to develop nation's roadways
1917	Congress passes stringent new immigration laws
1917	United States enters World War I
1917	United States takes over nation's railroads to support World War I
1918	World War I ends
1919	Eighteenth Amendment for prohibition of alcohol is ratified

predatory pricing."[8] Although the cases against Standard Oil and American Tobacco became watershed moments in antitrust legislation, they were more important in setting the standard for future cases, establishing a precedent that endured for decades. With these cases, the burden of proof for the government was not simply trade restraint but "unreasonable" restraint of trade. This seemingly inconsequential difference, in fact, became a huge burden for the government. No longer was the size of a business in and of itself a valid reason for deploying antitrust legislation; the government had to demonstrate that a business was effectively restraining trade in an unreasonable manner. Far from clarifying the antitrust legislation, this new "rule of reason" added a level of subjectivity to the investigative process.

In an attempt to definitively determine the meaning of "unreasonable re-straints of trade," the government passed the Clayton Antitrust Act of 1914, which "prohibited a company from discriminating in price between pur-chasers, engaging in exclusive sales, and tying purchases of one good to the purchases of another if the effect of any of these actions was 'to substantially lessen competition or tend to create a monopoly.'"[9] The act further prohib-ited mergers with competitors if the mergers lessened overall competition within an industry. Though it was designed to strengthen the antitrust move-ment, the Clayton Antitrust Act had the almost opposite impact by narrowly classifying what was illegal. With a narrow definition in place, corporations were free to function almost unfettered for nearly five decades. Though the final Clayton Antitrust Act did not have the regulatory bite that its early sup-porters had envisioned, its passage coincided with the establishment of a new regulatory agency that did have a long-term impact on business and govern-ment relations—the Federal Trade Commission (FTC). Established two weeks before the passage of the Clayton Antitrust Act, the FTC became the de facto governmental body with sole discretion to define the nature and extent of un-fair competition.[10]

In addition to strengthening antitrust legislation during this decade, the government established a national banking system, transformed its tariff legis-lation, expanded its collection of taxes, and, most importantly, enlisted the sup-port and cooperation of businesses with America's entry into World War I.[11] With the passage of the Federal Reserve Act of 1913, the country gained greater control of its financial situation. The act established a central banking system with twelve regional banks and an oversight authority appointed by the president. For the previous several decades, the government was virtually helpless in protecting the country from the wild speculation that often led to financial panics and bank failures. In many cases, the government turned to business financiers like J. P. Morgan to bail out the country. With this act and its subsequent creation of a central banking system, the dependence on busi-ness executives was significantly reduced, but did not diminish entirely.

In conjunction with this massive undertaking, President Woodrow Wilson also fought for and won tariff reform. The Underwood-Simmons Tariff Act of 1913 was designed to reduce the protectionist tariffs on hundreds of imported goods. The high tariffs on many of these goods resulted in consumer prices often disproportionate to their values. Given America's expanded productivity and overall global competitiveness, the existing tariff system was considered oppressive and overtly protectionist. The Underwood-Simmons Tariff Act, writes Steven Weisman, "marked the first time a tariff bill was enacted to serve the interests of American consumers, as well as those of American industrialists and owners. It did so by dramatically lowering the cost of living for Americans, reducing the added cost of goods from about 40 percent to 27 to 29 percent."[12] The early provisions of the Underwood-Simmons Tariff Act were reinforced in 1916 through the creation of a permanent Federal Tariff Commission, which often functioned as a barometer of the protectionist or open-market sentiments in the country.

To make up for the revenue deficit caused by the lowering of the tariff rates, the Sixteenth Amendment to the U.S. Constitution was ratified in 1913. The new law, which established the first personal income tax since the Civil War, called for a 1 percent tax on incomes from $3,000 ($4,000 for married couples) to $20,000, with graduated provisions to increase the tax to 7 percent for incomes over $500,000.[13] Though it had a dramatic impact on the country over the course of the century, the new income tax was of little concern to most Americans. It was estimated that fewer than 500,000 well-off individuals (approximately 0.5 percent of the population) would be expected to pay, given the high-income threshold of $3,000.[14] As a point of comparison, the average annual income for one of the 8 million factory workers in the country was $700 in 1914.[15]

By the middle of the decade, it appeared that Wilson's presidency would be defined by Progressive domestic policies. He professed to have a great love for, and interest in, domestic reform legislation and a reluctance to embrace global concerns. Before his inauguration, he said that "it would be an irony of fate if my administration had to deal chiefly with foreign affairs."[16] This "irony of fate" came to be a stark reality for Wilson as war broke out in Europe.

Global Presence Emerges

Prior to the outbreak of World War I, Wilson's global policies were focused on protecting America's influence and control (some would say, imperialistic motives) in its own hemisphere. Wilson was particularly concerned about the various transfers of power that were rippling through Mexico, even providing military and financial assistance for a coup attempt in the spring of 1914.

Though he was willing to involve the United States in the affairs of Mexico, Haiti, Nicaragua, and other Latin American countries throughout his early administration, Wilson was extremely reticent to commit the country to the war effort in Europe.

The vast majority of the country supported this isolationist policy and celebrated the president's declaration of U.S. neutrality in 1914. The business community was also an early proponent of this policy. Fearing that the instability in Europe would create havoc for the U.S. financial markets, the governors of the various stock exchanges, including the New York Stock Exchange, voted to suspend operations for the first six months of the war (from July to December 1914). The governors feared that the war would cause Europe to quickly dump securities and create a collapse in the U.S. stock markets.[17] Far from creating the feared collapse, World War I actually increased the demand for U.S. goods. The war provided a significant boost to the business and labor community while generating increases in productivity and advances in standardization. Throughout its three years of neutrality, the United States provided mostly nonmilitary goods for both sides—the Allied Powers (Great Britain, France, Italy, and Russia) and the Central Powers (principally Germany, Austria-Hungary, Bulgaria, and Turkey).

Though there was strong American sympathy for the Allied Powers in Europe, the calls for neutrality were much stronger and more vocal. Wilson did not turn a deaf ear to those pleas. His promise of continued neutrality became a significant component of his reelection in 1916; his campaign slogan was "He Kept Us Out of War."[18] That promise, of course, did not last long. The United States entered the war in 1917 on the side of the Allies after failing to diplomatically dissuade Germany from attacking neutral ships (namely, U.S. commercial vessels) in the northern waters of the Atlantic and after Wilson's failure to broker peace between the enemies. The United States had lost hundreds of lives and several million dollars in random attacks by Germany over the preceding three years, and with those losses, the sentiments of Americans began to change. These sentiments changed in a dramatic way when Wilson positioned U.S. involvement in the war in moral terms; it was not a war for conquering land but a war to protect and defend democracy.

Though America entered the war in 1917, its army and munitions were scarcely adequate to mount a quick and serious threat. On April 1, 1917, the U.S. standing army, combined with the national guard, stood at 295,000.[19] At the same time, the "air army" consisted of only fifty-five planes.[20] With the help of the Selective Service Act of May 1917, which sanctioned the draft or conscription, the army eventually brought in 2.8 million men, with another 1.2 million entering the service as volunteers.[21] To support the country's mobilization efforts, the government enlisted the help of industry through the creation of the War Industries Board. Chaired by presidential appointee Bernard Baruch, a Wall Street financier, the board created a system for streamlining and otherwise organizing the nation's mobilization efforts. The board was granted wide latitude to ration commodities, set prices, and fix wages and working hours to support the production effort required to build the country's arsenal. The board played a significant role in quelling labor unrest during the war and in setting the tone for management-labor relations at the war's conclusion.

One of the principal mechanisms deployed by the government in conjunction with the War Industries Board was the adoption of cost-plus contracts for military orders. By adopting a cost-plus contract system for the manufacture of war munitions, the government was able to increase the speed with which orders were delivered. By agreeing to cover any costs associated with the military orders, the government enabled companies to focus on speed and efficiency; time, not cost, was the primary motivator during the war. To meet the demands of the war effort, the government often asked non-military supply companies to convert their operations to military production. Through the cost-plus contract system, the government essentially minimized the risk for businesses embarking on the conversion process, enabling them to develop new processes and procedures without having to absorb the traditional investment costs.

One of the primary concerns of the cost-plus contract system today is that it has the potential to encourage inefficiency. Opponents of the system argue that a company could easily stretch project costs unnecessarily. As project profits are based on a percentage of costs, the higher the cost basis, the higher the profits. These concerns barely registered during the war effort. The contracting system provided an efficient means for quick mobilization. Beyond its immediate contribution to the war effort, the cost-plus system brought business and government closer together, encouraged standardized manufacturing processes to ensure efficiency, and gave the burgeoning field of cost accounting added legitimacy and importance.[22] Many of the manufacturing advances that were achieved through the war mobilization effort continued after the war, and for some businesses, the advances provided a significant competitive advantage.

Samuel M. Vauclain's Baldwin Locomotive business, Eugene G. Grace's Bethlehem Steel Company, and Pierre S. du Pont's war munitions supply company prospered immensely during the wartime buildup of supplies. In addition to his innovative locomotive designs, Vauclain's sales skills allowed him to generate lucrative production deals with the United States and its World War I allies, including Russia, France, and Britain. Combining his vision for Baldwin with his support of postwar rehabilitation in Europe, Vauclain expanded the company into twelve countries, eventually positioning it as one of the world's largest locomotive producers.[23] Grace's Bethlehem Steel increased production of steel from 1.1 million tons in 1915 to 3.3. million tons by 1919.[24] In a similar burst of productivity, du Pont's company provided over 1.5 billion pounds of explosives during the war.[25]

Even companies like Gillette and R.J. Reynolds profited from the war. Gillette, headed by Frank J. Fahey at the time, prospered when its shaving sets became standard issue for new soldiers. More than 3.5 million razors and 36 million blades were distributed to servicemen during World War I.[26] Richard J. Reynolds added a significant marketing boost to his new cigarette brand, Camel, when he distributed them for free to soldiers. These opportunists more than seized the moment in expanding their businesses for the war effort; they also used the accelerated investments in their companies to improve their operational procedures.

Though the government looked to businesses to physically support the war effort, it also expected businesses to play a major role in funding the effort. To that end, the War Revenue Act, which increased the business tax from 1 percent to 12 percent of profits, was enacted in 1917. Before the passage of the act, business income taxation was considered largely irrelevant. For most companies, it amounted to nothing more than a minor nuisance.[27] The new tax law was accompanied by a significant and far more complex set of rules than those applying to its predecessor—the Tariff Act of 1909. With the higher tax rate and associated income reporting rules, businesses turned to the fledgling accounting profession for assistance, and Arthur Andersen was one of the first individuals to capitalize on this opportunity.

America's ability to rapidly mobilize its industry and its citizens did much to energize the Allies and to accelerate the war effort in Europe. Though Germany

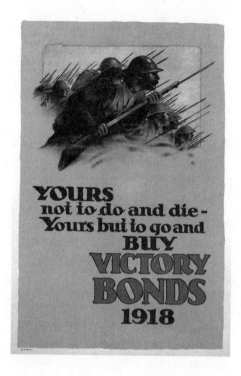

One of many posters encouraging Americans to do their part to pay for the war effort by purchasing victory bonds (1918).
(Source: Swim Ink/CORBIS)

had obtained a significant victory when Russia (having succumbed to the Bolshevik Revolution) agreed to drop out of the war and negotiate a separate treaty, the German troops were essentially demoralized. While the Allies and the Central Powers had been fighting for four years on French soil (the Western Front), both sides were locked in a stalemate. The result was the death of thousands of soldiers, with neither side making any significant advances.[28] The infusion of American troops and, not insignificantly, their enthusiasm did much to bolster the battered Allies, who were able to hold off German offenses throughout 1918. By the autumn of 1918, the Allies were on the offensive and had moved the Western Front more than fifty miles, setting the stage for the final armistice, which was signed on November 11, 1918.[29]

With the conclusion of the war, America's demobilization efforts were swift, indicating that the country planned to revert back to the comfort of isolationism. Though on many levels the country did move in this direction, several businesses that had expanded rapidly through the war effort looked for new opportunities in the ruins of Europe. The continued investments by businesses after the war helped stave off a U.S. recession until the early

1920s while simultaneously opening new markets for American products. The postwar pro-American sentiment almost overwhelmed the conscience of the country, which for years had been deeply troubled. In this decade, the United States was forced to look hard at what it meant to be an American.

Who Is a Real American?

By 1910, more than one-third of America's population of 92 million were considered "hyphenated Americans"—German Americans, French Americans, Irish Americans, Chinese Americans, and so forth, whose ethnic origins had typically been hyphenated (e.g., *German-Americans*) in those days.[30] Most were first- or second-generation immigrants struggling to make their way in America but still maintaining strong ties to their homeland. When he ran for a second term, Wilson made a concerted effort to ask Americans to be "real" Americans and cease to be "hyphenated Americans," a gesture that many historians consider to have been a shrewd campaign tactic.[31] This less-than-subtle denunciation of ethnic pride set a new tone for America's openness to immigration.[32]

Through 1914, immigration rates were consistent with the last several years of the previous decade—between 800,000 and 1,200,000 each year.[33] Given America's bias for neutrality, it is not surprising that antiforeign sentiment peaked during the war years. This sentiment was heard in the walls of Congress and was legitimized through the passage of an immigration law that required new entrants to pass a literacy test and pay a head tax, both extremely effective barriers to entry. Initially targeted at all immigrants, the law was largely meant for Europeans and was often loosely enforced for Latin Americans, who were needed to support the labor shortages during the war years.[34] The net effect of the stricter laws was a significant reduction in the number of immigrants— falling from 1,218,480 (in 1914), to 326,700 (in 1915), to 110,618 (by 1918).[35]

The anti-immigration sentiments lasted beyond the end of the war into the early 1920s as a wave of conservatism spread throughout the United States. With the end of the war came a yearning to return to some semblance of familiarity and comfort in the country. There was a longing for the way things used to be (more often than not, this was defined by the white middle class). Through the war effort, there were many new entrants to the workforce, especially women and blacks. Though many women did enter the workforce, most offered little resistance to surrendering the majority of their positions

TABLE 2-2

Social and demographic facts about the 1910s

- 92 million Americans in 46 states (42 million urban residents and 50 million rural residents) in 1910; grows to 106 million in 48 states by 1920
- National debt: $1.15 billion
- Movie attendance: 30 million per week
- Less than 10 percent of all automobiles are closed models, with windows and doors
- First parachute jump
- *Titanic* sinks in 1912, killing more than 1,500 passengers
- 76 lynchings
- Nevada grants divorces after 6 months of residence
- Margaret Sanger, who coined the term "birth control," is arrested in New York for distributing information on contraception
- Fads: hobble skirts, striped trousers, ballroom dancing, the fox-trot, speeding
- Games: Erector sets, Lincoln Logs, Tinkertoy sets, pogo sticks
- New words: *movies, GI, D-day*
- Average annual earnings (1910): $517
- Life expectancy (1910): 51.8 years for females, 48.4 years for males

when the soldiers returned from the war to reclaim their jobs. Far from being disillusioned by the change in events, women used their newly acquired economic power to further champion the right to vote. A woman's ability to successfully hold a job that had been traditionally occupied by a man was a strong reinforcement for greater equality.

There was, however, much greater resistance and resentment on the part of black Americans, who moved in great numbers from the South (the migration was often referred to as the Great Migration) to fill vacant and essential positions within the factories of the Northern cities. Though blacks had been called on to fight for America in Europe and work for America at home, they were expected to relinquish their positions and what some deemed any associated "temporary privileges" at the end of the war. Tension between whites and blacks escalated and finally erupted with massive race riots in major U.S. cities in 1919, creating further divides in economic opportunity and prosperity.

Society's Loss of Innocence

Part of the tension that came to the fore during the race riots was due to the underlying trepidation that existed in the country. Many historians characterize the 1910s as the decade in which America began to lose its innocence.[36] In a sense, the country moved from the rambunctious exuberance of its early childhood into the complexities, ambiguities, and uncertainties of adolescence. World War I was the ultimate catalyst for the country's transformation of its internal and external identity. America was forced to look beyond its own nation-building motives and designs in the Western Hemisphere and toward its own role in global affairs. The image of America as a welcoming port of immigration was critically reexamined in the midst of the war. What seemed important to the middle-class advocates of Progressivism seemed less so in the "fight for democracy." The rights of workers and the rights of businesses were subordinated, for a time, to the rights of the nation. And from time to time, the maintenance and expansion of those rights were even under attack from within.

Shortly after the United States entered the war, Congress passed the Sedition Act of 1918, which made it unlawful to criticize any aspects of the government's war efforts. Although this curbing of liberties was temporary, there remained in the country a strong anxiety about maintaining order in the face of violent economic, political, or social change, especially the changes brought on by immigration.[37] One thing that became increasingly unacceptable was alcohol consumption. In 1919, the United States enacted the Eighteenth Amendment, which prohibited the sale and consumption of alcohol (the Prohibition Act). The Prohibition Act did not achieve its proponents' stated objectives—namely, reduced crime and greater urban stability. Instead, the act spawned a plethora of underground illegal businesses during the fourteen years that it was a law of the land.

Postwar anxieties were further fueled by the political climate and activism in Russia. With the Russian Revolution in full swing, a "Red Scare" swept through America and, for a time, created a sense of hysteria and irrationality. In an effort to root out the "evils of communism," the Justice Department established a new General Intelligence Division, with a young J. Edgar Hoover at its helm.[38] The goals of this division were to arrest and eventually deport suspected communist sympathizers. Though the fervor of their cause fell out of popular favor in the early 1920s, the anticommunist warriors' activities had a longer-term impact on the underlying psyche of American suspicion, a paranoia that resurfaced significantly at the end of World War II. The Red Scare had a more immediate impact on the labor movement. Given that the labor movement, rightly or wrongly, was considered by many to be actively collaborating with socialists, unions were viewed as havens for radical foreign-born residents and communists and, as such, were viciously attacked as anti-American.[39]

Labor Rises, Then Falls

Throughout the decade, the power balance between employers and employees was still heavily weighted on the side of business, though labor would, for a time, take advantage of its increased bargaining clout during World War I. On the whole, business conditions at the beginning of the decade were still very poor, consisting of long hours, unsafe working environments, and low wages—less than 5 percent of the 37 million estimated workers had union representation.[40] Between 1910 and 1914, the number of manufacturing jobs in the United States increased by 5.1 percent, from 7.8 million to 8.2 million.[41] This growth of 400,000 positions in the largest industry sector in the country paled in comparison to the number of immigrants who came to the United States during the same period—5.2 million.[42] With a ready supply of available labor and a high unemployment rate, businesses had relatively few exogenous incentives to change working conditions or pay rates. Despite these conditions, there were two significant boosts to the labor movement prior to the outbreak of war in 1914.

In a move that generated greater symbolism than immediate practical benefits for labor, President Wilson separated the Department of Labor from the Department of Commerce in 1913 and appointed William B. Wilson as the first cabinet member for this position. William B. Wilson had been the president of the United Mine Workers Union, and his cabinet-level appointment was seen as a strong win for labor.[43] President Wilson's other labor reform efforts during this time had only limited impact. In 1916, he pushed through laws prohibiting the employment of children under age fourteen for firms engaged in interstate commerce, but two years later, the laws were ruled unconstitutional.[44]

Though it was not then viewed as a win for labor, the second significant prewar labor boost came in the most unlikely of places—Ford's automobile business. While it seems almost absurd to claim that Ford was progressive in his treatment of employees (given his well-documented inflexibility, autocratic management style, and anti-Semitism), he was one of the first major employers to share the profits of his business with his workforce. He did so by more than doubling the wages of his assembly-line workers in 1914 (to an unprecedented $5 per day); he used almost 50 percent of his $25 million in profits to do so. Not only did he double the day's labor wage, but he also reduced the workday from nine hours to eight. Ford's actions were, in his own words, motivated by a desire to maximize productivity, which he believed increased when workers were paid appropriately.[45] An apparently obvious sentiment today, it was considered radical at the time.

Regardless of his motivation, Ford's move became national news and was reported by the *New York Times* on January 11, 1914: "[Ford] shocks businesses by agreeing to share profits with workers."[46] The shock that reverberated throughout the business community was also acutely felt by the growing union movement. Remarkably, the unions strenuously objected not to the increase in pay, but to the reduction in the length of the workday. They feared that other businesses would follow Ford's lead in reducing the workday but without an equivalent salary adjustment.

Ford's actions during this decade were far from the norm. Business executives continued to pay little attention to the needs of their workers. This attitude changed somewhat in the war years between 1915 and 1918, when the number of manufacturing jobs swelled to over 11 million with a simultaneous drop in immigration. The reduction in the available labor pool played a large role in decreasing the U.S. unemployment rate from a prewar high of 15 percent to a postwar rate of roughly 2 percent.[47] When the United States entered the war in 1917, unions seized this short-term opportunity to advance their cause. America's businesses needed to find replacement workers for the nearly 4 million individuals who joined the army. Unions utilized massive recruiting efforts and a corresponding wave of work strikes to build their power base, eventually doubling union membership between 1915 and 1920 (from 2.5 million to 5.0 million).[48] Unions were also successful in increasing wages, especially in the manufacturing sector. The average factory worker who earned twenty-two cents an hour in 1913 earned sixty cents an hour by 1920.[49]

Although the increased strikes, low unemployment, and expanded membership base strengthened the labor movement, the government's intervention through the creation of the War Industries Board did much to stymie any further progress in the decade to come.[50] Through its power to fix wages and ban strikes, the board essentially halted the momentum of labor and reaffirmed the power balance between businesses, government, and employees.

Technology Drives Forward

While Ford's labor practices were considered anomalous in the 1910s, his automobile business was the primary driver of technological innovation during this decade. Several key technical innovations were instrumental in making the automobile affordable, accessible, and safe. They included the invention of the electric self-starter by Charles Kettering, the development of hydraulic brakes by Malcolm Lockheed, and the application of interchangeable parts in the assembly and repair process by Henry Leland. The new self-starter, which eliminated the need for manual cranking, and the safer braking mechanism helped improve the reputation and consequently the demand for automobiles. Before the invention of hydraulic brakes, it was considered a competitive advantage if a car stopped in only twice its length at eighteen miles per hour.[51] While both of these innovations were significant, it was the assembly line that brought automobiles truly within the reach of the masses. In 1908, Leland, president of Cadillac Motor Car Company, demonstrated that interchangeable parts could be successfully deployed in the manufacture of automobiles. Leland's work was a pivotal step in the early mass production of automobiles, and no one took greater advantage of the productivity gains associated with interchangeable parts than Ford.

Ford, an early proponent of Frederick Winslow Taylor's time-and-motion studies, used the concept of interchangeable parts to create an assembly-line structure within his manufacturing operation. The automobile magnate described the ideal process for building automobiles: "The way to make automobiles is to make one automobile like another automobile, to make them all alike."[52] When the assembly line was introduced at Ford's manufacturing plant in 1913, the chassis of the car was originally pulled along a production line by rope, stopping at predetermined intervals that allowed work teams to complete specific tasks in the building of the automobile. Through a series of improvements, the assembly line was eventually automated using an endless chain and placed at the waist level of workers to minimize both unnecessary lifting and strain. The introduction of the assembly line reduced the production time of a Model T automobile from twelve hours to one and one-half.[53] The dramatic growth and expansion of the automobile industry was characterized by the accelerated pace of production of Ford Model T cars. With the introduction of the modern assembly line, which may have been an even greater innovation

An early version of the automobile assembly line at a Ford plant in the 1910s. (Source: Underwood & Underwood/CORBIS)

than the automobile itself, Ford was able to significantly increase production and reduce prices. In 1912, Ford produced 82,000 Model T cars, which retailed at $850; by 1916, Ford produced over 585,000, at a retail price of just $360.[54]

Leaders: Reincarnation Specialists

Although the use of interchangeable parts was a new discovery in the automobile industry, it had been firmly established as a core operating approach in the production of typewriters and clocks for decades. With the typewriter's several raw material components and hundreds of parts, the complexity of its assembly made it a natural candidate for interchangeable parts. In fact, the typewriter has been called "the most complex mechanism to be mass produced by American industry in the nineteenth century."[55] To achieve efficiency of production and standardization of design, several typewriter manufacturers, including Remington, Dinsmore, and Smith-Premier, organized themselves into the Union Typewriter Company in 1893. As the proprietors of a young company, the Smith brothers (Wilbert and Lyman) jumped at the opportunity to collaborate with other industry leaders. The association gave them both a close-up view of the mass production of typewriters and a distinct role in defining that process. Believing that there was a better way to manufacturer typewriters, the Smith brothers, after ten years of affiliation with the Union Typewriter Company, decided to embark on their own. They brought new innovations to the design of typewriters while borrowing existing, proven processes. In particular, the Smith Company perfected the first typewriter to produce both upper- and lowercase letters, which soon became a product standard.[56]

In similar fashion, Seth Thomas Jr., the great-grandson of the founder of the Seth Thomas Clock Company (founded in 1812), continued the family's tradition of innovating within the hundred-year-old clock-making business. The younger Thomas continued to perfect the use of interchangeable parts by applying them to the production of both watches and wall clocks. When Thomas took over the firm in 1919, it had produced its last batch of pocket watches (having produced over 4 million) and was in the process of converting its operations to new watch designs.[57] Thomas oversaw the transformation that enabled the company to continue to prosper and grow while essentially protecting itself against product obsolescence.

Like Thomas, many leaders of the 1910s inherited businesses at critical stages in their development. The decisions that they made to invest, to convert, or to harvest were often difficult gambles requiring great risk with uncertain returns. In terms of far-reaching business altering decisions, no one did more to help a company on the brink of ruin than William A. Fairburn, who rekindled the hopes and prospects of not only a single business but an entire industry.

When Fairburn joined the Diamond Match Company in 1909, almost thirty years after its founding, the company was suffering on a number of fronts. While it had long enjoyed the prosperity of controlling most of the U.S. market for matches, Diamond Match was beset with problems. It had seriously depleted its supply of timber resources, and its cost structure had skyrocketed. Furthermore, Diamond's employees were constantly subjected to poisonous vapors, which caused a condition called phosphorous necrosis (company records cited thirty-seven cases of worker poisoning prior to Fairburn's arrival).[58] Finally, Diamond Match had become the target of public scorn for producing a toxic home product. The company's most serious business threat was from international suppliers that had recently developed a prototype of a safety match, a nonpoisonous match that worked when used on a specific surface. If this technology were perfected by the European match industry, it could essentially destroy Diamond Match. Fairburn, characteristic of his nature, systematically and diligently attacked each of the threats to the company's operations.

To address the depleting timber resources, he embarked on both new land acquisition and an early version of reforestation. He developed a plan to rotate different tree species that could adequately supply the raw materials for the matchstick, the box, and the cover. A major factor impacting the rising costs of match production was the inability to control the climate within the factory, which typically limited operations to eight or nine months per year. In an effort to address the climate concerns, Fairburn designed an air-conditioning and ventilation system (prior to the invention of modern air-conditioning) that would allow the factories of Diamond Match to effectively operate for the full year. While the ventilation system greatly enhanced the conditions for productivity, it also provided a safer working environment, essentially functioning as an external filter for the poisonous vapors.

Finally, Fairburn set up a new chemistry department to develop a match that could be consistently produced from nonpoisonous phosphorus. His earlier work in controlling the climate of the factory enabled him to experiment in better conditions than those endured by his failed predecessors, and he was able to oversee the production of a new safety match. Fairburn could have easily retained the exclusive rights to the new patent or even sold the patent for a hefty royalty to competitors, but he did neither. At the urging of Congress and the Bureau of Labor, Fairburn, remarkably, decided to give the new patent to the public for free. In so doing, he essentially leveled the playing field for all competitors and ensured both a safe work environment for factory employees and a safe and reliable product for consumers.[59]

Entrepreneurs: Masters of Marketing

The consumer was also the key focal point for the decade's entrepreneurs who embraced and enhanced the opportunities for national distribution. These business executives were heavy investors in sales and marketing strategies and were early adopters of new technologies to promote their products—predominantly radio, which became a national phenomenon in the 1920s. Representative brand builders included John T. Dorrance, Joyce C. Hall, and Elizabeth Arden. Dorrance invented the process for making condensed soup, reducing canning and shipping costs by two-thirds. As a result of Dorrance's invention, Campbell Soup Company became the first soup company to achieve national distribution. Hall pioneered the use of radio and later television advertising for greeting cards and revolutionized the industry with a display case that allowed the seller to accurately monitor sales and inventory. Through her salons and cosmetics line, Arden targeted the "discriminating woman" who would spend more to pamper herself. During her career, Arden owned 150 salons throughout the world and sold her one thousand products in twenty-five countries.

As these individuals developed their brands, the advertising industry was correspondingly blossoming. Developments included the launch and expansion of the Batten, Barton, Durstine and Osborn (BBDO) and the Lord & Thomas agencies. Each of these firms profited immensely in the 1920s and beyond, as product advertising became ubiquitous. Bruce Barton of BBDO was responsible for helping to develop a more favorable public image for U.S. Steel Corporation after the steel strike of 1919. He employed a heretofore little-used strategy to impact public sentiment; that strategy was later called public relations. During his career, Barton also created many advertising pillars, including "Betty Crocker" for General Mills. Taking a different approach, Albert Lasker of Lord & Thomas embraced and perfected hard-hitting advertising. He directed campaigns for such products as Palmolive soap, Quaker Oats, and Pepsodent toothpaste. Later in his career, Lasker was instrumental in gaining public acceptance for the advertisement of Kotex sanitary napkins, and through his promotion of Sunkist, he popularized the idea of drinking orange juice.

Many entrepreneurs were initially ridiculed for their seemingly counterintuitive business practices. Charles Merrill, for instance, built his initial brokerage business on the fledging retail sector. Considered a highly suspect industry at the time, Merrill received little initial funding support. As the population centers began to dramatically expand, Merrill was eventually proven correct, but he needed to rely on his own headstrong vision to sustain his operation. Another headstrong visionary who was originally castigated for his ideas went on to revolutionize the way Americans shopped for groceries.

Clarence Saunders (1881–1953), Piggly Wiggly Stores, Incorporated

The story of Clarence Saunders is one of triumph and corresponding despair, of unbelievable wealth and bitter poverty, and of incredible innovation and paralyzing stubbornness, but mostly it is a story of perseverance, rebirth, and renewal. Just when he was apparently firmly defeated, Saunders rebuilt himself and pushed the envelope of innovation to its outer limits once more. A tireless entrepreneur and perpetual inventor, Saunders answered to no one but himself and therein was a major source of his problems; sometimes his self-counsel was laced with gold, but just as often poisoned with lead. Saunders was an inventive creator first and a businessman second.

The son of a successful tobacco farmer and plantation owner, Saunders was born in Virginia and raised along the banks of the Cumberland River in Clarksville, Tennessee. Like many founders of the early decades, Saunders had little formal education; he received approximately four years of schooling between the ages of ten and fourteen. Beginning as a grocery store clerk earning four dollars a month, Saunders went on to work in a variety of different functional areas within the grocery industry. His outgoing personality and charm were particularly well suited to the life of a traveling grocery wholesaler-salesman, and as such, Saunders formed his own independent grocery cooperative, which functioned as an intermediary between the local grocers and the product producers. His interactions with hundreds of grocers also enabled him to view firsthand the frustrations of both customers and grocers, and his role as a wholesaler gave him a unique perspective on the fundamental shifts that were impacting the industry.

With the amount of national advertising skyrocketing, customers yearned for access to branded products at low prices. In the meantime, grocers sought to increase the inventory turnover of their private-label items while simultaneously limiting the amount of goods sold on credit. Most grocers at the time were small independent operations that could not afford to sell a vast array of both branded and private-label products. Grocers made up for the dearth of product selection with liberal credit policies, which Saunders observed often became the cause of their demise. The average grocery store by 1915 carried between 750 and 1,000 products and the basic business premise was high margin and low turnover.[60] That business premise was beginning to change in the mid-1910s as the Great Atlantic & Pacific Tea Company (A&P), the largest grocery retailer in the country, attempted and succeeded in flipping the equation—opening new "economy stores" that were designed to sell low-margin products in high volumes. A&P was able to lower its product margins by eliminating the wholesaler and negotiating directly with manufacturers. In some cases, A&P even processed and distributed its own products. Without the margin afforded to wholesalers, A&P could pass along price reductions to the consumers, which essentially changed the entire dynamics of the grocery trade.[61] As a wholesaler during this time, Saunders was undoubtedly aware of the changes happening within grocery retailing, and instead of watching the changes, he chose to drive them.

In 1915, after more than a decade as a successful grocery wholesaler, Saunders left the life of a salesman for the life of a retailer. Taking stock of his observations and insights, Saunders embarked on an ambitious plan to design and build a radically new grocery store operation. He borrowed new approaches from his wholesaler customers, particularly those stores that were beginning to institute cash-and-carry policies that depended on high product volumes to secure low prices. The low prices, in turn, made a no-credit policy more palatable to the consumer.

His plan for a self-service grocery establishment where customers entered the store through secure turnstiles, selected their own items from display shelves, and placed them in a wooden basket while walking through serpentine aisles that ended at a payment counter could not have been more different from the traditional shopping experience. The new store, which he called Piggly Wiggly, included end-aisle displays situated at eye level to encourage impulse purchases and products containing a patented hanging tag identifying the price of the merchandise. This tagging practice was the first recorded instance of a retailer's providing individual, visible prices for all its products.[62] Adding to the aesthetics of the experience were uniformed personnel who were required to abide by strict employee work guidelines. The new model also required that customers pay for their goods as they left the store, virtually eliminating the age-old store credit policies. To build and outfit his store, Saunders had to essentially create most of its fixtures and components, including his trademarked Checking and Settlement Counter at the end of the store maze.[63] He developed and patented most of the store fixtures and display cases and established a separate company, Saunders Manufacturing Company, to produce and distribute them.

A consummate salesman, Saunders created his own brand of Southern, homespun advertising to draw attention to weekend specials, which in the case of Piggly Wiggly, actually lasted all week (another new notion in store advertising). His early advertising was centered on a friendly pink pig that

The innovative grocery shopping design created by Clarence Saunders of Piggly Wiggly (1918).
(Source: CORBIS)

seemed to capture the essence of Southern hospitality. In addition to his own advertising, Saunders courted the producers of nationally branded products, believing that his new store could piggyback on their wide-scale advertising. He was convinced that consumers wanted access to these products, which would sell quickly—a key component of his volume strategy.

While the preceding shopping experience sounds very familiar today, it was an absolutely foreign concept in the 1910s. Grocery stores at the time revolved around a model in which the grocer controlled all aspects of the customer interaction. Under the traditional approach, there were a limited number of items available for purchase and even those items were not accessible to the customer. The shopping scenario required the customer to provide a grocery clerk with a list of desired products, which were then gathered and bundled by a clerk scurrying about the store. After the cost of the items was tallied on the customer's credit account, the completed order was either delivered to the customer's home or given to the customer on the spot. Most items for sale were not individually wrapped or packaged and had to be secured and measured from large barrels or crates throughout the store. The entire purchasing process required the intervention of several individuals and the completion of a multitude of tasks. In many cases, local grocers selected the brand of items that a customer received and willingly substituted their own choice of products if the store was out of stock on a specific request.

The ridicule that Saunders initially endured when he opened Piggly Wiggly dissipated quickly as the economics of his revolutionary grocery store emerged. By shifting the labor associated with grocery shopping to the customer, Saunders operated his stores with a minimum number of employees. This enabled him to offer much lower prices than traditional grocery stores could while simultaneously providing access to nationally branded products. "Traditional stores had done $400 to $500 a week in sales at a cost of 12–17 percent. Piggly Wiggly grossed $7,000 a week at a cost of 3 percent."[64]

Saunders left little to chance. Though a whimsical name like Piggly Wiggly might suggest a lighthearted operation, a visit to the store was actually designed to be a very streamlined experience; it was an experience focused on efficiency, cost-savings, and service. As a student of scientific management, Saunders was quick to apply the concepts of efficiency and order to the grocery trade. Within a year of opening Piggly Wiggly, Saunders had hired a time-and-motion expert to continually refine his operation.

The early success of the first Piggly Wiggly operations in Memphis gave way to a rapid expansion program that involved both internal development and franchising. Within the first year of operations, Saunders opened nine Piggly Wiggly stores, and that number grew to over 1,200 in forty states by 1922 (half of these stores were franchised operations, buying the store layout, design, and operational procedures from Saunders). Within a few years of launching Piggly Wiggly, Saunders became a multimillionaire, and his company was estimated to be worth over $100 million. Saunders was quick to embrace his new status and began to build a life of opulence. He bought country homes and built a massive pink mansion, dubbed the Pink Palace, in downtown Memphis. His success, however, was short-lived.

To rapidly expand his operation, Saunders had listed his business on the New York Stock Exchange in the early 1920s. In November 1922, a Northeast franchise chain of stores operating under the Piggly Wiggly name, though not part of Saunders's company, declared bankruptcy. A few speculators on Wall Street seized this opportunity to sell short the Piggly Wiggly stock, hoping that the public would confuse the bankrupt Northeast company with the official Piggly Wiggly operation. The speculators assumed that the price of Piggly Wiggly shares would drop precipitously. And, for a short time, they were right. Prior to the "bear raid" by the speculators, Piggly Wiggly stock was trading at around $50 per share. The speculators had lowered that price to $39 per share.[65] In a desperate attempt to bolster his company's stock price, Saunders borrowed over $10 million to buy back as much stock as possible. His actions quickly boosted the stock price to over $70 per share. He continued to buy stock in Piggly Wiggly, eventually pushing its price to over $120 a share and essentially cornering the market. Saunders fully expected to "beat Wall Street at its own game," but he did not expect that the New York Stock Exchange would aggressively attempt to break his corner on the market.[66]

When Saunders demanded delivery of the shares that he had purchased, the exchange, in an effort to retain market stability for what was now a vastly overpriced stock, decided to suspend trading of the stock and extend the normal twenty-four-hour delivery period to five days. To make matters worse, the exchange then removed the stock listing altogether. With the extension for the delivery of shares, the speculators were able to meet Saunders's call, and he was left heavily in debt. He was now the holder of stock so highly priced there was no market for it. Unable to settle his debts even after attempting to sell off some of his properties, Saunders was forced to resign from the company and turn over all his professional and personal assets, including his uncompleted Pink Palace. He declared personal bankruptcy in February 1924.[67] In eight short years, Saunders had gone from rags to riches and back again. He was forty-three years old and had lost everything.

Although his stubborn and unwavering faith in his business ironically led him to lose control, he was not defeated. He set his sights on new frontiers and, within a few years, was back in the grocery retail business as the proprietor of a store he called "Clarence Saunders, Sole Owner of My Own Name." The name was a "rebuff to the Piggly Wiggly Board's effort to keep [Saunders] from using his name in food retailing."[68] Commonly called Sole Owner, this grocery chain was modeled after Piggly Wiggly and achieved considerable success after its founding in 1928, but it did not last long, either. Saunders again employed an aggressive growth plan and overextended the company's debt burden. By the beginning of the Great Depression, Saunders was bankrupt and had lost control of the company with his name.

Undaunted by his previous two failures, Saunders continued to tinker with new designs for shopping and introduced yet another revolutionary shopping experience in 1937. His vision for the future entailed a fully automated grocery store (the Keedoozle, for "Key Does All"), in which the customers selected items behind glass cases by inserting a special key at the product location. The product was then dropped onto a conveyer belt and sent to a packaging station, where a clerk tallied the bill and bundled the goods.

Saunders believed that this new store design would virtually eliminate the need for more than two employees. His design was well ahead of its time, and mechanical problems were a persistent headache for Saunders. Though he expanded slowly with the concept, the store's constant need for mechanical readjustment forced him to close the operation by 1941.

After the demise of the Keedoozle, Saunders kept himself busy through the war years of the 1940s by designing and building wooden toys. By the end of World War II, Saunders had hit on his second version of the Keedoozle, which he called the Foodelectric store. He had worked through many of the operational glitches with the Keedoozle and was set to launch his latest store prototype when he died in 1953. Upon his death, the two-time millionaire had left a personal estate of just two thousand dollars.[69] Historians have estimated that Saunders's Keedoozle and Foodelectric stores were fifty years ahead of their time. In many ways, the online grocery shopping portals of today are symbolic representations of Saunders's automated shopping dream. Though he had many failures, Saunders left an indelible mark on America's shopping landscape. He deftly tapped into the American consumer's desire for self-reliance and control, and his store designs and approach foreshadowed fundamental changes in the retail grocery trade.[70]

A Yearning for More

The openness of America's frontier was ripe for the business executive of the 1910s. The spoils were there for the taking. Those who succeeded knew how to exploit the opportunities presented by the changing composition of the country, the proliferation of the automobile, the opening of the oil industry, and the bittersweet requirements of the war effort. As the decade came to a close, Americans were yearning for something more. The optimism of the fight for democracy quickly gave way to bitterness and disillusion as the treaty process dragged on and as it became apparent that democracy would not reign throughout Europe and Russia. A creeping cynicism developed as the country slipped into a recession. Americans longed for an escape from the pain of war, the pain of recession, and the uncertainty of the world order. There was an overriding sense of entitlement in the country—a feeling that Americans deserved more for their efforts. For many, these yearnings would be satisfied in the 1920s.

TABLE 2-3

Entrepreneurs, managers, and leaders of the 1910s

Entrepreneurs

Arthur E. Andersen, Arthur Andersen
Elizabeth Arden, Elizabeth Arden Company
Bruce Barton, Batten, Barton, Durstine and
 Osborn
Leon L. Bean, L.L. Bean
William E. Boeing, Boeing Company
Willis H. Carrier, Carrier Corporation
John T. Dorrance, Campbell Soup Company
Camille Dreyfus, Celanese Corporation of
 America
William Fox, Fox Film Company
Daniel F. Gerber, Gerber Products Company
Samuel Goldwyn, Samuel Goldwyn
 Productions
Joyce C. Hall, Hallmark Cards
John D. Hertz, Yellow Cab Company
Henry J. Kaiser, Kaiser Industries
Carl Laemmle, Universal Pictures Corporation
Albert D. Lasker, Lord & Thomas
Charles W. Nash, Nash Motors Company
Helena Rubinstein, Helena Rubinstein
Clarence Saunders, Piggly Wiggly Company
Elmer A. Sperry, Sperry Gyroscope Company
Adolph Zukor, Paramount Pictures

Managers

Archie A. Alexander, Alexander & Repass
Earl D. Babst, American Sugar Refining
Stephen Birch, Kennecott Copper
Edward G. Budd, E. G. Budd Company
Ralph Budd, Great Northern Railroad
David Burpee, W. A. Burpee Company
Floyd L. Carlisle, St. Regis Paper Company
Harry Chandler, Los Angeles Times
Joshua S. Cosden, Cosden & Company
Richard T. Crane Jr., Crane Company
Arthur V. Davis, Alcoa
Henry S. Dennison, Dennison Manufacturing
James C. Donnell, Ohio Oil Company
Pierre S. du Pont, DuPont Corporation
William Durant, General Motors Corporation
Frank J. Fahey, Gillette Company
Otto H. Falk, Allis-Chalmers Company
James A. Farrell, United States Steel
 Corporation
Truman K. Gibson, Supreme Life Insurance
 Company
Eugene G. Grace, Bethlehem Steel Corporation
Howard Heinz, H. J. Heinz Company
Alanson B. Houghton, Corning Glass Company

James W. Johnson, Johnson & Johnson
 Company
Henry P. Kendall, Kendall Company
George H. Mead, Mead Corporation
John P. Morgan Jr., J. P. Morgan & Company
John H. Pew, Sun Oil Company
Frank Phillips, Phillips Petroleum Company
Marjorie M. Post, Postum Cereal Company,
 Limited
Frederick H. Prince, Chicago Stock Yards
 Company
Stanley B. Resor, JWT Advertising Agency
Arthur Reynolds, Continental & Commercial
 Bank
Richard J. Reynolds, R.J. Reynolds Tobacco
 Company
Julius Rosenwald, Sears, Roebuck and Co.
Harry F. Sinclair, Sinclair Oil and Refining
 Company
Theodore E. Steinway, Steinway and Sons
Ross S. Sterling, Humble Oil and Refining
 Company
William L. Stewart, Union Oil Company
Jesse I. Straus, Macy (R. H.) and Company
Harold L. Stuart, Halsey, Stuart & Company
Walter C. Teagle, Standard Oil of New Jersey
Robert L. Vann, Pittsburgh Courier
Samuel M. Vauclain, Baldwin Locomotive
Solomon D. Warfield, Seaboard Air Line
 Railroad
John P. Weyerhaeuser, Weyerhaeuser Company
Albert H. Wiggin, Chase National Bank
Charles S. Woolworth, Woolworth and
 Company

Leaders

William A. Fairburn, Diamond Match Company
Frank L. Gillespie, Liberty Life Insurance
Samuel Insull, Middle West Utilities Company
George S. Lannom Jr., Lannom Manufacturing
Clifford D. Mallory, Mallory (C. D.) and
 Company
Robert R. McCormick, Chicago Tribune
Edward J. Noble, LifeSavers
Joseph M. Patterson, New York Daily News
Richard S. Reynolds, Reynolds Corporation
Wilbert L. Smith, L. C. Smith & Corona
 Typewriters, Inc.
Seth E. Thomas Jr., Seth Thomas Clocks
John W. Van Dyke, Atlantic Refining Company
Thomas J. Watson Sr., IBM
Daniel Willard, Baltimore and Ohio Railroad

THREE

1920–1929

From Prosperity to Despair

*It is only those who do not understand our people, who believe our national
life is entirely absorbed by material motives. We make no concealment of
the fact that we want wealth, but there are many other things we want much
more. We want peace and honor, and that charity which is so strong an element
of all civilization. The chief ideal of the American people is idealism.
I cannot repeat too often that America is a nation of idealists. That is the only
motive to which they ever give any strong and lasting reaction.*

—Calvin Coolidge

THE MONUMENTAL MOBILIZATION that occurred in business and
society to sustain the war effort in the 1910s continued after the last guns
were fired and the last soldiers returned home. Though the United States embarked on a swift disarmament process, there was still considerable momentum in the economy, mostly fueled by the demand for basic necessities in
Europe and America. The war mobilization effort also brought about fundamental social changes that not only impacted businesses, but also influenced the types of businesses that emerged and created a subculture that no
longer promoted products simply for utility but for material possession. The
new American hero was not just the returning soldier from World War I;
he was joined by the business executive who could indulge a consumer's
wildest desires. New consumer products and services emerged at a rapid pace,
and the 1920s became an era of consumerism. Those who prospered knew

how to reach the customer and, probably more important, began to value the customer.

The marketing of the automobile demonstrated how different companies accepted or rejected the challenge of satisfying the customer. For all his brilliance and efficiency, Henry Ford failed that challenge. He not only shunned consumer preferences, but actually derided them. His famous quote that "customers can get any car and color that they want as long as it is a black Model T" is the epitome of his rejection of the consumer. Being the first to market and being the low-cost producer, as Ford was, certainly enabled him to prosper for many years. By the mid-1920s, Ford manufactured 50 percent of all cars produced in the world. His standardized mass production, then called "Fordism," enabled him to sell the ten millionth Model T for one-third the price of the original model.[1] Despite these triumphs, Ford was not prepared for the age of consumerism. He balked at simple, basic consumer desires such as color and style and major new developments such as the closed-car model.

An automobile executive who chose a different path sparked a transformation in customer management. Taking the helm of General Motors Corporation in 1923, Alfred P. Sloan Jr. revolutionized the growing automobile business by giving consumers a choice of color, size, and style. He understood the underlying current in America at the time, a current that longed for individuality, freedom, and status. Instead of one car for all people, Sloan's General Motors produced a suite of cars, each aimed at a particular social status. Beyond freedom of choice, Sloan also gave consumers "freedom of purchase" by offering cars on installment plans. He gave the consumers the illusion that they could have it all, a higher-priced, uniquely designed car on credit. By 1927, one-third of all cars were purchased on credit.[2] The annual automobile model change (as heralded by Sloan) was a symbol of the consumer culture as much as the Model T was the symbol of production efficiency.[3]

Though Sloan is most known in academic circles for his contributions to organization design (decentralized, autonomous business units delivering a broad range of products to specific audience segments), he left a broader legacy in his willingness to embrace and satisfy the customer. Heretofore, customers were often considered a necessary evil, not a rich and untapped well of opportunity. Sloan was not the first to recognize the value of targeting unique consumer desires, but he took some of the greatest risks in defying the

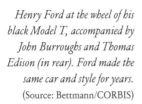

Henry Ford at the wheel of his black Model T, accompanied by John Burroughs and Thomas Edison (in rear). Ford made the same car and style for years.
(Source: Bettmann/CORBIS)

prevailing wisdom that uniformity in product design was the only path to cost-effective manufacturing. Through Sloan's efforts, General Motors' market share increased from 13 percent in 1921 to 20 percent in 1925, while Ford's market shared dropped from 56 percent to 40 percent.[4] By the end of the 1920s, General Motors surpassed Ford as the largest automobile manufacturer in the world.[5]

The tale of the Ford and Sloan car wars reflects the conflicting nature of the 1920s. Ford was an uneducated son of a midwestern farmer, whereas Sloan was the educated and refined son of an East Coast merchant. Ford was a traditionalist, shunning consumer preferences and staunchly adhering to a cash-only payment policy. Sloan was a consumerist who catered to customer desires and embraced the liberalism of credit. While Ford focused on the product for the masses, Sloan focused on the product for a given market segment. In management style, Ford wielded an autocratic iron fist, whereas Sloan diffused his own power through the adoption of a decentralized management structure. In the end, Ford was the epitome of the business executive of a generation gone by, while Sloan was the new breed of chief executive.[6]

Adopting more of Sloan's style than Ford's, in 1924, Walter Chrysler defied the prevailing conventions of the time by making larger and more powerful automobiles for the public; these car designs had been originally targeted for the high-end race-car circuit. Chrysler, like Sloan, chose to build his business by first understanding what customers wanted instead of simply delivering what they needed. From this point forward, the purchase of an automobile would depend on its symbolism as much as its utility. With the success of his enterprise, Chrysler joined Ford and General Motors as one of the Big Three in U.S. automobile manufacturing.[7] General Motors, Ford, and Chrysler dominated the automobile market and demonstrated the clear advantage of size and scope in the industry. In 1921, there were eighty-eight automobile manufacturers in the United States. By 1927, that number had been cut in half and was continuing to decline.[8] Automobile production was forevermore the domain of big business.

Historians often point to the automobile as the defining icon of the 1920s, equally heralded as a symbol of the country's spectacular boom period and vilified as the culprit for the country's economic downturn. Critics cite the adoption of installment payment plans in the automobile sector as a major contributor to the growth of unmanageable personal debt. The availability of liberal credit for an expensive item like an automobile opened the floodgates to the use of credit for a multitude of household items, including refrigerators, washing machines, and other appliances.

1929 advertisement for a new General Motors Pontiac—heralded as the "biggest car value" in America. (Source: Bettmann/CORBIS)

On the positive side, the automobile created a wave of businesses, including upstream suppliers of components and raw materials and downstream services such as replacement parts, repair shops, and gasoline service stations. In particular, the used-car market boomed in the mid-1920s, with pre-owned automobile sales outstripping new car sales in 1927.[9] Beyond these direct businesses, the automobile gave Americans a sense of mobility and freedom that was unprecedented. Americans could now live outside the city, they could travel great distances, and they could seek new employment.

Managers: Giving Customers What They Want

Embracing the needs and desires of the customer became a hallmark of the 1920s, and this emphasis created a major advertising boom. Between 1919 and 1929, advertising grew from a $1.4 billion to a $2.9 billion industry.[10] For some less-than-scrupulous business executives in the 1920s, it also became an easy outlet for developing marketing scams. To induce fears and galvanize purchases, these snake-oil merchants "educated" consumers about a number of new diseases. For instance, if you suffered from bromodosis, your life was not in jeopardy; you simply had an unforgivable case of bad foot odor. Some believed that a homemaker's worse nightmare in the 1920s was homotosis—the unenviable "disease" caused by the lack of nice furniture. If you wanted to avoid coalitosis, you would heat your home with oil and not with coalitosis-causing coal. Advertisers saw an incredible opportunity to market their clients' products as remedies to diseases that Americans didn't even know they had.[11] And the American public was all too willing to be swept into this frenzy.

Beyond the public's acceptance of these so-called diseases, there was little regulation on the part of the government, and there were most certainly no consumer protection agencies picketing manufacturers. Manufacturers and their advertisers had free rein to seduce and sell. Interestingly, the term *media* first became part of the advertisers' lexicon in the early 1920s. They used the term as a broader means of defining the communication vehicles (mostly newspapers and magazines at the time) in which they placed their advertisements.[12] From the 1920s forward, the American public would become "media targets."

One individual who tapped into not just a fleeting desire but the long-term essence and core of what it meant to be an American with his product

Advertisement for La-Mar Reducing Soap, one of many similar ads of the 1920s that took excessive liberties with actual product performance. (Source: Bettmann/CORBIS)

was Robert W. Woodruff. Though it was only sugarcoated water, Coca-Cola became as American as apple pie, baseball, and motherhood. Woodruff, more than most business executives of the time, understood what Americans truly yearned for. He was a consummate salesman who effectively deployed advertising and elaborate marketing schemes to satisfy that yearning.

Robert W. Woodruff (1889–1985), Coca-Cola Company

Woodruff was raised in a life of affluence in Georgia, yet in many respects, he could have been born into a family of much lesser means. His father, Ernest Woodruff, was a very successful and influential Atlanta banker who strongly believed in the biblical maxim "Every one to whom much is given, of him will much be required; and of him to whom men commit much, they will demand the more."[13] Having given his first-born child a life of wealth and status, Ernest expected much from him. He expected his son to apply himself to his studies, graduate from college, and join him as a respectable Southern banker. He did not expect a son to squander his resources, abandon school, and pursue "ordinary labor."

By all accounts, Robert Woodruff was not a gifted student. He struggled through elementary school, flunked out of Boys' High School in Atlanta, and barely graduated from the Georgia Military Academy, where he had been sent to finish his studies. What he lacked in academic skills, he made up in his leadership positions at the military academy. Though even his teachers at the military academy recommended a life of industry for Woodruff, his father insisted that he attend Emory College. Given that Robert spent time cutting classes and carousing, it is hard to know if he could have succeeded. After just one semester, he was strongly encouraged by the college president not to return. He gladly obliged, much to the chagrin of his father.

At age nineteen, Woodruff became a laborer, shoveling and sifting sand for the General Pipe and Foundry Company, where he was soon promoted to a position as a machinist's apprentice. From there, he moved on to a sales position with the parent organization, General Fire Extinguisher Company. In this position, he found the roots of his real desires and talents. He was a natural and gifted salesman. As his sales territory quickly expanded, his success caught the eye of his still befuddled father. Finally giving up his dream of a college education for his son, Ernest Woodruff offered Robert a position as a purchasing agent at one of his companies, the Atlantic Ice and Coal Company. In this capacity, the younger Woodruff successfully negotiated the purchase of a trucking fleet from the White Motor Company to replace the horse-drawn wagons currently used to deliver ice and coal. Having become enamored by the new truck models while attending an automobile exhibition in New York City, Robert struck the deal with White Motors without consulting his father or others at the company. According to Coca-Cola historian Frederick Allen, Robert Woodruff did more than just purchase the fleet: "In exchange for the low price [that he had extracted], Woodruff suggested that White keep the trucks on display for the rest of the show and exhibit them as the largest fleet [fifteen vehicles] ever sold to a Southern company."[14] Through this act, Woodruff displayed an early appreciation for promotional flair. His father was less impressed. In fact, he was furious with the rashness of his son's actions and blocked a pre-negotiated pay raise that Robert was anticipating.

Robert quit the Atlantic Coal and Ice Company and joined the Cleveland-based White Motor Company in 1913. The executives of White Motor were so impressed with young Woodruff's negotiating skills that they were all too willing to offer him a sales position as their representative in the Southern region. Woodruff's natural sales abilities and personal connections in the South were a formidable combination. He targeted potential customers who needed not just one or two trucks, but a fleet of vehicles, and his first prospects were the county road commissioners. His strategy paid off, and he quickly rose through the ranks of the company. During the years of World War I, Woodruff secured a position in the government's ordinance department, where he helped design special transportation trucks. Interestingly enough, the truck specifications were an almost perfect match to the White Motor truck chassis. By 1921, Woodruff had become a vice president with White Motors and had relocated to the home office in Cleveland. Two years later, at age thirty-three, he had become the heir apparent to the firm's founder.

While Woodruff was excelling at White Motors, his father had purchased the ailing Coca-Cola Company from the Asa Candler trusts in 1919 for the unprecedented sum of $25 million. At the time, it was the largest business transaction in the South. When Woodruff purchased Coca-Cola, the company was struggling as a result of its restrictive relationships with its bottling franchises. Early on, the company had negotiated a fixed price for selling its ingredients to the bottlers, but when sugar was rationed during the war, its cost skyrocketed. Not wanting to detract from volume sales, the company refused to increase the price of Coca-Cola to consumers. As such, the company had to absorb the increased sugar price. After buying the company, Ernest Woodruff and his associates renegotiated the contract with the bottlers to include a provision for a fixed price for all ingredients with the exception of sugar, which would fluctuate with the prevailing market conditions. By 1923, the company had weathered the worst of the war rationing and postwar recession and was looking to grow on a new scale. Woodruff and his associates believed that the person to take Coca-Cola to the next level was Robert; they offered him $36,000 in salary to run the company. Though he was making $50,000 more per year, he accepted the position. Whether he accepted to move back to Atlanta, where he felt a strong bond, or whether he was still trying to prove his abilities to his father is not known. He publicly stated that he returned to Coca-Cola to recoup his investment in the company; he had acquired and been given shares over time.

Taking the helm of Coca-Cola, Woodruff concentrated first on what he knew best: sales and marketing. Jumping on the advertising bandwagon, Woodruff employed Archie Lee of D'Arcy Advertising in St. Louis to reenergize the image of Coca-Cola. The agency created the enduring tagline "The Pause That Refreshes," giving Americans a reason and a need to slow down their increasingly hectic lives. Placing a bottle of Coke in wholesome images of American life, Woodruff and Lee captured the hearts and minds of the mainstream public. His images transcended the differences between North and South, between urban and rural, and between liberal and conservative. They skated on the thin middle ground that appealed to America's collective ideal of itself by evoking subliminal sex appeal but not too sexy, celebrating traditional values but not too hokey, seemingly indulgent but a good alternative to bootleg liquor. Woodruff helped make Coke's appeal universal, not partisan.

He embraced the opening of the frontier made possible by the automobile and bought a tremendous amount of advertisement space along America's new highway network. In the late 1920s, he also championed the radio as a new medium for extolling the virtues of Coke. Woodruff was a master of promotion, even orchestrating a highly publicized retrieval of the original secret recipe for Coca-Cola that had been held in the vault of a New York bank as collateral for the early sugar loans that the company needed during World War I.

Like his counterparts of the 1920s, Woodruff was focused on the reach and scope of his business. More Americans had become mobile, and with that mobility came opportunities for broader distribution. Bottled sales of Coke were soon becoming more important than the company's flagship soda-fountain sales. Woodruff restructured the company's distribution model to create a much stronger bottling network. Obsessed with product quality and standardization, he forced bottlers to adhere to strict sterilization procedures and precise mixing guidelines. On his occasional surprise visits to bottling operations, his pleasure or displeasure was always evident. He did not expand by merging with other companies or creating product line extensions as he was urged to do, but expanded instead through a dedicated, almost obsessive, singular focus on one product: Coca-Cola. He believed that service—not sales—was the key to the future success of distribution. In a dramatic move, Woodruff held a company meeting in which he fired his entire sales staff. He rehired them the next day as members of the newly created "service department." Their new role was to help retailers, soda fountains, service stations, and other outlets create an environment that was conducive to selling more Coke.

Between his start in 1923 and the end of the decade, Woodruff tripled profits from $4.5 million to $13 million. As noted by one of the many biographers of Coca-Cola, "the company typified the major corporation in the twenties—the era of the first professional managers, who relied increasingly on lawyers, public relations experts, market researchers, psychologists and advertisers."[15] Woodruff employed them all. By the outbreak of the Great Depression, the company seemed surprisingly poised for continued success. Woodruff understood that even in tough times, Americans would spend a nickel for a brief respite. He did not retreat during the Depression, but instead increased the company's advertising by continuing to depict an ideal America. In fact, if a person only looked at the Coca-Cola advertising of the 1930s, he or she would be hard-pressed to discover any images of the harsh reality of the times.[16] The company was added to the Dow Jones Industrial Average in 1932 and was trading at $200 a share in 1935, the highest industrial stock price in the country before its four-to-one split.[17] Coke's success generated both strong competition from the likes of Pepsi-Cola and a host of cola-wannabes. Woodruff was vigilant in his legal battles against any actual or potential infringements on the company's secret formula and trademarked branding.

Looking beyond America's shores for world dominance, Woodruff solidified Coke's international presence when he announced during World War II that Coca-Cola would be available to any U.S. soldier overseas for five cents, regardless of the cost to the company. This remarkable publicity stunt enabled Coca-Cola to maintain its access to rationed sugar during the war. Coca-Cola had been initially limited to 80 percent of its sugar consumption in 1940, but the ration could be lifted if the end product had a significant military use. Woodruff set out to make Coke a military necessity. With the benefit of government subsidies, the company built sixty-four bottling plants throughout the world and U.S. soldiers consumed over 5 billion bottles of Coca-Cola. After the war, Woodruff had a ready-made global infrastructure. Through his global network of bottling plants and his unofficial product ambassadors (U.S. soldiers), Woodruff built Coca-Cola into a world beverage. He did so by holding firm to his conviction that the formula never be changed, regardless of local or cultural taste differences. It seems almost fitting that his death at age ninety-five came one month before the release of the New Coke in 1985—a decision that Woodruff would probably never have made.[18]

Coca-Cola was representative of the modern organizational structure that emerged in the 1920s, designed to better control, utilize, and measure resources. Companies like General Motors and Coca-Cola adopted smaller corporate offices with defined staff functions that provided services to decentralized

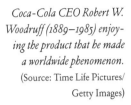

Coca-Cola CEO Robert W. Woodruff (1889–1985) enjoying the product that he made a worldwide phenomenon.
(Source: Time Life Pictures/ Getty Images)

and, often, autonomous business units headed by independent general managers. Many individuals anticipated the needs of the new corporation and established businesses to fulfill them. One such person was James O. McKinsey, who founded the largest management-consulting firm in the world. His greatest contribution was to focus attention on the importance of budgeting as a major instrument of management. He asserted the need for continued education for future executives and foresaw the era of the "scientific man" in business, an era characterized by careful planning, research, and aligned organizational frameworks.

Turning Inward: America Embraces Isolationism

With the end of World War I, the only country that emerged from the experience stronger, richer, and more powerful was the United States, but the country did not use its newfound status to take a leadership role in global affairs.[19] On the contrary, it retreated to the comfort and familiarity of isolationism. Aside from its "intervention at will" policies in Mexico and Latin America, where the United States continued to interject its might whenever such action served the country's economic or political agenda, the United States, on the whole, stayed out of foreign affairs. U.S. foreign policy during this time consisted of helping maintain stability in East Asia and enforcing the payment of loans for the war and reconstruction efforts.[20]

Though many nations throughout the world initiated a disarmament program after World War I, Japan continued to build its naval presence in East

TABLE 3-1

Business events that shaped the 1920s

Date	Event
1920	Supreme Court rules U.S. Steel Corporation not a monopoly
1920	KDKA in Pittsburgh—first licensed radio station
1920	Sears introduces installment payment plans
1920	Alfred P. Sloan Jr. presents first reorganization plans for General Motors; fully implemented by 1924
1921	Congress passes Emergency Immigration Act to restrict immigration
1921	Secretary of commerce chairs first Commission on Unemployment (5.7 million jobless)
1921	Supreme Court rules that Clayton Act does not protect secondary boycotts by labor movement
1921	U.S. Post Office Department experiments with airmail
1921	General Accounting Office created
1922	Teapot Dome Scandal
1922	Congress adopts protectionist tariffs
1922	First radio commercial aired by AT&T's WEAF
1922	Country Club Plaza opens near Kansas City—first U.S. planned shopping center
1922	Insulin invented by Sir Frederick Grant Banting
1923	First traffic signal invented
1924	Employee productivity studied at Western Electric's Hawthorne plant
1925	MIT engineer devises first "modern" computer
1925	AT&T sends photo by wire to three cities simultaneously
1925	Kelly Act passed to privatize airmail service
1926	Income tax reduction act signed
1926	Air Commerce Act gives Department of Commerce control of nation's airways and airports
1926	Robert H. Goddard launches first liquid-fuel rocket
1927	Federal Radio Commission formed
1927	Charles Lindbergh is first to fly nonstop from New York to Paris
1927	First talking movie—*The Jazz Singer*
1927	U.S. wages become the highest in the world
1928	WGY of Schenectady broadcasts first scheduled television program in United States
1929	Frozen foods offered to the public by Clarence Birdseye
1929	Car radio introduced by Paul V. Galvin of Motorola
1929	AT&T—first corporation to record revenues of $1 billion
1929	Dow Jones Industrial Average hits high of 381.17 on September 3
1929	Dow Jones Industrial Average falls to 260.64; beginning of the market crash

Asia. The United States grew increasingly concerned that Japan would embark on an empire-building campaign that would result in a closed market in Asia, especially in China. In an effort to stabilize the balance of power in Asia and retain trading access to China, the United States helped negotiate the Five Power Naval Treaty, which set proportional limits for ship strength at 500,000 tons for Great Britain and the United States, 300,000 tons for Japan, and 175,000 tons for France and Italy. In addition, the five nations pledged to respect China's open-door policy and to respect each other's claims to prewar possessions in East Asia.[21] The U.S.-brokered arrangement brought much-needed stability to the region for many years and, in so doing, created what ultimately became a false sense of security.

The U.S. attempt to secure loan repayments from Europe characterized the contradictions evident throughout the 1920s. Within five years, from 1914 to 1919, the United States went from the world's leading debtor to the world's leading creditor.[22] While the United States held Europe accountable for its debts, the nation simultaneously made repayment more difficult. The U.S. Congress, through the passage of the Fordney-McCumber Tariff Act of 1922, restored high tariffs on many imported goods, which reversed the position taken by the Underwood-Simmons Tariff Act of 1913. This later action signaled a reinvigorated protectionist stance and a deep support for domestic business operations.[23] The new act was targeted mainly at the chemical and metal-processing industries that were dominated by Germany before World War I.[24] New U.S. enterprises had arisen to handle the dearth of products from Germany, and the government sought to protect many of these nascent businesses. One such business was Orlando F. Weber's National Aniline and Chemical Company, which was organized in 1917 to manufacture dyestuffs formerly made only in Germany. After the war, this enterprise formed the basis of the Allied Chemical and Dye Company.[25]

Though tariffs helped protect U.S. domestic industries, they also made it more difficult for European nations to repay their war debts. Without an open and available market to sell and distribute European goods, Europe's ability to build cash reserves was severely hampered. This inability of European nations (especially Germany) to manage their debt burdens to each other and to the United States contributed to the frightening nationalism that emerged, but its repercussions were of little concern to many in the United States.[26]

Business Has a Friend in Government

With the war over, unrest spreading throughout the country, and a crippling recession, Americans longed for a sense of comfort and stability. They yearned for a return to a semblance of normalcy, and they found the champion of their ideals in President Warren Harding and, to a much greater extent, his vice president, Calvin Coolidge. The election of Harding in 1920 brought back a sense that the old values were alive and well again.[27] Those values were not the prewar values or even the values of the Progressives, but the values of the country at the turn of the century. Through his policies and cabinet-level appointments, Harding restored government support for unfettered business development and growth, reestablished America's isolationist and protectionist stance, restricted the flow of immigrants into the country, and set an overall tone of laissez-faire management. He wholeheartedly believed that a vibrant industrial sector made a strong and healthy nation, and his government intervention policies (or lack thereof) were designed to support that goal.

Though the government had exercised its regulatory muscle in the preceding decade with the breakup of the Standard Oil Company and the dissolution of the American Tobacco Company, the efforts to pursue the monopolistic U.S. Steel Corporation and the Aluminum Company of America were soundly rejected. Though the U.S. Steel Corporation had the "power to act as a monopoly," the Supreme Court ruled that it did not exercise its prerogative.[28] Following the tenets of the "rules of reason" from the Clayton Antitrust Act of 1914, the court reiterated that market share (i.e., size) did not in itself constitute an antitrust violation. The court further believed that the dissolution of U.S. Steel would constitute a greater hardship for Americans than any ramifications from the company's acting as a monopoly.[29] The court's decision showcased the importance of prevailing economic conditions in determining government policies toward business. The government's defeat in the antitrust suit against U.S. Steel marked the first major failure of the trust-busting era.

Using the same reasoning applied in the U.S. Steel case, the Supreme Court struck down the allegations of monopolistic behavior on the part of the Aluminum Company of America (Alcoa). Alcoa had grown dramatically over the first two decades of the twentieth century, eventually controlling 90 percent of the market for primary aluminum alloy and mill-fabricated products used in the United States. As with the U.S. Steel case, the Supreme Court ruled that "large firms [like Alcoa] were legal as long as size was not accompanied by 'unreasonable' conduct."[30] The fact that Andrew Mellon, the treasury secretary, was a major stockholder of the company may also have played a role in swaying the court's opinion. Even an apparent antitrust victory like the government's 1927 case against the Eastman Kodak Company was weakly enforced. Kodak had been accused and found guilty of utilizing exclusive contracts, yet the government did little to enforce its ruling, allowing Kodak to operate unimpeded for years after the case was decided.

Though his tenure was cut short with his death from heart disease in 1923, Harding had done much to support the business community. Some would say he did too much. Unfortunately for Harding's reputation, many of his key administrators took their pro-business stance too far and were embroiled in political scandals and corruption. Most notably, his secretary of the interior, Albert Fall, was convicted of taking bribes from oil executives who had secured drilling rights in Teapot Dome, Wyoming, and Elk Hills, California—land that was part of the nation's federal reserves.[31] Fall awarded the drilling rights without a competitive bid process and received "personal loans" in return. The Teapot Dome Scandal helped set the stage for the creation of the Federal Oil Conservation Board, which functioned less as a regulatory oversight body and more as a planner and collaborator for the oil industry.[32] Just before Harding's death, his administration was racked with suicides and widespread resignations.

The scandals could have done much to reverse the pro-business sentiment in the country, but that was not to be. With Calvin Coolidge's ascent to the presidency in 1923, business had an even better ally in the White House. Coolidge deftly handled the scandals, which subsided in a few months, by appointing an independent investigative committee and easily won reelection in 1924. Coolidge was the epitome of a hands-off chief executive. He was fond of the motto "Don't hurry to legislate" and was known to spend only four hours a day on government business. He believed that problems would go away without intervention.[33] Like Harding, Coolidge was an ardent promoter of standardization and efficiency in business. Far from fearing the potential downsides of collusion, Coolidge encouraged the development of professional and trade associations as opportunities for businesses to share best practices and procedures. It was during this time that the American Management

Association was formed. The creation of this group placed management under a spotlight. Academics and business executives began to explore the implications of treating management as a profession.[34]

From a policy perspective, Coolidge continued the fiscally conservative approach of his predecessor. He encouraged Treasury Secretary Mellon to reduce taxes, especially for wealthy Americans, while curtailing national expenditures and managing the nation's debt level. During Coolidge's administration, the wartime excess-profit tax was repealed and the maximum tax rate on personal income was reduced from 50 percent in 1921, to 40 percent in 1924, and to 20 percent in 1926. At the same time, the national debt was reduced by 35 percent from $25.5 billion to $16.9 billion, and government expenditures fell from $6.4 billion to $3.0 billion.[35] With these provisions in place, the economy grew by 6 percent per year, productivity increased by 4 percent per year, and by 1929, 43.3 percent of the world's manufactures were made in America.[36] The prospects for America seemed limitless, but underneath the surface, there were severe divisions in the nation. The divisions came to a head in the 1928 presidential contest, when a Democratic, Catholic, and anti-prohibitionist from a Northern city (Alfred Smith) took on a Republican, Quaker, and prohibitionist from the Midwest (Herbert Hoover). This contest symbolized the stark divisions in the minds of Americans and exposed some of the country's deep-seated wounds and ugly bigotry.[37]

A Country Divided: Fractured Social Mores

Throughout the 1920s the nation struggled with the meaning of its identity—from the postwar recession that began the decade, to the exuberant prosperity and experimentalism of the middle years, to the depths of despair and panic in the closing years. Although the war years of the preceding decade had successfully masked many of the underlying divisions in American society, there was no such mask in the 1920s. The America of the 1920s was a country divided—between North and South, between rural and urban, between immigrant and native, and between traditionalist and liberal. The decade was awash in contradictions and seemingly irreconcilable differences. Though often referred to as the Roaring Twenties, a name that symbolized selfishness and decadence, the decade began with the enactment of a major conservative movement—prohibition. Despite the beginnings of progress in job opportunities for women and minorities during the preceding war years, their advances also fueled a new wave of resentment and bigotry not seen since the end of the Civil War. While urban settings benefited greatly from the massive advances of new technologies and seemingly endless money in the growing stock market, life changed very little for farmers and other rural dwellers, who continued to struggle to survive off the land.

The country struggled to reconcile its differences, especially regarding prohibition and suffrage. Though the intentions of those who fought for prohibition may have been noble, its enforcement bore little resemblance to the heated debates and conviction expressed during the run up to its passage. Prohibition did discourage alcohol consumption, but not through moral suasion as its proponents had hoped; instead, consumption was curtailed mainly among the lower classes, who could not afford the higher prices of illegal drinks. The enforcement of prohibition also romanticized the consumption of alcohol by making drinking alluring and secretive, thereby providing a new industry for organized crime.[38] The 1920s saw the rise of the crime syndicate with such notorious figures as Al "Scarface" Capone and Lucky Luciano, who made a mockery of prohibition through their gang-controlled bootlegging and bribery.[39] The number of speakeasies (the decade's euphemism for "bars") in New York City during the 1920s approximated 32,000, which was double the number of previous legitimate bars.[40] In Detroit, the second-largest business during the 1920s (behind only the production of automobiles) was bootlegging.[41] Prohibition did not bring the country together in moral righteousness and social conformity, but in fact expanded the philosophical divide.

While prohibition continued to fracture the country, one movement that did unite most social classes of women (not necessarily men) was the fight for suffrage, which won victory in the passage of the Nineteenth Amendment to the U.S. Constitution in 1920. Though the fight for suffrage was sidetracked during the war years, it ultimately received a boost as women increased their economic and political clout in the workforce. The number of women employed in nonfarm positions increased from 5.0 million in 1900 to over 8.3 million in 1920.[42] Many historians believe that women's new economic freedom played a pivotal role in supporting the passage of the amendment. The amendment had been defeated every year for the previous forty-two years that it had been presented before Congress.[43]

TABLE 3-2

Social and demographic facts about the 1920s

- 106 million Americans in 48 states (54.2 million urban residents and 51.5 rural residents); grows to 123 million by 1930
- For the first time, more workers employed in manufacturing than agriculture
- Average unemployment rate of 5.2 percent
- Women's Suffrage Amendment to the U.S. Constitution is ratified
- Divorce rate increases from 1 out of 17 marriages in the 1890s to 1 out of 6 by the 1920s
- Military force of 343,000 (down from 1.2 million in 1919)
- First Macy's Thanksgiving Parade, held in 1924
- John T. Scopes is tried for teaching evolution in a Tennessee school
- Fads: yoga, nudist colonies, dance marathons, flagpole sitting
- Games: Ouija boards, crossword puzzles
- New words: *racketeering, media, normalcy, motel, speakeasies, mass production, sex appeal*
- Average annual earnings (1920): $1,236
- Life expectancy (1920): 54.6 years for females, 53.6 years for males

Despite the conflicting opinions about the value and worth of prohibition and suffrage, the positions of each side were relatively clear. There was no such clarity in the conflicts between liberal social mores and fundamentalism. Though the lines were not drawn by strict geographic boundaries, there were clear and undeniable differences in the nation. For many rural Americans, cities were thought to be breeding grounds for perverse ideologies, widespread experimentation, and social depravation.[44] In exaggerated images, cities were portrayed as islands of decadence where crime festered unchecked and corruption ran rampant.[45] Urban dwellers held just as many stereotypes—albeit not as sensational—about what they perceived as the quiet, uninformed, and unexamined life of the rural inhabitant. Though part of the same country, the urban and the rural dweller of the 1920s could easily have been a world apart.

Demography: The Doors Are Closed

The composition of the nation's leading urban centers, essentially the major Northern cities of New York, Boston, Detroit, Chicago, and Cleveland, was impacted by the migration of many black Americans who left the predomi-

nantly agrarian-based Southern economy for better-paying jobs and prospects in the North. The migration began during the war years and continued
throughout the 1920s, when 615,000 black Americans (representing 8 percent
of the native black population) moved from the South.[46] As their numbers
grew in major Northern cities, so too did their economic and political clout,
which helped spark the cultural, literary, and artistic movement known as the
Harlem Renaissance. The Harlem Renaissance symbolized black pride, white
fascination in all things African, and intercultural curiosity. Up until the outbreak of the Great Depression, the Harlem Renaissance helped break down
barriers between white and black cultures, especially in the elite intellectual
circles of the North.[47]

The influx of immigrants to America played an even larger role in widening
the divide between urban and rural communities. Immigrants were far more
likely to settle in cities than in farming communities. Immigration had stalled
during and immediately after World War I, but it was on the rise again in the
early 1920s. Almost 806,000 immigrants came to America in 1921, compared
with 141,000 in 1919, and unlike preceding patterns, the composition of the
immigrants changed.[48] More people were coming from Eastern and Southern
Europe and Mexico.[49] With the bitterness of the war a recent and inescapable
memory, the country experienced a growing level of nationalism, which sometimes bordered on outright nativism. The nativism cause was embraced on a
number of fronts. It became a rallying cry for a mainstream rural America that
longed for a return to traditionalism and for the older generation of immigrants who sought to protect their proportional standing in the U.S. population. It was even a celebrated cause for radical groups like the Ku Klux Klan,
which saw a resurgent rise in the popularity of its hate-based propaganda.
The Klan was particularly concerned in the 1920s with the influx of Jews and
Catholics from Eastern and Southern European nations. America was more
like a garbage can than a melting pot, the Klan's founder, William J. Simmons, warned: "When the hordes of aliens walk to the ballot box and their
votes outnumber yours, then that alien horde has got you by the throat."[50]

The combination of the country's isolationist sentiments, the resentment
between urban and rural dwellers, the swelling ranks of the unemployed, and
the protectionist rhetoric of the Klan became fertile ground for the enactment
of immigration quotas aimed at Europe and Asia. The Emergency Immigration Act of 1921 imposed a nationality quota, whereby annual immigration

was restricted to 3 percent of each represented group (nationality) living in the United States in 1910. The Immigration Act of 1924 added further restrictions. The revised quota was set at 2 percent for each nationality represented in the census of 1890. By going back to the 1890 census, the law was intentionally trying to reflect more Western European individuals, who had settled in the country before the turn of the twentieth century.[51] The new immigration quotas essentially resulted in a 50 percent reduction in the number of immigrants from Europe and Asia between the beginning and end of the decade.

Overall, the U.S. population grew from 106 million to 122 million, but more important, it was the first decade in which the balance tipped in favor of urban communities. By 1920, 50 percent of all Americans lived in communities with greater than five thousand inhabitants.[52] While cities thrived, farmers struggled to survive. Having overextended their operations to handle the food needs for the war, farmers were left with overcapacity and a much smaller market for their produce. The smaller market opportunities and lower income possibilities sparked a movement toward farm consolidation. As R. Douglas Hurt explains in his book on the twentieth-century American farmer, "by 1930 the farm population had fallen to 30.5 million, or about 25 percent of the population, after peaking in 1916 at 32.5 million, or 32 percent of the population."[53] Several attempts to support the plight of the farmers (e.g., efforts at subsidies and rationing) were soundly rejected by Congress or the president, or both. Farmers were not alone in being forsaken. In the pro-business 1920s, labor struggled to gain a solid footing.

One Step Forward, Two Steps Back for Labor

Whatever gains labor achieved during the war years had all but disappeared by the 1920s. Union membership that stood at 5.0 million in 1920 was a mere 3.4 million by 1929.[54] Beyond the 32 percent reduction in its membership rolls, labor experienced major setbacks in two U.S. Supreme Court cases. In an action that essentially nullified the labor movement's exemption from antitrust suits, the Supreme Court in 1921 ruled in the *Duplex Printing Press Company v. Deering* case that it was legitimate to hold injunctions against union actions that supported secondary boycotts. Unions had often appealed to the public to boycott a company's products or services in an effort to reinforce their bargaining position. The court ruled that this activity was in violation of the free flow of interstate commerce and constituted illegal restraint of trade.[35] On the heels of this blow to labor, the Supreme Court overturned minimum-wage legislation in 1926. Though the law was initially aimed at children and women, the court believed that establishing minimum wages was a clear violation of the right and freedom of any individual to enter into working contracts at will. The ruling set a new precedent and provided a foundation for effectively challenging state minimum-wage laws throughout the 1920s and 1930s.[36] The struggles of the labor movement were exacerbated by the government's strong support of big business. As labor historian Eli Ginzberg has noted: "In the opinion of the Republicans, the very best that the federal government could do [for the workers] was to do nothing and to leave the initiative where it properly belonged, in the hands of the leaders of the business community."[37]

With the support of the government's laissez-faire approach, employers felt emboldened to hire workers who did not belong or did not want to belong to a union, creating a surge in open shops. In a further effort to discourage unionism, employers introduced a series of employee benefit programs under the title of "welfare capitalism," which could include profit sharing, pension plans, bonus programs, and unemployment insurance, among other benefits. In conjunction with the adoption of welfare capitalism, employers like Endicott-Johnson, Wrigley's Gum, and Johns-Manville began to reexamine their operational processes and procedures.

Although George Johnson built a successful shoe company, his most enduring achievements were in his progressive labor practices that included the introduction of the eight-hour workday, forty-hour work week, and comprehensive medical care for his employees. Philip Wrigley made his mark on the family chewing-gum business by instituting an income insurance plan, a gradual retirement program, and an extensive pension system. Finally, while building the world's largest producer of asbestos-based building materials, Lewis Brown introduced collective bargaining, the eight-hour workday, the forty-hour work week, and employee attitude surveys (using the results to change working conditions). It would take years before the efforts introduced by these trailblazers became commonplace, yet their actions influenced how managers treated and viewed their employees and also impacted overall working conditions. Like welfare capitalism, though, the early motivations underlying the assessment of workers were driven less from a sense of altruism and more from a desire to maintain a productive, thriving, and nonunion workforce.[38]

Technology Makes Life Easier

Business-driven technology became one of the few unifying factors that helped level the playing field for Americans. Many innovations of the time were centered on enhancing the lives of ordinary Americans. The explosion of advertising and the abundant availability of credit made access to these new technologies easier than ever before. Less focused on product quality than appearance, advertisers believed that it was their duty to "show the great masses how advancements in science could be integrated into their daily lives."[59] The invention of the radio, the proliferation of entertainment, and the development of household conveniences all played a significant role in this process.

From an impact perspective, the introduction of the radio was a defining moment for business. Though radio had been around for almost a decade, the government had taken control of the medium during the 1910s to assist in national defense. By 1919, the government privatized radio through the establishment of the Radio Corporation of America (RCA), originally jointly owned by American Telephone & Telegraph (AT&T), Westinghouse, and General Electric (GE). The plan called for AT&T to manufacture transmitters and hold "radio telephony" rights while GE and Westinghouse produced radio receivers. There was no early provision for what would become the mainstay of radio broadcasting.[60]

Although station WWJ in Detroit went on the air in August 1920 to transmit bulletins from the *Detroit Daily News*, Pittsburgh's KDKA broadcast of the presidential election results on November 2, 1920, was considered the turning point in radio. Owned by Westinghouse, KDKA was the first station to broadcast regular programs instead of periodic news bulletins.[61] Westinghouse hoped to use radio to promote the sale of its own products. RCA and GE also adopted this self-funded philosophy for radio, but AT&T went in another direction. Through its WEAF station in New York City, AT&T broadcast the first radio commercial for a real estate firm—Queensboro Corporation.[62] The cost of a hundred dollars for ten minutes shocked radio purists, who believed that the airwaves should remain advertisement free.[63] The success of the early advertisements, however, produced an unstoppable groundswell of support. A new age of advertising began, just in time to exploit the feelings of prosperity and materialistic desires that pervaded many sectors of the country.

By the middle of the 1920s, AT&T, under the leadership of Walter S. Gifford, had built up a network of radio stations that were being funded by advertising revenues and continued self-investment. Besides these successes, the company saw greater financial rewards in the licensing of broadcasting rights than in the operation of the stations. In 1926, the primary radio operators instituted a new agreement among themselves. AT&T sold WEAF (the largest radio station in New York City) and its affiliated operations to RCA in exchange for a monopoly on the sale of network connections between stations. GE and Westinghouse concentrated on their patent rights to produce and sell radio receivers and transmitters. Under the leadership of David Sarnoff, RCA went on to build one of the largest affiliated networks of radio stations through a plan that called for the ownership of at least two primary stations in major U.S. cities. The business formula essentially attempted to dominate market share and reach. Sarnoff formed two networks: the Red Network, with the flagship WEAF radio station, and the Blue Network, with the flagship WJZ radio station in Newark, New Jersey. The Red Network became the National Broadcasting Company, and the Blue Network eventually became the independent American Broadcasting Company (formed after a court divestment order in the 1940s). Around the same time, William Paley formed the Columbia Broadcasting System, thus completing the early basis of the three major networks.[64]

David Sarnoff on duty at the Wanamaker radio station in New York City. (Source: Bettmann/CORBIS)

First used to broadcast sporting events and national news, radios soon became a full musical entertainment medium and an advertiser's dream. In fact, advertisers were primarily responsible for the early development of radio content. In an effort to gain more air time for their clients, advertisers often created independent programs to be sold to affiliated radio networks. By the end of the decade, it was estimated that advertisers produced all sponsored programs.[65] While radio provided a new mass-market medium, it often did so at the expense of individualism. Soon, people all across the country were tuned in to the same programs, recognizing the same kinds of stars and heroes and enjoying a new mass culture only hinted at before in mass-produced books and magazines.[66]

To a much greater extent than radio in the 1920s, movies became a recipe for how Americans should behave and look. Movie houses, which grew from 15,000 in 1919 to 20,500 in 1928, had become the most popular form of commercialized amusement in the country.[67] The acceptance of movies as a form of entertainment by the middle class did much to change the respectability of the medium. Even though movies gained social respectability, their content often reflected the transformation of social mores in the country. The alternative to traditional American behavior (in the 1920s) that movie audiences most clearly demanded was passionate behavior.[68] Helping Americans find refuge in movies, Harry M. Warner and his brothers developed the technology for adapting sound to motion picture production. When their *The Jazz Singer*, the first talking movie, debuted in 1927, it revolutionized the entertain-

A large crowd waits to see the first talking motion picture (produced by Warner Brothers) in 1927. The film featured Al Jolson in the title role in The Jazz Singer. (Source: John Springer Collection/ CORBIS)

ment business. The revolution continued with the launch of *Steamboat Willie*, the first talking cartoon, by Walter E. Disney, in 1928.[69]

While radio and film provided Americans with a source of entertainment, other seminal inventions of the 1920s helped make life easier on a day-to-day, practical level. During this decade, indoor plumbing, central heating, and in-home electricity and telephone service all increased significantly. The household chores of cooking, cleaning, and laundry consumed between sixty and seventy hours per week at the outset of the decade. With the advent of accessible electric-powered irons, refrigerators, Maytag washing machines, and Hoover vacuums, the time required to complete these chores was significantly reduced (ostensibly providing more time for leisure activities like movies and radio).[70] Many of these new appliances were available through installment payment plans, which further contributed to the soaring credit-based economy.

Entrepreneurs: Taking Flight

Though many technological advances were centered on the home, some of the most significant innovations continued to be in the transportation sector, which received a tremendous boost from the U.S. government. In an effort to improve the speed of mail delivery, the Post Office Department embarked on the development of a transcontinental airmail route in the early 1920s. With the development of a series of short-run air flights between major U.S. cities, the Post Office demonstrated the viability of airmail and secured $1.5 million in government appropriations in 1921 to improve landing strips and add lighting for night flying. Over the next four years, the Post Office continued to build a nationwide airmail system and generated momentum for further government subsidies. Being a pilot for the Post Office was not for the faint of heart. Early pilots flew in open cockpits with a parachute affixed to their backs. Of the first forty pilots hired by the U.S. Post Office Department, thirty-one were killed by crashes within six years.[71]

With the passage of the Air Mail Act (Kelly Act) of 1925, the Post Office was given the authority to privatize the airmail system in the country. With this act and the subsequent Air Commerce Act of 1926, the government awarded airmail contracts to private companies and provided funds for building and maintaining the safety of the nation's airports and airways.[72] The Post Office received more than five thousand applications for the first twelve air routes that it awarded in 1925.[73] Both Boeing and the precursor of United Airlines, National Air Transport, were among the firms awarded contracts.[74] The government's support of private air carriers did much to boost the development of safer and larger aircraft and set the stage for passenger transport.

Much as it does today, the government continued to take responsibility for the infrastructure and safety of the nation's airports while turning over the day-to-day operations of flights to private carriers. By 1928, just seven years after its initiation, all forty-eight states had airmail service, and more importantly, the airline industry had found a commercially viable (and nonmilitary) means for its existence.[75] Though domestic flying was just spreading its wings in the 1920s, one individual looked far beyond the U.S. airways to the international marketplace. Named one of *Time* magazine's business titans of the twentieth century, Juan Trippe was described as "having the great American instinct of seeing a market before it happened—and then making it happen . . . [H]e fathered the international airline business."[76]

Juan Trippe (1899–1981), Pan American World Airways

Juan Trippe came of age during the barnstorming, stunt-driven time of the early flight business. When he was ten years old, in 1909, his father brought him to an air race over Long Island. That first glimpse of a plane circling the Statue of Liberty was all the boy needed to find his calling. Once he experienced air flight for the first time in college, Trippe's fate was essentially sealed. By the time he was done with his life's work in 1969, he had built a network of eighty thousand air miles connecting the United States with eighty-five other countries.

Trippe was born into an upper–middle-class family in Seabright, New Jersey. His father was an investment banker and broker in New York City, and like Ernest Woodruff, he expected his son to follow him in the banking business. While not a brilliant student, Trippe developed a strong ability to debate his viewpoints; he always displayed an uncanny sense of patience and quiet self-righteousness. He attended high school in Pottstown, Pennsylvania, and graduated from the Sheffield Scientific School at Yale University in 1920. At Yale, Trippe found two assets that became invaluable for the rest of his life—a confirmed love of flying and a network of influential friends. Trippe took his first flying lessons in college and with a group of friends created the Yale Flying Club, which afforded him the opportunity to take part in intercollegiate air races. The friends who joined him in the Flying Club and on Yale's varsity athletic fields were not just run-of-the-mill college buddies. They were friends whose last names were a who's who of American industry—Whitney, Rockefeller, and Vanderbilt.

Trippe's time at Yale was interrupted twice. The first time occurred when he served in the naval air corps during World War I. The second time, he briefly left Yale when his father passed away. Trippe helped settle his father's estate and returned to finish his studies. As a tribute to his father and in an effort to support his mother, Trippe, on graduating from Yale, spent two years as a bond salesman for the Lee, Higginson and Company investment firm. He considered them the dullest years of his life, though he continued to solidify relationships with influential and wealthy colleagues.[77] In 1923, he left Wall Street and never turned back.

With a few friends from his days at Yale and in investment banking, Trippe bought seven World War I army surplus planes for five hundred dollars each and formed Long Island Airways. The airline was originally formed to provide sightseeing tours to the elite summer vacation crowd on Long Island. He realized that he could create more business if he converted the cockpits of the surplus planes to accommodate two passengers instead of the one, as was part of the original design. By substituting a powerful, yet smaller engine, Trippe was able to make the change.

Despite the success of his seasonal sightseeing trips, Trippe knew he had to secure steady business to sustain his operation. He acquired his first international opportunity by flying for the United Fruit Company in Honduras. He had learned that while shipments for United Fruit were docked at the port city of Tela, Honduras, the country's law required an official government stamp to properly receive the goods. The stamp had to be secured in the capital, which was accessed by a three-day road journey. Trippe convinced the United Fruit Company that it could become more efficient if it flew the papers to the capital, which was a service that Long Island Airways could provide. Trippe shipped one of his seven planes to Honduras, and so began his first international assignment. Trippe continued to look for additional opportunities to provide air service in remote regions. He reasoned that these areas were the most difficult to traverse, and though air flight was slow in its early days (often unable to compete with efficient interconnected railway lines), it was far superior to other transportation options in sparsely inhabited areas. Though

Long Island Airways had a unique international offering, its beach flying business suffered from intense competition. After eighteen months, Trippe sold Long Island Airways and began looking for a more viable airline opportunity.

While Long Island Airways was not a financial success, it did provide Trippe with a solid education on the economics of running an airline. He took that education and experience along with financial backing from some friends and created his second airline—Eastern Air Transport. The year was 1924, and the U.S. government was in the midst of deciding the merits of federally funded airmail routes. Trippe lobbied hard for the Boston-to-New York airmail contract, but given his tender age (only twenty-six), he was rebuffed. He learned that a competitor, Colonial Airlines, was doing better in the bidding process. Colonial was backed by a collection of political figures, including the governor of Connecticut. With his influential financial backers and board members, Trippe orchestrated a merger of Eastern and Colonial into Colonial Air Transport. The political clout and influence of the company's backers surely played a significant role in Colonial's receiving the first airmail contract awarded by the U.S. government. Given that the primary investors and organizers of the combined companies were occupied with other full-time pursuits, Trippe managed to secure the position as the head of Colonial Air Transport.

With no equipment, Trippe set his sights on outfitting the company with some of the latest aircraft. While others in the airmail business were planning to use single-engine aircraft (in fact, the airmail contracts specifically called for single-engine crafts), Trippe placed orders for trimotor planes (Fokker F-7s), which could accommodate both mail and passenger service. He believed that these new aircraft could travel greater distances and ultimately service international operations. To demonstrate the power of the aircraft, he embarked on a journey from New York to Havana with a demonstration plane borrowed from the manufacturer. He believed that an airmail route from Key West or Miami to the Caribbean would be inevitable. On landing to fanfare in Cuba, Trippe impressed the country's president with flight demonstrations of the technically superior trimotor Fokker F-7. Trippe's skills at international diplomacy were also tested on this trip, and he succeeded in securing landing rights for future airmail service to Cuba.

Despite the success of the trip, his board and financial backers were growing impatient. Though a year had passed since the trimotor planes had been ordered, Colonial Air Transport had yet to take flight. Unfazed by the delay in the delivery of equipment, Trippe continued to try to secure additional air-mail contracts. It was this zealous, almost reckless, disregard for cautious business practices that created a gulf between Trippe and many of his financial backers. Though he tried to secure enough support from key board members to retain his position, Trippe was ultimately removed from the company. It was 1927, and Trippe was unemployed.

Again, Trippe went back to the well; he sought assistance from Cornelius V. Whitney, William H. Vanderbilt, and Percy Rockefeller to build a new air-line. With ten additional backers, including Lehman Brothers, Trippe formed the Aviation Corporation of America (AVCO) with $300,000 in capital. With many of the domestic airmail routes already awarded, Trippe set his sights on the international stage—namely, the Key West to Havana airmail route. A few other less financially secure operations, one named Pan American Airways (which became Pan American World Airways in 1950), had also set their sights on the international stage. Pan American had secured the airmail route from Key West to Havana but lacked the equipment and landing rights to fulfill its contractual obligation, which called for the first airmail exchange to occur by October 19, 1927. A missed date would result in the revocation of the contract. In exchange for helping Pan American backers meet their date, Trippe secured the consolidation of his company into Pan American Airways. Once more, through his negotiation skills, he secured the presidency of the combined entities. It didn't hurt that he was bringing with him the landing rights to Cuba.

Pan American Airways was Trippe's third airline in less than five years. Having made the deadline for the first flight to Havana (using the trimotor planes that Colonial refused to accept when they were finally ready), Trippe focused his energies on other international airmail contracts. While other air carriers were struggling to justify their cost efficiency for mail service compared with railroads in the United States, Trippe was taking on a transportation competitor that he could easily defeat—the slow-moving shipping industry in the Caribbean and Latin America. He secured a dedicated team of professionals to run the operations of the business and spent a considerable amount of time in Washington, D.C., successfully lobbying for long-term, federally subsidized foreign airmail contracts. He found a receptive voice in Washington diplomats who believed that a strong U.S.-backed operation was essential to the country's foreign interests.

Three pilots for Colonial Air Transport are congratulated by Juan Trippe after their successful airmail trip. Trippe was a pioneer in expanding airmail services to the Caribbean and throughout Latin America. (Source: Bettmann/CORBIS)

Having negotiated landing rights throughout many Caribbean nations, Trippe was well poised to reap the advantages of new government contracts as they reached further into Latin America. To secure the routes, the company had to negotiate with local government offices. By staying well ahead of the curve, Trippe virtually eliminated any competition. His company won the first five foreign airmail service contracts from the U.S. government. To service areas with impenetrable terrain or inadequate facilities, Trippe deployed twin-engine amphibian planes that were capable of landing on water. Decades before it became commonplace with other carriers, Trippe also utilized aircraft that enabled him to carry both passengers and mail, essentially inaugurating international passenger air flights.

In the 1930s, while other companies were struggling through the Depression, Trippe focused on expansion by connecting the western United States with Asia. He initiated air service in the Alaskan territory using Seattle as an anchor site and, in 1933, bought a controlling interest in China National Aviation Corporation. He connected the two worlds through a series of island stops throughout the Pacific Ocean. To traverse such great distances, Trippe worked with the Martin aircraft company to develop the famous PanAm China Clipper, which in 1935 had the engine force and fuel capacity to fly the

8,200 miles from San Francisco to the Philippines. His success in the Pacific was rivaled four years later, when PanAm's Yankee Clipper (a Boeing B-314) made the first scheduled transatlantic flight from New York to France. By the beginning of the 1940s, just thirteen years after the incorporation of Pan American Airways, Trippe had built a truly global airline. With their giant capacity for hauling freight and passengers, the Clippers were fully deployed as military transport carriers during World War II.

With the end of the war, commercial flights resumed, and PanAm was in a position to dominate the international airways. Much to the dismay of his competitors, Trippe introduced low tourist-class fares as an incentive for more international travel, and he even allowed passengers to pay for their tickets on an installment basis. Though resisted by other airlines, these practices eventually became a permanent hallmark of the industry. Consistent with his practice of utilizing the latest technology, Trippe was one of the first to supply his airline with advanced jets, which were capable of extending the range of nonstop flying. PanAm inaugurated U.S.-based jet service across the North Atlantic with the Boeing 707 in October 1958—more than a year before another competitor did so.[78] PanAm's domination of international travel in the 1950s was so strong that Trippe even offered to make the company a regulated monopoly. When the government declined the offer, competition for the international passenger soon accelerated, and PanAm was ill prepared to handle it.

Having operated with virtually no competition, PanAm had developed a sense of arrogance over the years. This sense was, in many ways, a reflection of Trippe, who was known as an autocratic, controlling individual. Having built the world's leading global air carrier against tremendous odds, Trippe made decisions whose motives were rarely challenged. He refused to delegate extensively, believing his source of power rested with his unique understanding of the operations of the business. It was this knowledge that enabled him to push forth his plans for continued expansion, even when some of his board members advocated more cautious strategies. Heavy leverage and overextension ultimately caught up with PanAm, which succumbed to intense competition. Trippe's legacy lived on, not in one company but through the growth and development of an entire industry. Before almost anyone else, he understood the value and opportunity of a globally connected world, and he forged those literal connections.[79]

Leaders: Hitting a New Stride

While Trippe was blazing a new trail in the airways, others were attempting to navigate the rocky waters of business maturity and stagnation. This was especially the case for Robert T. B. Stevens, who took the helm of his family's 115-year-old textile mill, J. P. Stevens & Company, in the 1920s. Stevens inherited a loosely structured and largely inefficient organization that was struggling to grow. In response to these conditions, Stevens merged the manufacturing and selling sides of the business, which brought much-needed coordination to the operation. This new structural change was followed by vertical integration, plant closings and relocations, expansion into new fabric areas, and numerous other cost-saving measures. The results of his efforts enabled the large textile conglomerate to regain a position of prominence in the marketplace and to thrive for several decades.[80]

The challenges that Stevens faced in assuming the leadership of J. P. Stevens & Company paled somewhat in comparison to the task confronted by Francis B. Davis Jr. This businessman had the unenviable position of taking the helm of United States Rubber Company in 1928, just as it lost $10 million. Over the previous thirty years of its existence, U.S. Rubber had grown into a disparate collection of inefficient operating units with no formal reporting structure. Drawing on his prior experience with DuPont, Davis reorganized U.S. Rubber by adopting a multidivisional organizational form with a strong, centralized staff focused on financial management and strategic oversight. Through this transformation, various underperforming operations were eliminated. Between 1928 and 1933, Davis reduced the company's debt by $40 million, and in 1935, the company posted its first profit in seven years. Having restructured the organization, Davis invested in new research capabilities. As a result of this research, Kaylon, a foam-rubber cushion material, was developed in 1934, and rayon cord was introduced into tire production in 1938.[81]

While both Stevens and Davis were essentially forced to take drastic measures to reenergize their enterprises, other leaders began the transformation process much sooner. For instance, though General Electric was already very successful in manufacturing and marketing heavy electrical machinery and engineering systems, Gerard Swope was determined to diversify the company into what he called public products. Before its production of home appliances, GE's only other consumer product was the lightbulb. Though Swope sought

Workers flood the streets in a panic after the October 29, 1929, stock market crash on Wall Street. (Source: Hulton Archive/ Getty Images)

to maintain the company's dominance as a supplier to the utility sector, he believed that the company would have better prospects by catering to both consumers and commercial enterprises. He also believed that there would be significant reciprocal benefits from this transformation. Swope poured millions into new product development, especially smaller electronic appliances, which required the electricity that the company helped produce. Swope's consumer-focused expansion efforts were so successful that by 1930, consumer products accounted for 50 percent of GE's business. In many ways, Swope helped the company thrive on the consumer bandwagon of the 1920s.[82]

A Jolt to the System: Spiraling into Despair

Up until the stock market crash of 1929, business executives were admired and sometimes even revered. Businesses produced new products and services at an unprecedented rate, and in the process, their stock values skyrocketed—fueling the hopes of Americans to get rich quick. Hundreds of thousands of individuals entered the stock market for the first time, as brokers were willing to allow new investors to borrow up to 90 percent of the purchase price of stocks. Though the market was rising at an unprecedented rate through the 1920s, it seemed unstoppable. The margin loans, which ultimately totaled $8.5 billion (representing half the public debt in the United States in 1929), seemed like a good deal.[83] Hoover revealed these sentiments in his January

1929 inaugural address: "I have no fears for the future of our country . . . it is bright with hope."[84] Even one month before the collapse, there was little pessimism in the air. The Dow climbed to 381 in September 1929, up from 88 in 1924.[85] But, in a matter of a few days in October 1929, the stock market's value dropped by 37 percent and continued to fall until it reached bottom in 1932 (a mere 11 percent of its former high-water mark). The September 3, 1929, Dow Jones Industrial Average value of 381 would not be reached again for twenty-five years.[86] The causes of the crash have never been pinpointed to one specific element, yet economists and historians have pointed to a combination of contextual factors—too much credit, bloated inventory levels, stock speculation, protectionism, and, ultimately, greed. When the prosperity of the 1920s came to an abrupt halt, it unleashed a level of despair that the United States had not felt since the Civil War.

TABLE 3-3

Entrepreneurs, managers, and leaders of the 1920s

Entrepreneurs	Managers
Benjamin Abrams, Emerson Radio & Phonograph	Melvin H. Baker, National Gypsum Company
Howard F. Ahmanson, Ahmanson & Company	Edward Bausch, Bausch and Lomb Company
Clarence Birdseye, General Seafood's Company	Amos L. Beaty, Texaco
Walter E. Disney, Walt Disney Company	Hernand Behn, International Telephone and Telegraph
Donald W. Douglas, Douglas Aircraft Company	William B. Bell, American Cyanamid Company
Ole Evinrude, Outboard Motors Corporation	Horace Bowker, American Agricultural Chemical
Paul V. Galvin, Motorola	Stephen F. Briggs, Outboard Motors Corporation
Howard D. Johnson, Howard Johnson	Herman Brown, Brown & Root
William Levitt, Levitt & Sons	Lewis H. Brown, Johns-Manville Corporation
Royal Little, Textron	Charles A. Cannon, Cannon Mills Company
Henry R. Luce, Time Life, Inc.	Owen R. Cheatham, Georgia-Pacific Corporation
John W. Marriott, Marriott-Hot Shoppes	Colby M. Chester, General Foods Corporation
Louis B. Mayer, Metro-Goldwyn-Mayer Corporation	Walter P. Chrysler, Chrysler Corporation
George J. Mecherle, State Farm Insurance	Gilbert Colgate, Colgate-Palmolive Company
Samuel I. Newhouse, Newhouse Publishing	Carle C. Conway, Continental Can Company
Arthur C. Nielsen, A. C. Nielsen Company	Henry Crown, Material Service Corporation
William S. Paley, Columbia Broadcasting System	Otto D. Donnell, Ohio Oil Company
Frederick B. Rentschler, United Aircraft Corporation	Nelson Doubleday, Doubleday and Company
Igor I. Sikorsky, Sikorsky Aircraft Corporation	Lammot du Pont, DuPont Corporation
Juan T. Trippe, Pan American World Airways	Walter S. Gifford, American Telephone & Telegraph
DeWitt Wallace, Reader's Digest	Bernard F. Gimbel, Gimbel Brothers Department Stores
Harry M. Warner, Warner Brothers Pictures	

TABLE 3-3 *(continued)*

Bowman Gray, R.J. Reynolds Tobacco Company
Carl R. Gray, Union Pacific Railroad
Walter A. Haas, Levi Strauss & Company
Erle P. Halliburton, Halliburton
John A. Hartford, Great Atlantic & Pacific Tea Company
George W. Hill, American Tobacco Company
Hale Holden, Chicago, Burlington & Quincy Railroad
Herbert W. Hoover, Hoover Company
Jay C. Hormel, Hormel
George M. Humphrey, Hanna (M. A.) & Company
George F. Johnson, Endicott-Johnson Company
Herbert F. Johnson, Johnson Wax Company
Alexander Legge, International Harvester
James F. Lincoln, Lincoln Electric Company
Paul W. Litchfield, Goodyear Tire & Rubber
James S. Love, Burlington Industries
Oscar Gottfried Mayer, Oscar Mayer
Elmer H. Maytag, Maytag Corporation
Thomas H. McInnerney, National Dairy Products
James O. McKinsey, McKinsey & Company
William L. McKnight, 3M
Ward Melville, Melville Corporation
George W. Merck, Merck & Company, Inc.
Lorimer D. Milton, Citizens Trust Bank
Charles E. Mitchell, National City Bank
William L. Moody Jr., Moody & Company Bank
William Nickerson Jr., Golden State Insurance
Edgar M. Queeny, Monsanto Company
James H. Rand Jr., Remington-Rand Company

Gordon S. Rentschler, National City Bank
Eugene W. Rhodes, Philadelphia Tribune
William Rosenthal, Maidenform
Walter E. Sachs, Goldman Sachs
Nicholas M. Schenck, Loew's
John R. Simplot, Simplot Company
Alfred P. Sloan Jr., General Motors Corporation
Hurlburt W. Smith, L. C. Smith & Corona Typewriters, Inc.
Charles C. Spaulding, North Carolina Mutual Life Insurance
Robert C. Stanley, International Nickel Corporation
John Stuart, Quaker Oats Company
Ernest T. Weir, National Steel Corporation
Charles D. Wiman, Deere & Company
Sidney W. Winslow Jr., United Shoe Machinery
Robert W. Woodruff, Coca-Cola Company
Philip K. Wrigley, William Wrigley Jr. Company

Leaders

Charles S. Davis, Borg-Warner Corporation
Francis B. Davis Jr., United States Rubber Company
Robert Lehman, Lehman Brothers
Alex Manoogian, Masco Corporation
Thomas B. McCabe, Scott Paper
Henry B. Spencer, Fruit Growers Express
Robert T. B. Stevens, J. P. Stevens & Company
Gerard Swope, General Electric Company
Orlando F. Weber, Allied Chemical and Dye
Robert E. Wood, Sears, Roebuck and Co.

FOUR

1930–1939

Survival Through Adaptation
and Renewal

*What the country needs is a good big laugh. There seems to be
a condition of hysteria. If someone could get off a good joke every
ten days I think our troubles would be over.*

—Herbert Hoover, 1931

*The country needs bold, persistent experimentation. It is common
sense to take a method and try it. If it fails, admit it frankly
and try another. But above all, try something.*

—Franklin Delano Roosevelt, 1932

THE STOCK MARKET CRASH of October 1929 ushered in a decade of
despair, despondency, and desolation as America's deepest and darkest
period of economic instability and poverty unfolded—the Great Depression.
While the majority of Americans did not have money invested in the stock
market, the ripple effect of the market's collapse was tremendous. Many businesses that overextended themselves in the 1920s by taking advantage of lax
credit policies could not transform their operations quickly enough to survive.
The lack of both active self-restraint on the part of businesses and imposed
regulatory checks on the part of government created an atmosphere of bold
risk taking, fueling unrealistic expectations of growth and prosperity. As credit

spiraled and inventories swelled, the fragile house of cards that was propping up many companies (and personal portfolios) crumbled under its own weight.

In a matter of days, the stock market lost $26 billion in value.[1] It is estimated that almost sixty thousand businesses collapsed between 1930 and 1931.[2] In lockstep with the business collapses, the banking community imploded as nervous Americans rushed to withdraw whatever money they had left. For many, however, it was too late; between 1930 and 1933, over nine thousand banks shuttered their doors.[3] With no deposit insurance protection, thousands of individuals and families lost their savings in addition to their jobs. The collapse of tens of thousands of businesses and financial institutions, combined with the swift and continuing drop in the stock market (the market reached its low point in 1932), crippled the country's productivity. Although unemployment stood at a low of 3 percent in the summer of 1929, it reached an all-time high of 25 percent (with over 12 million Americans out of work) by 1933.[4] For Americans lucky enough to retain their employment, they often did so at a huge cost. In many cases, their income levels dropped by one-third.[5] Overall, the average annual American family income was reduced from $2,300 to $1,500 between 1929 and 1932.[6] With these conditions, the public's perception of the business executive changed drastically.

The irrationality that created heroes out of ordinary business executives in the 1920s quickly gave way to vilification and enmity for these same individuals in the 1930s, and this shift in attitudes was swift and unforgiving. What was once considered adventurous risk-taking was now considered foolhardy. What was once considered innovative and courageous was now considered unethical. Regardless of the underlying truth of the allegations, business executives were viewed as the main culprits in the demise of the American economy. They were seen as selfish swindlers who squandered resources. Moreover, they tarnished the American ideal that prosperity was inevitable for those who worked hard. It was no longer that simple (if it ever was).

Business executives in the 1930s were faced with severe economic instability, labor unrest, and, above all, significant government intervention. Opportunities nevertheless arose even in this hostile landscape, and those who seized these opportunities defined a new version of business leadership. They were able to transform themselves and, in some cases, their companies as new government policies were introduced and new relationships between employers and employees emerged.

TABLE 4-1

Social and demographic facts about the 1930s

- 123 million Americans in 48 states (60 percent urban); grows to 132 million by 1940
- Unemployment rate hits 25 percent (never below 14 percent)
- Dust Bowl storms destroy millions of farms
- "Star-Spangled Banner" named national anthem
- *Dick and Jane* children's books introduced
- New York City installs first traffic lights
- George Gallup introduces first market survey
- First drive-in theater opens in Camden, New Jersey
- Zippers replace buttons
- Ninth major planet discovered—Pluto
- Fads: stamp collecting, wide and high-waist pants for men, radio soap operas
- Games: Monopoly, parlor games
- New words: *streamline, mobile, skid row, hopefully*
- Average annual earnings (1930): $1,368
- Life expectancy (1930): 61.6 years for females, 58.1 years for males

---

Government Takes Charge

Herbert Hoover had the unfortunate distinction of serving as the country's president during its worst economic crisis, and he is often criticized for contributing to its debilitating impact. For the first three years of his administration, he was convinced that private enterprise would cure the Depression. Unfortunately, it did not. Though he was deeply ridiculed, Hoover was staunchly against any government intervention that impeded private enterprise or appeared to be a handout to Americans. In an effort to support both domestic business and one of his key constituents, farmers, Hoover strongly endorsed the Smoot-Hawley Tariff Act of 1930. Despite the objections of some one thousand economists, the act became the most protectionist tariff legislation ever enacted by Congress.[7] It increased tariff rates by an average of 18 percent on nine hundred manufactured goods and 57 percent on seventy agricultural products.[8] Far from providing the relief that Hoover sought, the act fueled a wave of retaliatory protectionist legislation from the country's key trading partners. In fact, U.S. farmers, who were supposed to be protected, were impacted more severely than any other group. The act essentially shut down many farming operations that could not find a sustainable market for their produce. By 1933, one-quarter of all farmers had lost their land.[9] The net impact of the countervailing protectionist actions was a 65 percent decline in world trade between 1929 and 1933.[10] The decline did not abate until 1934, when U.S. trading partners, ushering in a new period of antiprotectionism, signed reciprocal trade agreements.[11]

Despite his faith in business, Hoover watched the economy continue to decline. By the end of 1932, the U.S. gross domestic product was 50 percent of the level in 1929.[12] Through the creation of the Reconstruction Finance Corporation (RFC), Hoover tried to signal a new tone in government practices. Under Jesse H. Jones's presidency of the RFC, it became the nation's largest bank and biggest single investor. It not only provided loans to established banks, but also encouraged new ventures and sought to enlarge capital by buying bank-preferred stock, which, in turn, created a base for credit expansion. Between its inception in 1932 and its dissolution in 1954, the RFC made available more than $50 billion in loans.[13] Initially, however, Hoover was extremely cautious in expanding the scope and reach of the RFC. He strongly preferred a modest level of government spending even when faced with evidence that increased investment could stimulate the economy. His desire to retain a balanced budget became his economic Achilles heel. By the time he decided that more government intervention in the economy was warranted, it was essentially too late.[14]

The economic suffering of the country was only one part of the Great Depression. Of equal, if not greater, importance were the psychological ramifications from a loss of employment, loss of savings, loss of security, and loss of self-worth. Americans yearned for a new voice of hope. They found that voice in President Franklin Delano Roosevelt (FDR), who was elected to office by a landslide victory in the fall of 1932. On the day of Roosevelt's inauguration, bank liabilities stood at $41 billion versus a reserve of only $6 billion.[15] Roosevelt immediately called for an emergency session of Congress to deal with the financial crisis and declared a four-day banking holiday. In a matter of hours, Congress passed the Emergency Banking Relief Act, which strengthened federal oversight of the nation's banks and provided the government with greater authority for managing the currency through the Federal Reserve System.[16]

To address the banking crisis, Roosevelt also reached out to the American public. He was a master of using the growing popularity of the radio to calm and reassure the nation while simultaneously promoting new policies. His famous radio-based fireside chats enabled him to connect with ordinary

The alphabet soup of government programs during the Great Depression of the 1930s. (Source: Hulton Archive/ Getty Images)

Americans in a manner not possible for previous administrations. Roosevelt's first radio chat, on March 12, 1933 (the last day of the banking holiday), drew 60 million listeners and did much to stabilize the banking crisis.[17] With confidence inspired by Roosevelt's radio address and the provisions of the Emergency Banking Relief Act, individuals began to redeposit their savings. Within weeks, deposits outnumbered withdrawals, reversing a five-month negative trend.[18] By the end of Roosevelt's first month in office, 75 percent of banks in the Federal Reserve System had reopened.[19] The swiftness with which Roosevelt moved on the banking crisis was a precursor to the unprecedented speed with which his administration approached successive legislation.

Over the course of the next ninety-six days, Roosevelt's administration proposed and enacted fifteen sweeping legislative initiatives aimed to remedy the economic crisis in the country. Despite the failure of some of his experiments, Roosevelt's accomplishments during his first hundred days are still considered monumental in scope and impact. Legislation was enacted to reform banking, regulate security issuance and disclosure, stimulate business cooperation, provide relief to farmers, repeal prohibition, abandon the gold standard, generate home refinancing opportunities, and create employment opportunities through massive public works projects. In addition, the government authorized the development of the Tennessee Valley Authority, which, through land and water management initiatives and hydroelectric development, provided relief and opportunity to seven impoverished Southern states.[20]

Through these legislative actions a number of new regulations were imposed on businesses as the passage of the Glass-Steagall Act of 1933 split commercial banking from its speculative cousin, investment banking. By forcing banks to choose between commercial lending and underwriting securities, the government sought to avoid the unregulated speculation of the 1920s. Banks were also prohibited from engaging in the sale and distribution of insurance. The Banking Act of 1933 extended the provisions of Glass-Steagall and created the Federal Deposit Insurance Corporation (FDIC) to protect individual savings accounts (initially up to $2,500). By 1934, 96 percent of deposits were covered by FDIC protection, and bank deposits increased by 46 percent over the next five years.[21]

Congress also pushed through the adoption of the Securities Act of 1933 and the Securities Exchange Act of 1934. These acts required public entities to fully disclose information about new stock and bond issues and established a formal process for reporting quarterly and annual financial performance.[22] While the Securities Act regulated initial public offerings, the Securities Exchange Act protected investors by regulating the ongoing financial reporting and management activities of public companies. To this end, the Securities Exchange Act established the Securities and Exchange Commission (SEC) in 1934 to oversee the securities market and protect the public's interest. These acts made it illegal for company officers to "short sell" stock in their company (a widespread practice in the 1920s) and provided the initial guidelines for restricting insider trading. Given the legal and financial implications of the new reporting and regulatory compliance requirements for publicly traded companies, the role of corporate lawyers and accountants increased in value and scope.[23]

The regulation fervor continued with the establishment of the Federal Communications Commission for the oversight of radio, telegraph, and cable operators (and, later, television), and the Federal Housing Administration, which ensured that housing construction adhered to federal safety and quality standards. In what could be construed as reactionary legislation, businesses were further constrained by the passage of the Wheeler-Lea Act and the Food, Drug and Cosmetic Act in 1938. The Wheeler-Lea Act set stringent controls over false or otherwise deceptive advertising and broadened the Federal Trade Commission's purview in regulating unfair competition. The Food, Drug and Cosmetic Act strengthened the 1906 Pure Food and Drug Act signed by Roosevelt's cousin, Theodore. The newer act required product safety testing; enhanced product labeling, especially regarding the potential risks and side effects of drugs or therapeutic devices; and periodic factory inspections.[24] The provisions of the new act sought to ensure product safety, not efficacy; this issue of regulation would not be addressed again until the 1960s. Given many of the false hopes and unfulfilled promises of the advertisers of the 1920s, it is not surprising that Consumers Union (publishers of *Consumer Reports*) was also established in the 1930s. Its formation was another sign that the nation was ready for a new level of protection against unscrupulous businesses.

Though Roosevelt was often painted as a foe of business, the characterization was based less on reality and more on rhetoric. Roosevelt's stumping speeches often vilified business, but his actions were less constraining than they might have appeared. Throughout the 1930s, massive mergers and consolidations occurred in several major industries. For example, by 1935, the initial three hundred tire manufacturers had consolidated into twenty-six enterprises.[25] Merger activity was also especially brisk in the oil industry. Led by Standard Oil of New Jersey, a company that resulted from the U.S. Supreme Court—ordered dissolution of Standard Oil in 1911, the oil industry embarked on a renewed consolidation phase.[26]

Despite all the legislation, Roosevelt was in many ways fiscally conservative. Though he was encouraged by key economists to increase federal spending to stimulate private investment, he was unwilling to stray far from a balanced budget. Federal spending during the Depression was never more than 3 percent of the nation's gross domestic product.[27] As the economy showed signs of improvement in 1936 and 1937, Roosevelt chose to reduce federal spending in an effort to curb the growing budget deficit. Like Hoover, his efforts to balance the budget did more harm than good; it created a secondary recession. At its height, the federal deficit grew to $3 billion in the 1930s.[28] When the country finally spent its way out of the Depression, through the mass-mobilization effort for World War II, the federal deficit swelled to $40 billion.[29] While his relationship with business was complicated and often conflicted, Roosevelt's relationship with labor was simple; the worker had a friend in the White House.

Labor Seizes the Opportunity

Unemployment levels, which peaked at 25 percent, did not drop below 14 percent throughout the entire decade. When farmers are excluded from the employment rolls, the unemployment level never fell below 20 percent.[30] While the banking and securities reform acts transformed the financial centers of America and helped establish a consistent system of checks and balances, Congress also enacted sweeping legislation to address the plight of disadvantaged workers. The passage of the Social Security Act of 1935 was the government's first attempt to provide a small financial cushion for the terminally unemployed, the aged, and the disabled. The business community played a major role in shaping social security legislation. Business executives believed that overall productivity levels would increase as older workers retired and were replaced by more able and less expensive employees. Though the financial cushion from the new legislation was small, it did make retirement a more viable and attractive option for many. It also helped take out of the workforce many women and children who were often employed principally to support the needs of their elderly relatives.[31]

Beyond direct financial assistance, the government experimented with a series of employment initiatives, including the Civilian Conservation Corps (CCC), the Public Works Administration (PWA), and the Work Progress Administration (WPA). The CCC, which was created during Roosevelt's first hundred days, was designed to provide employment for young, single men between the ages of eighteen and twenty-five. In total, over 3 million men were employed in projects to improve forestry management, develop park and recreational facilities, and oversee soil conservation efforts. The PWA, which was also created during the first hundred days, was a similar relief program in which the government provided jobs to the unemployed to complete a variety of public works projects. With $3.3 billion earmarked for public improvement projects, PWA workers built New York's Triborough Bridge, the Overseas Highway from Miami to Key West, and Chicago's subway system.[32] In total, the program created over 400,000 jobs and initiated thirty-four thousand public works projects.[33] The WPA was created in 1935 and essentially expanded both the spirit and the charter of the PWA. In addition to funding a plethora of public works projects, including monuments, bridges, and urban parks, the WPA supported numerous artists and consequently sparked a revival in the celebration of traditional Americana in art, writing, and theater. The WPA also extended the aims of the CCC by creating the National Youth Administration to provide part-time employment opportunities for students. Prior to the expiration of its federal commission in 1943, the WPA allocated $11 billion in funds for the benefit of roughly 9 million unemployed workers.[34]

While the government created numerous employment opportunities to help the unemployed, it expected the business community to contribute as well. To that end, the National Industrial Recovery Act (NIRA) was passed in 1933. In addition to authorizing the creation of the Public Works Administration, the NIRA established the National Recovery Administration (NRA), which was designed to forge cooperation between businesses, employees, and government. Part of the basis for the establishment of the NRA was derived from the success of the War Industries Board that the government had commissioned during World War I to galvanize productivity.[35]

The goals of the NRA were to stabilize business operations by reducing competition, create more employment opportunities to increase overall purchasing power in the economy, and promote fair labor practices within specific industry sectors. These goals were to be achieved by the deployment of consistent business and labor practices across industry sectors. At the time, many believed that government-mandated industry associations (a formal and authorized extension of the trade association movement of the 1920s) would encourage and sustain fairer competition. To foster cooperation, the government even agreed to relax antitrust legislation. In exchange for the lessened regulatory oversight, businesses were expected to recognize the right of workers to organize into unions and bargain collectively. Over a two-year period, 450 industries and 23 million workers were impacted through this form of industrial cooperation.[36] Though many businesses were still considerably reluctant to recognize union organizing efforts, labor did benefit from industrywide agreements, which reduced the overall work week and promoted minimum-wage levels. To recoup their labor concessions, many industry sectors raised prices on their products and services, essentially nullifying the overarching intent of the NRA. After two years, the NRA lost a considerable amount of support and was ultimately deemed unconstitutional by the U.S. Supreme Court, mainly because of the potential for price fixing and trade restraint.[37]

The momentum of the labor movement, which was emboldened by the collective bargaining provisions of the NRA, was significantly enhanced by the passage of the National Labor Relations Act (also called the Wagner Act) in 1935. Workers not only were given the right to organize, but also received federal protection from unfair labor practices. The act also established a renewed National Labor Relations Board to oversee and enforce the unions' rights to organize workers and hold legitimate strikes.[38] The government's support of the worker was seen as a major victory for the union movement. In less than a decade, unions had moved from the despised havens of socialists and communists to the mainstream of America.

In an unprecedented wave of labor organization, union membership swelled to over 7.5 million by 1937, including a thirteenfold increase for the United Automobile Workers (UAW) union, which grew from 30,000 to 400,000.[39] The UAW was part of the Congress of Industrial Organizations (CIO), which was formed by John L. Lewis after the American Federation of Labor (AFL) refused to recognize unskilled workers. Formed in 1886 by Samuel Gompers, the AFL had long existed as a vehicle for the organization of the skilled labor trade.[40] Because of the AFL's reluctance to dilute its membership base with unskilled labor, however, the organization lost almost 1 million members.[41] With the creation of the CIO, Lewis, for the first time, created a sense of empowerment for some of the most disenfranchised members in the employment ranks, who mostly channeled their newly won power on the automobile industry.

Though Alfred P. Sloan Jr. of General Motors (GM) was a pioneer in giving consumers a choice and a voice, he, like his contemporaries in the automobile business, was loath to give his employees a similar platform. As the National Labor Relations Act was being debated, Sloan was quoted as saying, "Industry, if it has any appreciation of its obligation to future generations, will fight this proposal to the very last."[42] With 250,000 employees in 110 plants throughout the world, GM had produced profits of $196 million in 1936.[43] GM's success, despite the overall harsh economic climate, made it one of the first targets for the new sit-down strike, in which the workers took control of the manufacturing plant by refusing to leave. Though banned as an organizing device in 1939, the sit-down strike was extremely effective. Business executives like Sloan attempted to diffuse the unions with coercion and pleas for government intervention, but to no avail. After significant pressure and cost from a forty-four-day sit-down strike in six of GM's major plants, Sloan finally acquiesced to union demands, and in so doing, he set the tone for union negotiations throughout most of the automobile industry. Chrysler quickly followed suit and signed with the United Automobile Workers. He was followed by Ford, but not without a brutal and fatal fight. Even with the support of the government, most labor progress was not achieved without significant violence and hardship for both employers and employees.[44]

The transformation of the business landscape continued with the adoption of the Fair Labor Standards Act in 1938. This act sought to formalize a minimum wage and maximum working hours for employees of companies engaged in interstate commerce. The new law set forth a minimum wage of forty cents per hour and a maximum work week of forty hours to be phased in over an eight-year period. The act also prohibited the employment of children under the age of sixteen in all occupations and under the age of eighteen in certain hazardous occupations.[45] Unemployment remained high throughout the decade, yet real wages for those employed during the last five years increased significantly due to the momentum of the union movement combined with the support of federal legislation. Between 1935 and 1941, wages for factory workers increased by 30 percent.[46]

Though many business executives were cajoled into accepting the new realities of the labor movement, others did not need new laws or new movements to pursue progressive labor practices. These individuals led successful

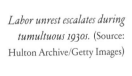

Labor unrest escalates during tumultuous 1930s. (Source: Hulton Archive/Getty Images)

businesses and independently pursued activities to support their base of employees. In many cases, they were proactive in creating a stabilized and sustainable business environment in a time of great uncertainty, confusion, and anxiety. Though Charles Hook built Armco Steel Company into the leading producer of sheet metal, he was better known for his fair and consistent treatment of employees. Hook advocated full disclosure of company information to all employees and displayed an impenetrable sense of loyalty through both good and bad times.[47] This sense of loyalty to employees was also shared by Robert W. Johnson Jr., of Johnson & Johnson, and Eli Lilly II, of Eli Lilly and Company; both refused to lay off workers throughout the down years of the Depression.

Beyond the empowerment of labor, the union movement played a significant role in influencing government policy regarding immigration. In an attempt to protect what few jobs were available to Americans, unions tapped into an all-too-common anti-immigration sentiment. Though many more Americans were informed about world issues through radio broadcasts (80 percent of Americans owned at least one radio by 1939), this awareness did little to change the country's isolationist tendencies.[48]

A View Across the Ocean

As events in Europe spiraled out of control during the years prior to World War II, most Americans were only passively interested. In fact, a strong undercurrent in America blamed the economic problems of the country on the unsustainable mass-mobilization effort for World War I. For many Americans, big business was culpable for a host of the country's postwar problems. Some Americans even believed that business executives had tricked the country into war for their own financial gain.[49] In particular, there was a tremendous backlash against war munitions manufacturers, bankers, and others that profited from the previous mobilization efforts. As the world economy contracted through the early years of the decade, all debtor nations except Finland defaulted on their loans from the United States. In the face of a global recession, Hitler's desire for a revitalized Germany seemed of little consequence to most Americans. In accordance, the U.S. Congress passed three neutrality acts during the 1930s, which imposed increasingly stringent prohibitions on travel abroad and selling war munitions to belligerent nations.[50]

Even in the face of growing atrocities in Europe, Americans turned away from both the war effort and, to a large extent, the fate of persecuted refugees. These feelings were shared not just within the union movement that sought to protect jobs, but also among all social classes and sectors. A 1938 *Fortune* magazine poll captured the prevailing sentiment when it reported that 83 percent of Americans were against relaxing immigration quotas to support refugees.[51] Roosevelt and the country held firm in these convictions. The neutrality stance only began to weaken when Germany attacked Poland in 1939 (a year after already taking control of Czechoslovakia and Austria), causing Britain and France to declare war. With the attack on Poland, Roosevelt offered a "cash-and-carry" policy to Britain and France.[52] Through this policy, sales of war munitions and other goods were made available to Britain and France if they were willing to transport the "cash-bought" provisions on their own ships. In this way, Roosevelt sought to avoid being drawn into the war by potential enemy submarine attacks on American cargo ships. With this policy, America took its first major step out of the neutral zone, but the overarching sentiment in the country remained firmly rooted in isolationism. The war in Europe seemed so far away, especially in the face of economic survival on the home front. As the Depression lingered on, Americans became convinced that tending to their own problems was the only prudent course of action.

Go West: Migration in America

The immigration numbers of the 1930s stand as a testament to America's entrenched isolationist sentiments; only 528,431 immigrants came to the United States between 1931 and 1940. This was by far the smallest number of immigrants in any decade of the twentieth century. In contrast, the number of immigrants in the 1920s was over eight times higher, even with the stringent immigration quotas set in 1921 and 1924. The last time the number of immigrants had been roughly 0.5 million was one hundred years earlier, between 1831 and 1840.[53] While America's borders were closed to new immigrants, there was no lack of population shifts in the 1930s. The migratory American farmer became the country's newest "immigrant" as rural flight reached new levels.

Hoover's ill-fated protectionist tariffs on agricultural products decimated the export market for farmers and created an overabundance of crops. Without viable export opportunities, crop prices slid further and further downward.

Fleeing the dust bowls and unemployment of the Midwest for new hope and opportunities in the West.
(Source: Hulton Archive/ Getty Images)

By 1932, farm incomes had dropped by 52 percent from 1929, and almost 1 million farmers lost control of their operations.[54] In an effort to assist farmers, Congress passed the Agricultural Adjustment Act in 1933, which essentially paid subsidies to farmers for not growing their crops. While the act did provide some relief to large farming operations, which had the capacity to downsize, it did not support smaller farmers, especially tenant farmers and sharecroppers. In addition, the artificial scarcity of crops actually produced higher prices for consumers. Like the National Recovery Administration, the Agricultural Adjustment Act was considered a failed experiment and was ultimately ruled unconstitutional.

While farmers were trying to cope with the pricing crisis, they were faced with an even greater foe. Overfarming, severe drought, and intense heat in the summers of 1934 and 1935 became a deadly recipe for dust storms that destroyed crops, farms, and entire livelihoods. The dust bowl stretched from New Mexico to Kansas, but its impact was felt throughout the country, both literally (12 million tons of dust landed in Chicago in 1934) and figuratively.[55] By 1938, more than 10 million acres of land had been stripped of five inches of topsoil.[56] Over the course of four years, 3 million farmers left their farms for the promise of a better life in the nation's cities or the fertile fields of California. By the end of the decade, over 60 percent of the U.S. population lived in urban settings.

The realities for the new migrants rarely measured up to their dreams, however. The lack of viable farming opportunities was often replaced by a lack of available jobs and crowded housing. Many who headed west or north returned home or simply wandered from place to place searching for employment.

The U.S. population that had grown by 17 million in the 1920s increased by only about 8 million in the 1930s. This 6.5 percent population increase from 123 million to 131 million was the lowest in the history of the nation. With immigration being virtually eliminated, the bulk of the population rise was attributable not to an increase in births but to a decrease in death rates. The number of babies born between 1930 and 1935 actually fell below a zero growth rate.[57] Throughout the Depression, couples delayed having children and delayed getting married; the number of marriages in this period declined by 22 percent.[58] There was also a corresponding drop in the divorce rate, notes David Kennedy. The rate dropped "by 25 percent, as the contracting economy sealed the exits from unhappy marriages."[59] Perhaps more out of financial necessity than choice, the 1930s brought forth a renewed focus on the family and traditional values.

Looking for an Escape

The experimentation of the 1920s was quickly replaced with pragmatism and conservatism, but at the same time that traditional values were being heralded, there was a significant increase in crime, prostitution, and panhandling. Some pointed to the repeal of prohibition in 1933 and the legalization of gambling as the culprits for the rise in crime, but for many people drawn to robbery, prostitution, or begging, the underlying reasons were much more complicated. Many believed that they had no other means to survive; a life of crime or begging often became the only viable option.

Throughout the decade, Americans turned to simple, small pleasures to escape, if only for a short time, the drudgery of their lives. With the significant decrease in leisure travel, families stayed close to home and sought new forms of inexpensive entertainment. Not surprisingly, then, there was a surge in home-based parlor and board games, escapist literature, and radio ownership. Introduced as much for social commentary as for fun, the game of Monopoly became a best seller shortly after its introduction in 1935. On the literature front, mystery novels by authors such as Erle Stanley Gardner (creator of Perry Mason) garnered widespread appeal. When not playing games or escaping in fiction, Americans often tuned in to radio soap operas that celebrated self-made men and women transcending the contextual realities of their times. The first soap opera, *The Puddle Family*, was introduced by Procter & Gamble in 1932.

This radio drama spawned a new direction in advertising by reinforcing brand icons like Oxydol and Ivory soap. Sporting events, especially baseball and boxing, and the comedic antics of Freeman Gosden and Charles Correll (otherwise known as Amos and Andy), George Burns and Gracie Allen, and Jack Benny (sponsored by John Dorrance's Campbell Soup Company) were also popular radio fare. The radio quickly became a centerpiece of the American home by bringing families together for a few hours of programmed escape.[60]

Americans also sought relief and freedom in movies. The 1930s became the golden age for movie producers as five thousand films were released and more than 70 million Americans (60 percent of the population) saw at least one of these movies each week.[61] Though money was sparse, a quarter for a few hours of relief seemed like a bargain. Movie content spanned the spectrum of escapism, from the Marx Brothers comedies to the classic horror films of *Dracula*, *Frankenstein*, and *The Mummy* to elaborate musicals and epics. In a strange twist that was inconsistent with the prevailing focus on traditional values, audiences flocked to movies that celebrated the lives of gangsters and criminals. In an odd way, there was sympathy for anyone who could conquer despair. Taking escapism to a new level, Walt Disney Company introduced the first feature-length animated movie, *Snow White*, in 1937. The film cost an unbelievable sum of $2 million, yet became one of the highest-grossing films produced to date. A year later, the *New York Times* aptly called Disney's movies and other ventures "industrialized fantasy."[62] Technological advances in radio

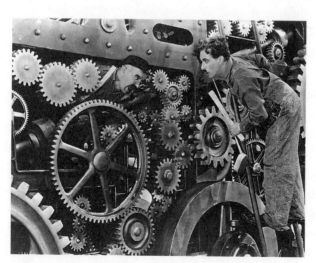

Charlie Chaplin in a scene from the 1936 movie Modern Times, *a scathing parody of industrialization.* (Source: Bettmann/ CORBIS)

and movie production like those advanced by Disney provided the means by which Americans could, without guilt or condemnation, indulge in their fantasies of a better life, one that had been ravaged by the Depression.

Technology Soars to New Heights

Despite the overall economy, technological innovations blossomed during the Depression. This decade saw the introduction of air-conditioning by Willis H. Carrier, DuPont's discovery of a "miracle fiber" called nylon, and the development of fiberglass by Owens-Illinois. Innovators at these companies not only launched sustainable business enterprises, but also transformed whole industries. Carrier, for instance, is credited with making the modern skyscraper a more viable business structure through the incorporation of climate-controlled air-conditioning and ventilation systems. Air-conditioning was also instrumental in the development of industry in both the Western and the Southern states.[63] DuPont's discovery of nylon after almost ten years of research and development and Harold Boeschenstein's perfection of fiberglass helped legitimize the notion of active investment in innovation. Nylon, the first synthetic fiber, became a fundamentally important component not just in the world of fashion but for hundreds of military applications, including parachutes, apparel, and tires, which were all critical to the mobilization effort for World War II.[64] Recognizing the commercial and scientific opportunities for fiberglass in the mid-1930s, Boeschenstein convinced Owens-Illinois to create a new company. With the launch of Owens-Corning Fiberglass, Boeschenstein built a new industry from scratch. He tirelessly promoted the potential uses and applications for fiberglass for over twenty-five years and is considered one of the "pioneers of the plastic age."[65]

While these innovators were creating and extending major industries, other business executives were transforming the American frontier. At the forefront of the aviation revolution was aircraft manufacturer Donald W. Douglas. Douglas, through the creation of the DC-3 aircraft in 1935, was largely responsible for the viability, safety, and comfort of passenger travel. His aircraft could hold twenty-one passengers, cruise at a speed of 195 miles per hour, and fly one thousand miles without refueling. The DC-3 quickly surpassed the then state-of-the-art Boeing aircraft, which could hold ten passengers and cruise at 165 miles per hour.[66] The DC-3 could also be built quicker and

TABLE 4-2

Business events that shaped the 1930s

Date	Event
1930	President Hoover signs protectionist Smoot-Hawley Tariff Bill
1930	State Department prohibits almost all immigration of foreign workers
1930	World's largest bank formed with merger of Chase National and Equitable Trust
1931	Procter & Gamble introduces brand management
1931	Empire State Building completed (tallest in the world), only 46 percent occupied
1932	Reconstruction Finance Corporation authorized
1932	First Glass-Steagall Banking Act expands federal credit
1932	Unemployment reaches all-time high: 13.7 million U.S. and 30 million worldwide
1932	Dow Jones Industrial Average hits low of 41.22 on July 8
1932	5,000 banks are closed
1932	Instant photography invented by Edwin Land
1933	Four-day banking holiday declared; Emergency Banking Relief Act passed
1933	Creation of Civilian Conservation Corps
1933	Agricultural Adjustment Act provides subsidies to farmers to not grow crops
1933	Tennessee Valley Authority created
1933	Federal Securities Act regulates public companies
1933	National Industrial Recovery Act forms Public Works Administration
1933	National Recovery Administration establishes fair labor standards
1933	Banking Act creates deposit insurance protection
1933	National Labor Board created
1933	Frances Perkins named secretary of labor, first female cabinet member
1933	Prohibition repealed
1933	First recorded sit-down strike—Hormel plant in Minnesota
1933	Frequency modulation (FM) radio invented

cheaper than any other aircraft, enabling a host of airline operators (including Juan Trippe's Pan American World Airways) to efficiently expand their businesses. By the end of the decade, 90 percent of the world's airlines had DC-series planes in their fleets, and passenger revenue was on par with airmail delivery revenues.[67]

With the technological advances in aircraft design and structure, many airlines that were originally launched for mail delivery quickly grew into full-fledged passenger service. Among these airlines were William A. Patterson's United Airlines, Jack Frye's Trans World Airlines, Cyrus R. Smith's American Airlines, Edward V. Rickenbacker's Eastern Airlines, and Robert F. Six's Continental Airlines. In many ways, the growth in the airline industry

TABLE 4-2 *(continued)*

Date	Event
1934	Securities and Exchange Commission created
1934	Federal Communications Commission created
1934	Federal Housing Administration created
1934	Reciprocal Trade Agreements Act passed, lessens protectionist tariffs
1935	Works Progress Administration created
1935	National Recovery Act and Agricultural Adjustment Act ruled unconstitutional
1935	National Labor Relations Act provides employees with right to join unions and to strike
1935	Banking Act revises Federal Reserve System
1935	Social Security Act passed
1935	First of three Neutrality Acts passed
1935	John Lewis forms Committee for Industrial Organization, later called Congress of Industrial Organizations
1935	First DC-3 jet engine flight
1936	Imports exceed exports for the first time in ten years
1936	Consumers Union formed
1936	Hoover Dam completed
1938	Nylon introduced by DuPont
1938	Fair Labor Standards Act passed, sets minimum wage and maximum working hours
1938	Radio advertising expenditures exceed print advertising for first time
1939	Igor Sikorsky invents helicopter
1939	Silicon Valley begins, with William Hewlett and David Packard
1939	Germany invades Poland
1939	Roosevelt endorses cash-and-carry policy for war supplies for Britain and France

paralleled the growth in the automobile sector in how it spawned numerous associated enterprises (parts, transportation, delivery, hospitality, etc.) and made new frontiers even more accessible. The innovations in aircraft design also laid the foundation for the rapid growth and transformation of air travel that was so important to World War II and beyond.

Entrepreneurs: Providing an Escape

Though business executives took advantage of many technological advances in the 1930s, the average American could no longer afford expensive items like automobiles and major appliances. The installment plans that had made those items so attractive and seemingly affordable during the 1920s were now non-existent. Inventories continued to swell in many industries, further exacerbating the financial and employment turmoil of the times. Though overall investment in heavy industry fell by 87 percent in three years (1930–1933), the consumer goods sector performed better than most during the 1930s. As a whole, the consumer products sector declined by only 19 percent.[68] While consumers had considerably less money to spend, what little they had went toward necessities, including food, clothing, and personal care. Whether by choice or necessity, Americans turned their backs on the lavish spending of the 1920s for a simpler life, yet they did not completely forgo luxuries. The luxuries they sought were small and inexpensive.

The 1930s saw the birth of Revlon cosmetics under Charles H. Revson and the expansion of personal-care products by Hollywood makeup artist Max (Francis) Factor Jr. Conventional wisdom would have suggested that personal-care businesses would not have been viable during the Depression. Who would spend what little money they had on such seemingly frivolous items as nail polish, lipstick, and other makeup? Revson and Factor correctly assumed that millions of women would do just that.

Known for his autocratic and direct management style, Revson built Revlon into the second-largest cosmetics company in the United States. His unique talent of grasping the female psyche, bolstered by his fiercely competitive nature, allowed Revlon to grow from a small nail-polish maker into a huge cosmetics conglomerate that eventually produced over 3,500 products. Revson was especially adept at portraying hidden desires and fantasies in his print advertising campaigns and, later, in his use of models in television sponsorship.[69]

Taking over the family company after the death of his father in 1938, Max Factor is also regarded as a pioneer in the cosmetics and makeup business. He transformed the company from a Hollywood makeup studio into a worldwide provider of name-brand cosmetics, bringing the makeup of the "stars" to the main streets of America and beyond.[70]

The branding in the personal-care sector helped create illusions of luxury and high culture at a very low price. In so doing, it gave many Americans a brief chance to escape the drudgery of the times. Despair and despondency created a formidable shield in the 1930s. One individual who penetrated that shield was Margaret F. Rudkin. This business entrepreneur took a basic and necessary product and created a brand icon that spoke to Americans who longed for something extraordinary and special in their lives.

Margaret F. Rudkin (1897–1967), Pepperidge Farm, Incorporated

In many ways, the first half of Margaret Fogarty Rudkin's life and career closely paralleled the prevailing social and economic conditions of the early decades of the twentieth century. She took advantage of employment opportunities for women in the late 1910s (during World War I), which ignited an early interest in business and finance. She enjoyed a life of comfort, wealth, and leisure in the 1920s, building a country estate farm that was landscaped with Pepperidge trees. Moreover, she survived a bitter reversal of fortune in the 1930s—a reversal that became a catalyst for a new life and a revived business career at the age of forty. Had Rudkin not been affected by the Depression, she most probably would not have founded one of the most enduring bakery brands in the United States: Pepperidge Farm. In the process, she broke several molds, including the role of women in business; the viability of upscale, niche retailing; and the high-priced branding of a lowly commodity product.

Margaret Fogarty was born into a life of relative privilege in New York City, and for the first twelve years of her life, she and her parents shared a four-story brownstone home with her Irish grandparents in the Tudor neighborhood of Manhattan. With personal servants on staff, Margaret and her mother were shielded from many typical household chores. Though her mother lacked an interest in cooking, Margaret often liked to watch her grandmother bake. At times, the young girl experimented with her own recipes. An academically gifted student, Margaret graduated at the top of her high school class and secured a position as a bank bookkeeper. As the first woman to be employed in this position at the firm, she felt the pressure to excel. Margaret recalled some of the pressure of this position: "At the end of the day you had to add up the debits and credits—the bank didn't have an adding machine—and if they didn't balance, you had to sit there until you found the mistake."[71] Margaret's focus on quality was a common theme throughout her career.

Her early success in the bookkeeping venture led first to a promotion to bank teller and subsequently to a position in public relations for a Wall Street brokerage firm, McClure, Jones & Company, in 1919. She later used this early exposure and experience in public relations to catapult Pepperidge Farm to the national marketplace. It was at this brokerage firm that Margaret Fogarty met her husband, Henry Albert Rudkin, a successful stockbroker and partner in the firm. After they were married in 1923, Margaret, at the age of twenty-six, retired to a life as a "society wife." She became part of the jet-setting, afflu-ent community of New York City. Henry Rudkin rode the wave of prosperity in the 1920s, and in 1928, the Rudkins built an estate in Fairfield County, Con-necticut, on 125 acres of land. Being from the city, they had idealized the life of a country farmer and wanted to explore it on their own. They hired servants to tend to the household upkeep and lived a life that could have been taken from an F. Scott Fitzgerald novel—hobnobbing in the city and attending horse shows and polo matches (Henry was a skilled player) in the country.

As the Great Depression unraveled in the nation, so did the Rudkins' idyl-lic life. With the stock market crash, Henry Rudkin's brokerage business be-came a shadow of its former glory. This alone forced the Rudkins to stream-line their lifestyle. The readjustment was further exacerbated when in 1931 Henry suffered a severe polo accident that left him bedridden for months. Through the early years of the 1930s, Margaret Rudkin was forced to dismiss all her servants and sell many of her possessions, including four of the family's five cars, to survive. While her husband tried to salvage his job on Wall Street, Rudkin looked for opportunities to create income-producing ventures from their country estate. Luckily, her life of affluence had not left her with a con-stricting sense of pride and entitlement. Her resourcefulness was demon-strated when she sent for a government brochure (Department of Agriculture Pamphlet number 1186) on how to properly slaughter pigs, and then she did so.[72] After several marginally successful ventures, including raising turkeys, Rudkin stumbled into a business that transformed her life and transformed niche grocery retailing.

The inspiration for the transformation came from Rudkin's son, who suf-fered from severe asthma. Convinced that the young boy's condition was aggravated by both the damp climate of the North and the additives in processed food (especially bread), the family doctor suggested that the Rud-kins either move to a drier climate or begin preparing and cooking their own baked products at home. Without the funds to move, Margaret turned to the second alternative—baking bread. Recalling her early attempts to bake bread,

Rudkin remembered: "I never saw a cookbook in my house, and I never saw my grandmother or my mother write anything down. So my recipes came out of my head—just memories of how things tasted and looked."[73] She was often quoted as saying that her first loaf of bread should have been sent to the Smithsonian Institution's collection of geologic artifacts: "it had the consistency and texture of a brick."[74] When she finally succeeded in producing a product reminiscent of her childhood days, she discovered that it was much more than edible. It was delicious and, in many ways, comforting. As an added and somewhat unexpected bonus, the whole-wheat bread seemed to cure her ailing son.

After their family doctor asked for several loaves of bread for some of his other asthmatic patients, Rudkin and her husband began to explore the possibilities of creating a business. They first approached other physicians, believing that they had stumbled on medicinal bread. Their success in targeting the physician community was almost instantaneous, and they soon had a thriving mail-order enterprise. On the heels of this success, Rudkin approached her local grocer in Fairfield. He agreed to try the bread as a favor to a loyal customer, not believing that it would be good or sellable. He was wrong. After tasting the bread, he quickly agreed to stock the item. Given her local success, Rudkin sought out Charles & Company, an upscale grocer in New York City. To convince the grocer of the quality of her product, she brought with her a basketful of warm bread and butter. Her product-sampling approach worked. The grocer agreed to order twenty-four loaves a day.

Starting in her country kitchen, Rudkin baked whole-wheat bread, which her husband took on the 7:38 a.m. train into New York City on his way to Wall Street. In this way, Henry Rudkin became the company's first distributor. It did not take long for the bread to become extremely popular, even though it sold for two and a half times more than commercial white bread (25 cents versus 10 cents). Though grocers at first scoffed at the price differential, consumers quickly purchased the product. Rudkin had hit on a viable and sustainable niche for high-end bakery products. At the time, she was modest about her accomplishment: "I am only trying to please the minority who want a good loaf of bread and are willing to pay for it."[75] That focus served as an underlying credo for all Pepperidge Farm products. Rudkin reinforced this approach by only targeting niche retailers whose clientele represented her intended audience.

Given her early background in public relations, it is not surprising that one of Rudkin's first attempts to expand the business involved the hiring of a publicist. The first story about Pepperidge Farm appeared in the year of the company's founding, 1937. The article, written for the *New York Journal and American*, extolled the wholesome nature of the bread. Within a year, the company was selling four thousand loaves of bread a week and had moved operations from the family kitchen to a stable on the Pepperidge Farm property. Serving a regional marketplace, Pepperidge Farm had a delivery company take over the distributor role that Henry Rudkin had originally performed. After her publicist landed a *Reader's*

Margaret Rudkin displaying the bread that became the foundation for the success of Pepperidge Farm. (Source: Bettmann/CORBIS)

Digest story about a former society matron baking bread in the country in 1939, the demand and popularity of Pepperidge Farm bread blossomed. It became a national sensation, and Pepperidge Farm was well on its way to becoming one of the most well-known brands in the niche grocery-retailing sector.

The national exposure forced Rudkin to move her operations off the farm and into a much larger facility. In 1940, having borrowed fifteen thousand dollars, Rudkin converted a former automobile showroom in Norwalk, Connecticut, into a full-service baking center. Within a few years, Rudkin's operations were selling over twenty-five thousand loaves of bread per week, and the company was beginning to extend its product offerings. The first two additions were melba toast and pound cake. These products were followed by the company's introduction of mixes for stuffing, a move that was, in many ways, a testament to Rudkin's ingenuity and creativity. One hallmark of Pepperidge Farm bread was its quality and freshness. Any bread not sold within two to three days was returned to the company. Rudkin created the stuffing as a by-product of the returned bread, and this convenience product became phenomenally popular.

Rudkin's focus on quality and the use of all-natural ingredients permeated the culture of the company. To that end, Rudkin sought suppliers that were skilled at producing premium raw materials for her baking operation. She was known to "commission farmers to grow high-quality wheat, then arrange for stone grinding at vintage mills throughout the Northeast."[76] When she exhausted the premium capacity in the supply chain, Rudkin decided to pursue a strategy of backward integration by opening milling operations throughout the Midwest. By the end of the 1940s, Rudkin had built a vertically integrated operation, from raw material production to baking to distribution. She continued to expand the product line but only after new or enhanced products passed a strict quality threshold. If Rudkin believed that the company could not produce a better product than its competitor could, she refused to introduce it. Her greatest satisfaction was holding true to this strategy despite several temptations to exploit the company's hard-earned goodwill. Rudkin's most significant product introduction came in the 1950s, when she added a line of distinctive, high-end cookies to her portfolio. The search for the perfect cookie took over ten years. On a European vacation (and cookie-tasting tour), Rudkin found what she was looking for. After orchestrating an agreement to buy the cookie recipes of Delacre, a Belgium baker and chocolatier, she brought the recipes to the United States and established a dedicated operation to produce a line of high-end cookies, each representing a name of a famous European city (Milan, Brussels, Geneva, etc.).

Throughout her leadership of Pepperidge Farm, Rudkin embraced marketing and advertising, and she used both radio and television to promote the wholesomeness of her products and her company. The Pepperidge Farm advertising consistently stressed both the high quality of the products and their natural ingredients. Rudkin even inserted herself into the company's advertising mix by taking on the persona of Maggie Rudkin, vouching for the natural ingredients and consistent quality of her products. Serving on a panel of public-relations experts, Rudkin noted that the "basis of developing public relations is to protect your product so intrinsically that it honestly constitutes the best value obtainable by the public for the price."[77] She believed that her products should fill a definite need in the marketplace and should be sold principally on their merits.[78] Through her skillful product line additions and integrated advertising, Rudkin built Pepperidge Farm into the largest independent bakery operation in America.[79]

Leaders: Survival Specialists

Facing declining market demand, excess capacity, and labor unrest in the 1930s, business leaders attempted to redefine their operations for survival. Many leaders transformed their businesses to serve new market requirements, often moving from commercial to consumer production. One such leader was Amory Houghton, of Corning Glass. Houghton was instrumental in converting Corning Glass from a wholesale distributor of commercial lighting and glass fixtures into a consumer product company. He sharply reduced the prices of oven ware and lightbulbs to make the products more palatable to the consumer market. Houghton further expanded the business by creating subsidiaries to test-market additional consumer products, lessening the company's dependence on the struggling industrial marketplace.[80]

Two individuals who took advantage of the end of prohibition to reinvent their businesses were Joe Thompson Jr. and Erwin Uihlein. Having established a small retail operation as an outgrowth of his block-ice business, Thompson seized the opportunity to build on the convenience-store concept when ice sales precipitously declined. The expanding American landscape, combined with the end of prohibition, contributed to the growth and popularity of these conveniently located and easily accessible stores. Through the reinvention of his block-ice operation, Thompson created the 7-Eleven convenience-store chain. The ability to sell beer contributed greatly to the success of this new enterprise (beer and cigarettes are two of the biggest sellers in this distribution channel).[81] Uihlein also capitalized on this renewed selling opportunity. Though his company was not producing during prohibition, Uihlein quickly revived the family brewery business through massive investment and retooling. His Schlitz Brewing Company became the second-largest beer producer in the United States and held that position for three decades.[82]

While these business leaders redirected their operations for a new base of customers, many in the financial services sector tried to navigate the complicated and somewhat unpredictable role of government intervention in their operations. The passage of strict banking regulations in 1933 and 1935 forced a number of business leaders to rethink their operations. This was especially true for financial institutions that engaged in both securities underwriting and commercial banking.

Harold S. Stanley (1885–1963), Morgan, Stanley & Company

When contemplating the history of Morgan, Stanley & Company, most people automatically think of the larger-than-life figure of J. P. Morgan, who was considered one of the most successful bankers (and business executives) of the twentieth century. Morgan wielded an immense level of power during the early decades of the twentieth century, a power that enabled him to control whole industries and to exert tremendous pressure on proposed government regulations. His financing abilities and power are nothing if not legendary, but Morgan, aside from posthumously contributing his name, was not involved in the creation and ultimate success of Morgan, Stanley & Company. In fact, he was long since deceased at its founding in 1935 (Morgan died in 1913). The fate of Morgan, Stanley & Company rested on the shoulders of Stanley, not on the legacy of Morgan.

Harold S. Stanley was a banker's banker, spending his entire life in the epicenters of the banking community. Born in a small town in Massachusetts, Stanley enjoyed a life of privilege and comfort in his early years. He attended well-heeled private schools and enjoyed lavish vacations. His father, William Stanley, was an inventor, and it was his name that the General Electric Company used in the creation of Stanley Works in Pittsfield, Massachusetts. The younger Stanley summed up his life's purpose in his 1908 college yearbook from Yale University with the phrase "will enter business."[83] A more appropriate and precise phrase might have been "will enter banking."

After travel in Europe, Stanley's banking career began when he joined the National Commercial Bank of Albany. Two years later, in 1910, Stanley joined the bond house of J. G. White and Company as an assistant treasurer. His early success in the endeavor led him in 1916 to the Guaranty Trust Company, where he produced stellar results as a vice president in the bond department. He was so successful in growing this business that Guaranty decided to establish a separate trust company, with Stanley as its president. In this role, he underwrote and sold millions of dollars of bond issues for both the public and the private sectors. More importantly, Stanley's devotion, determination, and perseverance opened the doors to the elite banking community in the country. His achievements were not unnoticed by the House of Morgan, and in 1927, J. P. Morgan's son, John P. Morgan Jr., invited Stanley to become a partner in the banking and brokerage business, J. P. Morgan & Company.

At the age of forty-two, Stanley became one of the youngest partners in the most prestigious financial house in the world. His appointment also came at a time when business executives were heralded as geniuses. Stanley understood that the urbanization of America created tremendous opportunities for a multitude of utility providers, from gas to electricity to phone service. His expertise in this arena quickly became a tremendous asset in underwriting security issues for utility providers and consolidators. His uninterrupted success seemed unstoppable, yet two years after joining the House of Morgan, the stock market collapsed, which brought forth a wave of government intervention and massive regulation in the banking community.

Stanley, like the rest of the financial world, was faced with a new context, one that could not have been more divorced from the past. In his history of the investment banking sector, Vincent Carosso summed up the times: "The crash and the Depression transformed the image of the investment banker from one with halo to one with horns and spiked tail. The shortsighted, occasionally two-faced behavior of financial leaders during and immediately following the crisis shook the public's confidence in bankers as expert custodians of other people's money. The subsequent failure of hundreds of firms, including some of the strongest ones, damaged still further the investment bankers' image by demonstrating how incompetent many of them had been in managing their own affairs."[84] It was within this new framework that Stanley's next moves in the financial world were defined.

To comply with the Glass-Steagall Act, which split commercial banking from investment banking, Stanley left J. P. Morgan & Company in 1935 to create Morgan, Stanley & Company, an independent bond house that would carry forth the security trading business that his former employer was forced to exit. With a handful of executives, $7.5 million in capital, and a tremendously powerful name, Stanley began to build a new business.[85] During his first full year as the head of Morgan, Stanley & Company—and despite being in the depths of the Depression—Stanley oversaw the issuance of more than $1 billion in public offerings and placements.[86] Through the next several years, Stanley and his company continued to garner a large share of the investment banking business in the country. When Morgan, Stanley & Company joined the New York Stock Exchange in 1941, the company had managed 25 percent of all bond issues underwritten since Glass-Steagall took effect.[87] In fact, Stanley was so successful in managing business relationships that Morgan, Stanley & Company twice came under attack by renewed government intervention.

In the late 1930s, the government, under pressure from investment houses based outside New York (most notably, Halsey, Stuart & Company of Chicago), chaired the Temporary National Economic Committee (TNEC) to aggressively pursue the issue of competitive bidding for securities. Heretofore, many corporations did not engage in competitive bidding for the issuance of their securities. These deals were made on personal, professional, and historical relationships, just the type of relationships that Harold Stanley was so adept at managing. Stanley believed that relationships between investment bankers and issuing corporations should model personal relationships in all walks of life—relationships based on integrity, mutual respect, and balance.[88]

As a major beneficiary and leader of the status quo, Stanley vehemently opposed the concept of competitive bidding, and he became the industry's most ardent defender. Testifying before the TNEC, Stanley stated his belief that competitive bidding would undermine smaller operations that did not have the wherewithal to compete with larger firms. He asserted that the only true asset of smaller, boutique operations was their ability to establish close personal relationships with issuing firms, and he believed that this advantage would be obliterated if price wars ensued.[89] In a 1939 memorandum, "Competitive Bidding for New Issues of Corporate Securities," Stanley articulated his position: "in the world of private enterprise, business managers should have the right to decide whether their companies are best served by such relations [knowledgeable and personal], or by the casual contacts that would result from competitive bidding for new security issues."[90] Stanley was concerned that casual contacts emerging from competitive bidding would lead to pricing based on opportunistic, short-term motives and not serve the long-term objectives of the firm. Though the government did not adopt his point of view against competitive bidding, Stanley's

Harold Stanley waiting to testify during the reopening of the Senate Banking and Currency Committee Inquiry in 1933. The hearings set the stage for the passage of the Banking Act, which provided the impetus for the formation of Morgan, Stanley & Company.
(Source: Bettmann/CORBIS)

performance in the defense process further solidified his position of prominence in the tight-knit financial circles of the times.

Though his business suffered immediately after the 1941 ruling (losing many bids to Halsey, Stuart & Company), Morgan, Stanley & Company was back on top by the mid-1940s. In fact, the company was doing so well that in 1947, the government charged it, along with sixteen other investment houses and the Investment Bankers Association, with monopolistic practices. At the time, Attorney General Tom Clark commented that the antitrust action "was one of the biggest and most important cases ever brought under the Sherman Act."[91] The case dragged on for six years, and again, Harold Stanley became the principal witness for the defense. Throughout the extended trial, Stanley was an outspoken advocate for his own company, his industry, and his affiliated trade association. In this instance, his defense was a success; the case against the seventeen investment banking houses was formally dismissed in 1955. It was virtually impossible for the government to prove that a collusive and monopolistic pact existed between seventeen independent companies. More than defending the protective environment that had engulfed Wall Street, Stanley helped recalibrate the public's perception of the banking community. At this point, Stanley felt that his life's work had come to a natural end. He resigned as the managing partner of Morgan, Stanley & Company at the conclusion of the trial. True to his character and love of finance, Stanley remained a limited partner of the firm until his death in 1963.[92]

Managers: Extending the Line

Capitalizing on the declining stock market and the availability of distressed companies, many business executives pursued an expansionist policy through mergers, acquisitions, consolidations, and new organizational designs. The collapse of the export market played a significant role in influencing these strategic approaches. Cost management became the watchword, and managers sought ways to survive by generating increasing operational and production efficiencies. Managers also took advantage of the buyer's market in the 1930s by expanding their operations through low-cost investments.

In particular, individuals who headed major railroad lines used the availability of relatively inexpensive labor and supplies to upgrade and invest in their operations. This investment was handsomely rewarded when the railways were again "federalized" during World War II. Some of the key railroad executives who embarked on a plan of expansion were representatives from the East (Robert R. Young), the Midwest (Matthew S. Sloan), and the South (Ernest E. Norris).

Young set out to take over the holding company that owned the Chesapeake & Ohio (C&O) Railroad, and despite losing substantial backing from a group of General Motors executives, he eventually gained control of the company. Though he struggled with securing capital for the improvement of the rail lines, Young was instrumental in eventually opening up the financial markets for all railroad executives. The financing struggle for the C&O resulted from the battle over competitive bidding for securities and bond issues. The House of Morgan bitterly fought Young in his quest for competitive bidding. Despite the financing battle, the C&O railroad itself was completely revitalized under Young and eventually became one of the strongest railroads in the East.[93]

While Young was battling with the railroad establishment in the East and the financial circles in the North, Sloan was overseeing the rapid development of the Missouri-Kansas-Texas Railroad lines that grew in conjunction with the dynamic population explosion in the southwestern United States. Sloan led the company in a massive investment campaign to extend the railroad lines to keep pace with westward expansion. Though his tenure as president (1933–1944) coincided with the depths of the Depression, Sloan was able to increase the company's revenues threefold, from $26 million to over $80 million.[94] In lockstep measure, Norris is largely heralded as invigorating the railroad establishment in the South through his management of the Southern Railway System. Norris expanded Southern Railway through solid, traditional business principles, including heavy capital investments in new railway cars, but also through his championing of the Southern lifestyle. By forming an explicit link between the Southern Railway and the community it served, he created a sense of pride for both employees and riders.[95]

The efforts of Young, Sloan, and Norris are extremely impressive, but the scope of their work pales in comparison with the challenge faced by Martin W. Clement, who took the helm as the eleventh president of the Pennsylvania Railroad, in 1935. At that time, it was the largest railway network in the world, with operating revenues of over $350 million and thousands of miles of track. The Pennsylvania Railroad weathered the Depression not by retreating from expansion or through consolidation, but through massive investment.

Throughout the decade, the company spent over $500 million in "betterments, improvements, and additions to its equipment, roadway, structures and other parts of the plant."[96] This investment, in the face of bitter economic troubles, enabled the Pennsylvania Railroad to emerge from the 1930s as a more vibrant enterprise, ready to tackle the monumental challenge of managing transportation logistics for the United States during the war years.

Throughout his tenure, Clement sought to improve the major assets of the railroad, taking advantage of easily accessible labor, supplies, and financing. Early in his presidency, he embarked on a $200 million program to electrify certain key routes. Through his investment in electrification, Clement introduced more streamlined locomotives and passenger cars produced by the Pullman Company. The streamlined nature of the new equipment, in turn, enabled the railroad to reduce its travel time to major U.S. cities. The success of these lightweight aluminum trains gave prominence to the word *streamlined*, which originally implied aerodynamic design but soon became so popular that it came to represent anything efficient.[97]

Clement sought to reinforce the railroad's competitive positioning by expanding the company's full transportation network. So that the railroad could offer its freight customers door-to-door shipping and delivery service to and from more than one thousand train stations, he increased the company's affiliated trucking fleets and added new water ferry routes. Between 1935 and 1939, "net tons per train in freight service increased from 1,006 to 1,164 or by 15.7 percent."[98] In line with his focus on greater operational

Crowds watch as Pennsylvania Railroad's new electric locomotive begins its inaugural trip from Philadelphia to Harrisburg. (Source: Bettmann/CORBIS)

efficiency, Clement enhanced the company's safety record. Through the installation of better brakes and signaling devices, Clement dramatically reduced the number of injuries and deaths of railroad workers. By the end of the decade, the annual injury rate of workers had been reduced to 264 on a base of over 130,000 employees. Five years earlier the annual injury average was 998, and ten years earlier it stood at over 2,000.

Through his refurbishment of the rail cars, Clement also sought to improve passenger comfort. To that end, he became a strong advocate for the use of air-conditioning, and by the mid-1930s, the Pennsylvania Railroad "boasted the largest fleet of air conditioned cars of any railroad in the world."[99] His improvements had a dramatic impact on passenger travel. Between 1935 and 1939, passengers carried one mile increased from 2.2 billion to 3.1 billion.[100] Despite this massive investment during the Depression years, Clement was able to reduce the overall debt load of the company while continuing the railroad's uninterrupted streak (over ninety years) of annual dividend payments. Clement kept the Pennsylvania in the black through skillful use of favorable government financing and through access to subsidized labor, including assistance from the Public Works Administration. During his first five years in office, the railroad's revenues increased by 26 percent, from $342 million to $431 million, and operating income also increased by 26 percent, from $61 million to $77 million.

This five-year buildup of the Pennsylvania Railroad was but a precursor to the phenomenal investments that were required for the railroad's critical role during World War II. During the war years, freight traffic doubled and passenger traffic quadrupled. The Pennsylvania Railroad handled 1.4 billion tons of freight and moved more than 17.5 million military personnel. To manage just the increased requirements for military traffic, Clement commissioned the use of 29,670 additional trains, composed of 400,000 cars.[101] Clement's railroad met the demands of vastly heightened wartime production and service, even though by 1944 almost one-third of its male employees (over 51,000) had been called to military service. By 1944, the railroad employed 100,000 fewer employees while conducting four times as much business.[102] The giant leaps in efficiency brought forth a corresponding leap in revenue and profitability. By the war's conclusion in 1946, the Pennsylvania Railroad accounted for 5 percent of the rail track in the United States but 9.4 percent of the freight load and 16.7 percent of the passenger traffic.[103]

Unprecedented Changes Ahead

Although business held the balance of power over both government and employees in the 1920s, the fate of business was reversed in the 1930s. The context changed from business expansion to business collapse, from unfettered business growth to strident government intervention, from full employment to massive unemployment, from open shores with limitless possibilities to closed borders and isolation. The 1930s were a period of heavy government intervention and intense labor mobilization. Though a war was brewing in Europe, America chose to ignore it for the bulk of the decade. In conjunction with this cocooning of America, the social mores of the times reflected a new conservatism. Business executives who not only survived but also prospered in this context were skillful at transforming themselves and their businesses to meet the new realities of the time. These skills of transformation would be put the ultimate test in the 1940s.

TABLE 4-3

Entrepreneurs, managers, and leaders of the 1930s

Entrepreneurs

Stephen D. Bechtel, Bechtel
Arnold O. Beckman, Beckman Instruments
Harold Boeschenstein, Owens-Corning
  Fiberglass
Thomas E. Braniff, Braniff Airways
Leo Burnett, Leo Burnett Company
Curtis L. Carlson, Gold Bond Stamp/Carlson
  Company
Max (Francis) Factor Jr., Max Factor Company
Herman G. Fisher, Fisher-Price Toy Company
Jack Frye, Trans World Airlines
Andrew J. Higgins, Higgins Industries
Howard R. Hughes Jr., Hughes Aircraft
  Company
Edwin H. Land, Polaroid Corporation
William P. Lear, Lear
James S. McDonnell, McDonnell Aircraft
John K. Northrop, Northrop Aircraft
David Packard, Hewlett-Packard Company
William A. Patterson, United Airlines
Milton J. Petrie, Petrie Stores
Elmer F. Pierson, The Vendo Company
Charles H. Revson, Revlon
Edward V. Rickenbacker, Eastern Airlines
James W. Rouse, Rouse Company

Margaret F. Rudkin, Pepperidge Farm
David Sarnoff, Radio Corporation of America
Robert F. Six, Continental Airlines
Cyrus R. Smith, American Airlines
Carl E. Wickman, Greyhound Corporation

Managers

Kenneth S. Adams, Phillips Petroleum
  Company
Winthrop W. Aldrich, Chase National Bank
Howard L. Aller, American Power and Light
Beatrice F. Auerbach, G. Fox & Company
Sewell L. Avery, Montgomery, Ward and
  Company
Sosthenes Behn, International Telephone and
  Telegraph
John D. Biggers, Libbey-Owens-Ford Glass
Alvin G. Brush, American Home Products
Arde Bulova, Bulova Watch Company
Louis S. Cates, Phelps-Dodge Company
Martin W. Clement, Pennsylvania Railroad
Samuel B. Colgate, Colgate-Palmolive
  Company
John L. Collyer, B. F. Goodrich Company
Charles L. Coughlin, Briggs & Stratton
  Corporation

TABLE 4-3 *(continued)*

Richard J. Cullen, International Paper
Bernard M. Culver, Continental Insurance
Company
Nathan Cummings, Consolidated Foods
Richard R. Deupree, Procter & Gamble
Alfred B. Dick Jr., A. B. Dick and Company
Arthur C. Dorrance, Campbell Soup Company
Willard H. Dow, The Dow Chemical Company
Benjamin F. Fairless, United States Steel
Corporation
William S. Farish, Standard Oil of New Jersey
Clarence Francis, General Foods Corporation
Walter D. Fuller, Curtis Publishing Company
Ernest Gallo, Gallo (E. & J.) Winery
Arthur G. Gaston, Booker T. Washington
Insurance
Lawrence M. Giannini, Bank of America
Tom M. Girdler, Republic Steel Corporation
James A. Gray Jr., R.J. Reynolds Tobacco
Company
Robert E. Gross, Lockheed Aircraft Corporation
Leon Hess, Amerada Hess
Paul G. Hoffman, Studebaker Corporation
Charles R. Hook, Armco Steel Company
Haroldson L. Hunt, Hunt Oil Company
Robert W. Johnson Jr., Johnson & Johnson
Daniel C. Keefe, Ingersoll-Rand Company
Kaufman T. Keller, Chrysler Corporation
Herbert V. Kohler, Kohler Company
Eli Lilly II, Eli Lilly and Company
Leroy A. Lincoln, Metropolitan Life Insurance
Daniel K. Ludwig, National Bulk Carriers
John H. MacMillan Jr., Cargill
David H. McConnell Jr., Avon Products
Ernest E. Norris, Southern Railway System
Robert A. Pinkerton II, Pinkerton's
John G. Searle, Searle (G. D.) and Company
Matthew S. Sloan, Missouri-Kansas-Texas
Railroad

Elbridge H. Stuart, Carnation Company
Gustavus F. Swift Jr., Swift and Company
Guy W. Vaughan, Curtiss-Wright Aircraft
Company
Charles R. Walgreen Jr., Walgreen Company
Dwane L. Wallace, Cessna Aircraft Company
Walter H. Wheeler Jr., Pitney-Bowes
Horace C. Wright, Sunbeam Corporation
Robert R. Young, Chesapeake & Ohio
Railroad

Leaders

Garner A. Beckett, American Cement
Corporation
Robert F. Bensinger, Brunswick
J. Chadbourn Bolles, Chadbourn
Herman Cone II, Cone Mills Corporation
Frederick C. Crawford, Thompson Products
C. Donald Dallas, Revere Copper and Brass
Victor Emanuel, Aviation Corporation of
America
Albert H. Gordon, Kidder, Peabody
Ray W. Herrick, Tecumseh Products
Amory Houghton, Corning Glass Company
Jesse H. Jones, Reconstruction Finance
Corporation
John S. (Jack) Knight, Knight-Ridder, Inc.
Richard K. Mellon, Mellon National Bank
Theodore G. Montague, Borden
Willard F. Rockwell, Rockwell International
Henry A. Roemer, Sharon Steel Corporation
Joseph P. Routh, Pittston Company
Joseph P. Spang Jr., Gillette Company
Harold Stanley, Morgan, Stanley & Company
Joe C. Thompson Jr., Southland Corporation
Erwin C. Uihlein, Schlitz Brewing Company
Langbourne M. Williams Jr., Freeport Sulphur
Samuel M. Zemurray, United Fruit Company

FIVE

1940–1949

Reaching New Heights
Through Standardization

To American production, without which this war would have been lost.

—Joseph Stalin, toasting the
United States at the Teheran Summit in 1943

M OVING FROM the high consumption and free spending of the 1920s
into the dark days of the Depression was a shock for the nation. From
the vantage point of the 1930s, the leap into full employment and mass mobilization of the wartime 1940s would have seemed almost impossible—but that
is exactly what happened. Again, the landscape of business changed on a
monumental scale. The business survival skills of the 1930s quickly gave way
to a new form of leadership that tested the limit of America's ingenuity, productivity, and compassion.

Beyond its impact on the country's own identity in the world, America's
full entry into World War II (after the Japanese attack on Pearl Harbor) had
far-reaching implications on the structure and nature of business and its
workforce. These implications stretched into the rest of the century.[1] Nearly
overnight, businesses needed to transform into mass mobilizers, and the scale
with which they needed to transform was unprecedented in the history of the
United States and the world. Businesses were stretched to the limit; no obsta-
cle seemed too large, no barrier too secure, and no boundary too fortified. In

many ways, World War II was a war of machines and science, and no country built more machines or made as many advances in science than the United States. Referring to the unprecedented productivity gains and gigantic leaps in manufacturing during the war years, historians have described business in the 1940s as "the redemption of capitalism," "the wonder of war," and "the production miracle."[2] American business "turned out 86,000 tanks, 2 million army trucks, 193,000 artillery pieces, 17 million handguns and rifles, and 41 billion rounds of ammunition," historian Thomas McCraw writes. "Most remarkably of all, aircraft companies in the United States built almost 300,000 planes during the war years. By comparison, the leading American postwar producer of airliners, Boeing, manufactured about 6,000 passenger jets during the entire 30-year period from 1960 to 1990."[3]

A Spirit of Cooperation

To achieve this seemingly impossible manufacturing feat, a new working order emerged—one that focused on standardization, innovation, and cooperation. The mandate for cooperation, in particular, created for American business a new paradigm in which the government, unions, and business executives worked together in a variety of alliances. Although the business executive had been vilified in the 1930s, this individual was seen in a new light in the 1940s—not as a 1920s-style individualistic hero, but as an American patriot. Business executives were measured by the contribution that their company made to the war effort. The 1940s' hero was the collective manufacturing operation, and the businessperson who could marshal company resources to support the war was rewarded with new insights into operational efficiency, skyrocketing profitability, and a foundation for postwar sustainability.

Business executives who assumed their positions during this volatile decade, of course, not only had to mobilize their companies for the war effort, but also had to convert their operations to a new postwar reality. Founding a company or becoming a CEO in the 1940s presented individuals with a new set of challenges—building for record levels of productivity through investments in innovation and standardization, while remembering that overinvestment could spell disaster during peacetime.

An individual who was extremely adept at managing this balance was Louis B. Neumiller, who led Caterpillar Tractor Company through the war and into peacetime production. Rather than manage his company for short-term, war-driven profits, Neumiller built it for longevity, making Caterpillar into arguably the most efficient producer and distributor of earth-moving equipment in the world. Having never left his hometown of Peoria, Illinois, and working for only one company his entire life (from 1915 to 1962), Neumiller is not your prototypical business maverick. But under his quiet leadership and guidance, Caterpillar's revenues increased sevenfold to become one of the five largest exporters in the United States.

Louis B. Neumiller (1896–1989), Caterpillar Tractor Company

Fatherless at age five, Neumiller received little formal education other than one year of training at the business college in Peoria. Then in 1915, at age nineteen, he landed a job at Holt Manufacturing Company—a company that later became Caterpillar. Founded in the late 1880s by the Holt brothers, who had left their New Hampshire home to join the California gold rush, the company had its early roots in manufacturing agricultural implements. Under the direction of the youngest brother, Benjamin, the company began developing "track-laying" steam tractors, which could cultivate the soft California soil far better than the existing heavy, wheel-based tractors could. Though Benjamin Holt did not invent the first tracklaying machinery, he perfected the design and created a viable tracklayer, which, more importantly, could be produced through standardized manufacturing processes. The photographer Charles Clement, whom Holt employed to help publicize his new machine, observed that its movements mirrored a crawling insect, and he coined the name "Caterpillar."[4]

Holt expanded his Stockton, California–based operation by purchasing in 1909 a factory in Peoria, where his company manufactured the next version of the Caterpillar tractor using gasoline instead of steam as the source of power. It was at this factory that Neumiller embarked on his first job with the company as a stenographer's clerk—earning sixty dollars a month. Neumiller spent a short tour of duty in the U.S. Ordinance Corps to support the World War I mobilization efforts, and when he returned from his military service obligation, he assumed the parts manager position at Holt. When the company merged with its prime competitor, C. L. Best Tractor Company, in 1925, he was promoted to general parts manager for the combined entity. The newly formed corporation was headquartered in Peoria and took the name of its best-selling product—the Caterpillar Tractor Company.

As Neumiller progressed through the ranks of management, the company abandoned its exclusive focus on agricultural machinery to concentrate on the more-promising heavy-construction industry. Transforming Caterpillar's product line for large-scale earthmoving opportunities aptly positioned the company for the government-funded equipment-building projects of the 1930s. Taking on the construction market as a customer segment, Caterpillar staked its reputation on consistency, reliability, and quality. During this time, the company also began to build a distributed dealership network to ensure that parts and product line extensions were available wherever and whenever needed.

By the early 1930s, Neumiller was promoted to sales representative and later to labor relations director. In all these positions, he built a reputation of unassuming confidence and integrity—qualities that would become as much a part of the Caterpillar culture as they were hallmarks of Neumiller's personality. In his capacity as the director of labor relations, Neumiller honed his management skills. After a bitter struggle with management, the CIO (Congress of Industrial Organizations) organized Caterpillar's workers in 1937, during the heyday of the U.S. union movement. Having grown up in the company, Neumiller felt equally at home among both factory workers and executives and was able to bridge the gap between the two camps.

Recognizing Neumiller's abilities, Caterpillar's senior management appointed him CEO in 1941. Two months later, Japan attacked Pearl Harbor, and the United States officially entered World War II. Like many business executives of the 1940s, Neumiller was called on to retool his manufacturing operation for artillery production. But rather than blindly following the military request, he believed that the company should not attempt to fundamentally change its business. He convinced the government that large-scale earth-moving equipment would be needed on the battlefields.

Having painstakingly built and maintained a reputation for quality and service, which allowed the company to charge 5 to 10 percent more for its earth-moving equipment than other manufacturers, the company was very reluctant to abandon its core capabilities. To stay his course while still trying to service the artillery needs of the military, Neumiller proposed a compromise whereby Caterpillar would build a new plant in neighboring Decatur,

Illinois, for the production of an air-cooled diesel engine for the army's M4 tank. Within one year (1942), the new plant was operational under the name of Caterpillar Military Engine Company. In addition to producing diesel engines, the new company produced howitzer carriages, shells, and other bomb parts.

Neumiller's strategy and steadfast determination to stay on course paid off. There was, indeed, a strong need for both military supplies and earth-moving equipment. During most of the war, bulldozers had the same priority status held by planes and tanks. In fact, the demand for tractors and bulldozers was so strong that the Decatur plant was converted to traditional manufacturing lines by 1943. As an unofficial endorsement of Neumiller's strategy, Admiral William Halsey, a commander of the South Pacific Allied Fleet, declared that the bulldozer was a primary contributor to winning the war in the Pacific.[5] Bulldozers and tractors were especially crucial to the development of make-shift landing strips throughout the Pacific isles and were used extensively to build military roads, clear timber, traverse swamps, and dig protective trenches and bunkers. Over the next four years, Caterpillar sold over $500 million worth of equipment to the government—this amount was five times the company's 1941 total revenue—and doubled its employment from 11,000 workers to over 20,000.[6] What was more important, this growth was not a

Louis Neumiller (left) of Caterpillar oversees the production of tractors and bulldozers for the war effort in the Pacific (1947). (Source: Time Life Pictures/Getty Images)

short-term aberration but the continuation of a long-standing and steady expansion plan.

At the end of the war, Caterpillar received unexpected assistance in its international expansion efforts as its bright yellow, easily recognizable Caterpillar-branded equipment stayed behind when the U.S. troops came home. Most of the U.S. government–purchased Caterpillar machinery left behind in Asia and Europe was taken over by local governments and businesses, which, in essence, created a new market opportunity. Under Neumiller's direction, Caterpillar established dealer/service centers in these international areas for training, maintenance, and, most importantly, follow-on purchases. This did much to boost Caterpillar's international presence and brand recognition—in a similar way that Coca-Cola received a marketing boost by supplying its products to the troops well below cost.

Neumiller took advantage of the company's newfound international presence and expanded Caterpillar's dealership network throughout the globe to service remote customers. For many years, Caterpillar had a thriving export business, with the centers of production still in the heartland of America. As Caterpillar's international presence expanded, Neumiller oversaw the development of manufacturing plants in Europe, Latin America, and Asia. Throughout the company's expansion efforts, Neumiller insisted that all manufacturing plants, regardless of location, use standardized production processes and techniques—ensuring that a part produced in Belgium had the same specifications and tolerances as a part produced in Peoria. The accessibility and interchangeability of its parts was a key element of Caterpillar's selling proposition.

As the U.S. landscape began its rapid expansion after World War II, Caterpillar was there to fill the growing need for earth-moving equipment, providing machines for roadway construction, suburban expansion projects, and other large-scale development. Biographers John Ingham and Lynne Feldman note: "As America prepared to embark on the greatest orgy of road and superhighway building in its history, Caterpillar, as the dominant firm in the industry, was ideally placed to take advantage of that boom."[7] Given that Neumiller had insisted that Caterpillar stick with its principal production process and product lines throughout the war years, the company was well equipped to produce tractors, bulldozers, and a full line of other earth-moving equipment for the changing American landscape.

Although this dedicated focus made peacetime conversion relatively easy, the company was not fully prepared for new innovations and competitive pressures that resulted from a bulging domestic market opportunity. The company was caught off guard by its singular focus on its core product lines. While Caterpillar was perfecting its line of tractors, competitors were introducing faster and more powerful tractors using rubber-tired wheels. In addition to fending off the faster wheel-based tractor, Caterpillar was ill prepared for the introduction of the front-wheeled loader introduced by Clark Equipment and International Harvester after the war. Caterpillar's dedication to production efficiencies and standardization left little room for new product introductions or research-based investment. This situation changed quickly, and though Caterpillar lost some initial domestic market share, it pursued a new investment and product launch strategy with a vengeance. In a few short years, Caterpillar introduced its own version of the faster and more versatile earth-moving equipment.

Though its products were dubbed "copy-Cats," the company's reputation for quality was so strong that it quickly dominated the market. At the time, Neumiller commented on his company's late-market-entry approach: "We do it the second or third time, and we do it better."[8] From this point forward, Neumiller maintained a steadfast concentration on consistently improving Caterpillar's core strength—the production of high-quality tractors, bulldozers, and other earth-moving equipment—but also invested heavily in new product development. It was at this juncture that the company began to follow a strict strategy of specialization and depth—a strategy that enabled it to become the only full-service provider of construction equipment for extremely large projects. This focus on product line depth was accompanied by the company's continued focus on standardization and the interchangeability of parts. Because its factory lines had become standardized and its parts were very compatible, there was very little downtime involved in changing from one product run to another.

Throughout his tenure, Neumiller was committed to the success of the company's dealer network. He expanded the network to several hundred locations, employing thirty thousand individuals throughout the world, and made it a goal of the company to source a customer part anywhere in the world within twenty-four hours. He centralized logistical control in Peoria and invested in technology that would help local dealers better estimate the needs of their ultimate customers. In the late 1950s and early 1960s, Caterpillar was one of the first large-scale manufacturers to adopt computerized technology for managing their logistical tracking needs.

During Neumiller's tenure, Caterpillar's net assets tripled, plant space doubled, sales and profits increased sevenfold, and the company secured over 50 percent of the earth-moving-equipment market, outpacing its nearest competitor by a factor of three to one.[9] In addition, Neumiller laid the foundation for the company's formidable international presence. This success without fanfare was a testament to Neumiller's humble management approach. His office was always sparse—no corporate symbolism, no works of art, and no personal accolades. Neumiller stepped into the chairman's role in 1954, making way for his successor, Harmon Eberhard. *Fortune* covered the transition in its 1954 article, "The Art of Modest Management," and spoke of both men's modesty: "neither individual [Neumiller or his successor] claimed credit for any one advance or innovation."[10] Although Neumiller was not larger than life, in many ways he epitomized the greatness of the 1940s: he let his company become a hero instead of himself.[11]

Government Mobilizes

At the onset of the decade, the ability of the United States to win the war was far from certain. The country was still reeling from the effects of the Depression, its industrial infrastructure was struggling to survive, and its military arsenal was hardly a force to be reckoned with. With a standing army of around 175,000 soldiers, the U.S. military was far smaller than those of most major nations of the world in 1940.[12] McCraw notes: "the task of mobilization presented the most serious administrative challenge the nation ever faced."[13] The nation met this challenge through the cooperative efforts of many parties and specifically through the adoption of several new legislative initiatives.

To build the country's military might, the U.S. Congress authorized the first peacetime conscription in 1940. During the course of the war, the military ranks swelled from 175,000 to over 15 million. As one historian notes, two-thirds of all men from the ages of eighteen to thirty-four eventually joined the military during the war.[14] In addition to building the military strength of the country, the growing ranks of men joining the army helped

TABLE 5-1

Business events that shaped the 1940s

Date	Event
1940	Office of Production Management created
1940	War Production Board created
1940	Boeing 307 Stratoliner—first pressurized commercial aircraft
1941	Lend-Lease Act passed
1941	Office of Price Administration created
1941	United States enters World War II
1941	300 businessmen join government service for $1-per-year salary
1941	"Rosie the Riveter" campaign encourages women to enter workforce
1941	Unions pledge no strikes during war
1942	Emergency Price Control Act passed, sets ceiling on prices and rents
1942	Rationing begins with gasoline (followed by rubber, sugar, and coffee)
1942	Secret Manhattan Project commissioned to develop atomic bomb
1942	All automobile production halted for duration of war
1943	Tax Payment Act authorizes federal withholding of taxes
1943	President Roosevelt authorizes 48-hour workweek for defense contractors
1944	Servicemen's Readjustment Act (GI Bill) passed
1944	International Monetary Fund and World Bank created
1945	Atomic bomb deployed
1945	Axis Powers surrender, ending World War II
1945	Union membership hits 14 million
1945	Alcoa convicted of antitrust violations
1946	Atomic Energy Commission created
1946	U.S. farm prices reach all-time high
1946	Baby boom begins; 76 million births by 1964
1946	ENIAC, world's first all-electronic computer, displayed
1947	All food rationing ends
1947	Taft-Hartley Act passed, placing severe restrictions on union activities
1947	House Committee on Un-American Activities initiated
1947	Three Bell Lab scientists invent transistor
1947	General Agreement on Tariffs and Trade enacted
1948	President Truman authorizes federal takeover of striking railroads
1948	Marshall Plan commissioned to provide relief and support for Europe
1948	Supreme Court orders movie production houses to divest of their theater chains
1948	General Motors signs industry's first union contract including a cost-of-living adjustment clause

lessen unemployment figures. It was also during this time that Roosevelt championed one of his most important pieces of legislation, the Lend-Lease Bill, which provided Britain with billions of dollars in defense weapons, without committing U.S. troops.[15] The bill's provisions eventually resulted in the authorization of over $50 billion in defense spending between 1941 and 1945.[16] To coordinate the massive mobilization effort required for the Lend-Lease Bill and then for America's direct entry in the war, the U.S. government passed the War Powers Act in 1942, establishing the War Production Board that oversaw the mobilization for military preparedness on a whole new scale.

Granted wide latitude to set production priorities, determine rationing schemes, and allocate specific manufacturing contracts, the board reassigned companies from civilian production to military production. For instance, no radio sets, washing machines, shavers, irons, toasters, stoves, mixers, waffle irons, or heating pads were manufactured for civilian use during the war.[17] All the manufacturers of these consumer products moved to military production. Vacuum cleaner manufacturer Eureka converted its operations to gas-mask production, a typewriter manufacturer made machine guns, and even Steinway refrained from making pianos—diverting its wood supply to the war effort. In a remarkable twist, a corset company became a grenade belt manufacturer.[18] Similarly, Avon replaced lipstick making with bullet production, and Procter & Gamble employed fourteen thousand to stuff gunpowder into artillery shell casings.[19]

Because of the board's ability to control the use of raw materials, it was able to drastically reduce nonessential production while rewarding those businesses that supported the war effort. The board's broad-reaching powers eventually resulted in over 350,000 contracts awarded to forty thousand contractors.[20] Since the demands of rapid mobilization favored big business, however, a full 75 percent of those military contracts went to just fifty-six prime contractors. This concentration of contracts in the hands of big business sparked the establishment of the Smaller War Plants Corporation. Designed to direct subcontract work to new and smaller organizations, its success led to the creation of the Small Business Administration at the end of the war.[21]

War production soon buoyed the whole American economy. From 1937 to 1944, the nation's output of goods and services doubled.[22] All told, the United States spent nearly $288 billion to fight World War II—thirty-two times the annual federal budget in 1940 ($9 billion).[23] To pay for the war, the United States broadened the tax base in the country through the passage of the Revenue Act of 1942. In addition to the adoption of the graduated income tax, the act authorized an additional 5 percent Victory Tax for 1942 on all income over $624.[24] To make the tax payments more palatable to Americans, a weekly tax withholding system was adopted. Before 1943, income taxes were generally paid once a year in one lump sum. The new tax system endorsed by the Internal Revenue Service was accompanied by a far-reaching public-relations plan. Entertainment companies like Walt Disney even donated animation services, creating a "cartoon in which Donald Duck computed his tax bill, marking out standard deductions for Huey, Louie, and Dewey."[25] The income derived from the expanded tax base covered approximately 45 percent of the country's war debt, and the remainder was funded through the sale of Liberty Bonds and large-scale deficit spending. Most economists point to this massive spending (peaking in 1943 at $53 billion) as the major impetus for breaking through the iron grip of the Depression.[26]

As more and more products were being rationed and as employment continued to increase, the gap between disposable income and available consumer goods expanded. During the war years, disposable income increased 64 percent, from $92 billion to $151 billion, while the value of the civilian supply of goods increased by only 23 percent, from $77 billion to $95 billion.[27] To control this recipe for inflation, the government passed the Emergency Price Control Act to enforce a series of wage, rent, and price controls. Administered through the Office of Price Administration (OPA) between 1942 and 1947, the act took measures to regulate prices on over 8 million items and to ration a number of scarce goods, including sugar, butter, coffee, and gasoline.[28] The OPA also set rent controls in areas where defense production was high and established wage caps in several key industry segments. The wage caps helped control some of the growth in disposable income and served as a deterrent to union activities.[29]

Businesses reaped enormous profits through the war years and were given much latitude from the government in their operations, yet they were not immune from antitrust legislation. At the outset of the decade, the Federal Communications Commission (FCC) ordered the National Broadcasting Company (NBC) to sell off one of its radio networks. David Sarnoff's NBC controlled two networks (the Red and Blue Networks) in many major U.S.

cities. As radio increased in popularity and use, the FCC sought to control attempts at monopolization of the airwaves by allowing a company to own only one station per major metropolitan market. To avoid the charges of monopolistic practices, Sarnoff sold the Blue Network to Edward Noble, founder of the LifeSavers candy company, for $8 million in 1942. Noble changed the network's name to the American Broadcasting Company in 1945 and eventually quadrupled his investment by selling the company to Paramount in 1953.[30] The central antitrust case of the decade involved Alcoa (Aluminum Company of America)—a company that had previously defeated several suits. At the time of the renewed antitrust suit in 1937, Alcoa controlled 90 percent of the market for aluminum ingot, and the U.S. Supreme Court sought to break up the company (see Chapter 3). After a series of case dismissals and recharges, the court ruled in 1945 that "mere size, as measured by share of the product market, could be an offense" of the Sherman Antitrust Act.[31] This ruling was a turning point in antitrust legislation. Heretofore, antitrust suits were initiated on the basis of allegations of anticompetitive or monopolistic business practices, not mere size. Alcoa's 1945 conviction for violating the antitrust law set a new tone for business expansion. By the time of the settlement, war mobilization was in full swing and the aluminum market had become more diversified. Under these new conditions, Alcoa was able to avoid a sell-off of some of its operations, but it was prohibited from buying military production plants after the war.

Though the effects of the war mitigated the impact on Alcoa, the case sparked a series of antitrust suits based on market size. Antitrust legislation was initiated in 1946 against cigarette manufacturers, in 1949 against DuPont and American Telephone & Telegraph (the first of many to come), and in 1956 against Eastman Kodak and RCA.[32] All cases were settled through consent decrees, which limited market expansion but avoided major corporate restructuring activities. The net impact of the renewed antitrust legislation prompted the initial moves toward conglomeration—a movement that became prominent within the next two decades. It is interesting to note that the Federal Trade Commission first used the term *conglomerate* in a 1948 cautionary warning to the public.[33] The commission applied the term to the unusual practice of acquiring unrelated business entities. If market share and vertical integration were paths to antitrust suits, diversified acquisitions were the new path to business expansion.

Despite some intensified antitrust activity, there was a pervasive cooperative spirit between business and government. The first major wave of such cooperation, during the wartime military mobilization period, led to staggering productivity growth and standardization, which advanced new technologies in many business sectors. Many historians point to this alliance between industry and government as a key linchpin in the Allied victory. The second wave of cooperation came as the nation confronted the Cold War.

The World at War (Again)

Though World War II raged on for roughly the same amount of time as did World War I, the greater dependence on machines (e.g., military weapons) resulted in twice as many deaths for the later war.[34] The combination of genocide and military casualties exceeded 60 million.[35] U.S. reliance on technology and machinery kept total American casualties relatively low: in contrast to the millions who died from other nations, the United States suffered 405,000 deaths along with 670,000 wounded.[36]

The same industrial might and productivity that contributed to the massive loss of lives also eventually helped win the war for the United States, Britain, and their Allies. Japan's final surrender, on the heels of atomic bomb explosions in Hiroshima and Nagasaki in August 1945, signaled the end of war and a new beginning for international relations. Italy had fallen months earlier, and Germany had succumbed to a two-pronged attack by British and American forces in Southern Europe and by Russian forces in Eastern Europe. The 1945 Yalta Conference brought Britain, the United States, and the Soviet Union together to divide the spoils of the war—setting the stage for new power struggles.

As in World War I, the United States was again the only nation to end the war in a stronger overall state than when the war began. The U.S. Depression had ended, its factories were full, its workforce was utilized to capacity, and its continental landscape was virtually unscathed. The war's end resulted in a new positioning for the United States, not unlike the role that it rejected after World War I. The difference now was that the United States was forced to face its new global role. Isolation was no longer a viable long-term option.

Several activities demonstrated America's increasing involvement in world affairs and further solidified its position as a global power. A coalition of the

United States and forty-four other nations created the International Monetary Fund to minimize global currency fluctuations. At the same time, the coalition created the World Bank (originally called the International Bank of Reconstruction and Development), which was initially fashioned after the Reconstruction Finance Corporation, in an effort to provide relief and support for rebuilding war-torn countries.[37] The focus for both entities centered on increasing global stability and self-sufficiency—and to avoid a 1930s-era global postwar recession. The United States further recognized its new role in global affairs by adopting the General Agreement on Tariffs and Trade (GATT), which, among other things, reduced tariffs on more than fifty thousand items. Originally signed by twenty-three countries representing 75 percent of the world trade volume in 1947, this global pact curbed the pattern of reciprocal protectionism so pervasive throughout the twentieth century. The impact on the United States was a one-third reduction in its prevailing tariffs.[38]

Extensive lobbying by President Harry Truman and Secretary of State George C. Marshall led to yet another U.S. global commitment in the postwar years: the European Recovery Program, also called the Marshall Plan. Although the stated goals of the Marshall Plan lacked any hint of self-interest, providing economic and humanitarian relief for war-torn Europe, Congress ultimately supported the plan because of its implied endorsement of democratic governments friendly to the United States.[39] The idea was rooted in an impassioned directive by the president, in what would become known as the Truman Doctrine: "the policy of the United States [must be] to support the free peoples who are resisting attempted subjugation by armed minorities or by outside pressures."[40] Still, the plan's provisions were hotly debated until the Soviet Union's occupation of Czechoslovakia. Coming on the heels of Soviet-backed communist uprisings in Greece and Turkey, the occupation left the plan's passage virtually uncontested.

In many ways, the $13 billion Marshall Plan helped continue the massive industrial expansion that had emerged in American business during World War II.[41] Through substantial government spending over five years, U.S. companies helped to physically rebuild Europe by providing labor and producing millions of necessary products. The spending of the Marshall Plan, which peaked at 2.4 percent of the U.S. gross national product in 1949, kept factories in high gear, providing a continued cushion for large-scale employment while simultaneously defending the benefits of capitalism.[42]

Though its infrastructure was badly damaged by the war and, in sheer numbers, it lost more lives than any other nation, the Soviet Union also emerged from the war as a new world power. Its path to Germany through Eastern Europe had garnered the Soviet Union a base of support (albeit sometimes forced) for communism. As the Soviet Union began to assume control of many formerly German-occupied countries, a frost developed between it and the United States. The countries had starkly contrasting styles of government: centralized and autocratic versus decentralized and democratic. To deter the expansionist ambitions of the communist state, the United States adopted a "policy of containment" in its relationship with the Soviet Union. The policy involved a large-scale U.S. military buildup, which, in turn, created many business opportunities.[43] For instance, Joseph Crosby of Thiokol Corporation built a small $3 million military supply (jet propulsion fuels) company into a $275 million advanced research and development operation between 1947 and 1963. During his tenure, Thiokol designed sophisticated rocket launch equipment used for the Mercury and Gemini space programs and developed missile components required for operating the Minuteman missile, a weapon of containment.[44]

The suspicions and fears of communism played a major role in the passage of the National Security Act of 1947. The legislation made the Joint Chiefs of Staff, which was founded during World War II, a permanent entity. The prevailing concerns also helped establish the Central Intelligence Agency and played a role in the authorization of the nation's first large-scale peacetime standing army. The National Security Act was followed by U.S. membership in the North Atlantic Treaty Organization, which bound together the forces of democracy throughout the Atlantic region; the U.S. standing army would now be "on call" for protecting democracy throughout the world.[45] As the United States and the USSR continued to flex their muscles (including the 1949 Soviet test of its own atomic bomb), forty years of enormous defense spending and scientific research ensued, all in the name of protection and alleged superiority. Businesses that had prospered during the defense buildup of the war had a new reason to continue investing in innovation. This defense spending and scientific research fueled both the economy and several industrial corporations for decades—triggering the longest and largest economic expansion in U.S. history.

Innovation Drives Technology

The speed with which extremely large amounts of complex machinery were produced during the war effort could not have been achieved without a move toward standardization. Although Henry Ford had done much to standardize his automobile factories through the movable assembly line, the funneling of enormous amounts of war machinery to the front required a new level of precision and focus. This dedicated commitment to standardization, which drove simplicity and order into manufacturing processes, enabled the United States to achieve unprecedented productivity gains: between 1940 and 1943, U.S. manufacturing output increased twenty-five-fold, from $1.5 billion to $37.5 billion. During the same period, output only doubled for Germany and Russia, tripled for Britain, and quadrupled for Japan.[46] Within the first full year of the U.S. entry in the war, manufacturing productivity increased by a staggering 25 percent—up from an average of 1.9 percent for the preceding forty years.[47]

These massive gains were felt throughout all industries, but the results were most notable in the aircraft, shipbuilding, and automobile sectors. The automobile industry alone ultimately produced 75 percent of all aircraft engines and 20 percent of all war goods.[48] Ford, for example, built a massive plant in Willow Run, Michigan, which eventually produced 8,524 B-24 bombers.[49]

In addition to supplying the military with bombers and aircraft engines, Ford joined forces with Willys-Overland Motors to produce the new workhorse of the army—the jeep. Willys had won the design competition for a "small personnel-arms carrier" in 1940.[50] Though Ford had entered the design competition and lost, the company went on to produce Willys engines in its factories, and the two companies eventually manufactured 660,000 jeeps.[51] The vehicle became one of the most significant products to bridge the gap between military and civilian use. It essentially launched a whole new class of automobiles and became the precursor to the ubiquitous sports utility vehicle.

Speed in production was especially evident on the water and in the air. Borrowing from the mass-production techniques of the automobile sector, Henry Kaiser revolutionized the shipbuilding industry by reducing the time

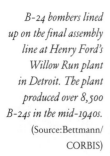

B-24 bombers lined up on the final assembly line at Henry Ford's Willow Run plant in Detroit. The plant produced over 8,500 B-24s in the mid-1940s.
(Source:Bettmann/ CORBIS)

required to build a Liberty cargo ship from two hundred days to one day.[52] Another dramatic example of seemingly incomprehensible production speed was demonstrated by Boeing, which produced a B-17 bomber aircraft every ninety minutes at its peak of production in June 1944.[53]

The standardization that drove these manufacturing feats was a direct by-product of innovation. War-motivated investment in research and technology accelerated the product development life cycle. For instance, before the war, the United States was the world's largest importer of natural rubber. When its access to Axis-controlled rubber plantations was blocked, the United States, within months, built its own synthetic-rubber industry, virtually from scratch. Contributing to this effort was Harvey S. Firestone Jr.'s Firestone Tire and Rubber Company. Firestone invested in synthetic-rubber technology while simultaneously producing over 50 percent of all mobile antiaircraft gun units during World War II. By the end of the war, the United States had become the largest exporter of synthetic rubber in the world.[54]

The war also sped up the development of the first computer—the ENIAC (Electronic Numerical Integrator and Computer). As a product of the War Department, the ENIAC was developed to support strategic and tactical military planning. Introduced in 1946, the machine weighed thirty tons, housed eighteen thousand vacuum tubes, cost $487,000,and consumed a room that measured thirty by sixty feet.[55] The initial development of the transistor by

The world's first computer—the room-sized ENIAC, Electronic Numerical Integrator and Computer—was used initially by the War Department. (Source: Bettmann/CORBIS)

Bell Laboratories in 1948 would later revolutionize and miniaturize computer technology. The advances in manufacturing and technology were mirrored in the scientific community, most notably with the development of penicillin. Alexander Fleming had unearthed the fundamental antibiotic properties of *Penicillium* fungal cultures in the late 1920s, but not until World War II was the drug refined and finally mass-produced. Called a wonder drug, penicillin fundamentally changed the medical treatment protocols throughout all theaters of war.[56]

Although inventors, businesses, and government officials often receive credit for the massive war mobilization effort, labor's role was essential to the overall success. With the war in full swing, new individuals entered the workforce in unprecedented numbers, bringing with them a fresh perspective on business operations. Unconstrained by "what had always been done," many people questioned the working order of manufacturing, and in so doing, they helped propel productivity to new levels. The long, hard years of unemployment that preceded the war had not bred complacency. When the employment floodgates opened, it unleashed a torrent of untapped potential and desire.

Labor Mobilizes

The unemployment rate at the beginning of World War II stood at 17.2 percent, representing 9.5 million Americans. This figure dropped to 1.2 percent, or 670,000, in just five years. The last time the unemployment figure had approached this low level was in 1918, during World War I, when unemployment dipped to 1.4 percent. Moreover, during the fourteen years between 1929 and 1943, the changes in the U.S. labor force were overwhelming.[57] While the ranks of farmers continued to decline, those employed in the manufacturing sector increased by 7.4 million—corresponding almost exactly to the drop in unemployment. By 1943, the country had effectively reached full employment levels.

The magnitude of the unemployment shift during World War II was much swifter and much more dramatic than at any other time in the country's history, and it held far-reaching implications for the labor movement and society as a whole. As in World War I, women entered the workforce in unprecedented numbers, more than 5 million between 1941 and 1945.[58] In a February 18, 1942, report on the female workforce in Detroit, the center of war production, the *New York Times* noted: "Blue denim dungarees are displacing afternoon dresses, and tea cups are giving way to riveting hammers in the hands of Detroit women who, in increasing numbers, are taking their places in the war production work."[59] The government launched a large-scale national campaign to attract women to the manufacturing shop floor, featuring "Rosie the Riveter," a former housewife (portrayed by a model) who was doing her part by leaving the home to wield a rivet gun. For a brief time, the

TABLE 5-2

Shifts in U.S. employment

Year	Agricultural employment	Nonagricultural employment	Unemployed
1929	11.5 million	35.6 million	1.5 million
1940	9.5 million	37.9 million	8.1 million
1943	9.0 million	45.3 million	1.0 million

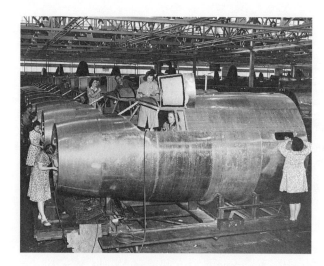

*Women working in the
Douglas Aircraft assembly
plant during World War II.*
(Source: Bettmann/CORBIS)

historically negative attitudes about women in the workforce and questions about the appropriateness of women in male-dominated occupations were suspended.[60] But, unfortunately, that did not translate into equal pay for women. On average, during the war years, women earned 60 percent of what men earned for equivalent jobs.[61] With the end of the war, the prevailing attitudes and social norms about women in the workforce quickly reverted to prewar views and practices.

African Americans also entered the workforce at an unprecedented pace—continuing the black migration from the South to the factories in the North and West. The migration extended throughout the 1940s and into the 1950s, when over 2.5 million African Americans relocated. Many historians point to the struggles of African Americans to be recognized both for their military service in World War II and for their contributions to business as the beginning of the modern civil-rights movement. To that end, the ranks of the National Association for the Advancement of Colored People (NAACP) grew from a relatively small organization to almost half a million members.[62] Though African Americans were beginning to have a voice, it would still take decades for improvements to occur in their social and economic lives.

Despite some gains in job security and salary, the power balance between employers and employees was weighted on the side of business during and after World War II. For the most part, labor was quieted by the patriotic mobilization efforts. But after the war, pent-up frustration was unleashed and a series of high-profile strikes swept through American industry. In the eighteen months after the end of the war, unions throughout the country organized 550 strikes, which affected 1.4 million workers throughout key industries, including steel, automobiles, petroleum, meatpacking, and transportation.[63] The surge in the number of strikes, which began to impact the public interest, became a strong impetus for a postwar antiunion movement.

On the heels of the renewed union activity and with strong backing from big business, the Republican-controlled Congress moved to restrict the union movement, reversing significant gains that unions had achieved in the 1930s under the Wagner Act. With the passage of the Taft-Hartley Bill (Labor Management Relations Act) in 1947, certain aspects of unions, such as closed shops (unions within companies that required only union employees), were outlawed, and union leaders were forced to take an oath that they did not have communist ties or loyalties. It became much more difficult to fight for collective union rights without being branded a communist supporter, despite the fact that many workers were employed to build the country's defenses to contain communism.[64] As reported in the *New York Times* on June 23, 1947, one of the bill's sponsors, Robert A. Taft, noted: "Where employers at one time had 'all the advantage' in dealing with workers, Federal policy had so altered the balance that now 'the labor leaders have every advantage.' The one purpose of the bill, he added, is to 'swing the balance back to where the two sides can deal equally with each other.'"[65] The labor movement, however, regarded the law not as a balancing act but as a "slave labor bill."[66]

In addition to navigating through the troubled waters of renewed antiunion sentiment, the labor movement had to contend with soldiers who were returning from military service seeking employment. With millions of men returning to the workforce, the unemployment rate began to creep upward (reaching 5.5 percent by 1949), despite the departure of women from the employment ranks in droves.[67] To mitigate some of the impact of the returning soldiers, the U.S. Congress passed the GI (for Government Issue) Bill, also called the Serviceman's Readjustment Act, in 1944. The act created the Veterans' Administration to oversee a variety of new benefits for returning veterans, including reduced mortgage rates, vocational training, and unemployment insurance. By 1950, the government had spent $20 billion to fund

TABLE 5-3

Social and demographic facts about the 1940s

- 132 million Americans in 48 states; grows to 151 million by 1950
- Unemployment rate drops to low of 1.2 percent during height of war mobilization
- National debt hits $43 billion
- 55 percent of U.S. homes with indoor plumbing
- Antarctica discovered to be a continent
- Cold War begins; United States and USSR become global superpowers
- Three times as many college degrees granted in 1949 versus 1940
- Commercial television appears
- Jackie Robinson joins major league baseball—first black player
- Joe DiMaggio of New York Yankees—first player to receive over $100,000 in salary
- Fads: victory gardens reinstated, jitterbug, zoot suits, patriotic movies, Superman
- Games: Slinky, Silly Putty, Frisbee
- New words: *jeep, iron curtain, Cold War, snafu*
- Minimum wage: $0.43 per hour, rises to $0.75 per hour by end of decade
- Average annual earnings (1940): $1,299
- Life expectancy (1940): 65.2 years for females, 60.8 years for males

special veterans' benefits, not the least of which was guaranteed unemployment compensation. The most significant benefit for GIs was the tuition remission program, which in addition to providing GIs with an essentially free education, took many men off the employment rolls for four years. All told, the GI Bill helped educate 450,000 engineers; 360,000 teachers; 243,000 accountants; 180,000 physicians, dentists, and nurses; 150,000 scientists; and 107,000 lawyers.[68]

Mass Migration

The mobility of veterans was just one of several shifts in the U.S. population, which swelled by 19 million, from 131 million to 150 million, during this decade. Most of the population increase was driven by internal growth factors, especially with the beginning of the baby boom. New immigrants accounted for only about 5 percent of the increase (approximately 1 million).[69] Though the number of immigrants had doubled from the depressed years of the 1930s, the actual increase was still quite small (less than half the average of any preceding decade). Even with the massive persecution throughout Europe, only a few hundred thousand immigrants came to the United States from Germany, Italy, France, Poland, and Austria, and many of those came after the war. The one country that did see a significant rise in its emigration numbers to the United States was Mexico.

With many U.S. farmers joining the military or taking on factory employment during the war years, there was a dearth of labor to till the soil. The U.S. and Mexican governments cooperated to create the Bracero Program, which brought Mexican laborers to the United States for much-needed help in the agricultural sector, in 1942. Under this program, which lasted until 1947, the employer of record was not the independent, local farmer but the U.S. government. The Mexican government had negotiated with the United States to ensure that Mexican farm laborers would be paid and treated appropriately and consistently—not underpaid, not drafted, and not deported when economic or social conditions waned. During the course of the program, official records indicated that over 220,000 Mexicans immigrated to the United States, though unofficial estimates were much larger.[70]

As with the influx of immigrants from Mexico, the overall growth of the population was far from evenly dispersed throughout the country. In addition to veterans returning home, Mexicans emigrating to the farming belt, and African Americans relocating North, the country's composition was experiencing "the greatest internal mass migration in American history."[71] Whole sectors of society were on the move. At first the goal was employment in the defense sector industries, but it soon became a search for a better life. The migration was made easier through heavy spending on the nation's highway system. Between 1945 and 1950, some 340,000 highway miles were added to the national network, effectively doubling the covered mileage.[72]

As the national highway system expanded and as air-conditioning became affordable for individual families, the population centers of the United States shifted westward. One historian explains that between 1940 and 1960, the population of the "Pacific states rose by 110 percent . . . Half of the population in the Far West now lived in a state different from the one in which they were born. And one-fifth of the nation's new population had settled in California, which surpassed New York by 1963 as the most populous state."[73] The shifting migration throughout the country eventually brought many new families to the suburbs, where they hoped to build and live their version of the American Dream. New housing construction exploded to shelter these growing families, increasing from 114,000 in 1944 to over 1.7 million by 1950.[74]

One of the most instrumental players in the development and expansion of the suburb was William Levitt, who applied standardized construction techniques to the production of new housing. Levitt identified twenty-seven distinct steps in the construction of a new home. According to the *Wall Street Journal*: "Bill Levitt's home building ideas borrowed liberally from Henry Ford and World War II production factories. At Levittown [nineteen square miles of undeveloped land on Long Island] trucks dropped identical piles of lumber, pipe and shingles at 60-foot intervals. Nonunion workers moved from house to house, doing identical tasks . . . When the system was in high gear, houses were completed at a rate of 30 a day."[75] In describing Levitt's role in the development of the suburbs, the *Wall Street Journal* noted: "There are moments when economic forces fall into line and a well-prepared entrepre-

Levittown, New York, was representative of the massive suburban expansion that occurred after World War II (1949). (Source: Bettmann/CORBIS)

neur can make a killing."[76] Levitt had the right idea at the right time. Though he was hailed as a construction genius, his social policies were less than progressive. He refused to sell to blacks until forced to do so by law and was often criticized for establishing a sense of uniformity and banal consistency in the American landscape. While the American dream of home ownership became a reality for many (whites), the equally strong American ideal of rugged individualism suffered.

Society Confronts the Face of Self-Righteousness

The sacrifices that Americans made during the Depression (delaying purchases, stretching resources, buying used clothing, etc.) were generally made out of necessity; the sacrifices made during the 1940s were driven by a commitment to the war effort. Somehow, rations of even basic commodities like sugar, butter, and coffee felt more bearable than they had in the 1930s; the deprivations were for a greater cause. Beyond rationing, there were few goods available for purchase as companies converted their operations to war production. Americans felt self-righteous about their sacrifices during the war years, but had more trouble coming to grips with some of the country's outright racism and oppression. The deep-seated resentment and fear harbored by many Americans after the attack on Pearl Harbor made it relatively easy for the government to intern more than 100,000 Japanese Americans during the war.[77] There was virtually no public outcry. Stripped of their every possession and sent to remote camps for the duration of the war, Japanese Americans were the subjects of both verbal and physical attacks. The nation's treatment of its own citizens underscored the brutal reality that the true melting pot did not really exist.

Many business executives were heralded for their heroic conversion efforts during the war effort, but those with German or Japanese ancestries were often stripped of their businesses, regardless of their allegiances or support. One such individual was Peter F. Hurst, who founded Aeroquip Corporation. In 1940, Hurst, an engineer by training, invented two new products that were critical to the growing aviation industry—detachable, reusable hose fittings and self-sealing couplings. As aviation took hold during World War II, these safety products became crucial, but Hurst's German heritage and citizenship forced him to relinquish his business for five years. After the war, Hurst regained control of his business and built it into a full-scale supplier of parts for conveying and moving dangerous fluids.[78]

Even though blacks fought and worked for America's defense, they were not welcome in the military, not welcome in unions, and not welcome in work. Blacks throughout the country rallied under the cry, first articulated in the black-owned *Pittsburgh Courier*, for "Double V," which stood for victory at home and abroad. Despite the many closed doors, some were slowly beginning to open. In 1941, Roosevelt signed an executive order that required the recipients of defense contracts to provide equality in opportunity and pay for blacks and other minorities, yet for the next six years, little progress was made.

Actual progress did occur in 1948, when Truman ordered the formal integration of the military. The military integration occurred three years after the end of World War II, and though late in coming, this change marked the beginning of a more serious civil-rights consciousness by some in government. A major component of Truman's 1948 reelection campaign also centered on what he called the Fair Deal, which would provide more equality in access to government-subsidized housing, education, and other benefits. Many of his far-reaching provisions were rejected, but the National Housing Act of 1949 was passed. This legislation provided 1 million subsidized homes for the disadvantaged and established an aggressive slum clearance program. Lefrak Corporation, under the direction of Samuel Lefrak, was the first private company to participate in city-financed housing projects in the United States. Lefrak completed several housing projects (such as King's Bay in Brooklyn, Parc Vendome in Queens, and Lefrak City in Queens, a forty-acre, $150 million housing development consisting of twenty 18-story buildings), which supported the urban renewal of New York City.[79]

In many ways, the 1940s brought forth so many social changes in such a short time frame that it rocked Americans' idealistic views about the world and themselves. Americans were confronted with their own racism, their own paranoia and fear of communism, and their own sense of vulnerability (after the development and deployment of the atomic bomb). The war and its aftermath forced Americans to reevaluate their lives on a number of fronts. Some began to yearn for simplicity and conformity. Others blazed a new path toward commercialism and innovation—reflecting Americans' sense of entitlement for what they had endured. In either case, opportunities were ripe for business.

Entrepreneurs: Riding the Boom

Many entrepreneurs attempted to exploit opportunities that accompanied the nation's changing population centers (suburbs) and the beginning of what would become the baby boom. For instance, Toys "R" Us founder Charles Lazarus revolutionized the toy industry with his chain's cookie-cutter uniformity, the precursor to today's retail category killers—The Home Depot, Circuit City, Staples, and others—that have become ubiquitous fixtures on the American suburban landscape. Robert E. Rich also tapped into the growth of postwar suburbia and the need for household convenience. With his invention of a frozen whipped topping in 1945, he created a whole new industry of frozen nondairy products. The increasingly efficient refrigerators introduced after the war helped establish Rich Products Corporation as a viable entity. Moreover, Cold War paranoia and its attendant stockpiling of food and water contributed to the purchase of home-based freezer units, yet another foundation for Rich's product lines. Rich's business was so successful that it ignited fierce competition with the country's dairy producers, who believed that Rich Products would severely undercut their livelihoods. Rich successfully fought the dairy interests and continued to introduce innovative products for over two decades.[80]

While many entrepreneurs attempted to exploit new market opportunities, others focused on influential customer segments. One of the most dramatic changes occurred in the publishing sector. Walter H. Annenberg of Triangle Publications launched the magazine *Seventeen* in 1941, sparking a new trend in publications targeted to America's youth. Annenberg again anticipated the times by launching *TV Guide* in 1953, which, by the mid-1960s, became the largest-selling U.S. magazine, with a circulation of over 20 million.[81] John H. Johnson of Johnson Publishing tapped into the growing economic and political influence of African Americans during the war effort with the creation of *Negro Digest* in 1942. Called a black version of *Reader's Digest*, the publication was followed by the 1945 launch of *Ebony*, which many considered the black version of *Life* magazine.[82] Other postwar entrepreneurs included Leonard S. Shoen, who, sensing the demand for relocating families and veterans after the war, founded the truck rental company U-Haul, and William R. Kelly, who built America's largest temporary-employment agency, Kelly Services, and placed millions of workers in newly created administrative office positions.[83]

These entrepreneurs could not have predicted the impact that the baby boom would have on their enterprises, but they did sense a fundamental change in the composition and movement of the American family. Building businesses to serve these new self-contained communities on the outskirts of major metropolitan areas was fraught with risk. It often took a gambler's disposition to make a leap of faith. One person who made just such a bet was Edward J. DeBartolo, who proclaimed that the suburban shopping center would replace the Main Street of American cities. Although his shopping centers would later identify him as a contributor to the decline of the traditional American downtown, he was not offended by the accusation. Rather than regretting the demise of Main Street, he celebrated his part in the transformation.

Edward J. DeBartolo (1909–1994), Edward J. DeBartolo Corporation

Cleveland Magazine called DeBartolo's life "a testament to the Great American Dream."[84] Where he ended up in life, however, was a far cry from his beginnings as a fatherless infant in the old-line steel town of Youngstown, Ohio. The son of Italian immigrants, he was born Anthony Paonessa in 1909, the same year that his birth father died, but he later changed his name to DeBartolo out of respect for his stepfather, who raised him and nurtured his interest in business. Young DeBartolo was educated in the local public schools and began his business life as a teenager. In addition to working as a mason's apprentice for his stepfather's business, DeBartolo was often called on to submit and evaluate construction bids on behalf of the senior DeBartolo, who could not read or write English. Between the ages of thirteen and eighteen, DeBartolo took on increasing levels of responsibility in the negotiation process.

Upon graduation from high school, DeBartolo envisioned a career as a truck driver. It was 1927, and the expansion of the automobile sector and the development of the nation's road infrastructure appealed to his sense of adventure. But his mother soon squashed that dream: "Jackass!" she said. "Your cousin will be a college graduate, and you will be a truck driver!"[85] The cousin was headed to the University of Notre Dame, and though DeBartolo had no admissions letter or references, he headed to Indiana with his cousin and used his well-honed negotiation skills to gain admittance. Almost sixty years later, DeBartolo acknowledged Notre Dame's fateful decision; he donated $33 million to the institution.[86]

DeBartolo studied civil engineering and paid for his education taking night jobs and working in general contracting. He graduated in 1932 and returned to Youngstown to work in his stepfather's contracting business. Five years later, DeBartolo decided to start his own company, building tracts of single-family residences throughout Youngstown. In 1941, however, after the outbreak of World War II, DeBartolo enlisted in the army and attended Officers' Candidate School. During the war, DeBartolo refined his skills in topography, becoming an expert in evaluating terrain for military action and troop maneuvers. Upon his return to Youngstown, he continued building prefabricated homes and joined forces with his stepfather to construct supermarkets and drugstores to service the growing metropolis. His business boomed with the return of veterans, the increase in family size, and the availability of inexpensive, government-backed mortgages. As home building expanded further away from the city center, suburbs were born, and DeBartolo recognized a much broader opportunity. He reasoned that families living on the outskirts of Youngstown's downtown would prefer to shop closer to their homes.

Banking on this notion, DeBartolo formally organized his company under the name Edward J. DeBartolo Corporation, in 1948. His first gamble was the development of a shopping center called Boardman Plaza on the outer reaches of Youngstown. The plaza encompassed a total of twenty-three stores, including a supermarket, drugstore, and other specialty stores, in an L-shaped design, now commonly referred to as a strip mall. Boardman Plaza was so far from the city limits that many believed that DeBartolo's gamble would go bust in a matter of months. Instead, the plaza was an almost instant success, essentially foreshadowing a fundamental shift in the shopping patterns of Americans. It wasn't long before his "country" shopping center was accompanied by the development of medical offices and other service businesses, all focused on meeting the demands of the growing numbers of suburbanites. William Kowinski, in *The Malling of America*, notes: "All those single-family homes [in suburbia] connected by highways lacked centers of informal social activity—places that don't have a rigidly defined purpose, like schools . . . Housewives were stuck out there twenty-four hours a day. Kids had nowhere to go. Families had no place to go together."[87] The shopping center solved that problem.

From his success with Boardman Plaza, DeBartolo built dozens of suburban shopping centers throughout the midwestern and southeastern United

States, sparking a construction boom with regional developers throughout the nation. Though he did not invent the original shopping center concept, he was the first to expand it nationwide. By the mid-1950s, the handful of shopping centers built before the war (mostly in California) had mushroomed to over 1,800, many bearing the DeBartolo trademark. DeBartolo's initial L-shaped designs eventually evolved into U-shaped configurations and, finally, parallel strips. From there, it was a relatively easy leap to enclose the shopping center with a roof, which DeBartolo did in the early 1960s, taking an active part in the next evolution of suburban shopping—the mall. The first enclosed mall (Southdale) had been built in Edina, Minnesota, in 1956 by the architect Victor Gruen. Gruen "anchored" two major department stores at either end of the plaza and incorporated a central enclosed courtyard design, which was bordered by a string of smaller shops on either side. The enclosure of the shopping center had an additional benefit; it protected the shopper from the extremes of the climate, which was an important issue for winters in Minnesota.[88] Though DeBartolo's wife urged him to sell his shopping centers to enclosed-mall developers, DeBartolo chose instead to do the job himself. Refusing to retire early, DeBartolo bought an airplane and began to search the highways and byways of the Midwest for locations on which to place his next bet, in so doing he put to use his strong topography skills.

By this time, the field of market analysis had become a central component in identifying high-potential locations for new shopping malls. Underscoring the increased competitiveness in the market, the Urban Land Institute issued a bulletin in 1958, which stated that opportunities for shopping center development were "no longer wide open . . . [it] is highly competitive."[89] DeBartolo's earlier training made him especially well suited for this new climate; he was said to have "one of the keenest knacks in the business for evaluating the potential of mall sites from 2,000 feet overhead."[90] He built a full-service operation, from market analysis to site development to ongoing management, and ruled his shopping empire with an iron fist.

In every aspect of his business, DeBartolo was driven by the details, believing that proper attention to even the smallest element of the operation could be the difference between an exceptional shopping experience and an ordinary one. He was not an absentee owner after the development phase was completed. On the contrary, he took pride in his company's maintenance record, explaining that "our whole idea is easy maintenance, prevention of decay, keeping the place from looking seedy." He believed that "disorder was costly . . . mental disorder, physical disorder, all disorder is costly."[91] By spending more on up-front development, DeBartolo reasoned that the on-going costs for back-end maintenance would be significantly lessened.

DeBartolo carried his early appetite for long hours throughout his lifetime. In many ways, his workaholic nature enabled him to stay one step ahead of the competition. He regularly worked thirteen- to fifteen-hour days (beginning at 5:30 a.m.) and expected his management team to do the same. He held regular senior staff meetings on Saturday mornings and even put in a full eight hours on Sundays. In explaining his work ethic, DeBartolo noted: "I was shaped by [growing up poor, the Depression, the war]. What the hell, I was hungry when I was a young boy. I was hungry when I was in my teens. You weren't accustomed to money, to anything being handed to you. I never knew anything more than just banging my brains out working."[92] His work consumed his life, and it was not long before he arranged his personal lifestyle to fit the requirements of his position. To reduce wasteful time in commuting, DeBartolo built a home a few blocks from his office in Youngstown, and he kept a private single-engine plane on a runway behind his headquarters. This enabled him to quickly fly over to the main airport in Youngstown, where he housed a larger jet that would carry him to meetings with retailers, bankers, investors, or real estate agents and would also allow him to easily survey his vast holdings.

Beyond hard work, DeBartolo demanded respect and unconditional loyalty from his employees, but with these expectations came significant rewards. DeBartolo was fond of saying, "I will accept a person with average ability who excels in loyalty."[93] His employees were paid handsomely in salary as well as in equity for their loyalty. For every fifth mall that he developed, DeBartolo distributed 35 percent of the equity ownership among his employees. While most entrepreneurs would strive to "work hard and play hard," DeBartolo lived by the credo "work harder than you play."[94] Though part of his motivation was driven by his humble origins, DeBartolo also believed that as an Italian American, he had to work harder to disprove some of his vocal critics who believed that his success was not totally self-made. Throughout his career, he had to deflect allegations of being connected to the Mafia—allegations that were never proven yet clung to him like a constant shadow. His reputation came under greater scrutiny when he later began developing horse tracks and bought several sports franchises, including the San Francisco 49ers football team and the Pittsburgh Penguins hockey team, among others.

Though DeBartolo and other developers of suburban shopping districts were often ridiculed for promoting ugly sprawl, they were equally heralded for their astuteness and courage. The *New York Times Magazine* reported on the cultural transformation brought forth by the suburban mall—"a shopping mall is consumerism transformed into social experience: A place to dress for, meet friends in, take a leisurely browse, have a meal, see a movie, bring the kids, bring the spouse, bask in the warm, sly suggestion that families that spend money together have more fun."[95] The mall had indeed become America's new downtown, and DeBartolo was its mayor.[96]

Leaders: Expanding the Possibilities

Entrepreneurs like DeBartolo who built solid postwar businesses had fewer challenges than leaders who had to oversee operations before, during, and after World War II. While leaders such as William M. Allen of Boeing and Henry Ford II of Ford Motor Company ran businesses that manufactured products that were core to the war effort, other business leaders faced the challenge of converting their non-military-specific operations to war-related production, only to reconvert at war's end. Others, who were able to produce a sustainable commercial product during the war, took the opportunity of government-funded manufacturing conversion to reinvent their entire operations after the war. In some cases, it was the perfect chance to develop a new capability while exiting a dying business sector. For still others, it was merely an opportunistic chance to enhance the company's portfolio.

Boeing's adaptation from defense contractor to civilian production was not achieved without significant difficulty and determination. Allen had been appointed the company's new CEO in 1945 and was almost immediately faced with the cancellation of $1.5 billion in wartime contracts, yet he held the company together and put it on a path to civilian production.[97] Allen gambled, author Thomas McCraw explains: "[When Allen realized] that the airline industry was about to enter a period of expansion, he directed that large passenger planes be constructed even though he had no orders in hand from customers."[98] Though this effort was not immediately successful, it did much to bolster the engineering division during a period of uncertainty and set the stage for future development—both for commercial applications and for military defense (especially as a result of brewing Cold War tensions). He weathered the immediate postwar downturn and led Boeing to emerge as a commercial success.

When Henry Ford II took over Ford Motor in 1945, the company was losing $9.5 million per month. He implemented an audit system for the company while introducing greater automation in the manufacturing facilities, and Ford Motor was the first major car manufacturer to introduce a new model after World War II. As a result of Ford's leadership, the company boasted net profits of $265 million in 1950. Three years later, Ford Motor overtook Chrysler and claimed second place in industry sales. Ford Motor continued to innovate by introducing new models and revamped car designs to meet the needs of suburbanites.[99]

One individual who made a habit of reinventing his business was Eugene Morehead Patterson. The second-generation leader of American Machine and Foundry Company (AMF), Patterson oversaw the company's transformation from a manufacturer of cigar-rolling equipment to a developer of sophisticated radar antennae during the war and, finally, to a producer of bowling machinery. When Patterson stepped into the president's position, the company's core product line was automated tobacco machinery produced in one factory, and its $5 million in revenues came primarily from long-term lease arrangements on its patented technology. Patterson immediately worked to adapt AMF's mechanical designs for a broader range of industrial machinery, including ornamental-stitching machines and pretzel-tying machines.

When, during World War II, Patterson converted his factory for military production, he decided to push the limits of his firm's engineering ingenuity to develop radar antennae for aircraft carriers, battleships, B-29 bombers, and a range of artillery components. After the war, Patterson set the company on a path of acquisitions and investment in both its tobacco and its defense contract businesses. While AMF's radar antennae technology continued to prosper during the ensuing Cold War years, the company further enhanced its defense offerings with ground-handling and launching equipment for guided missiles. The company eventually won a $29.3 million bid

The two faces of atomic energy. American Machine and Foundry showcases an exhibit on the peaceful application of the atom, part of a World Fair exhibit, which is a far cry from the mushroom cloud produced by an atomic bomb blast along Bikini Atoll in 1946. (Sources: left, Bettmann/CORBIS; right, CORBIS)

to design and develop the Titan intercontinental ballistic missile-launching device.[100]

As the company enhanced its reputation in defense contracting, it simultaneously reestablished its presence within its core industrial machinery businesses. Patterson's inquisitiveness and mechanical inclinations were unleashed on what would become one of America's favorite pastimes and ensure the future legacy of the company: bowling. The most revolutionary advancement in bowling was the development of the automatic pinspotter in the early 1940s—the apparatus that resets bowling pins after each throw of the ball. Patterson believed that his company could manufacture the invention on a broad scale, lease it to bowling centers nationwide, and, in so doing, create a new source of ongoing rental income (similar to its strategy with tobacco machinery).

Though he purchased the invention before the war, its debut was delayed until the war's end, in 1946. The venue for the launch was the Forty-Fourth American Bowling Congress (ABC) Tournament, which was held in Buffalo. Since the Bowling Congress had an exclusive arrangement with Brunswick, AMF's new product design could not be displayed within tournament-sanctioned bowling alleys. With AMF's backing, the inventors set up two makeshift bowling lanes in the armory building across the street from tournament headquarters. The fascination with the automatic pinspotter was so widespread that it drew more visitors and broader media coverage than the tournament itself. The ABC decided that year to endorse the automatic pinspotter in all future tournaments. True to his mechanical nature, Patterson tinkered with the design of the automatic pinspotter, ultimately receiving a patent in 1956 as a coinventor of an improved version. More "intelligent" than the original design, the improved version knew when a gutter ball had been thrown and avoided the unnecessary resetting of the pins.

As he had done with his tobacco and other industrial machinery, Patterson leased the automatic pinspotter and eventually produced a full line of bowling equipment that could also be leased to effectively franchise a full-scale bowling center. AMF's base of operations had grown from the one factory that Patterson stepped into in 1941 to more than forty-five factories and nineteen research and development laboratories throughout the world. In each of its products lines, AMF dominated the market.[101]

An Ending and a New Beginning

After the war, the traditional conflicts between government, business, and labor reemerged, and old patterns of distrust were difficult to contain. Labor struggled to gain a new foothold after the sacrifices made during the war, and the government attempted to determine an appropriate postwar role that would require less regulation. Certainly, President Roosevelt's own death in 1945 signaled the figurative and literal split in the decade. Within months of his death, the United States was ending one phase in its role in the world and embarking on an entirely new one. Successful business executives of this decade had to navigate this bifurcated landscape, shifting from full-scale, war-driven production to postwar production driven by pent-up commercial and consumer demand.

As the 1950s approached, the despair and uncertainty so evident ten years earlier were becoming a faint memory. The close of the 1940s brought forth a wave of prosperity that lasted for decades and a heightened appreciation of the individual consumer. Where the government was businesses' primary client for much of the 1940s, the individual consumer now assumed this position. Business legacies were formed and fortunes were made by targeting individual population segments and tapping into the country's new optimism. The next half of the century belonged to the consumer.

TABLE 5-4

Entrepreneurs, managers, and leaders of the 1940s

Entrepreneurs

Walter H. Annenberg, Triangle Publications
Edward W. Carter, Carter Hawley Hale
F. Trammell Crow, Trammell Crow Company
Edward DeBartolo, Edward J. DeBartolo
 Corporation
Georges F. Doriot, American R&D Corporation
John C. Emery Sr., Emery Air Freight
Conrad N. Hilton, Hilton Hotels Corporation
Peter F. Hurst, Aeroquip Corporation
John H. Johnson, Johnson Publishing
 Company
William R. Kelly, Kelly Services
Estée Lauder, Estée Lauder
Charles Lazarus, Toys "R" Us
James J. Ling, Ling-Temco-Vought
Charles E. Merrill, Merrill Lynch & Company,
 Inc.
Alexander M. Poniatoff, Ampex Corporation
Robert E. Rich, Rich Products Corporation
Leonard S. Shoen, U-Haul
Henry Taub, Automatic Data Processing

Managers

Stanley C. Allyn, National Cash Register
 Company
William Bernbach, Doyle Dane Bernbach
Harold Blancke, Celanese Corporation of
 America
Walter S. Carpenter Jr., DuPont Corporation
Catherine T. Clark, Brownberry Ovens
Joseph W. Crosby, Thiokol Corporation
James E. Davis, Winn-Dixie Stores
John A. Ewald, Avon Products
Marshall Field III, Field Enterprises
Harvey S. Firestone Jr., Firestone Tire and
 Rubber
John M. Franklin, United States Lines
Daniel F. Gerber Jr., Gerber Products
 Company
Leonard H. Goldenson, American
 Broadcasting-Paramount
J. Peter Grace, W. R. Grace & Company
Crawford H. Greenewalt, DuPont Corporation
Henry J. Heinz II, H. J. Heinz Company
Eugene Holman, Exxon Corporation
Norman O. Houston, Golden State Insurance
Edward C. Johnson II, Fidelity Investments
 Limited
W. Alton Jones, Cities Service Company
Donald S. Kennedy, OGE Energy Corporation

Bernard Kilgore, Wall Street Journal
Mills B. Lane Jr., Citizens & Southern National
 Bank
Fred R. Lazarus Jr., Federated Department
 Stores
Samuel J. Lefrak, Lefrak Corporation
Joseph M. Long, Long's Drug Stores
Joseph A. Martino, National Lead Company
Frederick L. Maytag II, Maytag Corporation
Fowler McCormick, International Harvester
Donald H. McLaughlin, Homestake Mining
Andre Meyer, Lazard, Freres and Company
Joseph I. Miller, Cummins Engine Company
Louis B. Neumiller, Caterpillar Tractor
 Company
LeRoy A. Petersen, Otis Elevator Company
Philip W. Pillsbury, Pillsbury Mills
Helen R. Reid, New York Herald Tribune
Richard S. Reynolds Jr., Reynolds
 Corporation
O. Wayne Rollins, Rollins
Dorothy Schiff, New York Post
Dorothy Shaver, Lord and Taylor
Philip Sporn, American Electric Power
 Company
Jack I. Straus, Macy (R. H.) and Company
Watson H. Vanderploeg, Kellogg Company
Lew R. Wasserman, Music Corporation of
 America
John P. Weyerhaeuser Jr., Weyerhaeuser
 Company
Uncas A. Whitaker, AMP
Charles Edward Wilson, General Electric
 Company
Charles Erwin Wilson, General Motors
 Corporation

Leaders

William M. Allen, Boeing Company
Francis C. Brown, Schering
Justin Dart, United Drug Company
Leland I. Doan, The Dow Chemical Company
Henry Ford II, Ford Motor Company
George H. Love, Consolidation Coal
 Company
Roger Milliken, Milliken & Company
John R. North, Ringling Brothers, Barnum &
 Bailey Circus
Eugene M. Patterson, American Machine &
 Foundry
Norton W. Simon, Hunt Foods & Industries
Joseph C. Wilson II, Xerox Corporation

SIX

1950–1959

Feeding the Machine of Consumption

Richard Nixon: There are some instances where you may be ahead of us, for example in the development of the thrust of your rockets for the investigation of outer space; there may be some instances in which we are ahead of you—in color television for instance.

Nikita Krushchev: No, we are up with you on this too. We have bested you in one technique and also in the other.

Nixon: We do not claim to astonish the Russian people. We hope to show our diversity and our right to choose. We do not wish to have decisions made at the top by government officials who say that all homes should be built in the same way. Would it not be better to compete in the relative merits of washing machines than in the strength of rockets? Is this the kind of competition you want?

Krushchev: Yes that's the kind of competition we want. But your generals say: "Let's compete in rockets. We are strong and we can beat you." But in this respect, we can also show you something.

—Vice President Richard M. Nixon and Premier Nikita Krushchev,
Moscow "Kitchen Debate," July 24, 1959

TWO GLOBAL CONVERSATIONS permeated U.S. life in the 1950s—consumption and fear. On the one hand, the war-mitigated rationing and self-sacrificing in the 1940s created pent-up consumer demand that was unleashed with a fury as businesses converted their operations to commercial production. On the other hand, Americans lived in constant fear of both communist domination and another world war—a war that would be defined not by the age-old military arsenal and front line, but by the nuclear age. The spread of communism in China and Eastern Europe and Russia's possession of atomic weapon technology reinforced these fears. Massive consumption proved to be one of the few antidotes that enabled Americans to soothe their unease. Although historians often view the 1950s as a time of social conservatism, robotic complacency, and mindless conformity, this approach to life provided one means for people to make sense of their world.

By purchasing the same homes, the same appliances, the same automobiles, the same clothes, the same records, and the same books, Americans established some predictability in an otherwise chaotic world. Between 1948 and 1958, over 13 million new homes were constructed, mostly in the outskirts of major metropolitan areas, and all these homes needed to be filled with the latest in household conveniences.[1] As Americans were filling their new cookie-cutter homes with Hoover vacuums, Maytag washers, GE refrigerators, and RCA televisions, however, they were also likely to make plans for their very own bomb shelter. Preparations for home bomb shelters progressed in earnest after the government issued the how-to guide *You Can Survive* in the early 1950s. The publication included tips on preparing for and withstanding an atomic blast. The hypnotic manner in which Americans went about stocking their bomb shelters while simultaneously planting their uniform flower beds seems almost unreal, but faced with the bitter complexities of the times, Americans of the 1950s could hardly be considered unusual. School children started their class sessions with duck-and-cover bomb drills, and the new, ubiquitous medium of television showcased Senator Joseph McCarthy's attacks on communist infiltrators in the sacred halls of government.[2]

While conformity often constricted opportunities for individual expression and diversity, it provided fertile ground for business development. Material possessions were the new social markers of success, and business executives such as Harry B. Cunningham of S. S. Kresge (later Kmart) and H. Stanley Marcus of Neiman Marcus did much to exploit this notion across socioeconomic classes. Despite, or maybe because of, the changes in social mores, businesses and especially big businesses thrived throughout the decade. In fact, many did so well that a sense of invincibility began to creep into the executive suite. The baby boom was in full swing and American families were ready to spend money and consume. In many respects, big business experienced a renaissance—there was a growing economy, a booming population, a supportive government, and minimal international competition. In

Fallout shelters became popular during the Cold War escalation in the 1950s and 1960s. This gasoline-generated Walter Kiddie Nuclear Laboratory model could sustain a family of four for three to five days.
(Source: Bettmann/CORBIS)

1953, Charles E. Wilson of General Motors Corporation seemed to sum up the general mood of the country: "for years, I thought what was good for our country was good for General Motors, and vice versa."[3] As the contextual factors coalesced to create a vibrant and explosive environment, big business did indeed permeate all walks of life.

The Population Booms

Probably the most significant contextual factor that opened up opportunities for business executives was the massive growth of the U.S. population. Between 1950 and 1960, the population grew by 19 percent, or by 28.6 million (from 150.7 million to 179.3 million)—an increase in sheer volume that was larger than any other decade of the twentieth century.[4] Of the 28.6 million, only a small fraction came from immigration—roughly 2.5 million.[5] The population increase was also only marginally impacted by the addition of Alaska and Hawaii to statehood status in 1959; these new states' combined population was less than 800,000.[6] The single biggest determinant of the population growth was the explosion in the birth rate, which peaked at 25 per 1,000 in 1955. The birth rate was so high that more babies were born in the early 1950s than in the preceding three decades put together.[7] Medical advances and, what was more important, access to medical care also expanded rapidly during the 1950s. The polio vaccine was identified and perfected in 1953 by Jonas Salk, and in that same year, the molecular structure of DNA (deoxyribonucleic acid) was discovered. These remarkable developments ushered forth an unprecedented era of medical and scientific discoveries and breakthroughs. The combination of record levels of births and extended life spans fueled the phenomenal population boom.[8]

In addition to the swelling of the population, accelerated internal migration fundamentally altered the country's demographic composition. During the 1950s, it was not uncommon for 25 percent of the population to move each year, which was a marked increase from previous decades and a precursor to future mobility trends.[9] During the decade, the number of farms dropped from 5.3 million to 3.9 million.[10] In addition to farm flight, there was a corresponding urban flight. For the first time in the century, the major urban centers, especially in the populous Northern cities, experienced outward migration to the suburbs—mostly among white middle-class families. More than 83 percent of the overall population increase from the 1950s to the 1960s was centered in suburbia, where 11 million new homes were built.[11] Despite the movement of many families to the suburbs, the nation's cities still experienced growth (albeit on a slower pace), largely as a result of the continued black migration from the South.[12]

The popularity of the suburbs for many former farmers or urban dwellers was dramatically enhanced by the affordability of single-family homes, and home ownership reached a high of 60 percent of the population.[13] Clarence Shaver, who headed United States Gypsum Company, and William Levitt of Levittown fame achieved tremendous business success from the bulge in home construction. With the increase in home ownership on the outskirts of metropolitan areas, there was a corresponding growth in the two-car family—one for commuting to work and one for family errands, community activities, and trips to the mall (very few stores were within walking distance). The term *bedroom community* was first used in the 1950s to describe the new lifestyles of suburbanites who generally sought employment and entertainment in the city and relaxation and rest in their home communities.[14] Though individuals and businesses could take comfort in the security and protection of their suburbs, they could not insure against the fear and paranoia that pervaded many aspects of life in the 1950s. There was no insurance policy for unpredictable world affairs.

Communism and Capitalism's Debut Fight

Just five years after the end of World War II, the United States came face-to-face with its new role as the strongest Western democracy in an antagonistic standoff with communist nations. From time-to-time the United States would accept this role, but only with some ambivalence and uncertainty and often with great physical and psychological costs. The stage for America's inevitable role in the new world order had been set in the late 1940s, when President Truman endorsed National Security Council Paper Number 68. This UN document warned that because communist countries (notably the Soviet Union) were seeking world domination, it was the duty of the United States to ensure that this did not occur.[15] Specifically, the United States felt empowered to protect the status quo—containing communism—and to do so, the United States justified the buildup of conventional military forces and the expansion of its nuclear arms program.

America's resolve for its role as protector was first tested in Korea. With the Japanese surrender in 1945, Korea became one of the spoils of the war, and its fate was similar to that of Germany. Korea was divided in half at the thirty-eighth parallel, which created two "temporary" independent nations, a Soviet-backed North Korea and a U.S.-backed South Korea. After five years of uneasy coexistence, North Korea, with backing from Stalin and the Soviets, crossed the thirty-eighth parallel to embark on its own brand of reunification. Truman left little doubt about the firmness of American resolve when he spoke before Congress, urging U.S. intervention. Even so, Truman's conception of victory would simply restore an unstable peace at the thirty-eighth parallel, rather than overthrow North Korea altogether. This compromise seemed foreign to many Americans, who continued to believe in U.S. invincibility. But after much seesawing of the front line, Truman won the backing of the UN allies, and an initial truce was declared on July 10, 1951. The finalization of the truce did not come for another two years, during which time sporadic fighting continued. Though begun by Truman, the final peace treaty between North Korea and South Korea was orchestrated by his successor, President Dwight D. Eisenhower.[16]

With Eisenhower's ascension to the presidency in 1953 and Krushchev's taking power after the death of Stalin that same year, the original protagonists of the Cold War had passed the baton. Both new leaders tried to remodel the confrontation on a premise of peaceful coexistence, which would be achieved, however, through an ever-expanding nuclear arms race. Though America's resolve as the protector of democracy was constantly challenged throughout the decade, the nation's rhetoric remained unshakable. Throughout the 1950s, Eisenhower walked a fine line between overt intervention, covert support, and outright neutrality.[17] His somewhat contradictory approaches often reflected the uncertainty of many Americans, who simply longed for a protracted peace and a return to the comfort of domestic issues.

An Uneasy but Reassuring Calm in Government Policies

Americans found the comfort that they were looking for in Eisenhower, who brought a sense of calm and quiet complacency to the intensity that characterized the times. On the home front, Eisenhower sought to maintain a balanced budget throughout his administration, fearing that unencumbered bureaucracy would lend itself to creeping socialism. Surprisingly, given his military career, Eisenhower focused his budget cuts on traditional defense funding. He believed that putting more money into nuclear arms development, rather than conventional forces and artillery, placed America in a strong position. Given the massive devastation that could be unleashed with nuclear weapons, he reasoned, the showcasing of traditional military might was unnecessary.[18]

The swift curb in defense spending that Eisenhower instigated at the end of the Korean War, however, forced the country into recession in late 1953 and early 1954. In an attempt to stimulate investment in nonmilitary capital, Eisenhower backed the Tax Reform Act of 1954. One of the key provisions of the new tax reform allowed businesses to accelerate depreciation on their capital assets. In approving this tax legislation, Eisenhower believed that the initial reduction in tax revenue would be more than offset by incremental investments in new technology and capital. He further believed that these investments would subsequently result in the development of new businesses and, hence, a broader overall tax base.[19]

In addition to trying to generate more investment in the economy, Eisenhower attempted to streamline government bureaucracy by disbanding the Reconstruction Finance Corporation (RFC), eliminating wage and price controls, and reducing overall subsidies to farmers. Though he believed that the RFC had already served its purpose in moving the country through the Depression and the war mobilization effort, he did support the continuation of one RFC department, the Small Business Administration (SBA). The Eisenhower administration formalized the SBA to protect the interests of small businesses and to make the agency a repository of information and support for new business development and enhancement. In addition, Eisenhower approved the distribution of food stamps for excess farm crops instead of large-scale direct subsidies and expanded federal expenditures for public health and public works projects, most notably the expansion of the federal highway system. His administration's approval of adding over forty-two thousand new miles to the nation's interconnected roadways over a ten-year period contributed in no small way to the rapid expansion of the suburbs.[20]

Although Eisenhower's endorsement of tax reform, the support of the SBA, and the investment in the country's infrastructure clearly labeled him as pro-business, he supported two key pieces of legislation that placed certain restrictions on the general liberties afforded corporations: the Celler-Kefauver Act and the Delaney Amendment to the Food, Drug and Cosmetic Act. Originally passed in 1950 as an amendment to the Clayton Antitrust Act of 1914, Celler-Kefauver closed a loophole in Clayton that had inadvertently allowed mergers and acquisitions of companies within the same industry through asset purchases. Under the Truman administration, Celler-Kefauver was weakly enforced, especially during the outbreak of the Korean War, when the government sought the cooperation of businesses. The Eisenhower administration, however, did enforce the provisions of the amendment and prohibited several important mergers, but another loophole was exploited. The amendment to the Clayton Act did not prohibit mergers and acquisitions of nonrelated companies, which left the door open for conglomeration. A wave of unrelated diversification swept through the country in the late 1950s and found its stride in the 1960s.[21] Two individuals who were early to capitalize on this opportunity were Charles B. Thornton and Charles B. Bluhdorn.

Thornton built Litton Industries from a small electronics company into a huge conglomerate by acquiring twenty-five companies between 1953 and 1961. Bluhdorn transformed Gulf and Western's auto parts business into a major conglomerate composed of media holdings, mining operations, and food products.

Through the Delaney Amendment, the government sought to mandate premarket clearance for any foods produced with preservatives or other additives. Before passage of the amendment, the burden of proof regarding harmful ingredients rested with the Food and Drug Administration (FDA). The FDA could obtain that proof only after a product had been distributed and caused harm. The Delaney Amendment essentially reversed the burden of proof to manufacturers, which were prohibited from selling and distributing foods and drugs with additives until they could prove the products were safe in general, as well as noncarcinogenic.[22] Although the amendment still did not address the issues of efficacy and false advertising, it marked the beginning of consumer protection legislation that became a hallmark of the following decade.

Eisenhower's success in keeping the balance in world affairs and on the domestic front was rewarded in 1956, when he easily won reelection. His margin of victory was considered a landslide and a strong endorsement for business as usual. For the most part, Eisenhower's second administration was more of the same, which was reassuring to many Americans. Despite social changes brewing on a number of fronts, Eisenhower's preferred strategy was to shy away from controversy unless it involved foreign policy. Even throughout some of the ridiculous machinations of Senator McCarthy's communist witch hunts, Eisenhower maintained a deafening silence. Although McCarthy inevitably self-destructed (never actually producing any concrete evidence on any suspect), the cost of Eisenhower's inaction, of course, was high, leaving countless reputations and lives destroyed.[23]

Despite his stance on McCarthy, it was important to Eisenhower and, so he thought, to many Americans, to maintain a unified front in the face of the communist threat. Anything that chipped away at this uniformity was considered dangerous and suspect. In a peculiar way, America's growing sense of conformity, and desire for it, resulted in a self-anointed view of superiority. Many believed that America was the chosen nation. Given this sense of destiny, it is not surprising that the words "one nation under God" were added to

TABLE 6-1

Social and demographic facts about the 1950s

- 151 million Americans in 50 states; grows to 179 million by 1960
- Alaska and Hawaii admitted to statehood in 1959
- Number of drive-in movie theaters hits 2,200 by 1950
- United States produces 52 percent of the world's goods
- First air-conditioned cars, offered by General Motors
- 98 percent of U.S. population supplied with electricity
- Senator McCarthy fuels communist paranoia in the country
- Rosa Parks's refusal to give up bus seat sparks yearlong Montgomery bus boycott
- In *Brown v. Topeka Board of Education* the Supreme Court rules against "separate but equal"
- Bomb shelter plans widely available
- Fads: hula hoop, poodle skirts, blue jeans, Davy Crockett coonskin caps, 3-D movies
- Games: Barbie dolls, Mr. Potato Head, Hopalong Cassidy guns and western wear
- New words: *rock and roll, DJ, fast food, UFO*
- Labor force male–female ratio: 5 to 2
- Minimum wage (1950): $0.75 per hour
- Annual average earnings (1950): $2,992
- Life expectancy (1950): 71.1 years for females, 65.6 years for males

the nation's Pledge of Allegiance and the words "in God we trust" were added to the country's currency. There was a deep-seated belief that America stood for what was right, and any contradictory notion was viewed with disdain.[24]

The Sounds of Silence

McCarthy's scheming early in the decade and the overwhelming paranoia associated with the Cold War undoubtedly exacerbated the tendency in the 1950s toward conformity: if you did not stand out in any material way, you could not be branded a liberal, or worse, a communist. Social conformity was especially evident in the growing suburbs. It was the first time that this social class reached a majority in the country, and their dominance and purchasing power enabled them to influence a host of social patterns. For example, membership in organized religion reached new heights. Between 1950 and 1956, 5 million members were added to the Roman Catholic Church, and 8 million joined various Protestant denominations.[25] For the three years between 1952 and 1954, the best-selling nonfiction book in the United States was *The Holy Bible: Revised Standard Version*, followed closely by Norman Vincent Peale's *Power of Positive Thinking*.[26] If Americans weren't looking for spiritual guidance and affirmation, they were looking for cooking or decorating advice—no less than seven of the top best sellers during this decade provided advice on being a better homemaker.[27] In many ways, these suburbanites, many of whom had relocated for employment opportunities, were trying to define a new sense of community and a nucleus of belonging—one that was easy to understand, easy to blend into, and easy to replicate.

The conservatism of the times did much to squelch the progress of women in the workforce. While women worked in greater numbers than ever before, they were relegated to low-level office positions and paid disproportionately less than men in equivalent jobs. Though women were generally silenced in the 1950s, two other groups would not be silenced—teenagers and African Americans. The teenage rebellion that emerged in the 1950s was driven less by ideals than by a need for expressing freedom. Middle-class incomes grew, and families relocated to the suburbs, where teenagers had more time and disposable income on their hands. As their parents tuned in to Lawrence Welk and his *Champagne Bubbles* and drove bigger and bigger sedans, teenagers found their rebellion embodied in the records of Elvis Presley and the hot rods and motorcycles driven by James Dean.[28] The popularity of such rebellious icons did not go unnoticed by the business community, and new manufacturers and advertisers emerged to cash in on the phenomenon. Although teenagers scoffed at their parents' general conformity, they embraced their own version of conformity by purchasing the same records, clothes, and cars. They became one of the hottest target markets, as advertisers began to understand the potential of developing early brand allegiances and of teenagers' ability to create and sustain fads. One individual who tapped into the rebellious spirit of teenagers was Walter Haas Jr., who helped Levi Strauss capitalize on denim blue jeans as a symbol of nonconformity and independence.[29]

For the first time, teenagers became a viable consumer market. The hula hoop was one product in a long line of both enduring and fleeting fads. (Source: Hulton Archive/Getty Images)

Although the teenage rebellion forced many to address social discontinuities in their individual families, a far more volatile rebellion by African Americans forced a whole society to confront fundamental stereotypes and abuse. Two hallmark events in the 1950s set the stage for the progressive civil-rights legislation that would define the 1960s: the *Brown v. Topeka Board of Education* Supreme Court ruling and the Montgomery, Alabama, bus boycott. In *Brown v. Topeka Board of Education*, the U.S. Supreme Court ruled in 1954 that educational separation of the races was unconstitutional. In arguing the case for desegregation, future Supreme Court member Thurgood Marshall provided ample evidence that, on average, funding for black schools was 50 percent of the level for comparable white schools.[30] Though it took fifty years to reverse the "separate-but-equal" ruling that enforced segregation, it would take longer to achieve the sought-after goals of true integration (which arguably still remain an idealized vision).

While one turning point in the civil-rights fight played itself out in the highest court of the land, another pivotal moment unfolded on the back of a bus in Montgomery. Like almost all aspects of society, the bus system in Alabama was segregated, with whites sitting in front and blacks in back. Moreover, on an overcrowded bus, it was expected that black passengers give up their seats for white passengers. On December 1, 1955, Rosa Parks refused to give up her seat to a white passenger and was arrested and charged with a federal violation of the segregation ordinance. Parks's arrest became a galvanizing force for the burgeoning civil-rights movement through a year-long boycott of the Montgomery bus system. During the boycott, more than twenty thousand black passengers (almost 80 percent of the total riders) used alternative transportation each day. The nonviolent form of protest worked, leading the Alabama Supreme Court to rule in December 1956 that bus segregation laws were unconstitutional.[31]

The clear and timely images of brutality and bigotry that were pervasive throughout the early fight for civil rights forced Americans to face the reality behind the facade of tranquility and conformity. The same medium that fueled the consumption economy of the 1950s became an unlikely partner for the "cause" by galvanizing support for civil rights. Leaving little to the imagination, television helped end the pervasive silence. Yet television was also a technology that could easily be co-opted for specific agendas—for selling, for shocking, for entertainment, and for education.

Transformational Technology

In many ways, television was a strong unifying force in creating homogenous communities; it portrayed what was acceptable and what was suspect. It exposed, it celebrated, and it informed. Television gave families a new set of ground rules and, in the process, fundamentally changed the structure of family life. Watching television as a family often replaced reading, conversation, and many other forms of interaction. At one point, Americans devoted one-third of their waking hours to watching television.[32] The emergence of the Swanson TV dinner in 1953 (ninety-eight cents for frozen turkey, peas, and whipped sweet potatoes) gave families an even better excuse to move dining room conversation to living room viewing.[33]

Though television had been around for many years, TV sets were difficult to mass-produce cost-effectively. There were few broadcast stations and even fewer choices of program content. Despite these setbacks, over 7 million televisions were sold in the late 1940s at an average cost of five hundred dollars; this at a time when the average American family earned just three thousand dollars a year, and the picture quality of television was likened to "viewing through half-closed venetian blinds."[34] With the perfection of the cathode-ray tube in 1953, the average cost of a new television dropped to two hundred dollars, and by the end of the decade, 45 million sets were sold.[35] The speed with which consumers accepted television was only paralleled by the speed with which businesses attempted to exploit the medium for selling. As early as 1950, Arthur Nielsen adapted his market research system for monitoring radio broadcasts to television. His system alerted television producers and advertisers about who was watching, what programs they were watching, and when they were watching those programs.

It wasn't long before television research and development focused on full-color versions. In 1953, the FCC ruled against a totally new design by CBS in favor of technology developed and supported by RCA. This technology would be compatible with RCA's installed base of black-and-white televisions. The company's development of color television in 1954 was considered the most complicated consumer good ever manufactured. Color transmission required a complete overhaul of broadcasting technology, from new cameras to new facilities to new technicians. It took almost fifteen years for color television to gain wide acceptance and usage, which was roughly three

*Television became a favorite
pastime of Americans
throughout the country.*
(Source: Bettmann/CORBIS)

times longer than it took the black-and-white version.[36] Managers like Frank
M. Freimann at Magnavox and Joseph S. Wright at Zenith rode the wave
of television's proliferation. Under Freimann's direction, Magnavox sales increased more than tenfold between 1950 and 1967. While Zenith also experienced massive growth, Wright focused on product enhancements, including
the launch of the wireless remote controller.

The technology that made the remote controller a possibility had its foundation in the 1950s through the invention of the transistor. The invention of
the transistor and the microchip provided the initial impetus for two key individuals, John E. Jonsson and Patrick Haggerty, who led the transformation
of Texas Instruments (TI). Considered one of the most significant contributions to the advancement of electronics technology, the transistor essentially
provided more power than the vacuum tube, at a fraction of its size. Recognizing the transistor's commercial potential, TI's Jonsson acquired a license
for using the Bell Laboratories silicon transistor patent. He then hired a team
to conduct extensive research that enabled TI to take an early lead in the sale
and distribution of transistor-based electronics. Then, in the late 1950s, with
Haggerty as CEO, TI perfected its manufacturing operations, and the company became the first major producer of cost-effective transistors. Under the
technical leadership of Jack Kilby, TI continued to push transistor technology
to new limits. Kilby was one of the first scientists to place transistors on a
board with resistors and capacitors to form the integrated circuit board. The

result was greater power on a smaller scale, without the need to solder transistor wires. Kilby's scientific advances and Haggerty's focus on operational efficiency enabled Texas Instruments to capitalize on the commercial viability and potential of transistor technology.[37]

While Haggerty's team was building integrated circuits, Robert N. Noyce was developing a process for the inexpensive reproduction of circuit boards. Unaware of the other's work, Noyce and Kilby simultaneously developed similar circuit boards, and both men attempted to secure a patent. For years, the patent ownership bounced back and forth between Noyce and Kilby, until 1969, when it was finally awarded to Noyce. By then, Noyce, along with longtime business partner Gordon Moore, had been making cost-effective integrated circuit boards for a dozen years under the Fairchild Semiconductor name.[38]

The work of Texas Instruments, Fairchild, and Bell Labs became part of the building blocks for computer giant IBM, which was fundamentally reshaped by Thomas J. Watson Jr. Though his father had turned IBM into a tremendously successful company, the firm that Watson Jr. inherited in 1955 was a mix of loosely organized divisions that competed with one another for resources. After an intensive restructuring, which improved efficiency while still maintaining a decentralized structure, IBM continued to expand further, acquiring ten new plants in six years and increasing foreign investment. Watson also continued to invest heavily in research and development, and by 1956, IBM had captured 85 percent of the computer market in the United States and *Fortune* had name Watson "capitalist of the century."[39]

Although the United States celebrated the technical wonders of television, transistors, and their affiliated offspring, the country's heretofore dominance in the world of technological innovation was challenged in a very significant and public way in October 1957. The Russian launch of Sputnik, a 184.3-pound aluminum sphere capable of circling the globe every ninety-two minutes at eighteen thousand miles per hour, sent shock waves through the U.S. government and society as a whole.[40] The United States had been caught off guard and was deeply embarrassed by Sputnik's success. The launch not only exposed the complacency that had crept into government-backed research and innovation, but also fueled the ever-present fear of communism. One month after the first Sputnik, the launch of Sputnik 2, which brought a dog into space, accelerated the U.S. sense of urgency and thus the launch date for a U.S. satellite. Within weeks of Sputnik 2, the United States invited the world to watch as it sent its own satellite into orbit. The world did watch, but what they saw was not American innovation and ingenuity, but failure and disgrace. The U.S. Navy's Vanguard rocket that was to carry the American satellite burst into flames within seconds of takeoff in December of 1957, exposing to all the world the country's inferior space technology.[41]

Again, Americans' perceptions of their country were shattered. In 1958, Eisenhower created the National Aeronautics and Space Agency (later to be called Administration) to coordinate and monitor the country's space exploration efforts and signed the National Defense Education Act, which provided federal grants for training in math, science, and modern languages. These efforts not only reenergized the U.S. commitment to space exploration, but also sparked the country's competitive spirit and even its imagination of what was possible.[42]

Labor Meets the Organization Man

While imaginations were piqued by the space race, they were often stifled in big business as the "organization man" began to emerge in full force. The growing conformity in the workforce was well documented, most notably by C. Wright Mills in his sociological study, *White Collar Society*, and William A. Whyte Jr. in *The Organization Man*, both published in 1956. Career success within this period often involved an almost cultlike commitment to the corporation and a subjugation of individual expression. To succeed in business, one had to play by the rules—being willing and able to move wherever and whenever required and accepting the conformity and homogeneity of corporate life.

American business was still benefiting from the standardization and technology investments made during the preceding war years, and worker productivity continued to increase. Between 1945 and 1955, productivity jumped by 35 percent.[43] The conversion back to military production occurred quicker than anyone expected, when the United States entered the Korean War. Just as it had done in World War II, the government intervened in management-labor relations. In 1952, Truman ordered the seizure of many of the country's steel mills, fearing that union workers would strike and cut off the vitally important supply of steel for the war. The steel company executives had rejected the proposed 10 percent wage increase that had been endorsed by the steelworkers' unions and by the Wage Stabilization Board, a quasi-business-government administrative arm designed to prevent inflationary pressures on wages and prices during the war. Ruling that Truman's seizure of the steel industry was illegal, the U.S. Supreme Court set limits on presidential power over business operations. The court decision was significant in that it prevented a single individual (namely, the president) from unilaterally intervening in business affairs without congressional support. The steelworkers were allowed to strike, which they did for fifty-three days. After that, they settled for a wage increase that was a compromise between the recommended 10 percent and the position of the steel company executives.[44]

The steelworkers' strike was indicative of the increased labor activism during the decade—activism that further intensified as two of the largest labor organizations decided to pool their political clout. With its 10.3 million members, the American Federation of Labor (AFL) merged with the 4.5-million-member Congress of Industrial Organizations (CIO) to form the AFL-CIO in 1955. The CIO, which represented unskilled workers, had broken ranks with the AFL in the mid-1930s, during the height of the Depression. At the time, the AFL, which represented skilled craftsmen, believed that agreeing to recognize unskilled labor within its ranks would undermine its bargaining power. The dramatic growth in automation and technology that followed the split rendered certain jobs obsolete, but at the same time, made other positions, often those requiring lower-level skills, much more desirable. In an ironic twist, the CIO's ability and track record in organizing unskilled laborers was now seen as very desirable.[45]

In consummating the merger, the two organizations sought to reduce the inherent redundancies and costs associated with running two large-scale administrative infrastructures, and they hoped to eliminate the ongoing raiding of union members. Beyond these important business considerations, the combined entity enabled the union movement to put a fresh face on its activities. It had long suffered from its alleged links to both communism and organized crime. By joining together, the AFL-CIO sought to distance itself from both characterizations, and to that end, the merged union went to considerable lengths to rid its organizations of perceived and alleged corruption.[46] The real test of the AFL-CIO's new commitment to a fresh perspective occurred less than two years after its merger, when it made the decision to expel

The new seal of the merged American Federation of Labor and the Congress of Industrial Organizations. At its peak, the AFL-CIO boasted over 15 million members.
(Source: Bettmann/CORBIS)

the large and influential Teamsters Union from its ranks. The Teamsters, led by Jimmy Hoffa, had refused to cooperate with federal investigations into corrupt practices—many of the investigations were aimed at Hoffa himself. Though it was the highest-profile expulsion, the ouster of the Teamsters was not a singular event.

The labor rehabilitation effort was not left simply in the hands of the AFL-CIO. The government decided to weigh in with the passage of the Landrum-Griffin Act. This legislation aimed to control union corruption and coercion by setting forth penalties for the misuse of union funds, preventing individuals who had been convicted of certain crimes from holding union officer positions, and restricting the use of secondary boycotts. The act also imposed new regulations on union elections, required unions to file annual financial reports, and outlined a bill of rights for union members.[47]

In many ways, the peak of union activity in the 1950s was the beginning of the end. As automation moved onto the factory floor and as big corporations sought growth through related and unrelated diversification, the bargaining power of unions slowly eroded. Beginning in the 1960s, the percentage of workers represented by unions began a decline that continued throughout the rest of the century. The 1950s marked the first time that the number of white-collar executives exceeded the number of blue-collar workers in American industry.[48] Ironically, the one future peak and potential for renewed union activity would be the organization of the organization man—the unionization of white-collar workers, which came in later decades.

Managers: Selling to Suburbia

As the economy boomed, so did investors' expectations. Business executives were scrutinized more than their counterparts in the 1940s, especially regarding financial performance. Though proxy fights had long existed as a vehicle for major shareholders to exert influence on corporate performance, they were rarely used before the 1950s. Between 1954 and 1955, shareholders of various

TABLE 6-2

Business events that shaped the 1950s

Date	Event
1950	United States sends military forces to Korea
1950	President Truman authorizes production of hydrogen bomb
1950	Defense Protection Act reinstates wage and price controls during Korean War
1950	Celler-Kefauver Act closes loophole on asset-based acquisitions
1950	A. C. Nielsen adapts Audimeter to television
1950	Color broadcasting first authorized by Federal Communications Commission
1951	AT&T becomes first U.S. corporation to record over 1 million shareholders
1952	Texas Instruments produces first silicon transistor (from Bell Labs patent)
1952	Congress ends price and wage controls
1952	Videotape recorder invented by Charles Ginsburg
1952	Hasbro's Mr. Potato Head is the first television commercial aimed at children
1953	Small Business Administration created
1953	Triangle Publications produces *TV Guide*; achieves largest circulation of any U.S. magazine
1953	Swanson introduces TV dinner
1953	Initial structure of DNA discovered
1953	End of Korean War
1953	Jonas Salk develops vaccine for polio
1955	Two largest union organizations merge to form 15-million-member AFL-CIO
1955	First *Fortune* 500 list produced; General Motors tops list
1955	Disneyland opens in California
1956	White-collar workers outnumber blue-collar workers for first time
1956	Dow Jones Industrial Average hits high of 500
1956	First fully enclosed mall opens in Edina, Minnesota
1957	President Eisenhower signs Civil Rights Act
1957	Russia launches Sputnik satellite, beginning space race
1957	Fortran computer programming language invented
1957	First Japanese car sold in United States—a Toyota
1958	United States launches first satellite—Explorer I
1958	National Aeronautics and Space Agency (later called Administration) created
1958	American Express introduces first widely available credit card
1958	U.S. airlines carry more passengers than buses and railroads for first time
1958	Regular transatlantic jet service instituted
1958	Integrated circuit board invented
1959	Secretary of Agriculture authorized to distribute surplus food with food stamps
1959	Landrum-Griffin Act places additional controls on union activities
1959	Microchip invented
1959	United States launches first weather satellite—Vanguard II

American corporations initiated more than thirty proxy contests.[49] And so, though the 1950s have often been referred to as the decade of business prosperity, in some respects, it was more difficult to succeed and to retain a steady level of success with a heightened level of public scrutiny.

By far, the largest and most obvious opportunity for business executives was the growing material needs of suburbia. Commercially catering to these needs triggered an explosion of entirely new businesses and product line extensions. One individual who took advantage of this situation was Jack Eckerd. He introduced the self-service retailing model in his drugstore operations and, in the process, built the largest retail drugstore chain in the South. Eckerd was one of the first business managers to recognize the potential of anchoring drugstore chains next to successful supermarkets. Through careful acquisitions and by riding on the coattails of the supermarket expansion in the South, Eckerd doubled the size of his business every two years between 1959 and 1975.[50]

To enhance the scale and scope of their market reach, many businesses also invested in aggressive advertising. Notable individuals who embraced advertising included Bowman Gray Jr. of R.J. Reynolds Tobacco Company and Joseph F. Cullman III of Philip Morris. Cullman's crowning achievement at Philip Morris was the fundamental transformation of the Marlboro brand of cigarettes, which for thirty years had been marketed as a premium-priced cigarette for women. In 1955, Cullman began the transformation of Marlboro by redesigning the packaging and the advertising message. He introduced the red and white flip-top box, which was the "first major packaging innovation in the cigarette industry in a half a century," and rechanneled the market positioning through the creation of the rugged "Marlboro Man," which completely changed the product's image.[51] Heavy advertising investment led Marlboro to become the best-selling cigarette brand in the world by 1972, and Philip Morris became the world's largest cigarette exporter. The company's main competitor, R.J. Reynolds, was also quick to embrace the expanding possibilities of advertising. In 1954, Gray introduced Winston, R.J. Reynolds's first filter-type cigarette, which became one of the nation's top sellers.[52] The vehicle that propelled R.J. Reynolds and Philip Morris to phenomenal growth was mass advertising. What by today's standards could be construed as immoral—the marketing of a cancer-causing agent—was not considered suspect in the prewar consumerism of the 1950s. Irrefutable data on the link between smoking and cancer was still a decade away from the public consciousness.

While many prototypical managers embraced television as a new medium for promoting their products and services, Howard J. Morgens of Procter & Gamble (P&G) did not stop with promotion. As P&G's CEO from the mid-1950s to the mid-1970s, Morgens led the company as its revenues quadrupled, from $1.1 billion to $4.9 billion, and its earnings quintupled, from $67 million to $316 million. Ultimately, this unassuming man helped put the 120-year-old company on a path for success that set its strategic tone for the next half century.

Howard J. Morgens (1910–2000), Procter & Gamble

Born in St. Louis in 1910, Morgens studied liberal arts at Washington University. Hoping to become a playwright or journalist, he helped finance his education by "staging musical comedies, adapting plays for radios, and reviewing drama for the daily newspaper."[53] He supplemented his income by singing with the Municipal Opera and working for the local phone company. He also wrote dozens of short stories and scripts, but publishers failed to show interest. Unable to achieve success in the arts, Morgens sought his fortune in business, having been accepted into the Harvard University Graduate School of Business Administration.

Upon graduating in 1933, he secured a position with Procter & Gamble. Though he had never sold a script, he had little trouble as an entry-level salesman. Having faced countless rejection letters, he was well equipped to handle even the toughest sales calls. This quality was just what Neil McElroy, the pioneer of brand management, saw in the young Morgens when McElroy interviewed him. P&G historian Oscar Schisgall notes that, given the theatrical background of Morgens, "McElroy probably expected a brash young fellow with a multifaceted personality matching the diversities in his resume. Instead he saw a quiet, reserved man of 22, soft-spoken, with remarkably vivid blue eyes and an air of calmness and confidence."[54]

As a junior salesman for the southwest region, Morgens earned $150 per month selling products such as Ivory soap and Crisco from the back of his company-issued Ford Model A. The car bore the moon-and-stars insignia of

Procter & Gamble and served as a "virtual showcase or corner store" for the company's products. Keeping detailed logs about what could be improved in the selling process, he often summarized his findings and sent them to headquarters in Cincinnati. His ideas were so warmly received that he was relocated to Cincinnati in 1934 to work in the national advertising department.

There, Morgens became one of the first executives to assume a position as an advertising brand manager; he was responsible for a new detergent called Oxydol. The previous year, P&G had chosen Oxydol to sponsor its first radio serial—*Oxydol's Own Ma Perkins*. A widow who dispensed advice and told compelling stories, Ma Perkins "spawned an American phenomenon known as 'soap operas' or 'washboard weepers' because of the soap manufacturer's sponsorship and the serial's daily heart-wrenching plots."[55] The radio serial was just one example of the company's aggressive investment in advertising, and that commitment enabled P&G to post record sales and profitability levels despite the Depression. Oxydol's success instilled in Morgens a deep appreciation for the value of advertising.

Throughout the 1930s and 1940s, Morgens progressed through the company, and in 1948 he became vice president of advertising, following in the footsteps of McElroy, who had been named president. It was in this new position that Morgens attached the future of the company's advertising efforts to television. Though P&G had dabbled in television sponsorship in the early 1940s, its efforts were curtailed during the war. But after 1945, Morgens recommended starting an in-house production company to create content for television, and thus began P&G Productions. Although many of the company's first attempts to transform radio serials to television were unsuccessful, one exception was the P&G-sponsored *Guiding Light*. The show transitioned to television in 1952 and has remained on the air ever since. By the mid-1950s, P&G was sponsoring thirteen serial television dramas, including *Search for Tomorrow*, *Another World*, and *Edge of Night*. The content of the 1950s daytime serials was closely aligned with the conformity and wholesomeness of the times. In fact, P&G employed strict guidelines to ensure that the content was acceptable for mainstream audiences. For years, the company was uncompromising in upholding these standards, and as a result, a number of competing soap operas emerged without P&G sponsorship. Free from restrictions, these spin-off dramas often pursued much racier material.[56]

Between 1950 and 1955, P&G fundamentally altered its advertising mix between radio and television. Whereas 97 percent of P&G's broadcast expenditures were allocated to radio in 1950, radio spending had decreased to 20 percent by 1955.[57] P&G's investment in television was virtually unrivaled; only General Motors spent more on television advertising and sponsorship.[58] In naming Morgens to the Hall of Fame for U.S. Business Leadership, *Fortune* magazine noted: "Howard Morgens perceived the potential of television advertising better than any other businessman, and used the new medium to boost his company to colossal gains in revenues and earnings."[59] His success in heading the advertising unit earned Morgens a position on P&G's board of directors in 1950, seven years before he became president.

While functioning as head of the firm's central advertising unit, Morgens was given the added responsibility of running the drug products division. At the time, the division was minuscule compared with the flagship soap/detergent and shortening (food products) divisions. Morgens had only two products, Prell and Drene shampoo, and a national sales force of less than twenty individuals. The other divisions boasted full product lines and sales forces in excess of seven hundred. Despite the division's size, Morgens successfully lobbied to treat the division as an independent entity and secured funding to hire dedicated brand managers, advertising agencies, and product development teams. Even though he initially only had two products, he firmly supported the strategy of dedicated and competing brand managers. As Drene and Prell competed against each other, Morgens invested heavily in new product development and within a few years had two additional strong products—Lilt, a home permanent system, and Gleem toothpaste.

Both products were quickly successful when rolled out nationally, but it was not a quick trip to full release. Morgens was a strong advocate of the company's historical commitment to exhaustive test marketing. Prior to its release, Gleem was test-marketed for almost two years, and upon release, it received another P&G imprint—massive advertising. In 1954, *Advertising Age* reported that P&G had spent between $14 million and $19 million to promote Gleem, which captured 20 percent of the estimated $135 million toothpaste business within twelve months of product launch.[60] Even as Gleem was being test-marketed, Morgens continued to abide by his focus on research and development. In fact, the success of Gleem helped pave the way for the company's best-selling drug item, Crest. Crest eventually put Gleem out of business, but it was just this competitive spirit that fueled new innovations and enabled the company to keep pace with changing consumer trends.

The success Morgens enjoyed in treating the drug products division as a separate corporate entity became the basis for organizing the overall company. Following General Motors' example of organizational design, Morgens had strong decentralized management teams running independent businesses, supported by central administrative functions. On the heels of the new organizational realignment of the company, Morgens was promoted to executive vice president, and in 1957, when Neil McElroy was tapped to be Eisenhower's secretary of defense, Morgens was the board's unanimous choice to take the helm of Procter & Gamble. *Advertising Age* reported: "When P&G had to pick a new president, they went back to the place where they found the old one—the advertising department."[61] That year, P&G spent $57 million on advertising and delivered 79 million selling messages each day.[62]

Though P&G's success in advertising was heralded, it was also problematic for the company. In 1957, soon after he was named president, Morgens was served with an antitrust violation from the Federal Trade Commission for the acquisition of Clorox, a company that P&G had bought earlier that year. The suit was unique in that P&G did not have any similar product lines and therefore was not accused of outright monopolistic behavior. The company was, however, accused of monopolistic intent and potential. The strength of the company's advertising was considered so powerful that when it was unleashed on a product, it had the potential to dominate a market. Though Clorox was already the market leader in bleach products when it was acquired, P&G was accused of trying to defeat all existing or potential competition through the larger company's vast advertising resources. Morgens vigorously fought the suit for almost a decade, but the company eventually had to drop the business. Even so, he was not dissuaded from pursuing a targeted acquisition plan for the company, believing that P&G should diversify.

He expanded the company's product portfolio through acquisitions including Charmin Paper Mills, Duncan Hines, and Folgers & Company. The Charmin acquisition provided P&G with specific knowledge of, and insight into, the disposable-paper-products business, and the company continued to expand its product lines, opening new divisions and research centers. One of these initiatives led to the development of a new disposable diaper, Pampers, which became a best seller. Morgens was attracted to Folgers because of the growing popularity of coffee and its vast market opportunity. In many regions of the country, coffee consumption was higher than any other beverage, and Morgens believed that its characteristics blended nicely with P&G's focused growth strategy. Having no experience in the coffee business, P&G opted to "buy the experience." Folgers, the second-largest U.S. coffee manufacturer at the time, was the company's largest purchase to date, at $130 million. As it had done with Charmin and its fictional spokesperson, Mr. Whipple, P&G supervised a national rollout of the Folgers brand with the introduction of a new fictional character, Mrs. Olsen. This engaging character delivered heart-warming testimonials for the product.

The advertising push for Folgers again caught the ire of federal regulators, who served the company with another antitrust violation in 1966, three years after the acquisition. Hoping to avoid another ten-year legal battle, Morgens negotiated a settlement with the government whereby P&G would refrain from acquiring any household consumer products distributed through the grocery stores for seven years and would not promote Folgers with any other P&G product. Though it had lost the right to continue its acquisition strategy, the company, under Morgens, had developed a successful product-development capability: 75 percent of its offerings in the mid-1960s had been introduced in the previous fifteen years.[63]

Ultimately, Morgens guided P&G from an American-centric soap and shortening company into a diversified, international consumer-products company. Looking back on his success, Morgens credited "product quality, marketing experimentation and meticulous attention to detail—not unique services or in-house geniuses."[64] Though P&G may not have had unique products and services, the manner in which Morgens aligned the strengths of the company with the needs of the marketplace put Procter & Gamble in a league all its own.[65]

Entrepreneurs: Franchising the Landscape

Beyond its sheer size, the physical landscape of the United States and its expanding suburbanization provided fertile ground for some industrious entrepreneurs. By perfecting and capitalizing on a franchise network of affiliated business operations, Richard A. and Henry Bloch, C. Kemmons Wilson, and Raymond A. Kroc created market opportunities based on consistency, reliability, and national scope. In essence, each of these entrepreneurs stretched the decade's preference for conformity to the extreme—recognizing the potential of a mobile, dispersed population.

Richard and Henry Bloch pioneered the franchise tax-preparation business in 1955, as an alternative to the free service offered by the Internal Revenue Service (IRS). Though the IRS sought to simplify the completion of tax returns, it often increased the problems. Many tax forms were erroneously prepared, generating a tremendous amount of complaints and rework. When the IRS decided to discontinue its preparation services in 1955, the Bloch brothers placed a local advertisement for completing tax returns from their Kansas City office. They were inundated with requests, many from places far afield of Kansas City. Believing that they were on the verge of a growth opportunity but unable to personally develop it, they decided to franchise their operation with local accounting teams throughout the country. Beginning in New York City in 1956, the brothers made a profit from the start and soon developed a nationwide network of franchises. By 1978, one in nine tax returns was completed by H&R Block (the business name was changed from *Bloch* to *Block* for ease of pronunciation and spelling).[66]

While the Bloch brothers seized an opportunity in the financial services industry, Kemmons Wilson's entrepreneurial bent filled another kind of void created by Americans' increase in disposable income: child-friendly, affordable vacation lodging. After a family vacation from Memphis to Washington, D.C., exposed the need for a lodging alternative to tourist courts, Wilson decided that he would build a string of slightly upscale motels. Wilson was particularly perturbed at the customary practice of charging a fee for children sharing a room with their parents. He vowed that he would never charge extra for children. Opening his first Holiday Inn in 1951, Wilson expanded his chain through an extensive licensing program. Each Holiday Inn, though operated by a different owner, would be nearly an exact replica of the others, with such amenities as air-conditioning, color television, and a swimming pool. Because of Wilson's strict standards and intensive licensee training programs at Holiday Inn University, he was able to build Holiday Inns into an affordable and popular brand-name motel chain.[67]

The ultimate exploitation of the franchise-based business model, however, emerged from a fifty-two-year-old salesman. At a point in life when most people are planning for their golden years, Ray Kroc was focused on another

Ray Kroc (1902–1984), founder of McDonald's, eating a hamburger in front of one of his neon golden arches.
(Source: Time Life Pictures/Getty Images)

piece of gold—the golden arches of McDonald's. He reflected on his decision to launch a new venture late in life: "I was a battle-scarred veteran of the business wars . . . I had diabetes and incipient arthritis . . . But I was convinced that the best was ahead of me."[68] He was right. From the age of fifty-two to eighty-two, Kroc overcame a multitude of hurdles to build the world's largest franchise network. In summarizing the ascent of McDonald's to the upper echelons of corporate achievement in *McDonald's: Behind the Arches*, John F. Love notes: "The fundamental secret to McDonald's success is the way it achieves uniformity and allegiance to an operating regimen without sacrificing the strengths of American individualism and diversity. McDonald's manages to mix conformity with creativity."[69]

In many ways, Kroc was the epitome of these two seemingly contradictory forces—conformity and creativity. Although his operation was centered on a business strategy that benefited tremendously from consistency, conformity, and reliability, Kroc and his company recognized and rewarded creativity and innovation. The innovation came in the form of new product offerings and new standardized procedures that could be easily replicated. By the end of the century, McDonald's grew from one small operation in Des Plaines, Illinois, to over twenty-five thousand stores in one hundred countries. The McDonald's empire feeds more than 30 million people each day and has the distinction of employing more youth than any other organization in the country. Indeed, with a McDonald's opening every three hours somewhere in the world, the company has come to represent so much more than a quick bite.[70]

Leaders: Working the Food Chain

Where Kroc succeeded by breaking the business mold and creating an industry where there had been none, the leaders of the 1950s found a way to breathe new life into dying industries. As in other decades, opportunities for restructuring existed alongside possibilities for creation and growth. Nowhere was this more the case than in the packaged-foods industry, which wartime had fundamentally altered. As the population surged and as raw material restrictions and rationing were lifted, postwar food processors were faced with completely new market opportunities. Individuals who succeeded reenergized their businesses to serve suburban dwellers seeking convenience and affordability, but, above all, variety.

In the 1940s, food processors were focused on standardization and throughput; given the tight raw-material rationing that was in place, there was no better measure of success than speed and volume. The postwar environment allowed for massive expansion through product line extensions, new introductions, and mergers and acquisitions. Leaders who thrived included Alfred N. Steele of PepsiCo and William Wood Prince of Armour and Company.

Arriving at Pepsi after defecting from an alienating position at Coca-Cola, Steele immediately began a highly involved rehabilitation process at the battered soft-drink maker. Steele's style, considered overly aggressive and flamboyant at Coca-Cola, was just what Pepsi needed to challenge its arch rival. Steele installed a more autonomous management structure, instituted an extensive and aggressive advertising campaign that helped Pepsi grow out of its "poor man's cola" image, and created a vending-machine business. Steele did not stop with advertising; he redesigned the cola's packaging to be more contemporary and built stronger relationships with the company's bottling network. All these changes allowed Pepsi to gain a great deal of market share, which increased from 20 percent to 30 percent. During his tenure, which ended with his unexpected death, he grew income from $1.6 million in 1950 to $11.5 million in 1958.[71]

Meanwhile, Prince at Armour and Company employed a path to grow through investment and automation. After taking the helm in 1957, Prince closed unprofitable lines and incorporated greater automation in the factories, thus reducing overhead expenses by almost 50 percent. He also shifted the company's product focus from fresh meat to precooked specialty meats, which fit nicely with the desires of suburban families. Having revitalized the core business within three years, Prince led the company through a number of acquisitions throughout the 1960s.[72]

While these individuals restructured their operations and expanded product lines for the growing population, one of their peers was revolutionizing the process for transporting their goods. Malcom P. McLean, a truck driver, fundamentally transformed the centuries-old shipping industry, an industry that had long decided that it had no incentive to change. By developing the first safe, reliable, and cost-effective approach to transporting containerized cargo, McLean made a contribution to maritime trade so phenomenal that he has been compared to the father of the steam engine, Robert Fulton.

Malcom P. McLean (1914–2001), SeaLand Service, Incorporated

As a youth growing up on a farm in the small town of Maxton, North Carolina, McLean learned early on about the value of hard work and determination: his father was a farmer who also worked as a mail carrier to supplement the family's income. Even so, when young Malcom graduated from high school in 1931, the country was in the midst of the Depression and further schooling was simply not an option. Pumping gas at a service station near his hometown, McLean saved enough money by 1934 to buy a secondhand truck for $120. This purchase set McLean on his lifelong career in the transportation industry.

McLean soon began hauling dirt, produce, and other odds and ends for the farming community in Maxton, where reliable transportation was hardly commonplace. Eventually, he purchased five additional trucks and hired a team of drivers, a move that enabled him to get off the road and look for new customers. For the next two years, his business thrived, but when poor economic conditions forced many of his newly won customers to withdraw their contracts, McLean scaled down his operation and got behind the wheel again.

During this setback in his life, when he almost lost his business, McLean came across the idea that changed his destiny. The year was 1937, and McLean was delivering cotton bales from Fayetteville, North Carolina, to Hoboken, New Jersey. Arriving in Hoboken, McLean was forced to wait hours to unload his truck trailer. He recalled: "I had to wait most of the day to deliver the bales, sitting there in my truck, watching stevedores load other cargo. It struck me that I was looking at a lot of wasted time and money. I watched them take each crate off the truck and slip it into a sling, which would then lift the crate into the hold of the ship. Once there, every sling had to be unloaded, and cargo stowed properly. The thought occurred to me, as I waited around that day, that it would be easier to lift my trailer up and, without any of its contents being touched, put it on the ship."[73] It would be nineteen years before McLean converted this thought into a business proposition.

For the next decade and a half, McLean concentrated on his trucking business, and by the early 1950s, with 1,776 trucks and thirty-seven transport terminals along the eastern seaboard, he had built his operation into the largest trucking fleet in the South and the fifth-largest in the country. As the trucking business matured, states adopted a new series of weight restrictions and levying fees. Truck trailers passing through multiple states could be fined for excessively heavy loads. It became a balancing act for truckers to haul as much weight as possible without triggering any fees. McLean knew that there must be a more efficient way to transport cargo, and his thoughts returned to the shipping vessels that ran along the U.S. coastline. He believed "that ships would be a cost-effective way around shoreside weight restrictions . . . no tire, no chassis repairs, no drivers, no fuel costs . . . Just the trailer, free of its wheels. Free to be lifted unencumbered. And not just one trailer, or two of them, or five, or a dozen, but hundreds, on one ship."[74] In many ways, McLean's vision was nothing new. As far back as 1929, Seatrain had carried railroad boxcars on its sea vessels to transport goods between New York and Cuba. In addition, it was not uncommon for ships to randomly carry large boxes on board, but no shipping business was dedicated to a systematic process of hauling boxed cargo.

Seeing the feasibility of these types of operations may have inspired McLean to take the concept to a new level. Transporting "containerized cargo" seemed to be a natural, cost-effective extension of his business. McLean initially envisioned his trucking fleet as an integral part of an extended transportation network. Instead of truckers traversing the eastern coastline, a few strategic trucking hubs in the South and North would function as end points, delivering and receiving goods at key port cities. The ship would be responsible for the majority of the travel—leaving the trucks to conduct short, mostly intrastate runs generally immune from levying fees.

With the concept in mind, McLean redesigned truck trailers into two parts—a truck bed on wheels and an independent box trailer, or container. He had not envisioned a Seatrain type of business, in which the boxcar is rolled onto the ship through the power of its own wheels. On the contrary, McLean saw several stackable trailers in the hull of the ship. The trailers would need to be constructed of heavy steel so that they could withstand rough seas and protect their contents. They would also have to be designed without permanent wheel attachments and would have to fit neatly in stacks. McLean patented a steel-reinforced corner-post structure, which allowed the trailers to be gripped for loading from their wheeled platforms and provided the strength needed for stacking. At the same time, McLean acquired the Pan-Atlantic Steamship Company, which was based in Alabama and had shipping and docking rights in prime eastern port cities.

Buying Pan-Atlantic for $7 million, McLean noted that the acquisition would "permit us to proceed immediately with plans for construction of trailerships to supplement Pan-Atlantic's conventional cargo and passenger operations on the Atlantic and Gulf coasts."[75] He believed that his strong trucking company, combined with newly redesigned cargo ships, would become a formidable force in the transportation industry. Commenting on McLean's controversial business plan, the *Wall Street Journal* reported: "One of the nation's oldest and sickest industries is embarking on a quiet attempt to cure some of its own ills. The patients are the operators of coastwise and intercoastal ships that carry dry cargoes."[76] The cure, the article noted, was business operators like McLean who were breathing new life into the shipping industry.

Though McLean had resigned from the presidency of McLean Trucking and placed his ownership in trust, seven railroads accused him of violating the Interstate Commerce Act. The accusers attempted to block McLean from "establishing a coastwise sea-trailer transportation service."[77] A section of the Interstate Commerce Act stated that it "was unlawful for anyone to take control or management in a common interest of two or more carriers without getting ICC's approval."[78] Ultimately unable to secure ICC's endorsement, McLean was forced to choose between his ownership of his well-established trucking fleet or a speculative shipping venture. Though he had no experience in the shipping industry, McLean gave up everything he had worked for to bet on intermodal transportation. He sold his 75 percent interest in McLean Trucking for $6 million in 1955 and became the owner and president of Pan-Atlantic, which he renamed SeaLand Industries.

The maiden voyage for McLean's converted oil tanker, the *Ideal X*, carried fifty-eight new box trailers or containers from Port Newark, New Jersey, to Houston in April 1956. Industry followers, railroad authorities, and government officials watched the voyage closely. When the ship docked in Houston, it unloaded the containers onto trailer beds attached to non-McLean-owned trucking fleets and its cargo was inspected. The contents were dry and secure. McLean's venture had passed its first hurdle, yet it was just one of many obstacles that he encountered. He needed to convince lots of customers to rely less on his former business, trucking. McLean also needed to persuade port authorities to redesign their dockyards to accommodate the lifting and storage of trailers, and he needed to rapidly expand the scope of his operations

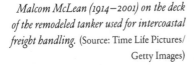

Malcom McLean (1914–2001) on the deck of the remodeled tanker used for intercoastal freight handling. (Source: Time Life Pictures/ Getty Images)

to ensure a steady and reliable revenue stream. Securing new clients proved the least difficult, since McLean's SeaLand service could transport goods at a 25 percent discount off the price of conventional travel, and it eliminated several steps in the transport process. In addition, since McLean's trailers were fully enclosed and secure, they were safe from pilferage and damage, which were considered costs of business in the traditional shipping industry. The safety of McLean's trailers also enabled customers to negotiate lower insurance rates for their cargo.

McLean's next challenge was convincing port authorities to redesign their sites to accommodate the new intermodal transport operation. Although he received his first big break with the backing of the New York Port Authority chairman, McLean continued to run into resistance. The tide did not change until the older ports witnessed the financial resurgence of port cities that had adopted containerization. His business got an additional boost when the Port of Oakland, California, invested $600,000 to build a new container-ship facility in the early 1960s, believing that the new facility would "revolutionize trade with Asia."[79]

The labor savings associated with McLean's intermodal transportation business was a major victory for shippers and port authorities, but it was a huge threat to entrenched dockside unions. The traditional break-bulk process of loading and unloading ships and trucks necessitated huge armies of shore workers. For some ports, the real threat to the industry was not McLean but other modes of transportation that were making ship transport obsolete. By endorsing McLean's business strategy, port officials believed that they were protecting the future of their business. If that meant fewer workers, so be it. They reasoned that it was better to have fewer workers in a prosperous enterprise than many in a declining one.

To achieve the dramatic reductions in labor and dock servicing time, McLean was vigilant about standardization. His efforts to increase efficiency resulted in standardized container designs that were awarded patent protection. Believing that standardization was also the path to overall industry growth, McLean chose to make his patents available by issuing a royalty-free lease to the Industrial Organization for Standardization (ISO).[80] The move toward greater standardization helped broaden the possibilities for intermodal transportation. In less than fifteen years, McLean had built the largest cargo-shipping business in the world. By the end of the 1960s, McLean's SeaLand Industries had twenty-seven thousand trailer-type containers, thirty-six trailer ships, and access to over thirty port cities.[81] With a top market position, SeaLand was an attractive acquisition candidate, and in 1969, R.J. Reynolds purchased the company for $160 million. When he set out to gamble on his idea of containerized cargo, McLean probably did not realize that he was revolutionizing an industry. McLean's vision gave the shipping industry the jolt that it needed to survive for the next fifty years. By the end of the century, container shipping was transporting approximately 90 percent of the world's trade cargo.[82] Though we have coded McLean as a leader in our research, some of his approaches and characteristics have more of an entrepreneurial flavor. There is often a fine line between creation and reinvention, and though the lines sometimes blur, we have generally tended to cite individuals as leaders when their innovations help restructure or reinvent an industry rather than create an entirely new one. For this reason, we see McLean as a leader.

Blinding Prosperity

For better or worse, the 1950s was ultimately a decade in which big business capitalized on the postwar ethos of "live for today, for tomorrow may never come." It was a widespread sentiment, given the destruction Americans had witnessed during World War II. The older, Depression-era generation observed, with wonder and disbelief, as the prewar and wartime values of thrift gave way to consumerism.[83] Indeed, between 1950 and 1955, debt carried by U.S. individuals almost doubled, from $58.7 billion to $110.6 billion.[84]

Although innovation and technical competence were the principal drivers of products in the 1940s, marketing, advertising, and standardization drove products and services in the 1950s. Sales volume was further increased because many products followed a planned-obsolescence life cycle. Successful businesses adopted this use-and-replace strategy, which was aided significantly with the rise in products manufactured with plastic or other synthetic materials. The lack of focus on product quality would eventually become a major liability for U.S. manufacturers, but that was hard to see in the general prosperity of the 1950s and 1960s as corporate profits continued to rise.

TABLE 6-3

Entrepreneurs, managers, and leaders of the 1950s

Entrepreneurs

Desiderio A. Arnaz, Desilu Productions
Ian K. Ballantine, Ballantine Books
Richard A. Bloch, H & R Block
Charles G. Bluhdorn, Gulf and Western
Richard W. Clark, Dick Clark Productions
Richard M. DeVos, Amway Corporation
Berry Gordy Jr., Motown Records
  Corporation
Hugh M. Hefner, Playboy Enterprises
Michael Ilitch, Little Caesar's Enterprises
Ewing M. Kauffman, Marion Laboratories
Raymond A. Kroc, McDonald's Corporation
Alden J. Laborde, Ocean Drilling &
  Exploration
Robert N. Noyce, Fairchild Semiconductor
Kenneth H. Olsen, Digital Equipment Corp.
Franklin P. Perdue, Perdue Farms
Simon Ramo, Thompson-Ramo-Wooldridge
Harland Sanders, Kentucky Fried Chicken
James E. Stowers Jr., American Century
  Companies
Charles B. (Tex) Thornton, Litton Industries
Rose Totino, Totino's Pizza
Jay Van Andel, Amway Corporation
An Wang, Wang Laboratories
C. Kemmons Wilson, Holiday Inn

Managers

Olive Ann M. Beech, Beech Aircraft
  Corporation
Marvin Bower, McKinsey & Company
Francis Boyer, Smith Kline & French
  Laboratories
Herbert P. Buetow, 3M
John T. Connor, Merck & Company, Inc.
Ralph J. Cordiner, General Electric Company
Joseph F. Cullman III, Philip Morris Companies
Harry B. Cunningham, S. S. Kresge Company
Harlow H. Curtice, General Motors Corporation
Morse G. Dial, Union Carbide Corporation
Earl B. Dickerson, Supreme Life Insurance
  Company
Frederic G. Donner, General Motors
  Corporation
Jack M. Eckerd, Eckerd Corporation
Frank M. Freimann, Magnavox Company
Robert W. Galvin, Motorola
Harold S. Geneen, International Telephone and
  Telegraph
Jean Paul Getty, Getty Oil Company

William B. Graham, Baxter International
Bowman Gray Jr., R.J. Reynolds Tobacco
  Company
Walter A. Haas Jr., Levi Strauss & Company
Patrick E. Haggerty, Texas Instruments
Henry F. Henderson Jr., Henderson (H. F.)
  Industries
John M. Hiebert, Sterling Drug
Samuel F. Hinkle, Hershey Foods Corporation
Herbert W. Hoover Jr., Hoover Company
William Irrgang, Lincoln Electric Company
Robert H. Johnson, Ingersoll-Rand Company
John E. Jonsson, Texas Instruments
John W. Kluge, Metromedia
Plato Malozemoff, Newmont Mining
  Corporation
Morton L. Mandel, Premier Industrial
  Corporation
H. Stanley Marcus, Neiman Marcus
Oscar Gustave Mayer, Oscar Mayer
John J. McCloy, Chase Manhattan Bank
John H. McConnell, Worthington Industries
Dean A. McGee, Kerr-McGee Corporation
Donald C. McGraw, McGraw-Hill
Howard J. Morgens, Procter & Gamble
Charles G. Mortimer, General Foods
  Corporation
Walter A. Munns, Smith Kline & French
  Laboratories
Fred M. Nelson, Texas Gulf Sulphur Company
William C. Norris, Control Data Corporation
Guy S. Peppiatt, Federal Mogul Corporation
Wallace R. Persons, Emerson Electric
  Company
Donald N. Pritzker, Hyatt Hotels
Ernesta G. Procope, E. G. Bowman
Lyle C. Roll, Kellogg Company
Frederic N. Schwartz, Bristol-Myers Squibb
  Company
Clarence H. Shaver, United States Gypsum
Elwyn L. Smith, Smith-Corona Marchant, Inc.
Henry Z. Steinway, Steinway and Sons
Robert A. Stranahan Jr., Champion Spark Plug
E. Gifford Upjohn, Upjohn Company
Lillian M. Vernon (Katz), Lillian Vernon
Ernest H. Volwiler, Abbott Laboratories
J. Basil Ward, Addressograph-Multigraph
Thomas J. Watson Jr., IBM
Henry S. Wingate, International Nickel
  Corporation
Paul B. Wishart, Honeywell
Joseph S. Wright, Zenith
Oscar S. Wyatt Jr., Coastal Corporation

TABLE 6-3 *(continued)*

Leaders

Henry C. Alexander, Morgan Guaranty Trust
William M. Batten, JC Penney
Wilton D. Cole, Crowell-Collier Publishing Company
Arthur J. Decio, Skyline Corporation
Armand Hammer, Occidental Oil Company
John R. Kimberly, Kimberly-Clark Corporation
Carl H. Lindner Jr., American Financial Group

Ian K. MacGregor, AMAX
William C. MacInnes, TECO Energy
Malcom P. McLean, SeaLand Service
Donald W. Nyrop, Northwest Airlines
David M. Ogilvy, Ogilvy and Mather
Generoso P. Pope Jr., National Enquirer
William W. Prince, Armour and Company
Robert A. Pritzker, Marmon Group
Alfred N. Steele, PepsiCo
Charles D. Tandy, Tandy Corporation

SEVEN

1960–1969

Business in a Bubble

Come mothers and fathers throughout the land
And don't criticize what you can't understand
Your sons and your daughters are beyond your command
Your old road is rapidly agin'
Please get out of the new one if you can't lend your hand
For the times they are a-changin'.

—Bob Dylan

T HE CRACKS in the social structure of the country were already evident
in the previous decade, despite the best efforts to mask them. By the
1960s, there was no need to search for the cracks; they were everywhere—in
the fight for civil rights, in the struggle for equality of the sexes, in the ques-
tioning of U.S. imperialism, in the clash between the values of the young and
the old, and in the search for meaning beyond material consumption.

America tried to reconcile its perception of itself as a land of freedom and
opportunity with the reality that existed for many. When President John F.
Kennedy uttered the oft-repeated phrase at the end of his inauguration
speech—"ask not what your country can do for you, ask what you can do for
your country"—he may have inadvertently ignited a passion and a yearning
to take up the mantle of both self-improvement and nation-improvement.
Many heeded the call, and the 1960s became embroiled in speeches, protests,
and demonstrations. The quiet certitude of the 1950s was gone, and it was

replaced with chaos and uncertainty. Yet amid this chaotic backdrop, businesses continued to thrive. Though they were impacted by the passage of affirmative action, consumer rights, and environmental protection legislation, businesses remained out of much of the social and political debate.

Business executives were not celebrated as they had been in the 1950s, but they were not under siege, and they were generally not the target of wide-scale protests. The backlash against all authority figures did damage the perception of the "organization man," but on the whole, business executives enjoyed the prosperity that came from continued consumption and growth. The 1960s saw the largest business expansion in American history, with the Dow Jones Industrial Average hitting a record 1,000 in 1966.[1] The intensification of the Cold War hostilities fueled defense spending, and the continuation of the baby boom more than maintained personal consumption. As the consumer revolution unfolded, credit card usage and merchant acceptance soared. For instance, within three months of the 1958 introduction of the American Express card, the company had signed up 253,000 members.[2] By the mid-1960s, under CEO Howard Clark's management, the memorable "Do you know me?" campaign was launched and membership reached millions. Consumers placed a premium on convenience, accessibility, and affordability, and business enterprises that could serve the new disposable society thrived. Service businesses, in particular, emerged to fulfill new consumer desires. For the first time, the number of individuals employed in the service sector exceeded those employed in manufacturing.[3] The nation was shifting the core of its competitive base, and new industry sectors (particularly high-tech sectors and electronics) began to experience dramatic growth.

The Shareholder Is King

Many businesses opted for a growth-oriented strategy that was predicated on unrelated diversification. Business executives could grow their enterprises through acquisitions without the threat of a costly or protracted government lawsuit, but only if the acquired entities consisted of diverse, unrelated operations. During the decade, the government intensified its antitrust intervention and succeeded in blocking all significant mergers, with the exception of one, in an eight-year period.[4] The conglomerate business form skirted much of this antitrust fervor and became a prominent new organizational structure.

The utter uniqueness of the conglomerate business approach has been fodder for considerable analysis and evaluation. Robert Sobel, in *The Rise and Fall of the Conglomerate Kings*, notes: "Conglomerates were the most exciting corporate form to appear in more than a generation, and they shook up the business scene as no other phenomenon had since the era of trust creation at the turn of the century."[5] The principle tenet of a conglomerate was that the "whole was worth more than the sum of the parts," and throughout the 1960s, that maxim appeared to be true. The *New York Times* got caught up in the excitement of conglomerates, even devoting a 1968 magazine story to the new business strategy.[6] The article reported on the financial maneuvering being employed by the wizards of the conglomerate strategy. These individuals included James J. Ling of Ling-Temco-Vought Enterprises, Charles "Tex" Thornton of Litton Industries, Harold Geneen of International Telephone and Telegraph, and Charles Bluhdorn of Gulf & Western Industries. By building their stock price, conglomerates could use the currency embedded in their stock to consummate an acquisition. As the stock market peaked and the economy grew, this strategy seemed to be both logical and profitable. Between 1950 and 1959, 4,789 firms were acquired within the manufacturing and mining sectors, representing $15.4 billion in assets.[7] Between 1960 and 1969, the number of acquired firms jumped to 12,614, with an asset value of $63.3 billion.[8]

Unrelated diversification was not simply the domain of portfolio builders; it became the preferred strategy for a number of mainstream organizations that sought rapid bottom-line growth: Quaker Oats bought a toy company, Johnson Wax entered the personal-care field, Chesebrough-Pond acquired a line of children's clothing, and Loew's expanded from theaters to hotels. These companies and many others like them were skilled at deftly avoiding the ire of government while pursuing a big-business approach. In fact, the takeover mania of the times was so intense that the New York Stock Exchange had to close on Wednesdays for much of 1968 to catch up on the backlog of paperwork.[9] Automation had not yet made its way to the stock exchange.

Shareholder wealth maximization was often the one and only goal of unrelated diversification. Many operators of conglomerates were convinced that what was right for a shareholder was ultimately right for the company—more so than what was right for the customer or what was right for the employee. Consequently, in the big-business search for cash, many employees became

casualties of the conglomerate era. As long as the stock price increased and acquisitions were affordable, no amount of debt seemed too high. Ultimately,
however, the debt burden became unsustainable. When the financial environment quickly changed in the beginning of the 1970s, few conglomerates
were able to survive. One individual who was an adept market watcher
was Henry Singleton. Singleton built one of the largest conglomerates in the
world in the 1960s, and when times changed in the 1970s, he changed with it;
halting all acquisitions and pursuing a much more conservative path. Singleton demonstrated an unusual flexibility in his operating style, but maintained
an unwavering focus on the one principle that got him started and kept him
motivated for three decades—cash flow.

Henry E. Singleton (1916–1999), Teledyne, Incorporated

Forbes magazine once referred to Singleton as "the Sphinx"—one who keeps
his thoughts and intentions secret. Though Singleton may have been hard to
understand, one has little difficulty interpreting the results of his success.
Within seven years, Singleton built Teledyne from scratch into one of the 150
largest and most profitable industrial corporations in the United States.[10] A
multiple-degree holder, Singleton possessed the unique ability to effectively
apply theory to real-world practice. His decisions were not hurried or rash;
they were deliberate and studied. He achieved dramatic and swift growth by
carefully reading the context of the times and adjusting his approach according to the dictates of market conditions.

The son of a successful cattle rancher and cotton farmer, Singleton was
born in 1916 and raised in the small town of Haslet, Texas, on the far outskirts
of Dallas. When he was a young man, he left the Texas farm and did not turn
back. Dreaming of a career as a naval officer, Singleton headed east with an
appointment to enroll in the Naval Academy in Annapolis, Maryland. After
three years at the academy, Singleton developed a stomach ulcer that forced
him to take a medical leave. When he returned to his academic studies, he
transferred to the Massachusetts Institute of Technology (MIT) to study electrical engineering. After earning his bachelor's degree, he stayed on to pursue
a master's degree and later a doctorate, both in electrical engineering. His
doctoral studies were interrupted when he worked for the U.S. Navy's Office
of Strategic Services in Europe during World War II. After the war, he con-

ducted research at General Electric's laboratories, secured a teaching post at MIT, and completed the requirements for his PhD in 1950.

In 1951, Singleton left academia to pursue a career in engineering at Hughes Aircraft in California. At Hughes, Singleton was a part of a team of financial whiz kids, including Roy Ash and Charles B. "Tex" Thornton, who had helped reorganize a struggling Ford Motor Company. After gaining experience at Hughes, Singleton moved to North American Aviation Corporation in 1952, where he assumed control for the development and engineering of navigation systems. Two years later, Singleton joined Litton Industries, an electronics-based conglomerate that had been organized the previous year by Thornton and Ash. At Litton, Singleton experienced the impact and potential of the conglomerate business model. Litton made a practice of acquiring small, financially sound electronics companies that were not the dominant player in their industry sector. In this manner, the company was able to avoid antitrust legislation and cobble together a formidable collection of profitable enter-prises. As its base of businesses grew, so too did its ability to undertake more and larger acquisitions. At Litton, Singleton became the first general manager of the electronic equipment division, and in six years, he built an $80 million business out of virtually nothing.

Singleton might have stayed at Litton for many years had he been able to convince Thornton and Ash that the company should invest in semiconduc-tor technology. His colleagues were adamantly opposed to semiconductors, believing that the sector was already overly crowded and highly competitive. Despite the intense concentration in the industry, Singleton believed that any successful electronics firm should ultimately possess the capability to produce as much as possible in-house. Unable to convince his fellow executives of the value of his proposed approach, Singleton resigned from Litton in 1960 to do it on his own. Fellow employee George Kozmetsky joined him, and both men personally invested $225,000 each in the new business venture. They were supported by an investment of $1 million from venture capitalists Arthur Rock and Tommy J. Davis.

With their initial capital, Singleton purchased the almost defunct Amelco in 1960. Singleton noted that Amelco had no strategic importance, with the exception of providing a base of employment. Having secured the Santa Monica facility, Singleton set up Amelco Semiconductor and lured Jay Last away from Fairchild Semiconductor to manage the operation. Within its first two years, Teledyne used its initial seed capital to acquire five additional small electronic companies, but the initial impetus for real growth came in 1961, when Singleton took the company public and aggressively utilized the exchange of stock to accelerate the pace of acquisitions. Between 1961 and 1964, Singleton orchestrated seventeen acquisitions and grew revenues from $4.5 million to $38 million. In a 1964 *Business Week* article, Singleton outlined his goals for Teledyne. He believed that Teledyne should make a wide variety of products in the fields of automatic controls and communications systems, should make all the components of the systems, and should develop strong capacity in growth-oriented electronics—namely, integrated circuits and semiconductors.[11] He was not about to wait for internal development on any of these fronts. He constantly sought new acquisitions and pushed his executives to the limit, believing that it was even better to "pay employees for vacations they don't take rather than slow production."[12]

Singleton's big break came in 1965, when Teledyne submitted a proposal to the U.S. government for the design and development of an "airborne computer system that would enable helicopters to fly in formation and to fire even under zero-visibility conditions."[13] Singleton's team of scientists was able to secure the lucrative government contract against fierce competition from much larger firms, including IBM and Texas Instruments. Teledyne's remarkable ability to secure the role of prime contractor had a quick and demonstrable impact on the company's stock price. Within one year, it rose from $15 per share to $65.[14] The boost in Teledyne's stock price was just what Singleton had been waiting for. Riding the crest of his own stock price increase and the overall growth in the economy, Singleton pursued a full-fledged, aggressive acquisition strategy.

Over the next four years, Singleton maximized the potential of the conglomerate business model by acquiring over one hundred firms. While he concentrated on acquiring small electronics companies, Singleton also bought firms that produced specialty metals, manufactured consumer products (Water Pik applications and shower massages), and sold insurance. Singleton believed that "the day of the old single-purpose company [was] passing: that to grow, in the future, a company must be prepared to follow where society and technology lead."[15] He understood and followed that technological lead. Throughout his heavy acquisition push, Singleton tried to ensure that no one product or service accounted for more than 3 percent of the company's total business.[16] Teledyne's performance was so strong that, by 1968, it ranked at the top of the *Forbes* list of companies with the highest growth in sales and earnings. As a consummate manager, Singleton had an impressive ability to identify companies that were on the cusp of rapid growth. He knew how and when to deploy scarce resources. Even without the continued acquisition push, the internal growth rate of Teledyne's business empire was often over 20 percent.

Unlike many other conglomerates, Teledyne sought mostly privately owned companies that could benefit from an infusion of cash and professional management. Singleton was not satisfied with steady improvement; he sought geometric growth. Despite a very lean corporate staff office, Singleton maintained tight financial controls. As long as company presidents achieved the set financial hurdles, they were allowed to function autonomously. If not, they were summarily removed. For Singleton, it wasn't personal; it was simply business, and his job was to "squeeze every penny he could to acquire more firms."[17] Singleton made no pretense about his business approach, which even inspired the company's name. *Teledyne* was derived from Greek roots meaning "force applied at a distance."[18] Commenting on his management style, *Business Week* reported that Singleton "is much more intrigued with finance and technology than with the niceties of management technique."[19] Singleton's disinterest even extended to his headquarters office, which, for the first several years, was located in the back alleyway of one of Teledyne's acquired companies in Century City, California.

By the end of the decade, the small plant that Singleton had acquired in 1960 had grown into a $1.3 billion conglomerate made up of 130 companies in a variety of industry sectors. Singleton had successfully leveraged Teledyne's soaring stock price to fund this staggering level of acquisitions. In 1969, the company seemed poised for more acquisitions, but Singleton sensed a softening in the market. He abruptly halted all merger activity and focused attention on shoring up the company's debt exposure. Through his efforts, Teledyne's debt level was reduced to 22 percent of total capital, compared with other conglomerates that had debt ratios hovering above 40 percent.[20] For the next decade, Singleton did not pursue a single acquisition. As the recession of the 1970s unfolded, Singleton's decision to reduce the debt exposure of the company enabled Teledyne to effectively weather the downturn. As the stock market receded, Singleton jumped on the opportunity to buy back his company's stock at often highly depressed prices. By 1976, he had acquired 22 million of the 38 million shares outstanding. Many stockholders were all too willing to surrender their shares in the depressed 1970s. Singleton had steadfastly refused to issue dividends, believing that stockholders could find no better value in which to reinvest their dividends than Teledyne. His argument was hard to refute. Between 1969 (the year the company stopped making acquisitions) and 1978, Teledyne revenues increased by 89 percent, earnings grew by 315 percent, and earnings per share rose by 1,226 percent.[21]

When the business environment changed again in the early 1980s, Singleton changed with it. Teledyne's strong cash position enabled him to pursue a different path. Instead of directly buying companies outright, he bought large blocks of noncontrolling stock in several operations, including his former employer, Litton Industries. Singleton's new portfolio approach to expansion enabled Teledyne to reap the investment return on growth-oriented enterprises without the liabilities associated with managing them and without overpaying for them. Once again, Singleton's timing was right on track, and Teledyne's stock price reached new heights, shooting to upward of $300 per share. Throughout his career, Singleton demonstrated a clear ability to understand market timing. Reflecting on his approach, Singleton once noted: "I believe in maximum flexibility so I reserve the right to change my position on any subject when the external environment relating to any topic changes, too."[22] Singleton's success with Teledyne and the success of business in general seemed almost surreal against the backdrop of the social discord that embroiled and gripped the nation.

Society Reaches the Boiling Point

As the melting pot boiled over, businesses often watched from the sidelines, even when they were directly affected by the fight for civil rights and women's equality. The civil-rights movement that began in earnest in the 1950s gained new momentum in the 1960s. Although the focus of the movement was still centered on greater rights for black Americans, there was an equal and oftentimes more difficult push for enforcement. Ten years after the *Brown v. Topeka Board of Education* Supreme Court decision, which ruled that segregated schools were unconstitutional, 75 percent of the school districts in the South had made no progress toward desegregation.[23] Young black students were the

TABLE 7-1

Social and demographic facts about the 1960s

- 179 million Americans in 50 states; grows to 203 million by 1970
- 850,000 wartime babies enter college
- California becomes the most populous state
- National Organization for Women founded
- Racial riots erupt in Los Angeles in 1966, Detroit in 1967, and 100 other American cities in 1968
- Assassinations of John F. Kennedy, Robert Kennedy, Martin Luther King Jr., and Malcolm X rock stability of nation
- Betty Friedan publishes *The Feminine Mystique*
- Thurgood Marshall, first black justice of the Supreme Court
- "Summer of Love" celebrated in 1967 in Haight-Ashbury area of San Francisco
- Woodstock music festival draws 350,000 in 1969
- Fads: miniskirts, bell-bottom pants, hip-huggers, troll dolls, go-go boots
- Games: skateboards, GI Joe dolls, slot car tracks
- New words: *sit-in, affirmative action, sexism, ageism*
- Minimum wage (1960): $1.00 per hour
- Average annual earnings (1960): $4,743
- Life expectancy (1960): 73.1 years for females, 66.6 years for males

first to take up the charge of enforcement, and they became some of the most devoted followers of Martin Luther King Jr.'s campaign for change. The Student Nonviolent Coordinating Committee (SNCC)—developed as a grassroots effort at high schools and colleges throughout the country—quickly emerged as a driving force in the struggle for recognition and enforcement. Through the use of sit-ins at whites-only lunch counters, theaters, and other public places, SNCC helped turn the tide of public support. The group's efforts were joined by freedom riders, activists who rode buses throughout the South in an effort to force federal protection for blacks.[24]

King's 1963 march on Washington (with 250,000 demonstrators) was the apex of the nonviolent movement. Through his efforts and those of the mostly unknown and unheralded "soldiers of freedom," in 1964 the government backed and passed new civil-rights legislation, which banned discrimination in all public places and in employment. The Voting Rights Act of 1965 paved the way for unrestrictive voter registration, and by 1968, 3 million blacks, representing 60 percent of the black population (the same percentage as for white

Martin Luther King Jr. leading the Selma, Alabama, March for racial equality and voting rights in 1965. (Source: Bob Adelman/Magnum Photos)

voters), had registered to vote.[25] Despite the passage of landmark civil-rights legislation, issues of enforcement still lingered. While King continued the nonviolent struggle, more activist groups took up the call of the disenfranchised. Impatient with the speed of nonviolent resistance, a group of Black Muslims under Malcolm X's leadership advocated swift and radical change.

By the mid-1960s, 70 percent of African Americans lived in metropolitan areas that had mostly been bypassed by the prosperity of the times.[26] Throughout the 1960s, the unemployment rate for blacks was double the rate of whites, and almost 50 percent of all unemployed blacks were at or below the poverty level.[27] The call to action by more militant civil-rights leaders, combined with the dearth of economic opportunities for blacks, sparked a series of riots throughout the country. The intensity of the inner-city violence escalated with the assassination of King in 1968.[28] Though he was but one of hundreds to die for the cause, King symbolized the heart and soul of the fight, and his death ignited riots and protests in over one hundred American cities. The riots and their aftermath made it clear that the fight for equality in legislation and in real economic opportunity would not be silenced.

Emboldened by the legislative success of the civil-rights movement and, more importantly, by the gradual shifts in public perception, the struggle for women's equality also gained new momentum. Betty Friedan struck a deep-seated chord with many women in her seminal work, *The Feminine Mystique*, in 1963. Chronicling the lives of suburban housewives, Friedan uncovered the concealed concerns and hidden dreams of many women who wanted more out of life than being a wife and mother. On the heels of her literary acclaim, Friedan and a small cohort of other social activists formed the National Organization for Women (NOW) in 1966. Friedan served as the organization's first president and fought for equal access to job opportunities and for legalized abortion.[29] Title VII of the Civil Rights Act of 1964, which prohibited job discrimination against race, color, religion, sex, or national origin, became a galvanizing focal point for NOW's legislative agenda. Though they had gained access to the country's premier business schools in the early 1960s and a handful of corporate offices, women still had to contend with the deeply embedded notion of a woman's role in society.[30]

No social group did more to push the limits of individual introspection, self-discovery, and free expression than the youth of the country. Some turned to "sex, drugs, and rock and roll" to find meaning in their lives, and it is often images of their search that one conjures when reflecting on the 1960s. The Federal Drug Administration's approval of the contraceptive pill (Enovid, by Searle) in 1960 did much to further sexual experimentation and lessen inhibitions.[31] The freedom that the contraceptive pill provided seemed tailor-made for the search for peace, harmony, and free love. Though the knee-jerk image of 1960s fashion is tie-dyed shirts, sandals, and love beads, the decade became a fertile ground for the establishment of a considerable number of well-respected designers and retailers.[32] New clothing styles, especially for the growing numbers of working women, combined with the proliferation of suburban retail establishments, enabled fashion-oriented business executives to ride the tidal wave of consumer consumption. During this decade, fashion designers Ralph Lauren, Calvin Klein, and Anne Klein brought respectability and profitability to American fashion.

Beginning his business in 1968, Lauren became one of the most influential contemporary designers, responsible for developing the American look and establishing New York City as a rival to Paris in fashion trends. Lauren manufactured as well as licensed his designs and demonstrated an unusual ability to combine form with function. While Lauren targeted the upscale, relatively conservative segment of the population, Calvin Klein sought to tap into some of the rebellious spirit that fueled the 1960s. He skirted the edge of acceptability with his provocative designs and equally provocative advertising. As Klein concentrated on pushing the envelope in "middle-class fashion," his business partner, Barry Schwartz, oversaw the operations of the business. Schwartz pursued a vertical-integration strategy that enabled the Calvin Klein company to both produce and distribute its designs. Finally, Anne Klein played a major role in targeting fashion designs to working women. Her unique style of interchangeable separates became so popular that it was later adopted by her peers, including Klein and Lauren as well as Liz Claiborne.[33] The ferment of self-expression that found an outlet in the fashion industry also seemed to be tailor-made for the launch of counterculture magazines like *Rolling Stone*, which was formed in 1967 by Jann Wenner, and *Essence* magazine, the first high-fashion magazine targeted to black Americans, launched by Edward Lewis in 1969.

As sensational as the 1960s experimentation process may have been, the reality of the youth movement was more complex. A much larger contingent felt empowered by Kennedy's call to impact the country, and their voices were heard on the lawns of college campuses throughout the country. Many students turned their backs on "the establishment," believing that they were markedly different from their parents and grandparents.[34] They did not blindly accept the government's call to arms—some fled the country, some burned their draft cards, some joined the Peace Corps, and many demonstrated. The single largest demonstration in American history was held in November 1969, when 700,000 people marched into Washington, D.C., protesting the war in Vietnam.[35] What began as a marginalized student revolt

Antiwar student protesters confront federal troops at the Democratic National Convention in 1968.
(Source: Raymond Depardon/ Magnum Photos)

eventually had the power to sway the policies of the nation. In 1965, 61 percent of Americans felt the war in Vietnam was justified. By 1971, the same percentage of Americans held an opposite position.[36]

As riots broke out throughout the country, the government attempted to calm the storm—sometimes with success and sometimes with an escalation of violence. In just a few years, the whole complexion of the nation had been transformed. The "new generation" of Americans that Kennedy had alluded to in his inauguration had taken up the mantle of change, yet their results would almost assuredly not have been recognizable to him when he took office at the dawn of the troubled decade.

Big Government, Big Business

In many ways, Kennedy's election to the presidency foreshadowed the turmoil to come. Though it was the narrowest presidential victory in the twentieth century, the election of the thirty-fifth president was also notable in the role that television played in the campaign process. Over 70 million Americans watched Kennedy debate his Republican rival, Richard M. Nixon.[37] Although political commentators and others who listened to the debates on the radio believed that the candidates had done equally well, those who saw the televised debate gave the edge to Kennedy. He was the first major political contender to successfully harness the power of television. He even acknowledged the power of the medium: "we wouldn't have had a prayer without that gadget."[38] Winning the election by less than 120,000 votes (out of 68 million), Kennedy did not possess the conviction of a popular mandate, and he was always cognizant of that fact.

Although many Americans associate Kennedy with the creation of expansive and inclusive government social programs, Lyndon Johnson was the president most responsible for leading the charge on the war on poverty. Through what became known as the Great Society program, Johnson used his political clout and acumen to shepherd legislation designed to end poverty and racial injustice, to provide economic expansion, and to advance the social and cultural agenda of the nation. Between 1964 and 1966, Congress passed more than 435 bills, including 90 of Johnson's initial 115 legislative actions in his first ten months in office.[39] In addition to the passage of civil-rights and voting-rights legislation, the Great Society program included the allocation of funds for the establishment of Medicare and Medicaid, the expansion of public housing, and broad-scale educational reform. Legislation was also enacted to fund the National Endowment for the Arts, to establish a myriad of job programs for youth, to preserve and protect national parks and landmarks, and to support cleaner environmental standards.

Businesses had a love-hate relationship with government throughout the Kennedy and Johnson administrations. On the one hand, government regulation and scrutiny were intensified, but on the other hand, generous tax concessions and increased defense spending fueled economic prosperity. Kennedy, in particular, did not hesitate to throw the weight of his office against business when necessary. In an effort to contain inflationary pressures early in his administration, Kennedy reached out to the steel industry to hold steel prices steady. Having worked with the United Steelworkers Union to accept only modest wage increases as part of their support for the economic welfare of the country, Kennedy was incensed when he learned that U.S. Steel had announced a major price increase. In a moment of intense frustration and passion, Kennedy was quoted in the *New York Times*: "My father always told me that all business men were sons-of-bitches, but I never believed it till now!" He later claimed that he was misquoted; he said that he was referring not to all businessmen, just steel executives. The passionate utterance was the beginning of an aggressive campaign against U.S. Steel. In a matter of hours, Kennedy unleashed a flurry of investigations into U.S. Steel practices and threatened to cancel government orders for its products. The threat of antitrust legislation, tax investigations, wage and price controls, and canceled contracts was enough for U.S. Steel to retract its price increase within three days.[40] Despite the U.S. Steel experience, businesses generally prospered during Kennedy's tenure. Kennedy reduced tariff rates between the United States and Europe, decreased corporate income taxes, and supported aggressive tax credits and accelerated depreciation allowances for businesses.[41]

Johnson continued Kennedy's efforts to use aggressive tax policies to stimulate the economy. The Revenue Act of 1964 cut taxes by $11.6 billion—$9.2 billion for individuals and $2.4 billion for corporations. In anticipation of more money flowing into the economy, businesses increased their inventory levels. As personal incomes swelled, consumer spending increased, and by 1965, the U.S. gross national product had expanded by over 25 percent in four years. During the same period, industrial production increased by 27 percent, and corporate profits grew by 64 percent.[42] The prosperity resulted in the unemployment rate's dipping below 4 percent in 1966—a rate not seen since 1953.[43]

Though businesses thrived in the 1960s, they were not totally immune from social activism, especially regarding consumer and environmental protection. In 1962, the Kefauver-Harris Amendment to the Food, Drug and Cosmetic Act was passed. This amendment forced pharmaceutical companies to conduct clinical trials for new prescription drugs in the United States and to disclose more fully the potential side effects associated with drug usage. The Food and Drug Administration's oversight was also expanded through the passage of more stringent inspection standards under the Wholesome Meat Act and Wholesome Poultry Act. Government intervention continued into the tobacco industry with the 1964 report that linked tobacco usage to cancer. At the time, tobacco was a huge industry, as almost 40 percent of American adults smoked.[44] Given this statistic, the surgeon general's report was initially released on a Saturday to avoid a dramatic impact on the stock market.[45]

Two prominent social activists used the public forum to advance their causes and, as a result, speed legislative action. In his book, *Unsafe at Any Speed: The Designed-In Dangers of the American Automobile*, Ralph Nader exposed the shoddy workmanship and widespread safety violations of the U.S. automobile industry. At a congressional hearing, he testified that "the automobile industry had permitted stylistic concerns to take precedence over safe design and proper construction." His vigilance against the big automakers helped secure the passage of the 1966 Vehicle Safety Act and Highway Safety Act, which set the foundation for the correction of countless quality flaws and the mandatory phased-in adoption of seat belts, tempered glass, and collapsible steering columns. Nader's efforts were also instrumental in helping set forth more stringent emission-control standards. He went on to be a consumer advocate for a host of products and services, including toys, flammable fabrics, radioactive materials, and consumer credit.[46] As Nader was fighting for consumer rights, marine biologist Rachel Carson began the fight for some of the earth's less vocal creatures. In her work *Silent Spring*, Carson shed light on the environmental impact of pesticide use—especially DDT, dichloro-diphenyl-trichloroethane, which had been heavily used for over twenty years. Her story helped ban the use of DDT in 1969 and laid the foundation for the 1970 establishment of the Environmental Protection Agency.[47]

Ralph Nader advocated for better safety and quality in U.S. automobiles. Nader appears at a Senate Commerce Subcommittee investigation into allegations that he was intimidated and harassed by General Motors for his viewpoints and writings. (Source: Bettmann/CORBIS)

As the economy continued to surge, the impact of the new consumer revolution seemed relatively tame. Increased scrutiny and regulation had not sidetracked business performance. President Johnson could and did take tremendous credit for the vibrant economy, and as the 1968 elections drew near, it seemed that the Democratic Party would be a formidable force. This was not to be, however. The Democrats fell victim to the social discord that was ripping through the fabric of the country, and the party imploded at the 1968 Democratic National Convention, when protesters and the Chicago police force brutalized each other on national television.[48] With Johnson already withdrawn from the presidential race, his Democratic colleagues could not muster the force to defeat Richard M. Nixon. Johnson, who should have been able to catapult his economic success and even his Great Society into further Democratic victories, was derailed and greatly overshadowed by his decisions regarding Vietnam.

Playing Global Dominoes

Historians have argued that Johnson's support of Vietnam was simply an extension of the spiraling commitments made by his predecessors. Kennedy, for his part, spent the bulk of his abbreviated time in office on global affairs. He was elected president at the height of the Cold War and was vigilant in the effort to contain the spread of communism. Even his often-heralded global human service effort, the Peace Corps, was justified as an "interventionist foreign policy [deployed] in parts of the world where ignorance and poverty would likely make the appeal for communism strong."[49]

While Kennedy chose a minimalist response to the almost stealthlike construction of the Berlin Wall in Germany, he was less reticent in dealing with America's neighbor off the coast of Florida. Not long after Fidel Castro overthrew the dictatorship of Fulgencio Batista in 1959, Castro declared the United States an enemy of Cuba and turned to the Soviet Union for both trade support and military protection. At the time of Castro's revolution, U.S. business interests had controlled 80 percent of Cuba's mines, utilities, and ranches and 40 percent of the country's leading export commodity—sugar.[50] Castro confiscated the business enterprises and seized much of the land. One of the last acts of the Eisenhower administration was to cut diplomatic ties with Cuba and authorize the training of a secret military force designed to facilitate a future coup attempt. The decision to deploy the military force rested on Kennedy's shoulders, and his decision to go forward resulted in the embarrassing fiasco at the Bay of Pigs. Kennedy had initially hoped to use the covert force to incite a wide-scale revolution by Cubans, but that never transpired and a humiliated United States withdrew from the island.[51]

Believing that the U.S. humiliation had weakened the country's resolve in the Cold War, the Soviets began to construct missile launch bases on Cuba. During a routine fly-over mission on October 15, 1962, U.S. reconnaissance planes detected eight such sites. The reconnaissance photographs did not indicate that any missiles had been placed on the sites, and Kennedy used this information to enact a naval quarantine. For thirteen days, the U.S. standoff against the Soviet Union played out on the world stage. As the Soviet ships made their way to Cuba, the nation held a collective breath. Kennedy and his administrative team worked behind the scenes to secure an agreement that would enable the two superpowers to pull back from the brink of war. In an exchange for agreeing not to attack Cuba and for the release of some non-strategic missile bases in Turkey, the United States secured Soviet commitment to turn back the ballistic missiles and dismantle the launching sites. The Cuban Missile Crisis did much to strengthen Kennedy's battered reputation and reinvigorated his resolve against communism.[52]

With Cuba's embrace of communism, the fight for Vietnam became an increasingly more important victory for America. Many in government believed that if Vietnam fell to communism, it would be the first domino to fall in Asia. Vietnam had secured its independence from France in 1954, and as part of the peace treaty, the country was split at the seventeenth parallel, with the communist North controlled by Ho Chi Minh and the pro-Western South led by Ngo Dinh Diem. The treaty called for a reunification election in 1956, but fearing that the election would result in a unified and communist Vietnam, the United States made every effort to prevent it.[53]

For several years, the U.S. role in Vietnam consisted mostly of money, arms, and small, strategic military forces. When Kennedy was assassinated in 1963, U.S. forces in Vietnam numbered 16,000.[54] Johnson could have pulled back from Vietnam, but he instead chose to escalate tensions under what became known as the Tonkin Gulf Resolution. Claiming that North Vietnamese communists had viciously attacked two American destroyers in the Gulf of Tonkin, Johnson sought and received authorization from Congress to "take all necessary measures to repel any armed attack against the forces of the United States and to prevent further aggression."[55] Johnson's erroneous claim that the attacks were unprovoked gave him the support he needed for a massive military action. His claim also secured the initial commitment of the American people. Within one year, an additional 160,000 soldiers had been sent to Vietnam, and over the course of the next three years, the number of forces reached a peak of 542,000.[56]

Despite the larger forces and a series of imposing and sustained bombing campaigns, the North Vietnamese were not deterred. They continued to hold their ground and even made inroads into key South Vietnamese towns and villages. As American soldiers returned home with stories of horror and despair, the public sentiment in the country changed. Despite the growing opposition, Johnson's administration maintained its steadfast commitment to prevent the domino from falling. The communist-containment ideology so central to the initial justification of the war was replaced by an even stronger emotional stance—the fear of global humiliation. As it became increasingly clear that an early victory was not at hand, Johnson continued to increase the power and strength of U.S. forces, but with little change in results.[57]

Racing to the Moon

The productive capacity of the United States was not a major factor in the Vietnam War. Unlike World War II and even the Korean War, Vietnam was not a battlefield that could be won with machines. It was a battle of wills fought by individuals. The toll of the war on Johnson and on the psyche of the country as a whole was devastating. America's spirit was broken, and it desperately needed an infusion of hope. The unifying event for the fractured nation came at the close of the decade, when on July 20, 1969, Neil A. Armstrong became the first person to walk on the surface of the moon.

The race to the moon began at the dawn of the decade after Soviet cosmonaut Yuri Gagarin became the first man to successfully orbit the earth. Having already been beaten in the race to launch a satellite into space, Americans became increasingly dismayed at being second best. Gagarin's feat prompted Kennedy to utter the famous statement: "I believe this nation should commit itself to achieving the goal, before this decade is out, of landing a man on the moon and returning him safely to earth."[58] Having invested $33 billion, the United States made good on Kennedy's claim with five months to spare. Armstrong's act of planting the U.S. flag on the rocky surface of the moon was symbolic on a number of levels. While the action demonstrated American technical prowess, it was far more symbolic for the entire country.[59] For a brief period, America could forget the social turmoil in its streets, the losing battle in Vietnam, and the glaring differences that seemed to conspire to rip the nation apart.

The road to space was paved with major advances in technology, especially computer hardware and software. In fact, over 450 computers provided the technical support for the mission to the moon.[60] With the perfection of the microchip in 1961, computers could harness more technical power in a smaller space. Although a major focus on technological development was centered on the space race, the commercial sector benefited tremendously from the advances. Microchips that were originally designed for space-age computer

Buzz Aldrin was one of the first men to walk on the moon during Apollo 11's historic 1969 space mission. (Source: CORBIS KIPA)

consoles found their way into hand-held calculators, watches, radios, and eventually televisions.[61] Though slow to emerge, color television took off in the 1960s and moved from a high-priced novelty to a necessary household item. Throughout the 1960s, U.S. television manufacturers controlled almost 100 percent of the consumer market and felt confident in their leadership role. Despite the emergence of lower-cost, alternative models resulting from highly standardized production processes, U.S. manufacturers continued to focus on technical prowess over cost-effectiveness.[62] TV manufacturers essentially ignored the business lessons from radio. In 1955, U.S. manufacturers controlled 96 percent of the radio production market. By 1965, that number had slipped to 30 percent, and by the middle of the next decade, it was zero.[63] Despite this experience, U.S. television manufacturers believed that technical superiority would trump price, marketing, and even quality. They would soon learn otherwise.

The consumer electronics industry was in full stride throughout the 1960s, as the growing U.S. population seemed insatiable. Companies focused their research and development efforts on new consumer conveniences, especially in the face of growing numbers of two-career families. One device that fit neatly into this new search for convenience was a "radar-based" cooking device, the microwave oven, which was introduced by Raytheon subsidiary Amana Refrigeration in 1967. Convenience and service also emerged within the banking community. The first automatic teller machine (ATM) was installed in 1968 by First Philadelphia Bank. The following year, Chemical Bank decided to make a significant investment in the new device and, in so doing, ushered forth the beginnings of a fundamental shift in its business operations.[64] The introduction and use of ATMs was the culmination of a long, concerted effort to search for automation, which would help companies move from customer service to self-service and from human to computer intervention.

Labor Strains

The initial proving ground for automation was not focused on the end-stage interaction with the customer; it was focused on the internal efficiency of the operating shop floor. As the push for factory standardization continued, numerical control devices were introduced as a means of replacing skilled machinists. Numerical control devices are programmable, general purpose machinery used to automate certain manufacturing functions. These automated machines were often deployed in hazardous work environments or in areas with a shortage of skilled labor. The movement to replace skilled laborers with automation was also motivated by factory managers who had long grown intolerant of work stoppages and union demands. The focus on productivity, especially for government contract work that required tight tolerances, also contributed to the focus on automation. The investments in numerical control devices and other forms of factory automation were part of the gradual process of shifting the skill levels and requirements of the nation's workforce. In the late 1960s, automation made inroads into the clerical sphere, as bookkeeping, payroll, and other financial-management tasks began to be performed more efficiently with the benefit of computer technology.[65]

The focus on standardization and productivity was further intensified during the age of conglomerates. Since the conglomerate business approach was based mainly on financial performance, any impediment to improved profitability was quickly removed. It was not unusual for an acquiring company to sell off or close down unprofitable operations or to attempt to orchestrate bargaining agreements across diverse business entities within its portfolio. Acquiring companies often took a very hard line with unions, threatening to eliminate entire product lines if unions did not acquiesce to management demands. In the late 1960s, General Electric, under the guidance of Vice President Lemuel Boulware, was especially vigilant in antiunion activities. In fact, the coined word *Boulwareism* came to represent tactics that undermine union activities and force offers on a take-it-or-leave-it basis.[66]

Despite the hardened attitudes of some business executives, the booming economy of the 1960s overshadowed the impact of automation and conglomeration on most of the nation's laborers. Certainly, the working conditions and opportunities for individuals (especially women and minorities) benefited from some of the social activism of the times. Though twenty-six states had already passed a local version of the Equal Pay Act, the federal legislation provided a legal basis for forcing equity in pay scales for the same jobs performed by men and women. While the act stopped short of defining pay standards for "equivalent" opportunities, it did provide a foundation for legislative action. The provisions of the Equal Pay Act were strengthened by the inclusion of Title VII in the 1964 Civil Rights Act. Title VII provided the first viable recourse for victims of employment discrimination and became the basis of affirmative-action programs.[67] Despite losing some ground as technology encroached on its domain, skilled labor benefited from more inclusive legal protection. What was more important, the government's effort to become more active in labor issues set a new foundation for trilateral cooperation between workers, managers, and government officials.

The conglomerate movement and the focus on automation also had a direct impact on the concentration of workers in large companies and in the nature of their work. By the middle of the decade, 42 percent of the civilian labor force was employed in companies with over 10,000 employees, and 15 percent were in firms with over 100,000 people.[68] In contrast, the number of farmers in the United States continued to decline. By 1966, only slightly more than 5 percent of the U.S. labor force was employed in agriculture, and as businesses continued to prosper, they were willing and able to absorb the mostly unskilled labor moving from the farm to the factory.[69] Automation had a two-pronged impact on opportunities for workers. On the one hand, new opportunities for unskilled laborers abounded as the need for numerical machine operators, keypunch operators, and maintenance clerks increased. On the other hand, automation provided opportunities for highly skilled workers who could devise the programs and procedures, which would allow computer technology to achieve its purported objectives. Individuals like H. Ross Perot of Electronic Data Systems Corporation and Max Palevsky of Scientific Data Systems contributed to, and benefited from, the move toward greater automation on the factory floor and in the office. As companies sought to maximize the potential of automation, they often looked outside the country's borders to broaden the available, skilled resource pool.

Population Boom Continues

The Immigration Act of 1965 fundamentally changed the discriminatory immigration quota practices in place since the mid-1920s. The new act, which was part of Johnson's Great Society, treated all nationalities on an equal basis, not as part of a specific numerical quota. The act set forth a stipulation of no more than 20,000 immigrants from any nation, with a total of roughly 290,000 immigrants per year—170,000 outside the Western Hemisphere and 120,000 within it. Though the new act provided broad-scale hemispheric restrictions, it did not place any such restrictions on the immigration of family members. Those seeking political asylum from persecution in their homelands and those who had unique skill sets (such as computer technology) were also granted preferential treatment. Over the ensuing years, the United States benefited from a "brain drain" of skilled and professional talent from around the world.[70] Businesses and unions supported the change in immigration policies; both believed that it provided access to a pool of new skilled members.

The immigration legislation changed the composition of new entrants into the United States (more from Asia and Mexico) and stabilized the overall process. Throughout the 1960s, the number of immigrants averaged 320,000 per year.[71] Although more than 3 million immigrants came to the United States during the decade, they represented just 13 percent of the nation's overall population growth. The 1960s saw the continuation of the baby boom, with a total increase in the population of roughly 24 million—from 179 million to 203 million. It was this growing population that helped fuel the consumption economy of the 1960s and became one of the fundamental factors in an ever-expanding business community.

Entrepreneurs: Recognizing the Value of the Consumer

In many ways, navigating the booming economy became a prerequisite for success for any business executive. While managers used their financial skills to build conglomerates, entrepreneurs used their understanding of finance in a very different way. Entrepreneurial executives focused on the core drivers of financial performance—employees and customers—and built businesses on the premise of value, volume, and cost efficiency.

Concentrating on a regional, low-cost, customer-focused strategy, entrepreneurs Herb Kelleher of Southwest Airlines, Sam Walton of Wal-Mart, and Paul Henson of United Utilities broke all the molds of past success within their respective industries. Though all these men began from a strong regional marketplace, they built companies of national scale and scope. In many ways, they were ahead of the curve in understanding the needs and, more importantly, the underlying desires of their consumers.

Kelleher developed the plan for the low-cost, highly profitable Southwest Airlines on the back of a napkin. His plan to initially offer twenty-dollar airfares from Dallas to Houston was vehemently opposed by larger carriers, which

TABLE 7-2

Business events that shaped the 1960s

Date	Event
1960	United States begins trade embargo against Cuba
1960	Enovid, first birth-control pill, approved for sale by FDA
1960	First laser created at Hughes Research Laboratory
1961	FDA requires cosmetic makers to pass safety clearances
1961	Valium invented
1961	Food Stamp Program initiated to combat poverty and boost farm income
1961	East Germany builds Berlin Wall
1961	Conglomerate boom begins
1962	Trade Expansion Act reduces tariffs
1962	John Glenn—first American to orbit the earth
1962	Cesar Chavez forms United Farm Workers
1962	Cuban Missile Crisis
1962	Rachel Carson's *Silent Spring* serialized in *The New Yorker*
1963	Equal Pay Act prohibits pay differences between men and women doing work of equal skill
1963	Clean Air Act passed
1964	President Johnson outlines "Great Society"
1964	Government study links cigarette smoking to lung cancer
1964	President Johnson signs $11.5 billion tax-reduction bill
1964	Anti-Poverty Bill passed
1964	Gulf of Tonkin Resolution passed, escalates U.S. role in Vietnam
1964	Civil Rights Act passed
1964	Economic Opportunity Act provides job-relief programs

feared their own demise. Their fears were not without merit. Once he gained approval for his low-cost airline, Kelleher dominated the market. Southwest redefined air travel through its low-cost, no-frills, no-reserved-seating approach. Kelleher knew early on that the only differentiating factor between Southwest and its competitors was its approach to customers and employees. The planes, gates, and destinations were the same. Southwest's highly participative corporate culture rewarded initiative and service and played a large role in a strike-free, unbroken record of consistent profits.[72]

Walton also achieved great success at Wal-Mart by focusing on customers. Walton was particularly interested in serving an often-ignored group of consumers, small-town, rural residents. He did so by doing the unthinkable—

TABLE 7-2 *(continued)*

Date	Event
1964	BASIC programming language invented
1964	IBM rolls out first mass-produced operating system, OS/360
1965	Antipollution bill requires emission standards for new cars and trucks
1965	Medicare and Medicaid created
1965	Ralph Nader publishes *Unsafe at Any Speed*
1965	Digital Equipment Corporation introduces first minicomputer
1966	National Traffic Safety Agency created
1966	Truth-in-Packaging Bill requires food labeling to identify contents
1966	Motor Vehicles Safety Act regulates emission controls
1966	First handheld calculator introduced by Texas Instruments
1966	Dow Jones Industrial Average tops 1,000 for first time
1966	National Football League merges with American Football League
1967	AT&T introduces "800" toll-free number
1968	Unemployment hits 15-year low—3.3 percent
1968	Truth-in-Lending Act passed
1968	New York Stock Exchange records highest trading day since October 1929—16.4 million shares
1968	Oil discovered in Alaska's Prudhoe Bay
1968	U.S. automakers required to add safety equipment
1969	DDT banned by Department of Agriculture
1969	Neil Armstrong first man to walk on the moon
1969	Artificial heart invented
1969	ATM invented

opening huge discount superstores that sold a wide variety of low-priced goods. Most major retailers believed that the base of consumption in rural areas was too small to generate significant return and virtually ignored them. Walton thought otherwise and proved that this underserved, undervalued constituent was a true gem. For almost twenty years, Walton was unchallenged in rural America, and during that time, he built a nationwide network of highly profitable discount stores.[73]

Henson took a small, regional telephone company in Nebraska and transformed it into the number-three telecommunications company in the United States. When Henson joined United Utilities, it had 500,000 customers, served five hundred rural communities, and generated sales of $42 million.

Stepping into the CEO role in 1964, Henson took advantage of the economy to embark on an acquisition spree, buying twenty-eight companies in five years. Henson differentiated his operation by offering lower costs and better technology. Through his foresight, the company was an early adopter of fiber-optic technology, which enabled the company to spring onto the national stage and leapfrog the outmoded equipment and infrastructure of its competitors. The new technology, in turn, provided a cost-effective platform in a highly price-sensitive market.[74] Generating a breakthrough idea or business structure often resulted in long-term market dominance if constant attention was paid to execution and differentiation.

Leaders: Making Businesses Young Again

Leaders demonstrated that a company was never too old to rejuvenate itself. The story of Black & Decker provides good evidence of this principle. When the Apollo 11 astronauts returned to earth in 1969, they brought with them sample particles they had collected from the surface of the moon. Hoping to better understand the composition of the lunar surface, National Aeronautics and Space Administration (NASA) astronauts, in a subsequent mission, brought with them a battery-powered Black & Decker drill, which enabled them to penetrate fifteen feet into the moon's core. NASA had chosen Black & Decker, because "like everything else that went to the moon, the drill had to be small, lightweight, and battery-powered."[75] The specialty-built, cordless drill included an advanced computer program that maximized the boring capabilities of the drill while minimizing the expense of power. Though dramatic in its application, Black & Decker's participation in the space race was a natural extension of Alonzo G. Decker Jr.'s efforts to build the do-it-yourself product market in the United States. Decker moved the family company from a 100 percent focus on business-to-business tools to one focused on the household consumer.

As the company moved into the consumer marketplace, Decker invested heavily in research and development. The company's investment in advanced batteries that would later become a critical component of the lunar drill was kept a secret, even from the sales force, until it was displayed before "incredulous Wall Street analysts."[76] The battery-powered drill was viewed as a turning point in credibly serving the individual market. From this base, the company pursued a massive effort to launch a series of home-based cordless products, including grass trimmers, hedge shears, screwdrivers, and saws. Decker's transformation of the company on the cusp of the suburban revolution enabled it to reap enormous benefits. Throughout the massive expansion of the 1960s, Black & Decker averaged a 15 percent annual growth rate for sales and earnings.[77] By the end of the decade, 60 percent of sales were derived from individual customers doing home repairs.[78]

The process of breathing new life into a tired or old business often became a matter of survival. Even when the stakes were extremely high and the investment almost insurmountable, business leaders often had no choice. They could gamble for a better future or settle for an inevitable slow demise. This was a choice faced by F. Kenneth Iverson when he was handed the reins of Nuclear Corporation of America.

F. Kenneth Iverson (1925–2002), Nucor Corporation

In their *Making It in America*, Jerry Jasinowski and Robert Hamrin aptly sum up the challenge that Iverson faced: "Should he follow conventional theory and practice a management style based on union power in an oligopolistic industry or should he break the mold and fashion a new type of steelworker?"[79] Time and again, Iverson chose to forge a new path. His courage and determination enabled him to face down age-old conventional wisdom and, more importantly, his own inner doubts. Although the implications of his actions have been compared to the legacy of Andrew Carnegie, working for a steel company was that last thing Iverson expected to do with his career. When he was a twenty-two-year-old master's student at Purdue University, Iverson took a field trip to an integrated steel producer. He recalled: "We were going through the plant, and we actually had to step over workers who were falling asleep there. I decided right then that I didn't ever want to work for a big steel company."[80] Iverson's conviction was only half right. He did not work for a big steel company; he built his own.

Iverson was born in 1925 in Downers Grove, Illinois, a small, rural community outside Chicago. Iverson's mother was from a farming family, and as a child, Iverson spent many vacations with his relatives on the farm. His experience with the work ethic and the pride of farmers would later strongly influence whom he hired and where he located his facilities. Iverson's father, an electrical engineer, was the superintendent of equipment for Western Electric and was principally responsible for all installations west of the Mississippi. Iverson followed in his father's footsteps, majoring in engineering at Cornell University. While at Cornell, Iverson also served in the U.S. Naval Reserves unit during the final years of World War II. Upon graduation from college, Iverson enrolled in a master's degree program in metallurgy and mechanical engineering at Purdue.

When Iverson graduated in 1947, he secured a position as a research physicist for International Harvester in Chicago. Iverson spent five years with International Harvester, the last big, established company he would work for. Though he enjoyed his experience there, he believed that the sacrifice for working for a big corporation was too much to pay. In his book *Plain Talk*, Iverson explained this view: "The behemoth that provides for you demands more than your honest effort in return. It extracts a measure of your individuality, as well."[81] Leaving International Harvester in 1952, Iverson spent the next ten years working for a variety of small, scientific-based manufacturers, including Coast Metals in New Jersey, where he served as executive vice president for this producer of hot-alloy welding rods.

Kenneth Iverson (1925–2002, center) of Nucor Corporation attends a meeting of the International Industrial Development Conference. Iverson's Nucor became one of the few U.S.-based steel mills to effectively compete with imports. (Source: Time Life Pictures/Getty Images)

When Nuclear Corporation sought to acquire Coast Metals, it encountered Iverson during the due-diligence process and was impressed with Iverson's capabilities. Nuclear Corporation hoped to secure his services as a future leader of the acquired company, but this plan did not sit well with the then current president of Coast Metals. To avoid a protracted legal battle, Iverson decided to leave the firm. Though the acquisition was not consummated, Nuclear asked Iverson to help it evaluate another acquisition target—Vulcraft Corporation in South Carolina. Iverson accepted the offer and ultimately recommended that Nuclear purchase the manufacturer of steel joists and industrial girders. Nuclear not only purchased Vulcraft, but also convinced Iverson to become the general manager of the facility.

In 1962, Iverson relocated from New Jersey to South Carolina. In many ways, Iverson was unprepared for the distinct segregation ingrained in the working environment of the company. At Vulcraft, there were separate work spaces, entrances, bathrooms, and cafeterias for black workers. Reflecting on his initial experience at Vulcraft, Iverson noted: "I didn't come to South Carolina to combat racism. I came to manage. I had a business to run, and I knew that to make Vulcraft perform the way I knew it could, I'd have to convince everyone to work together and to respect one another as equals."[82] Iverson knocked down the walls that separated the workers and began his battle against the we-versus-them mentality. His early experience with Vulcraft played a large role in his subsequent approach to managing employees—minimizing levels of management, providing tangible and achievable financial incentives, and listening to ideas and suggestions from every level. His commitment to the employees of Vulcraft was also a significant factor in defeating union-organizing activities.

Between 1962 and 1964, Iverson's efforts resulted in a tripling of sales and earnings. Vulcraft was the only bright star in the Nuclear conglomerate. Though its stated purpose was to build an organization that could keep the "US competitive in the atomic age," Nuclear Corporation had pursued a haphazard, opportunistic acquisition strategy. There was no link between the acquired companies, no apparent focus on atomic energy, and even less management oversight. By 1965, the company was on the brink of bankruptcy, and its managers were leaving in droves. Iverson was also contemplating his next move. In the midst of this upheaval, the corporate controller, Samuel Siegel, who had already tendered his resignation, offered to come back if Iverson was made president of Nuclear Corporation. As controller of the parent company, Siegel could not help but be impressed with Vulcraft's results. The board agreed to Siegel's conditions, and Iverson was named the head of the almost defunct conglomerate. Iverson and Siegel became a formidable pair, tempering expansive vision with financial practicality. The company that Iverson agreed to lead had 1965 sales of $22 million, with a net loss of $2.2 million.

Despite the otherwise booming economy, the acquisition days of Nuclear Corporation were over. Just twelve days after he assumed the presidency, Iverson announced a massive divestiture effort, which resulted in the sale or closure of more than half of the company's operations. The base of the business became Vulcraft, and in early 1966, Iverson decided to move the headquarters office from Phoenix, Arizona, to Charlotte, North Carolina, to be closer to the main assets of the firm. When the move was announced, twelve of the thirteen corporate staff members quit, believing the company was destined for extinction. Iverson and Siegel made the trip east and set up headquarters in a nondescript office strip, using a folding table and a few stray office chairs. Over the years, despite massive success, the two maintained the same level of frugality.

Within one year, the business was back in the black; it remained there throughout the next three decades. By concentrating on the joist and girder business of Vulcraft, Iverson had built it into a market leader. Despite his concentrated success, however, he was concerned with the volatility of the company's cost structure. The company was spending more than half of its sales dollars in steel costs and was securing 80 percent of its steel needs from Europe. Iverson believed that Nuclear Corporation could produce its own steel requirements, and though the company was just reemerging from the brink of disaster, he decided to gamble on its future.

Though virtually all steel in the United States was fabricated at integrated mills, Iverson decided to borrow a new continuous-casting technology prevalent in Europe and Japan: the steel mini-mill. As described by Iverson, the mini-mill "does not have ore mines, nor does it have blast furnaces, nor does it have coal mines."[83] It essentially reprocesses scrap metal through an electric furnace into reusable steel products like bars, structural shapes, and rods. The output was well suited for industrial applications such as joists and girders, not highly refined consumer products. Iverson's first mini-mill was built in 1968 in the farming community of Darlington, South Carolina. Iverson explained his rationale for building in small towns: "You generally get farm-oriented people. They have a good work ethic. They know which end of the wrench to hold. They are mechanically inclined."[84] He also understood the responsibility of being the largest employer in a region, and that knowledge played a significant role in crystallizing a key component of the company's management philosophy: "when times are tough, everyone shares the pain."

Iverson believed that his company could gain cost and time efficiencies by acting as its own general contractor, and with the construction of its first mini-mill, Nuclear Corporation began a long tradition of building its own facilities. Within nine months of breaking ground in Darlington, the mill was operational, and soon thereafter, it was also profitable. The investment in technology, combined with a nonunion workforce, enabled Nuclear to produce steel at a fraction of the cost of the large, integrated mills in the United States. What's more, without having to incur high shipping costs, Iverson was able to beat the prices of foreign competitors. With the success of Darlington, Iverson soon commissioned the construction of additional mini-mills, and in 1972, the name of the company was formally changed to Nucor Corporation.

Throughout the 1970s, Iverson continued to expand the company's mini-mill operations, even though investment in steel appeared to be counterintuitive. During this time, the U.S. steel industry suffered a major decline as a recession crippled both the construction and the automobile industries. To make matters worse, the steel market was flooded with cheap imports. The combination of these factors sent many long-standing steel giants to the grave, yet Nucor flourished. Within a decade, Nucor had become the most profitable carbon-steel-manufacturing operation in the world and the only U.S. operation to match or beat the prices of foreign imports. Iverson attributed only a small fraction of the company's success to its technology investments: "our culture accounts for more than half of our success as a business."[85]

That culture was based on a set of key business premises. First, Iverson placed decision-making control in the hands of his plant general managers, believing that they were in the best position to assess the needs of their individual operations. Iverson was a stickler for the minimization of management layers. Even as the company grew to become the second-largest steel producer in the United States, it retained no more than four layers in its organizational hierarchy and fewer than twenty-five employees in its headquarters. With this emphasis on local autonomy came a responsibility to push the envelope and to take risks, and it was often from these risks that additional productivity gains were achieved. Second, Iverson instituted an innovative incentive program, which enabled all workers to receive substantial performance-based compensation and became a strong deterrent to union organizing. While the base pay for Nucor employees (both on the production line and in management) was roughly 70 percent of comparable base rates for other steel firms, the addition of productivity incentives pushed overall compensation well ahead of rivals. For factory workers, incentive compensation was tied to team-based productivity. Factory teams were evaluated on their overall throughput and the quality of their final product. When teams earned incentive pay, it was included in their next paycheck. In that way, they could immediately see the tangible results of their efforts. During downtimes, Iverson adopted a "share the pain" plan, which resulted in a reduced work week for production workers and a decrease in compensation for management. Through this plan, Nucor avoided any staff reductions in an industry that had been notorious for its lack of security. Finally, all employees, regardless of level, were treated equally. There were no company cars, no reserved parking spaces, no executive dining rooms, no corporate jets, and no first-class airfare for executives.

From the beginning, Iverson was firmly committed to the company's culture. As Nucor became one of the largest industrial operations in the United States, his commitment did not waiver. In fact, his company's culture became a key ingredient in Nucor's success when it continued to launch new technologies to compete with the high-end products produced by other integrated steel mills in the United States. Iverson successfully challenged the heart of the old-line steel industry, but he did not just reinvent its technology base. Instead, he turned the practice of management on its head.[86]

The Bubble Bursts

The contextual landscape of the 1960s (e.g., heightened geopolitical tensions, higher government scrutiny, and massive social unrest) was generally more intense than the 1950s, but the conditions for an expanding economy still prevailed. In many ways, this business success in the face of a fundamentally changed context would fuel a sense of invincibility and arrogance. Throughout most of the post–World War II period, American businesses could operate without credible competition, without regard for the desires and needs of customers, and without fear of squandering the nation's seemingly unlimited natural resources. Many business executives were wholly unprepared for the new reality of the 1970s, when each of these dynamics fundamentally changed. As American homes became saturated with appliances, televisions, and other gadgets, it became clear that the quarter-century "wave of industrial expansion" had come to an end.[87] That it ended at a low point in the country's self-confidence and in the midst of a crippling oil-induced recession only exacerbated the problems for business. Business executives who blindly followed the path of the past were unprepared for international competition, scarcity of capital, and intensified government regulation. Where the 1960s had been about unbridled growth, the 1970s were about survival.

TABLE 7-3

Entrepreneurs, managers, and leaders of the 1960s

Entrepreneurs

Mary Kay Ash, Mary Kay Cosmetics
Frank Batten, Landmark Communications
Warren E. Buffett, Berkshire Hathaway
Mervyn E. Griffin Jr., Griffin Productions
Bruce D. Henderson, Boston Consulting Group
Paul Henson, United Utilities/Sprint Corporation
William R. Hewlett, Hewlett-Packard Company
Amos Hostetter Jr., Continental Cablevision
Herbert D. Kelleher, Southwest Airlines
Anne Klein, Anne Klein & Company
Ralph Lauren, Polo, Ralph Lauren
Mary W. Lawrence, Wells, Rich and Greene
Mark H. McCormack, International Management Group
Patrick J. McGovern, International Data Group
William G. McGowan, MCI Communications
Robert G. Mondavi, Robert Mondavi Winery
Thomas S. Murphy, Capital Cities/ABC
Jean Nidetch, Weight Watchers International
M. Kenneth Oshman, Rolm Corporation
Max Palevsky, Scientific Data Systems
Jeno F. Paulucci, Jeno's Frozen Pizza
H. Ross Perot, Electronic Data Systems
Thomas B. Pickens, Mesa Petroleum Company
Sumner M. Redstone, Viacom
Steven J. Ross, Warner Communications
Pete Rozelle, National Football League

W. Jeremiah Sanders III, Advanced Micro Devices
Richard M. Schulze, Best Buy
Muriel Siebert, Muriel Siebert & Company
Robert E. (Ted) Turner, Turner Communications
Samuel M. Walton, Wal-Mart
Leslie Wexner, Limited (The), Inc.

Managers

Terrence E. Adderley, Kelly Services
Robert O. Anderson, Atlantic Richfield Company
Paul R. Andrews, Prentice-Hall
Roy L. Ash, Litton Industries
J. Paul Austin, Coca-Cola Company
Edward J. Bednarz, Pinkerton's
Eugene N. Beesley, Eli Lilly and Company
Glen W. Bell, Taco Bell Corporation
William Blackie, Caterpillar Tractor Company
Fred J. Borch, General Electric Company
John Y. Brown Jr., Kentucky Fried Chicken
Willibald H. Conzen, Schering-Plough Corporation
Bert S. Cross, 3M
Fred DeLuca, Subway Sandwiches
Bernard A. Edison, Edison Brothers Stores
Louis K. Eilers, Eastman Kodak Company
John C. Emery Jr., Emery Air Freight

(continued)

TABLE 7-3 *(continued)*

Donald G. Fisher, Gap
Richard M. Furlaud, Squibb Corporation
Henry W. Gadsden, Merck & Company, Inc.
Edward G. Gardner, Soft Sheen Products
Maurice R. Greenberg, American International
   Group, Inc.
Robert C. Guccione, Penthouse International
   Limited
Ralph A. Hart, Heublein
Stuart K. Hensley, Warner-Lambert
   Corporation
Wayne Hicklin, Avon Products
E. G. Higdon, Maytag Corporation
Philip B. Hofmann, Johnson & Johnson
   Company
Carl C. Icahn, Icahn & Company
John K. Jamieson, Exxon Corporation
Mitchell P. Kartalia, Square D Company
Erwin Kelm, Cargill
Donald M. Kendall, PepsiCo
William F. Laporte, American Home Products
Edward T. Lewis, Essence Communications
Peter B. Lewis, The Progressive Corporation
Ray W. MacDonald, Burroughs Corporation
Forrest E. Mars Sr., Mars
Jack C. Massey, Hospital Corporation of
   America
Thomas S. Monaghan, Domino's Pizza
Ray T. Parfet Jr., Upjohn Company
Charles M. Pigott, PACCAR
Thomas M. Rauch, Smith Kline & French
   Laboratories
Jean Riboud, Schlumberger, Limited
Cedric H. Rieman, Gardner-Denver Company
Leonard S. Riggio, Barnes & Noble
David Rockefeller, Chase Manhattan Bank
Willard F. Rockwell Jr., Rockwell International
Francis C. Rooney Jr., Melville Corporation
Joseph L. Rose, Deluxe Check Printers
Barry Schwartz, Calvin Klein
Robert B. Shetterly, Clorox Company

Henry E. Singleton, Teledyne, Incorporated
William F. Souder Jr., Marsh & McLennan
Robert D. Stuart Jr., Quaker Oats Company
R. David Thomas, Wendy's International, Inc.
John P. Thompson, Southland Corporation
Laurence A. Tisch, Loew's
Jane Trahey, Trahey Advertising
Charles R. Walgreen III, Walgreen Company
Henry G. Walter Jr., International Flavors &
   Fragrances
Sigfried Weis, Weis Markets
Jann S. Wenner, Rolling Stone Magazine
George H. Weyerhaeuser, Weyerhaeuser
   Company
Walter B. Wriston, Citibank/Citicorp
Vincent C. Ziegler, Gillette Company

Leaders

W. Michael Blumenthal, Bendix Corporation
Howard L. Clark, American Express Company
Alonzo G. Decker Jr., Black & Decker
   Corporation
Jerry Della Femina, Della Femina and
   Travisano
Katharine M. Graham, Washington Post
Amory Houghton Jr., Corning Glass Company
F. Kenneth Iverson, Nucor Corporation
Samuel C. Johnson II, Johnson Wax Company
Howard B. Keck, Superior Oil Company
William F. Kerby, Dow Jones & Company
Edgar F. Luckenbach Jr., Luckenbach
   Steamship
Robert F. McDermott, USAA
Monroe J. Rathbone, Standard Oil of New
   Jersey
Herbert J. Siegel, Chris-Craft Industries
John E. Swearingen, Standard Oil of Indiana
Ralph E. Ward, Chesebrough-Pond's
Thornton A. Wilson, Boeing Company
William Wrigley III, William Wrigley Jr. Company

EIGHT

1970–1979

Managing Through the Malaise

This is an hour of history that troubles our minds and hurts our hearts.

—Gerald R. Ford

A Saudi Threat on Oil Reported

—*New York Times* headline, October 16, 1973

THE 1970S was a constant and often losing battle against malaise, discouragement, and even despair. Even more so than the Great Depression of the 1930s, the 1970s witnessed some of the darkest moments in the history of the country—the losing battle in Vietnam, the political scandals of Watergate, the crippling effects of oil embargoes, the senseless violence of Kent State, the bitter fight for equality, and the shocking helplessness of the Iranian hostage crisis. In the 1930s, Americans could and did turn to their president and their government for direction, support, and hope. That same recourse was not always available to Americans in the scandalous 1970s. Their anguish continued unabated as the morale of the country sunk to an all-time low.[1]

No image captured the helplessness of America more so than the lines at gasoline stations.[2] America's vast natural resources and ingenuity were not enough to stem a massive energy crisis that left the country's homes, businesses, and government at the mercy of oil-rich Middle Eastern nations. The glory days of the 1960s were gone, and they were replaced with an economic enigma—stagflation. The simultaneous growth of inflation and unemployment baffled economists. Until the 1970s, "it was generally believed that recession and inflation could not occur at the same time. A slowing economy was supposed to bring stable prices."[3] The nation experienced the highest annual rate of inflation since 1947, averaging over 8 percent, with peaks as high as 13 percent.[4] Meanwhile, unemployment hit 8.5 percent, a rate not seen since 1941.[5] High interest rates, high inflation, and high unemployment generated a series of crippling recessions.

For their part, businesses faced a scarcity of resources, a more demanding consumer base, a paucity of financing options, and an intensity of foreign competition. While growing inflation made U.S. goods more expensive and less attractive in the global marketplace, the lack of focus on quality and reliability exacerbated problems for business. For instance, the laissez-faire, arrogant approach of the "Big Three" U.S. automakers gave wide berth to lower-cost, fuel-efficient imports. When U.S. firms did enter the small-car market, they often failed to put the weight of their resources behind it. The high-profile quality problems of the Chevrolet Corvair, Ford Pinto, and American Motors Gremlin stand as enduring testaments to this shameful period of low quality. Even General Motors, the company that had succeeded against Ford by giving customers what they wanted when they wanted it, was very slow to address the small-car market. By focusing on quality, affordability, and safety, Japanese carmakers were well poised to exploit both the oil crisis and the fundamental loss of faith in U.S. business. By the end of the decade, Japanese

Japanese-made Toyota automobiles are unloaded in South Boston. The shipment represents part of the influx of smaller, high-quality, fuel-efficient vehicles that flooded the market in the 1970s and 1980s. (Source: Bettmann/CORBIS)

carmakers had captured 21 percent of the small-car market in the United States, up from 6 percent in the early 1970s.[6] The vulnerability felt by the Big Three and other businesses was not an isolated occurrence in the 1970s; vulnerabilities lurked around every corner and in every part of the world.

Global Vulnerabilities

When he was on the presidential campaign trail in 1968, Richard M. Nixon claimed that he had a plan to secure "peace with honor" in Vietnam. Like his predecessors, Nixon believed that he could force the North Vietnamese to acquiesce when they were faced with the full weight of American military forces. To that end, Nixon authorized more troops and an intensification of the air war campaign. Nixon also approved a massive fourteen-month air invasion of neighboring Cambodia, which had been used as a staging area and a sanctuary for North Vietnamese communists. Despite dropping four times the tonnage of bombs that were used against the Japanese in World War II, the attack on Cambodia did not achieve its stated objectives.[7] On the contrary, it emboldened the communist supporters and intensified the severity of antiwar protests in the United States, including the haunting scene of national guardsmen firing on student protesters at Kent State University in Ohio (four protesters were killed). Under intense pressure, Nixon agreed to a slow withdrawal of U.S. forces.[8]

The withdrawal occurred over a four-year period, during which time the United States attempted to negotiate a peaceful settlement with the North Vietnamese. In an irony reminiscent of the Korean War, the treaty that was signed in January 1973 was very close to the original negotiations in 1969. An additional four years of fighting left twenty thousand more American soldiers dead and countless others psychologically and physically damaged. The last American troops left Vietnam in March 1973, and though there was a tenuous peace in the region, the domino fell in 1975. Two years after the U.S. withdrawal, the North attacked the South, and this time, the United States did not intervene.[9]

Though Nixon often stumbled badly on the home front and was less expeditious than he should have been in ending U.S. involvement in Vietnam, he was considered a skilled statesman and opportunist on the world stage. Despite his vigilance in continuing the fight against communism in Vietnam,

Nixon simultaneously courted the two largest and most powerful communist nations in the world. The once-hardened accomplice to Senator Joseph McCarthy's communist purges in the 1950s, Nixon had become a pragmatist in his foreign policies, and he did more than any of his predecessors to open relations with communist stalwart nations. He eased trading restrictions and set forth the provisions that would garner most-favored-nation status for China. These efforts were backed by large industries, including textiles, petroleum products, and high-technology equipment. Executives like J. Paul Austin of Coca-Cola Company capitalized on the opportunity by securing in December 1978 an exclusive agreement to market Coke in China. Others quickly tried to tap into the enormous potential of the market. Nixon did not stop with China. In the same year, he initiated a period of détente with the Soviet Union by agreeing to a series of cooperative arrangements on space exploration, the environment, medicine, and, most importantly, military weapons.[10] Even before Nixon's efforts to reach out to the Soviet Union, Armand Hammer had already established a foothold in the communist nation. Hammer greatly expanded Occidental Oil Company by negotiating a $20 billion deal, which gave his company a supply of Russian ammonia and natural gas in exchange for the development of fertilizer plants in the Soviet Union.[11]

The muted celebrations of the U.S. withdrawal from Vietnam and the more vocal praise for the thawing of diplomatic relations with China and the Soviet Union were tempered by escalating tensions in the Middle East. The U.S. support for Israel in the Yom Kippur War of 1973 led to a crippling oil embargo by oil-rich Arab nations. Many oil-producing states had joined forces in 1960 to form the Organization of Petroleum Exporting Countries (OPEC) in an effort to combat the constant decreases in oil prices. Their efforts throughout the 1960s bore little fruit, but with the imposition of the oil embargo, the basis of power fundamentally shifted. In 1973, the United States relied on foreign oil for 36 percent of its domestic consumption requirements (up from 22 percent in 1970), and the loss of Arab oil had a starkly debilitating impact on American businesses.[12] In particular, multinational oil companies that had developed a long history of power and control in their operations were summarily downgraded to producing agents for oil-exporting states.[13] In response, executives at companies like Exxon and Mobil launched initiatives to develop synthetic fuels and engaged in ill-guided diversification in areas outside their core competence.

*Pump closings and long lines at service
stations were all-too-common experiences
during the energy crisis of the 1970s.*
(Source: Owen Franken/CORBIS)

Though the actual embargo was short-lived, its impact, especially the rapid acceleration of prices, lasted a long time. The price of oil rose from a pre-embargo rate of $1.50 per barrel to upward of $32.00 per barrel.[14] Such an increase had enormous repercussions, since it came at a time when 85 percent of Americans drove to work.[15] Throughout the decade, the administrations of Nixon, Gerald Ford, and Jimmy Carter experimented with a variety of measures to lessen U.S. dependence on foreign oil. In 1973, the U.S. Congress passed the Emergency Petroleum Allocation Act, which encouraged Americans to turn down their thermostats; increased the funding for alternative sources of power, including nuclear energy and coal; lowered highway speeds to fifty-five miles per hour; and encouraged better efficiency for automobiles and household appliances. Legislation was also passed to develop the Alaskan oil pipeline and to formally establish the Department of Energy. In addition to trying to lessen dependence on foreign oil, each administration sought to contain price increases through the adoption of explicit price controls, stringent regulatory measures, or higher taxation rates. Each effort brought only marginal relief, and by the end of the decade, President Carter signed legislation to deregulate all oil prices.[16] The impact of the regulatory price-control measures had actually discouraged U.S. firms from investing in costly oil exploration and inadvertently encouraged more dependence on already developed oil operations from OPEC nations.[17] Beyond its ultimate impact on the American economy, the Yom Kippur War forced the United States to play a more integrated role in the political landscape of the Middle East. Nixon's secretary of state, Henry Kissinger, helped negotiate a cease-fire between Israel, Syria, and Egypt and laid the foundation for the future Camp David peace accords.

Government Woes

Like Kennedy's optimistic start in the 1960s, Nixon's beginning did not foreshadow the monumental troubles of the 1970s. Nixon rode into the White House by appealing to what he referred to as the "silent majority," those law-abiding (mostly white) citizens who were not compelled to use public demonstrations and forums to promote their interests. They were the everyday Americans who were increasingly disillusioned and disgusted by what they perceived to be rampant permissiveness and irresponsibility in society. As the poster boy for disenfranchised whites, Nixon's appeal to the silent majority was not unlike Warren Harding's call for normalcy in the 1920s, and Nixon's election to the presidency in 1968 signaled a fundamental shift toward conservatism and traditionalism.

During his first administration, Nixon focused on shoring up the economy and was especially vigilant in his efforts to control inflation. He enacted a ninety-day wage and price freeze, abandoned the gold standard for the U.S. dollar, reduced spending for the space program, approved a series of tax cuts, supported a protectionist 10 percent surcharge on imports, and significantly curtailed defense spending. Social security benefits and food stamps were indexed to the rate of inflation, minority business owners were given preferential treatment in the awarding of government contracts, and a series of new health and occupational safety standards were approved. Nixon's appeal to the silent majority, his seeming ability to control the economy (pre–oil crisis), and his acquiescence on Vietnam made him an almost unstoppable candidate in the presidential elections of 1972. Garnering massive public support, Nixon won forty-nine of fifty states.[18] He had a clear and undisputed mandate, which made his spectacular fall from grace so tragic.

On the surface, the actual Watergate incident—the break-in and bugging of the Democratic National Committee offices—did not seem to have the makings to bring down a president. Certainly, when the incident was originally reported, it seemed relatively benign and received little public attention. When evidence at the scene of the crime suggested that the break-in had been conducted, allegedly without presidential knowledge or consent, by the Committee to Re-elect the President (CREEP), a media frenzy ensued. Though he was not directly linked to the original incident, Nixon was an active participant in trying to stymie an investigation that he had authorized. Over the course of two years, a web of presidential-level deception and deceit unraveled on national television. At the same time that Americans were facing an energy and economic crisis, they were subjected to a far more damaging crisis—the crisis of confidence in their leaders, in their country, and in their fellow man. By the time Nixon resigned from office to avoid almost certain impeachment, twenty-five government officials, including four cabinet members and the vice president, had been imprisoned or had resigned in disgrace.[19]

One month after taking the oath of the office of the president, Ford pardoned Nixon. The nation gasped in disbelief. What little momentum and leeway Ford may have been given by the American public was summarily extinguished. For his part, Ford retreated from massive legislative action. Within twenty-eight months, Ford vetoed sixty-six bills, one and a half times more than Nixon over sixty-eight months.[20] Ford was a strong believer in laissez-faire government, but his inaction did little to boost the economy, which hit rock bottom in 1974. The implosion of the Republican Party and the simmering

Nixon's scandals and subsequent resignation shook the confidence of the American people.
(Source: Owen Franken/ CORBIS)

economic turmoil paved the way for the election of Jimmy Carter in 1976. Carter was not swept into office in a wave of euphoria. The melancholy stupor of the country had cast a pall over the election, resulting in the lowest voter turnout in twenty-eight years.[21] At first, Carter's homespun character and outsider status were welcomed and admired. The charm, however, wore off when his inability and unwillingness to engage Congress stonewalled legislative action.[22] Carter did, however, enjoy some initial success internationally.

The 1978 Camp David Accords between Carter, President Anwar al-Sadat of Egypt, and Prime Minister Menachem Begin of Israel resulted in the Egyptian recognition of Israeli sovereignty in exchange for the Israeli withdrawal from the Sinai. Though tenuous, the peace talks helped formalize the U.S. role in high-level foreign diplomacy. Carter's success on the world diplomatic stage did not last long. Though heralded for his deftness in Middle Eastern diplomacy, Carter was maligned for being weak in the face of foreign oppression. The president's character was especially tested in November 1979, when Iranian militants stormed the U.S. embassy in Tehran and held fifty-three Americans hostage. The attack on the U.S. embassy came as retaliation for past support for the shah of Iran, and the U.S. public was subjected to an onslaught of television images of American flags and effigies of the U.S. president being burned and defaced.[23] Coming at the end of the decade, the images prolonged the sense of agony and helplessness that were so pervasive for so long.

Despite Nixon's scandals, Ford's relative inaction, and Carter's ineffectiveness, a considerable amount of consumer-rights legislation passed during the 1970s. This legislation was, in some ways, a backlash against the almost singular financial orientation of business in the 1960s—an orientation that often led to a neglect of consumer objectives such as safety, quality, and efficacy. In essence, legislation functioned as a means to tame poor business behavior. Nixon created the National Commission on Public Safety to collect and analyze data on products that had the potential to pose "unreasonable hazards to consumers."[24] The commission's initial report was shocking—20 million injuries, 110,000 permanent disabilities, and 30,000 deaths each year. The cost to the country was estimated to be over $5.5 billion.[25] On the heels of this report, the Consumer Product Safety Act was passed for the purpose of setting new marketing and product-quality standards for manufacturers. Consumer protection also extended to product warranty advertisements and financial credit. The Magnuson-Moss Warranty Act of 1975 forced manufacturers to specifically outline the provisions, scope, and limitations of their product warranties. Also benefiting the consumer, the Fair Credit Reporting Act established new standards for the accuracy and use of credit data and made credit reports accessible to individual consumers for the first time.

Arguably one of the most significant governmental actions for business in the 1970s was deregulation. Under severe opposition from most major airline carriers, Carter signed the Airline Deregulation Act in 1978. The act phased out the role of the government-controlled Civil Aeronautics Board, which had decided new air travel routes, determined which carrier would provide service, established prices, and reviewed merger requests. With deregulation, market conditions dictated routes, pricing, and network structures, while the government retained control for air safety. The concern that smaller communities would be hurt by deregulation was addressed by the government's requirement that current carriers continue service levels themselves or find a replacement carrier for the route. When the act was passed, there were forty-three certified airline carriers in the United States. By 1984, the number of carriers had doubled and severe price wars combined with overcapacity forced a marked decline in industry profitability.[26] By the mid-1980s, industry consolidation began in earnest.

Most of the economic stimulus policies of Nixon, Ford, and Carter failed. Inflation, unemployment, and interest rates continued to reach ever higher.[27]

President Carter signs the historic airline deregulation bill, which created a host of new competitors followed by massive industry consolidation. (Source: Bettmann/CORBIS)

As Americans continued to suffer, so too did some of the social and environ-mental efforts of the 1960s. In particular, the Environmental Protection Agency, which had been established at the beginning of the decade, endured a considerable amount of backlash.[28] When jobs were lost to new restric-tions and regulations, outcries from business and labor interests effectively squelched many environmental concerns.

Labor Disparity and Disillusion

While the labor movement was effective in winning some environmental concessions, it was relatively powerless in the face of the wage and price freezes that were intermittently applied throughout the decade. Though de-signed to control inflation, price controls actually hampered U.S. competi-tiveness and often contributed to job reductions. The rise in the U.S. un-employment rate, which grew from 3.5 percent in 1969 to 8.5 percent in 1975, came at a particularly inopportune time.[29] Between 1965 and 1980, the baby-boom children came of age, and the U.S. workforce grew by 40 percent as 30 million people joined the employment ranks.[30] On the whole, job cre-ation could not keep pace.

The accompanying rise in unemployment would have been bad enough on its own, but it occurred when the country was also experiencing a simul-taneous decline in overall worker productivity.[31] Less productive workers meant less output, which, in turn, resulted in an increase in inflation. In essence, Americans now had to work harder to stretch every deflated dollar. The pervasive disillusionment in the country was particularly heightened in the ranks of labor as two high-profile union murders scarred the already frac-tured movement. Joseph Yablonski, his wife, and his daughter were murdered in 1970 after choosing to challenge the allegedly rigged results of the United Mine Workers' presidential election. Five years later, Jimmy Hoffa's abduc-tion and apparent murder (no body was ever found) shocked the union movement again. In 1971, President Nixon had pardoned the former leader of the powerful Teamsters Union after Hoffa had been accused and officially convicted of pension-fund fraud and jury tampering. Nixon, a recipient of Teamsters Union campaign contributions, pardoned Hoffa on the condition that he would refrain from seeking his former position within the union. Had he abided by Nixon's pardon, Hoffa might have had a different fate.[32]

One individual who chose a different path was Cesar Chavez. This American labor leader made tremendous strides in improving the lives of migrant farm workers. Through high-profile boycotts, Chavez brought national attention to the plight of migrant farm workers, a group considered virtually impossible to organize. When violence erupted in the struggle for recognition, Chavez did not respond in kind; instead he chose nonviolent resistance—personal fasting. He was imprisoned for ten days in 1970 for organizing an illegal nationwide boycott of lettuce, but Chavez continued the struggle and orchestrated another national boycott of California grapes. This movement ultimately forced twenty-six grape growers to formally recognize the United Farm Workers (UFW). By 1975, the five-year-old organization was successful in tripling wages and improving working conditions for its fifty thousand members.[33]

As the labor movement struggled with its own internal issues, workers benefited from important government legislation and intervention, including the creation of the Occupational Safety and Health Administration (OSHA). Similar to the focus on consumer rights, the legislation on occupational safety was partly a response to the almost obsessive devotion to financial performance in the 1960s. Between 1964 and 1969, a national survey of manufacturing operations had uncovered a 25 percent increase in the on-the-job injury rate.[34] Congress hoped to redress this issue through the creation of OSHA, and within OSHA's first full year as an administrative agency, it conducted 28,900 inspections, cited 89,600 violations, and issued penalties totaling $2.1 million.[35] The real impact from OSHA did not come from the actual inspections, but from the original creation of the agency. In many ways, the mere existence of the agency forced businesses to reevaluate their operations in the event of a potential inspection.

The antidiscrimination and affirmative-action provisions of the civil-rights legislation also passed their first high-level judicial attacks. In 1971, the U.S. Supreme Court upheld the Title VII provisions that banned discrimination in hiring. The court ruled that "employers could not require qualifications for jobs that were discriminatory in effect unless those qualifications were proved necessary for the job."[36] In 1979, the Supreme Court in the *United Steelworkers of America v. Weber* case reaffirmed the use of preferential hiring to correct long-standing inequities in job opportunities. The court ruled that affirmative action was appropriate only when a distinct pattern of past discrimination occurred. In essence, it ruled that reverse discrimination was an acceptable outcome when an employer was attempting to correct long-standing employment inequities.

Society's "Pursuit of Happiness"

Two hundred years after the Declaration of Independence was penned, the country was still struggling with the meaning of one of its most noteworthy, yet elusive sentiments—"that all men are created equal, that they are endowed with certain unalienable rights, that among these are Life, Liberty, and the pursuit of Happiness." Just when America should have been celebrating its two hundredth birthday as a democracy, it was confronting the very meaning of its foundation. In particular, the struggle for black civil rights effectively forced the country to act on the very provisions of its Declaration.

As many black Americans were asserting their civil rights, a small, but influential group of black business executives were asserting their economic rights. By developing businesses that addressed the growing financial clout of black Americans, these individuals tapped into a vibrant economic wellspring. Through the creation of Motown Records, Berry Gordy Jr. set the stage for what was possible for black entrepreneurs in the 1960s. Backing such groups as Smokey Robinson and the Miracles, Diana Ross and the Supremes, and the Jackson Five, Motown Records became the most successful African American enterprise of its time. Although he mostly backed black artists, Gordy tapped into a musical genre that had tremendous appeal across a broad diversity of audiences.[37]

Thomas Burrell, Ivan Houston, and Earl Graves were African American entrepreneurs who followed Gordy's formula in the 1970s. In 1971, Burrell created an advertising agency to capitalize on the untapped potential of the African American market, and in the process, he became a pioneer of target marketing, building the largest black-owned advertising agency in the United States. He developed breakthrough advertising campaigns for Coca-Cola, McDonald's, and Procter & Gamble by focusing on the emotional appeal of the products—an approach that resonated with both whites and blacks. Houston was instrumental in streamlining Golden State Insurance Company's operations and enabling it to profitably expand. He moved the company from a sole focus on individual insurance for black Americans into the group insurance field, securing business from organizations such as Ford, General Motors, and AT&T. Over the course of his twenty-year tenure, Golden State became the third-largest black-owned financial services enterprise in the United States. After careers in the U.S. Army's Green Berets and in politics, Graves started *Black Enterprise* magazine as a news source for and about the growing community of black professionals and as a vehicle for promoting business and economic development. Profiling executives like Burrell and Houston, Graves succeeded in creating a vital resource for aspiring African American entrepreneurs.[38]

Black Americans were joined in the fight for economic and political parity by the organized women's movement. The National Organization of Women (NOW) became a strong advocate for equal rights and abortion. A watershed piece of legislation that did much to push the movement forward was Title IX of the 1972 Educational Amendment Act. The act required educational institutions to support affirmative-action programs for women. As a result, colleges and universities were required to ensure equality of opportunity for women in the classroom and on the athletic fields. The groundbreaking legislation opened the door for women to Harvard, Yale, and Princeton and, for the first time, gave female athletes a level playing field with their male counterparts.[39]

In 1972, Congress also approved the Equal Rights Amendment; after fifty years of struggle, formal recognition of women's equality would apparently be secured. Though the amendment had received an extension so that state ratification could be secured before the amendment was formally attached to the U.S. Constitution, the extension expired in 1982, three states short of the required thirty-eight needed for approval. What appeared to be a noncontroversial amendment became a battleground between conservatives and liberals.[40] The emotionally charged 1973 *Roe v. Wade* Supreme Court decision, which struck down state laws forbidding abortion in the first trimester, effectively splintered the women's movement. The *Roe v. Wade* decision galvanized the push for moderation, and the clash between moderates and activists fundamentally stymied further legislative action.[41] In addition to women, who were the most visible and vocal group to assert their rights, the struggle for recognition was embraced by homosexuals who sought protection against discrimination, by Native Americans who sought reparation and restitution for past government policies, and by prisoners who staged a series of high-profile riots to fight for better treatment.[42] These efforts to claim equal rights would have a dramatic impact on changing the composition of the U.S. labor force. Although they responded at different rates, businesses eventually became much more "integrated."

Women fought unsuccessfully for the passage of the Equal Rights Amendment. (Source: Flip Schulke/CORBIS)

In the midst of the turmoil and strife, many Americans chose to focus on what they could personally control, and more often than not, this meant their own lives. The decade was awash in self-help and self-indulgent best sellers, such as *Looking Out for Number One, How to Be Your Own Best Friend, Pulling Your Own Strings,* and *I'm OK—You're OK.* The search for new personal meaning also became fertile ground for self-discovery and analysis programs, including transcendental meditation and EST (Erhard Seminars Training). In some cases, the search was taken to the extreme, as evidenced by the proliferation of cult organizations. The most notorious of these cults was the one led by the eccentric Jim Jones, who orchestrated the mass suicide of 913 followers (drinking cyanide-laced Flavour-Aid) in 1978.[43]

The country's narcissistic focus became an escape from the constant dull pain of the 1970s. Watching their leaders circumvent the consequences of their actions, Americans increasingly looked to free themselves of personal burdens and even personal accountability. The decade saw the introduction of no-fault insurance and no-fault divorce and the expansion of guilt-free sexual experimentation. The playground for the self-indulgent crowd became the local discotheque, and by the end of the decade, there were ten thousand discos in America, and the industry had earned over $4 billion.[44]

The other side of the hedonistic culture of the 1970s was manifested in the health craze—especially the running craze—that swept the nation. A government report that linked reduced cholesterol intake and exercise to a lower risk of heart disease sparked a vibrant interest in jogging and contributed to a wave of exercise and diet books. Frank Shorter's gold-medal victory in the

1972 Olympic marathon and his silver-medal effort in 1976 did much to bolster the exercise industry, especially for athletic footwear. The nation's obsession with health became the foundation for a multitude of new businesses, including Philip Knight's Nike and Paul Fireman's Reebok. Through skillful advertising, endorsements from athletic icons, and innovative product development, Knight and Fireman successfully competed with each other while building a multibillion-dollar industry.[45]

Urban Blight

Many Americans were not satisfied with escaping the turmoil of the 1970s through literature, self-development programs, or exercise; they sought a literal escape. Urban flight reached a new level as Americans abandoned the riot-infested protest zones of the inner city for the quiet solitude of the suburbs. Many urban centers also suffered from the decline in major manufacturing industries, including steel, heavy machinery, automobiles, and tires.[46] The general demise in the economy was particularly difficult for the construction industry as the number of new housing starts dropped by nearly 2 million—from 12.2 million in the 1960s to 10.4 million in the 1970s.[47]

It became increasingly difficult to sustain a viable lifestyle, particularly in the manufacturing centers of the Northeast and Midwest. As businesses shuttered their doors, urban areas and their outskirts became vast underutilized and undervalued wastelands. Urban blight and decay became all-too-familiar symbols of the troubled times. The high inflation and unemployment that were epidemic in the nation's cities forced many people to relocate for new opportunities. Overall, the population of the United States increased from 203.3 million in 1970 to 226.5 million by 1980.[48] The increase of 23 million residents was roughly equivalent to the increase in the population of the 1960s, yet a much higher percentage of the increase in the 1970s (20 percent versus 13 percent) was attributable to immigration.[49] In particular, the total number of immigrants from Asia (especially China, Korea, the Philippines, and Vietnam) increased by a factor of three between the 1960s and 1970s. Delayed marriages, increases in the incidence of divorce, and lower birth rates all contributed to a reduction in organic population growth, though the impact of these demographic changes was somewhat mitigated by the continued medical advances that helped prolong life expectancy.

TABLE 8-1

Social and demographic facts about the 1970s

- 203 million Americans in 50 states; grows to 227 million by 1980
- President Nixon resigns after Watergate scandal
- United States celebrates bicentennial
- Twentieth Amendment to U.S. Constitution reduces voting age to 18
- Forced busing used to achieve racial integration ignites riots in major U.S. cities
- *Roe v. Wade* legalizes abortion
- Episcopal Church ordains female ministers
- Women admitted to military academies
- Women surpass men in college enrollment in 1979
- United Nations declares 1975 International Year of Women
- Antiwar protests, Kent State killings
- Environmentalists stage Earth Day
- Highway speed reduced to 55 mph
- Fads: pet rocks, disco, mood rings, smiley-face stickers, streaking, Earth shoes, leisure suits
- Games: Rubik's Cube, Star Wars figures, Atari's Pong video game
- New words: *Watergate, bottom line, sound bite, geek, couch potato*
- Minimum wage (1970): $1.60 per hour
- Average annual earnings (1970): $7,564
- Life expectancy (1970): 74.8 years for females, 67.1 years for males

A Brave New World in Technology

Advances in medical science were one of two primary drivers of technological innovation of the time. In the early 1970s, university laboratories perfected gene splicing to create recombinant DNA. Having read a paper on recombinant-DNA technology by Herbert Boyer of the University of California, Robert Swanson, a Kleiner and Perkins venture capitalist, became intrigued by the commercial possibilities for biotechnology. He sought out Boyer, and the two men eventually formed Genentech in 1976, the first organization devoted to commercializing biotechnology. One year after its founding, Genentech scientists cloned DNA in a bacteria culture to produce a human protein called somatostatin. The first human protein ever produced in a microorganism, somatostatin had limited commercial potential, but nevertheless demonstrated the viability of the technology. The following year, Genentech produced insulin through biotechnology. When Eli Lilly licensed it for the treatment of diabetes, this engineered insulin became the first recombinant-DNA product to reach the market.⁵⁰ Medical discoveries continued at an accelerated pace, reaching farther than anyone could have imagined. When the first successful in-vitro fertilization occurred in 1978, the news shocked the world. Though science had only joined the mother's embryo with the father's sperm in a test tube, the image of a scientifically produced "test-tube" baby evoked strong emotional reactions. Over time, the controversy surrounding artificial insemination subsided, but the debate over the extent to which scientific exploration and experimentation should interfere with human reproduction and disease management had just begun.⁵¹

The other significant technological development in the 1970s was much less controversial, although its impact on business and society was equally profound. During this time, the integrated circuit and microchip were fully exploited, ushering forth what business historian Thomas McCraw calls the Third Industrial Revolution—a revolution based on information, speed, and technological development.⁵² The microchip found its way into a host of new products, but its first broad-based commercial success was evidenced in the introduction of the pocket calculator. The integrated circuit on the microchip, which was imbedded in the first Texas Instrument pocket calculator, was one-quarter inch big and did the work of six thousand transistors.⁵³ Priced at more than four hundred dollars when it was initially introduced, the pocket calculator was thought of as a "gift for the person who has everything." The device soon gained widespread appeal, and in a matter of months, the price dropped to well below one hundred dollars and continued to decline. Within a year of its debut in 1972, over ninety companies were selling pocket calculators, but

Chips used as components of electronic circuit boards are balanced on the tip of a finger.
(Source: Bettmann/CORBIS)

by the end of the decade, only ten firms had survived the frenzy of market introduction, acceptance, and maturation.[54] The life-cycle pattern of the pocket calculator was dramatic and accelerated, but it continuously recurred with other electronic products, including the personal computer.

The acceptance and sustainability of computing technology has always depended on the availability and functionality of software. The first major productivity application to unleash the power of the computer was an electronic spreadsheet called Visicalc. Introduced in 1979, Visicalc was an almost instant success. In the course of six years, over one million copies of the productivity software were sold to individuals and professionals. The success of Visicalc sparked a number of imitators, and like the pocket calculator, the market was flooded with "me-too" products. The ultimate demise of Visicalc was a case study in software sustainability.[55] Without constant adjustments, enhancements, and support, any software, even a dominant one, is doomed to extinction. Technological innovation, especially in electronics and medicine, evolved more rapidly than ever before. Business executives who were able to capitalize on its potential often enjoyed a significant competitive advantage.

Managers: Facing a New Reality

Navigating the increasingly complex business landscape of the 1970s was extremely difficult—international competition, intensified government regulation, and tight monetary policies tended to constrain many businesses. The age of growth, even growth through unrelated diversification, was over. It became "hard for conglomerate managers to claim credibly that they were better at managing activities far afield from their core competence than other managers who focused their energies solely on managing a particular business segment."[56] The financial wizardry so characteristic of the 1960s no longer worked in a falling stock market. Wizardry was replaced with pragmatism—greater focus on product quality, better rationalization of resources, and prudent investment in research and development. Executives turned to strategic planning, cost management, and worker productivity programs to address the new contextual landscape. As Nitin Nohria, Davis Dyer, and Frederick Dalzell note in *Changing Fortunes: Remaking the Industrial Corporation*: "The key decisions were no longer which new products to introduce, or

TABLE 8-2

Business events that shaped the 1970s

Date	Event
1970	Environmental Protection Agency created
1970	Occupational Safety and Health Act mandates safe and healthful working conditions
1970	Racketeer Influence and Corrupt Organization Act passed to address organized crime
1970	Floppy disk invented
1970	National Association of Securities Dealers (NASDAQ) automates quotations of stocks
1971	National Railroad Passenger Corporation, Amtrak, formed
1971	President Nixon removes 20-year trade embargo against China
1971	Ninety-day wage and price controls enacted
1971	U.S. dollar devalued
1971	Intel invents microprocessor
1972	NASA space shuttle program approved
1972	United States and USSR agree to cooperate in science and technology
1972	Equal Rights Amendment introduced (abandoned in 1982)
1972	Bicycle sales outpace automobile sales for first time since 1900
1973	Peace treaty with North Vietnam signed
1973	OPEC oil embargo
1973	Alaska Pipeline Bill signed, authorizes 789-mile pipeline across Alaska
1973	U.S. economy encounters worst recession since Great Depression of 1930s
1973	Consumer Product Safety Commission created
1973	Gene-splicing, or recombinant DNA, discovered
1974	United States files antitrust suit to break up AT&T (settled in 1982)
1974	Equal Credit Opportunities Act eliminates discrimination in access to credit
1975	Securities Acts Amendments encourage competition in trading securities
1975	Metric Conversion Act passed, adopted by businesses
1975	Altair personal computer introduced
1976	Cray Research introduces first supercomputer
1976	Foreign Corrupt Practices Act prohibits bribes and commissions to foreign officials
1976	Genentech formed; first commercially successful biotechnology operation
1978	President Carter agrees to "bail out" New York City from impending bankruptcy
1978	Airline Deregulation Act eliminates federal control of airlines
1978	Health emergency declared at Love Canal; exposes danger of toxic waste sites
1979	President Carter ends controls on oil prices
1979	Inflation hits 15 percent, 33-year high
1979	Three Mile Island nuclear reactor shut down

which plant or distribution facility to invest in, but which existing operations to shut down."[57]

As the U.S. market contracted, many executives looked for opportunities outside the United States, and there was tremendous growth in the number and size of multinational corporations. In the 1970s, the three hundred largest U.S. companies (including seven banks) earned 40 percent of their profits in the international marketplace.[58] While many looked outward to bring stability to their earnings, others sought opportunities from careful and calculated investment in research capabilities. This was especially true for pharmaceutical companies that expanded dramatically in the 1970s.

Through heavy investments in research and development (R&D), John J. Horan led Merck to become the leading U.S.-based manufacturer of prescription drugs. While Horan doubled the amount of money that Merck spent on research, he also fundamentally changed the nature of the investment. Horan pushed the company away from researching chemical compositions and reactants to researching the development of diseases within the human body. This shift of focus brought a level of direct practicality and purpose to the ultimate development process and resulted in bringing drugs to market more quickly.[59] Another individual who embraced research and development was Edmund T. Pratt Jr., who assumed the CEO position of Pfizer in 1972. Over the course of Pratt's two-decade tenure, he built Pfizer into one of the most successful pharmaceutical companies in the world. In a time when short-term returns and financial performance were vital, he managed for the long term. The results of his efforts speak for themselves: a sevenfold increase in sales, an eightfold increase in earnings, and one of the strongest drug-development pipelines in the industry.

Edmund T. Pratt Jr. (1927–2002), Pfizer, Inc.

The methodical and dedicated manner in which Edmund Pratt attacked his position as the head of Pfizer dramatically contrasted with his overall outlook on life. Pratt once noted: "Through my life, I never had a clear vision of what I wanted to do. I sort of took opportunities as they came to me."[60] While he may have been opportunistic and carefree in his personal planning, he was very focused on his plans and objectives for Pfizer. When he stepped into the

CEO role, the company had a few marketable products, an impoverished re-search pipeline, a disparate collection of unrelated business entities, and an uncertain future. With sharp focus and clear objectives, Pratt sold off non-productive businesses, invested in new research, and consolidated operations. By the time he was finished, Pfizer had become one of the premier companies in the world—not bad for a man who lacked a clear vision.

Pratt was born in Savannah, Georgia, in 1927, and soon thereafter, his family relocated to Elkton, Maryland, where his father had secured a position as a guard in the Army Engineers Corps. Though the position did not pay well, it enabled Pratt, an only child, to have a happy childhood. As he explained: "I grew up in a very humble but completely comfortable, and I guess, typical American background. It was a simple but good life. And I appreciated what I had."[61] Lacking the personal funds to attend college, Pratt entered Duke University as part of the V-12 Navy College Training Program when he grad-uated from high school on D-day, June 6, 1944. Under this three-year college degree program, the U.S. Navy funded Pratt's education in exchange for a military tour of duty after graduation. The war ended during Pratt's second year in the program, and he completed his education through the GI Bill, graduating with an electrical engineering degree, magna cum laude, in 1947. Upon graduation, Pratt continued his education, pursuing an MBA from the University of Pennsylvania's Wharton School.

After receiving his MBA in 1949, Pratt joined the staff of International Business Machines as a salesman. He worked for IBM for almost fourteen years, including a two-year leave of absence to serve as an intelligence officer for the U.S. Navy during the Korean War. Pratt rose through the ranks of IBM, where his career culminated in the role of controller for the IBM World Trade Center from 1958 to 1962. His experience watching IBM grow as a multina-tional corporation proved to be invaluable in his later career with Pfizer. If not for the call from the Kennedy administration, Pratt might have been a one-company man. In 1962, when Kennedy's secretary of defense, Robert McNa-mara, asked Pratt to become an assistant secretary of the army for financial management, Pratt jumped at the opportunity to serve his country again. During his two years of government service, he oversaw the army's budgeting and planning operations and helped expand the use of data processing in over-all decision making and analysis. Like his international experience at IBM,

Pratt's exposure to government policy making and administration became very useful as Pfizer attempted to navigate the increasingly complicated waters of regulation in the 1970s.

Pratt left the public sector in 1964 and joined Pfizer as corporate controller in its New York City office. He had been recruited by former army chief of staff, J. Lawton Collins, who was then serving as vice chairman of Pfizer International. When Pratt joined Pfizer, the company was in the midst of a major diversification and expansion effort. The passage of the Kefauver-Harris Amendment to the Food, Drug, and Cosmetic Act in 1962, which insisted on extensive clinical trials for new prescription drugs, fundamentally changed the entire economics of the pharmaceutical industry. Drug approvals, which had previously been secured in a matter of months, now took years. Pfizer's answer to increased regulation was to diversify its overall business portfolio, and to that end, it acquired more than thirty companies in the early 1960s. The acquisitions, intended to circumvent the impact of an extended drug-approval process, were all related to one of Pfizer's core business lines—pharmaceuticals, specialty chemicals, hospital products, minerals, or agricultural medicines. In addition, like many other U.S. companies (as mentioned earlier, 40 percent of the profits of the largest three hundred U.S. companies were from overseas), Pfizer embarked on a dramatic international expansion effort, setting up research laboratories and manufacturing facilities throughout the world.

Pratt's strategic planning and strong organizational skills were considered crucial to the success of the international division. In 1967, he was tapped to be its vice president of operations. The rapid expansion of the company's international operations had been conducted at the expense of efficiency, and Pratt was charged with helping to bring order and control to the division without sacrificing growth. Pratt was less than enthused about the new opportunity: "Behind that wall, there were rumors that things weren't all that great . . . some people were leaving, and others were out looking for jobs. It was not a happy house."[62] Managers who were excelling in their international operations were not excited by what they saw as corporate encroachment on their growth. Pratt was very adept at walking the fine line between providing international operations with autonomy while also leveraging overall corporate assets and objectives. Although he left many elements of the international operations intact, he changed the reporting structure for their key financial resources; they reported directly to corporate headquarters, not their divisional presidents. He also encouraged cross-divisional communication and, when appropriate, consolidated operations to further streamline the company's haphazard growth. Pratt brought a sense of order and stability to the far-flung enterprise. Within two years, he was promoted to president of the international division and elected to the company's board of directors.

As Pratt was rising to prominence in the company, his counterpart, Gerald D. Laubach, was building a strong reputation as the head of Pfizer Pharmaceuticals. While Pratt was attempting to centralize and coordinate the company's international operations, Laubach was bringing order and structure to Pfizer's disparate research endeavors. Both men were focused on achieving greater productivity and improved financial performance, and both had achieved tremendous success. Given their track records, it was not surprising that both Pratt and Laubach were in line for the CEO position in 1972. Banking on their ability to work well together, the then chairman and CEO, John Powers Jr., designed a succession plan that named Pratt the CEO and Laubach the president. Pratt and Laubach's twenty-year partnership stood as a testament to their ability to share the leadership of the company. Pratt's international experience and marketing savvy were complemented by Laubach's deep scientific and technical expertise.

Pratt and Laubach inherited the leadership of a company with almost $1 billion in sales, but with a tired product pipeline. At the time, Pfizer was involved in several businesses, yet its largest division, health-care products, which developed and sold prescription drugs, was too heavily dependent on pharmaceutical products whose patents were on the cusp of expiring. Pfizer had also relied heavily on licensing products developed by other firms, which further increased its risk basis. Though the company's diversification efforts in the 1960s helped sustain growth while the core business adjusted to the new drug-approval process, the lack of attention to central R&D efforts left the health-care products division relatively vulnerable. Pratt summed up the company's position at the time he took the CEO helm: "We were new in the pharmaceutical industry. We had been lucky, we had a couple of good products . . . But we weren't even spending a fraction of what Merck and other people were . . . Hell, if we were going to survive in this business, we were going to have to be a player in their category."[63]

Pratt increased the company's R&D expenses from 5 percent of sales to a target of 15 to 20 percent of sales, concentrating the investment on drugs for treating chronic diseases. Pratt and Laubach also made the difficult decision to centralize Pfizer's research efforts. The freewheeling expansion in the 1960s had led to redundant and unproductive research endeavors, and the move to centralize resources was designed to facilitate the efficient delivery of new products. These decisions were riddled with controversy. With at least a ten-year lag time between initial drug development and approval, the performance horizon for Pfizer was fundamentally changed, and Pratt was constantly subjected to second-guessing and derision from Wall Street analysts who sought quick, short-term results. Pratt stood firm in his convictions and ultimately proved the skeptics wrong. Beginning in the early 1980s, Pfizer unveiled a string of new pharmaceutical products, which dramatically increased sales and positioned the company as a strong and viable player in the marketplace. Drugs that became blockbusters in the 1980s and 1990s—including Zithromax (antibiotic), Feldene (arthritis treatment), Novarsc (blood-pressure control), and Zoloft (depression)—all had their start in the 1970s.

By the end of the 1970s, Pfizer had streamlined its research efforts, coordinated its international operations, increased its productivity, and continued to pursue small, selective acquisitions. Sales more than doubled to $2.7 billion in 1979, and with this level, Pfizer had entered the domain of the one hundred largest companies in the United States. As Pratt's commitment to research investment continued, the firm spent upward of $3 billion in the 1980s. By 1989, Pfizer had over fifteen products going through FDA approval and was ranked as the second-most-productive drug research company in the world.[64] Spending close to 14 percent of sales on research and development, Pfizer had finally achieved parity with the market leader, Merck.[65] Pratt reflected on the commitment to research: "My colleagues and I realized that our industry was changing and that, more than ever, the name of the game was innovation. With shortened patent lives and an accelerating pace of new drug technology, we knew that only those companies with the technological resources to build strong new product pipelines would survive."[66]

As the company continued to work on its drug pipeline, Pratt became actively involved in protecting Pfizer's patents and intellectual property rights. Pratt was specifically concerned with the distribution of Pfizer's products in countries that had limited or nonexistent patent protection legislation. It was not uncommon for Pfizer to face competition against generic equivalents of its products even before the drugs had formally received FDA approval. For instance, when Pfizer launched Feldene in Argentina in the early 1980s, there were already six companies selling it under their own names without paying any royalties.[67] Pratt built alliances with large pharmaceutical concerns and other suppliers of intellectual property (software firms, music producers, etc.) in the United States, Europe, and Japan and established the International Property Rights Committee (IPC). The IPC worked with international trade organizations to develop a basic set of guidelines and minimum threshold levels for intellectual property rights protection in developing countries. Though his success was limited, Pratt was instrumental in bringing one of the major issues facing multinational corporations onto the world stage. The Carter and Reagan administrations recognized Pratt's efforts, naming him the chairman of the President's Advisory Committee for Trade Negotiations.

At the end of his tenure, Pratt had built Pfizer into one of the five largest pharmaceutical companies in the world. A year before his retirement in 1991, *Forbes* praised his efforts this way: "Those on Wall Street and elsewhere who used to complain about Pratt's fruitless heavy spending on R&D have changed their tune."[68] For Pratt, it was a small victory. The larger victory was the security of Pfizer's enduring legacy.[69]

Entrepreneurs:
Skating the Edge of Technological Innovation

In a period of economic recession, entrepreneurs took significant risks and invested heavily in new services and particularly in breakthrough technologies. While heavy investments may have seemed counterintuitive to many business executives, who were simply trying to survive, for the decade's entrepreneurs, investment was considered essential. Their metric of performance was not just financial achievement; these individuals valued speed, service, and, above all, technological advancement. During this decade of general despair and malaise, entrepreneurs conceived and developed businesses that had profound implications for the way Americans lived and worked. The companies that emerged read as a virtual who's who of business and market dominance— Microsoft, Apple, Intel, Federal Express, Oracle, The Home Depot, Charles Schwab, Ben & Jerry's, Price Club, and Visa International. These enterprises and sometimes their founders became part of American business folklore. Almost all these businesses used technology as a key differentiating lever.

The one product that emerged in the 1970s and fundamentally reshaped the personal and professional lives of Americans was the personal computer. Gordon Moore, Steve Jobs, and Bill Gates stood at the forefront of this revolution. Intel's development of the 8080 microprocessor in the early 1970s, under the direction of Gordon Moore and Robert Noyce, became the first key building block for personal computers. The 8080 microprocessor "incorporated all the essential parts of the personal computer," such as the central processing unit (CPU) and input and output circuits, on a single wafer-thin chip.[70] At one-eighth inch wide and one-sixteenth inch long, the microchip had more computing power than the room-sized ENIAC, the first digital computer, which had been developed in the late 1940s.[71] The development of the 8080 microprocessor made the personal computer a reality and formed the basis of the Altair, a mail-order home computer assembly kit.

The Altair was a hit with the electronic hobbyist crowd and caught the attention of both Steve Jobs and Bill Gates. Jobs and fellow electronics enthusiast Steve Wozniak treated the introduction of the Altair as the first throw of the gauntlet. Wozniak, in particular, picked up the gauntlet, determined to create a better and more useful personal computer, and his development of the Apple I in 1975 succeeded in that vein. Though fewer than two hundred Apple I machines were sold, its relative success caught the commercial imagination of Jobs. A stronger marketer than technologist, Jobs was instrumental in designing the second generation of the Apple with an eye toward the educated consumer instead of the electronics enthusiast. With financial backing from former Intel marketer Mike Markkula and strong product designs, Apple's rise to success was swift and spectacular. Within five years, the two garage hobbyists had built a $300 million business that reached the *Fortune* 500 list faster than any company in history.[72]

The Altair also inspired Bill Gates and Paul Allen, who together wrote a BASIC programming language for it. Though they tinkered with programming languages and operating systems throughout the decade, their big break came in 1980, when IBM asked them to develop an operating system for their new personal computer. Gates retained the rights to the operating system, MS-DOS (a system that was a modified version of code that he bought for fifty thousand dollars from a Seattle programmer), and struck deals with nearly all other manufacturers of personal computers, who felt their machines had to run on IBM-compatible systems. Gates's strategic maneuvering and creative alliances helped Microsoft become virtually synonymous with the power of the personal computer.[73]

Meanwhile, two other entrepreneurs applied technology to unique organizational models to build vibrant new enterprises—Frederick Smith of Federal Express and Dee Ward Hock of Visa International. Both men believed that technology would become a key component of their logistical infrastructure and would ultimately enable them to deliver on the promises of increased speed and productivity. Capitalizing on an idea that came to him while in college, Smith helped build and then dominated the overnight-delivery industry. Though Federal Express initially lost $29 million in its first two years (1973–1975), the need for express delivery services soon grew by geometric proportions. Smith achieved success at Federal Express by creating strategic partnerships with merchandisers and by leveraging technology to simplify a vastly complicated logistical process.[74]

In 1970, Hock used a technology infrastructure and innovative organizational design to create a reverse holding company, tying together thousands of independent banks as part of what would become Visa International. His aggressive marketing and sharp negotiation skills enabled Visa to quickly capture 20 percent of the U.S. charge-card business—outpacing the growth of both MasterCard and American Express. He developed the first computerized system for the electronic transfer of data between banks and pioneered the international magnetic strip, building bridges between domestic and foreign banking operations.

Dee Ward Hock (1929–), Visa International

Not long before he became the undisputed promoter of "plastic," Dee Ward Hock had disavowed any allegiance to credit cards. At twenty-five years old, married and the father of two toddlers and another child on the way, Hock was unemployed and in severe debt. Having overextended their financial liabilities on several credit cards, the Hocks were on the verge of personal bankruptcy. To make ends meet, Hock took any job he could and, in his own words, "swore that, with the possible exception of a home mortgage, we would never have more debt than cash in the bank . . . we shredded every credit card in our possession, swearing never to have another."[75] Fifteen years later, Hock was not worried about one credit card; he was worried about millions.

The financial struggles that Hock encountered when he was twenty-five were nothing new. It was an all-too-familiar experience for the last of six children growing up in a two-room cabin in rural Utah. The cabin had no plumbing, no bathroom, meager furnishings, and no heating source save a wood stove, yet the lack of material comforts did not diminish the sense of pride and tradition that flowed in the Hock household. Hock was raised to expect and appreciate hard work, commitment, and self-determination. As soon as he was able, he was expected to help support the family, first with household and farming chores and later with odd jobs in town.

At a young age, Hock acquired a fascination with books and became an avid reader, often gravitating to classic stories of leadership. Thinking back on his admiration for these historical figures, Hock noted: "Those people [Jefferson, Ghandi, Goethe, and Aurielius, among others] seemed able to put themselves into the future, to conceive of the world as it ought to be. They were able to bring that future into the present and live as though it was true."[76] His love for reading, however, did not translate into love for school; he found it utterly restraining and demotivating, except for debate. His gifted skills of persuasion, combined with an intense attention to detail and preparation, made Hock a natural debater. As a state tournament debate champion, Hock was entitled to a fifty-dollar "scholarship" to Weber Junior College, which he gratefully accepted.

Over the next sixteen years, Hock's career meandered through a variety of low-level management positions within various financial institutions. Never one to tow the company line, Hock often found himself on the street corner, a victim of his inability to play by the rules. The confinement and rigidity that he had so loathed in his early school days had not dissipated through the years. Even when his principles brought his family to the brink of survival, he was reluctant to change, and for years, his career was a virtual seesaw of modest success and bitter failure. In 1965, Hock decided it was time to balance the seesaw. He was thirty-six and again out of work. His last job had taken his family to Seattle, where his wife was pursuing a long-delayed university education and his children were beginning to feel a part of the community. Not wanting to uproot the family again, Hock decided to "make no more effort to climb the corporate ladder." Instead, as he wrote: "I would join the crowd and take up what may be the most common career in modern organizations: 'retirement on the job.' My victim would be one of the local banks where a modest living could be had at a cost of a pleasant demeanor, conformity, and fractional ability or effort."[77] His "victim" was the National Bank of Commerce, where Hock secured a position as a rotating management resource.

After floating through various assignments at the bank for a year, Hock was tapped by the bank's president, Maxwell Carlson, to help launch a credit-card program. The National Bank had agreed to be a licensee of Bank of America's personal-credit-card program, BankAmericard. Because Hock had agreed to "retire on the job," he was reluctant to accept the opportunity. He recalled telling Carlson: "I have absolutely no use for credit cards. All I had were destroyed fourteen years ago. I've not had one since and want none in the future."[78] Carlson listened but gave Hock the assignment anyway. For all his distaste for credit cards, Hock was a natural when it came to conceptualizing and delivering on their potential. Despite tremendous hurdles, such as lack of resources, lack of technology, and lack of applicable experience, the credit-card system for the National Bank went live on-time and on-budget. The chaos that surrounded the launch seemed utterly comfortable to Hock. With no rules and no predetermined game plan, Hock and his team could innovate on-the-fly. The bank recognized Hock's role in launching the program; within a year, the floating manager had found a permanent home as the head of the credit-card department.

In this capacity, Hock attended a 1968 meeting in Columbus, Ohio, for licensees of the BankAmericard program. Though Bank of America was profiting tremendously from the rapid expansion of licensing agreements, it was the only company making a profit. Its licensees were hemorrhaging cash. One account of the meeting noted the myriad challenges: "The licensees had no proper operating guidelines, no effective way to share information, and no organizing mechanism for sorting out their problems. Credit-card fraud was rampant, there were huge problems with the authorization system, and the licensees were facing huge mountains of paperwork."[79] Bank of America's lack of an efficient or even adequate system for reconciling fund transfers between banks and merchants was further complicated by the indiscriminate nature of securing credit-card customers by licensees. Believing that credit cards would bring enormous new bank business, licensees of Bank-Americard paid little if any attention to the creditworthiness of their customers and prospects. Children, felons, and even family pets were solicited for credit cards.

Bank of America was wholly unprepared to deal with the licensees' animosity and contempt. After the first day of the two-day meeting, it appeared that "the future of the entire BankAmericard program was in doubt."[80] With no other viable options, Bank of America decided to transfer accountability and ownership for problem solving to the licensees themselves. Hock was one of seven licensees asked to serve on a task force charged with recommending improvements to the BankAmericard program. Hock agreed not only to serve but also to chair the committee if its scope could be expanded beyond problem identification and solution to a full review of the overall program. When Bank of America agreed, Hock embarked on a new phase of his career.

Over the next two years, Hock, still drawing a salary from the National Bank of Commerce, organized the licensing banks into representative committees and essentially attacked every element of the BankAmericard program. Hock's key operating committee was locked in a sea of seemingly insurmountable problems until he suggested that they look at the credit-card system with a totally clean slate—no existing infrastructure and no boundaries. It was from this clean-slate perspective that the idea for a new system emerged—a system predicated on a cooperative organizational structure and futuristic technology. According to Visa historian Paul Chutkow, Hock "was convinced that digital technology, which was just beginning to emerge [in 1969], would radically change banking, credit cards, and our most basic concepts of money."[81] Long before it became reality, Hock envisioned a paperless and instantaneous ability to transfer and reconcile funds between entities twenty-four hours a day, seven days a week.

With the freedom to think creatively, Hock's committee developed a plan that called for a "self-governing partnership of banks [instead of the existing licensee structure] that would work together to manage and settle credit-card financial transactions from any place in the world."[82] Under the plan, Bank of America would cede control of the BankAmericard program and would shift from owner-controller to partner-member. It was a bold and unexpected move, and Hock's initial attempts to sell the proposal were soundly rejected. Having funded the initial investment for the BankAmericard program and spent millions to roll it out, Bank of America could hardly fathom giving up control. Hock eventually prevailed in securing the bank's approval through impassioned persuasion and a partially veiled threat. The threat entailed disbanding the committee effort and going public with Bank of America's refusal to cooperate with its licensees. Though the bank could withstand the impact of the negative publicity, Hock knew it had little appetite for a public fight. In 1970, Bank of America agreed to a transfer of ownership, and National Bank-Americard Incorporated (NBI) was created as an independent nonstock, for-profit membership organization.

Selling the NBI concept to Bank of America was just the first step in the transformation process. Hock had agreed that the effort would be disbanded if he failed to convince at least two-thirds of the 2,700 BankAmericard licensees to rescind their contract with Bank of America and sign a new, common licensing agreement with NBI. All joining banks would be equal members in NBI, with voting rights proportional to their percentage of overall credit-card charge volume. It was a delicate sales effort, as Hock recalled: "On the one hand, the member financial institutions are fierce competitors: they issue the cards, which means they are constantly going after each other's customers. On the other hand, the members also have to cooperate with each other; for the system to work, participating members must be able to take any BankAmericard issued by any bank anywhere."[83] Though Bank of America thought a nine-month window of opportunity was prudent, Hock set a deadline of ninety days and used a well-tested marketing strategy to win the support of the licensees. With significant assistance from Bank of America, he enlisted the support of several high-profile U.S. banks. Like a politician, Hock traveled throughout the country to explain the benefits and promises of the new program and quickly won acceptance from key banks. From these initial high-profile wins, the power of peer pressure and influence took over. At the end of the ninety days, Hock had convinced all 2,700 licensees to join NBI.

In July 1970, Hock formally resigned from the National Bank of Commerce and relocated to San Francisco to take the helm of NBI. The start-up nature of the new venture was exhilarating to the iconoclast. Under Hock, NBI had no official job titles, no definitive structure, and no formality, but the lack of traditional form did not cloud expectations. Hock was, in many ways, a tireless taskmaster who demanded results and was bitterly intolerant of mistakes. For Hock and NBI, the stakes were extremely high, and he was unwilling to leave anything to chance. The man who thrived without rules was not averse to enforcing his own rules and expectations on the organization. Despite his almost tyrannical management style, his vision and charisma could be infectious, and Hock tended to hire for passion and desire over applicable experience. To achieve his ultimate vision for a "seamless exchange of value," Hock had to first attack the key problems facing the new members of NBI—credit-card fraud, bad-risk cardholders, slow authorization, and mounds of paperwork. Within its first year of operation, NBI focused on the issues of bad debt and fraud. The organization reduced the number of total BankAmericard cardholders by 4 million (from 23.7 to 19.7 million) while increasing total charge volume by $1 billion.[84]

The linchpin to NBI's ultimate success depended on the digitized technology that Hock envisioned. He saw money as "alphanumeric data in the form of arranged electrons and photons that would move around the world at the speed of light, at minuscule cost, by infinitely diverse paths throughout the entire electromagnetic spectrum."[85] As Hock's team began to embark on the development of a system that matched his vision, he learned that American Express had similar plans. American Express had convinced NBI's largest member, Bank of America, that NBI should join its nationwide network development effort. NBI would provide some of the up-front development funds in exchange for lower usage fees when the system was rolled out. Against Hock's desires, the NBI board agreed to back the American Express system in 1971. Almost as soon as the contract was signed, Hock began a campaign to convince his board that the American Express system would ultimately result in a loss of control for its licensees; he was convinced that their needs would always be subordinate to the system owner. He believed that a proprietary system was the only solution for NBI. Hock's skills of persuasion worked again: though NBI was barely a year old and still struggling to gain solid footing, the board authorized the system.

NBI withdrew from the American Express deal, and Hock moved quickly to add technical depth to his team. There was no precedent for the development of an electronic payment system, no specific guidelines to follow, and no guarantee of success, but there was a clear vision of what the system should do. Hock pulled together a loose collection of consultants and team members and built what became known as BASE I—Bank Authorization System Experimental. When BASE I was introduced in 1973, it was the industry's first electronic payment system, and it was built on-time and under-budget. The American Express system had "withered on the vine," and another competitive effort by MasterCard was still months away from development.[86] In an ironic twist, American Express and MasterCard eventually became users of the NBI system. When the system was fully operational in late 1973, BASE reduced the authorization time for credit-card approval from five minutes to fifty-six seconds.[87] Hock's team continued to enhance the system, ultimately developing on the back of the credit card a magnetic strip, which was used for transmitting account information and verification.

At the same time that NBI was building its technological infrastructure, Hock was envisioning not just a domestic system for monetary exchange but an international one. To that end, he cultivated relationships with dozens of foreign banks and in 1974 helped create the international equivalent of NBI, called IBANCO. IBANCO functioned on the same principles as NBI, whereby banks issued and managed credit cards while the central membership organization handled electronic transactions and overall marketing and brand positioning. While the U.S. operation functioned under the single BankAmericard name, the IBANCO division had multiple card names. The lack of a common brand hampered the organization's overall efficiency, and to that end, Hock championed an effort to develop a new name, which could transcend unique cultures, customs, and norms. A company-sponsored brainstorming program produced the Visa name, whose image of freedom of travel and open access seemed to resonate on the global stage. In 1976, Hock and his team began the monumental task of converting millions of credit cards, merchant signs, and other collateral pieces to the Visa name and logo. What was expected to take four years was completed in pure Hock form—eighteen months.

Dee Ward Hock envisioned a world connected through digitized technology. His formation of Visa International changed the way banks operated and the way individuals consumed. (Source: Time Life Pictures/Getty Images)

By 1980, just a dozen years after attending the fateful licensee meeting, Hock had built BankAmericard/Visa into the largest credit-card organization in the world. With 53.5 percent of all U.S. bank-card transactions, it surpassed MasterCard and had a card-member base of over 64 million. Hock's organization had succeeded in eliminating cumbersome, manual-intensive tasks; decreasing fraud; and increasing overall efficiency. What was more important, credit-card departments went from being a money loser for banks into a viable profit center. Hock's Orwellian vision for "dancing electrons and photons" had become a reality, and his unique membership organization had demonstrated a keen ability to compete and cooperate in the marketplace.[88]

Leaders: Diversify for Survival

The difficult economy of the 1970s played havoc on a number of long-standing businesses and even whole industries. Not unlike their counterparts in the 1930s, leaders needed to focus on business survival, and for many, survival became a combination of cost containment and balanced diversification. The leaders did their share of cost cutting and realignment, but they also built a foundation for longer-term earnings potential. Leaders attempted to smooth cyclic earnings or lessen dependence on a few offerings with a well-balanced portfolio of businesses or products and services. Generally, the diversification efforts were far more focused than the "growth at any cost and in any industry" approach of the 1960s.

One would be hard-pressed to find a less glamorous business in the 1970s than ConAgra (short for Consolidated Agriculture). Though it certainly lacked glamour, it also lacked something much more fundamental—cash flow. This $633 million producer of grain, poultry, and flour was on the verge of bankruptcy when C. Michael Harper joined the company. What could have easily been a short-term, unspectacular venture became one of the greatest turnaround stories of the 1970s. Harper began a major divestment program, selling off vast real estate holdings, nonproductive business divisions, and even a profitable grocery distribution operation to shore up the company's balance sheet. Within a few years, the company had weathered the worst of the business downturn.

Having effectively managed the short-term financial problems of the company, Harper was ready to develop a long-term, sustainable business plan. He began the rebuilding process by recruiting several key executives, by looking for new growth opportunities, and by laying the foundation for a corporate culture and philosophy that stressed performance, openness, and accountability. He convened an off-site meeting with his new management team and developed what became known as the ConAgra Philosophy, a sixteen-page booklet that outlined the company's overarching goal to evolve from a grain and commodity business into a "basic food company with products and services across the food chain."[89] This broad positioning provided ample leeway in growing the company, but it was also coupled with specific operating objectives such as being the low-cost producer; maximizing shareholder wealth; encouraging entrepreneurial, risk-taking leadership; and fostering open and transparent communication.

While individual business units were given strict financial metrics (20 percent return on equity, debt no greater than 40 percent of capital, and 14 percent annual earnings growth), they were also given the autonomy to achieve these results in their own way. This blend of tight accountability and operational freedom became a key ingredient in ConAgra's culture. With the operating principles in place, Harper and his management team began a massive acquisition campaign to diversify the company. They acquired entities that suffered from lack of management attention, low investment, and uninspired marketing and provided these companies with the tools and resources needed for success. Technology played a pivotal role in supporting the needs of acquired companies. An early adopter of management information systems, Harper set up an elaborate computer system, which enabled him to "beam himself into ConAgra's many operating units," where he could monitor progress and expand the channels of communication.[90] The system provided the operating units with the reports and other information they needed to run their businesses. Harper also played a key role in setting an example for his enterprise by "shunning fancy titles, large staffs, and other forms of bureaucracy."[91] He explained his rationale for this approach: "When people surround themselves with huge staffs, they start craving power. That's not what we're about."[92]

When he retired in 1992, Harper had built ConAgra, with sales of over $23 billion, into the second-largest food company in the world. Its earnings growth and return-on-equity performance were unprecedented. Reflecting on his experience with ConAgra, Harper noted: "When catastrophe freed us from the company's past, it freed us to opt for a new ConAgra. And the cost of saving ConAgra deserved a lot better reward than simply restoring the average conditions that had prevailed."[93] A $3,000 investment in ConAgra stock in the year that Harper began as CEO was worth $500,000 in the year that he retired.[94]

Moving Beyond Stability to Growth

After two decades of constant struggles, Americans were tired of apologizing, tired of sacrificing, and tired of feeling bad. The sense of being ashamed and embarrassed by the nation's past deeds was not a natural one for many Americans; it was a feeling both uncomfortable and unwelcome. The transformation from the desolation and gloom of the 1970s to the hope and self-confidence of the 1980s was profound, but the path taken was tried-and-true. In many respects, the country bought its way out of despair, out of defeat, and out of depression. Personal and corporate debt of all kinds soared. Personal sacrifice and thermostat adjustment gave way to unbridled indulgence.

TABLE 8-3

Entrepreneurs, managers, and leaders of the 1970s

Entrepreneurs

John C. Bogle, The Vanguard Group
Thomas J. Burrell, Burrell Advertising
Elisabeth Claiborne, Liz Claiborne
Bennett R. Cohen, Ben & Jerry's Ice Cream
Richard J. Egan, EMC Corporation
Lawrence J. Ellison, Oracle Corporation
Debra J. S. Fields, Mrs. Fields Cookies
William H. Gates III, Microsoft Corporation
James H. Goodnight, SAS Institute
Lore Harp, Vector Graphics
Dee Ward Hock, Visa
Jon M. Huntsman, Huntsman Corporation
Steven P. Jobs, Apple Computer
Philip H. Knight, Nike
George W. Lucas, Lucasfilm, Limited
Alfred E. Mann, Pacesetter
Bernard Marcus, The Home Depot
L. Lowry Mays, CLEAR Communications
Gordon E. Moore, Intel
Allen H. Neuharth, Gannett Company
Michael Ovitz, Creative Artists Agency
Robert E. Price, Price Company
Barbara G. Proctor, Proctor and Gardner Advertising
Charles R. Schwab, Charles Schwab & Company
Frederick W. Smith, Federal Express Corporation
John G. Sperling, Apollo Group
James G. Treybig, Tandem Computer Company
Donald J. Trump, Trump Organization

Managers

Louis F. Bantle, UST
Howard O. Beaver Jr., Carpenter Technology
Henry W. Bloch, H & R Block
Joseph A. Boyd, Harris Corporation
Joseph D. Brenner, AMP
John W. Brown, Stryker Corporation
John H. Bryan Jr., Sara Lee Corporation
James E. Burke, Johnson & Johnson Company
Frank T. Cary, IBM
William K. Coors, Adolph Coors Brewing Company
Robert F. Dee, SmithKline Corporation
Robert E. Dewar, Kmart Corporation
Harrington Drake, Dun & Bradstreet
Walter A. Fallon, Eastman Kodak Company
Edward A. Fox, Student Loan Marketing Association
Earl G. Graves, Black Enterprise Magazine
Alan C. Greenberg, Bear Stearns Companies
Dick Griffey, Dick Griffey Productions
John P. Harbin, Halliburton
Edward G. Harness, Procter & Gamble
Stephen D. Hassenfeld, Hasbro Toys
Paul C. Henshaw, Homestake Mining Company
Raymond H. Herzog, 3M

TABLE 8-3 *(continued)*

John J. Horan, Merck & Company, Inc.
Richard H. Jenrette, Donaldson, Lufkin & Jenrette
Edward C. Johnson III, Fidelity Investments Limited
Reginald H. Jones, General Electric Company
Charles F. Knight, Emerson Electric Company
Harvey H. Lamm, Subaru of America
William E. LaMothe, Kellogg Company
Joseph E. Lonning, Kellogg Company
Whitney MacMillan, Cargill
J. Willard Marriott Jr., Marriott International
Thomas W. Mastin, Lubrizol Corporation
C. Peter McColough, Xerox Corporation
John G. Medlin Jr., Wachovia Corporation
Morton H. Meyerson, Electronic Data Systems
David W. Mitchell, Avon Products
Eugene R. Olson, Deluxe Check Printers
Warren H. Phillips, Dow Jones & Company
Robert T. Powers, Nalco Chemical Company
Edmund T. Pratt Jr., Pfizer
Donald T. Regan, Merrill Lynch & Company, Inc.
John M. Regan Jr., Marsh & McLennan
William J. Ruane, Sequoia Capital
Robert A. Schoellhorn, Abbott Laboratories
Irving S. Shapiro, DuPont Corporation
Vincent R. Shiely, Briggs & Stratton Corporation
Naomi Sims, Naomi Sims Collections
Goff Smith, Amsted Industries
Whitney Stevens, J. P. Stevens & Company
Dwight L. Stuart, Carnation Company
Diane S. M. von Furstenberg, Diane von Furstenberg, Ltd

Charles B. Wang, Computer Associates International
Richard D. Wood, Eli Lilly and Company
Alan L. Wurtzel, Circuit City Stores
John A. Young, Hewlett-Packard Company

Leaders

Leonard Abramson, US Healthcare
Michel C. Bergerac, Revlon
Charles L. Brown, American Telephone & Telegraph
Philip Caldwell, Ford Motor Company
Edward E. Carlson, United Airlines
Helen K. Copley, Copley Newspapers
Paul Fireman, Reebok International, Ltd.
Richard L. Gelb, Bristol-Myers Squibb Company
C. Michael Harper, ConAgra
Frank G. Hickey, General Instrument Corporation
Ivan J. Houston, Golden State Insurance
Harold J. Hudson Jr., General Reinsurance
Lido (Lee) A. Iacocca, Chrysler Corporation
Sidney Kimmel, Jones Apparel Group
Daniel J. Krumm, Maytag Corporation
Francisco A. Lorenzo, Texas Air Corporation
John C. Malone, Tele-Communications
Harold W. McGraw Jr., McGraw-Hill
Rene C. McPherson, Dana Corporation
Anthony J. F. O'Reilly, H. J. Heinz Company
William M. Rosson, Conwood Corporation
Donald H. Rumsfeld, Searle (G. D.) and Company
Robert H. Sorensen, PerkinElmer
Kenneth T. Wessner, ServiceMaster Company

1980–1989

Restoring Glory in American Business

Are you better off now than you were four years ago?

—Ronald Reagan

A FTER A DECADE of constant despair and discontentment, the nation longed for a new sense of hope, and more often than not, it found that hope in business. Businesses were seen as vital partners in the rebuilding of America. To this end, they were given immense latitude, which resulted in a host of new opportunities and sometimes immense wealth. Much of the wealth only benefited a small fraction of the population, but the aura that was created through reinvestment in America was seen as priceless. With high-profile business turnarounds (Chrysler), soaring stock prices (the Dow Jones Industrial Average tripled between 1982 and 1987), unprecedented deregulation, and merger mania on Wall Street, business executives were again vaulted to hero status in the 1980s.

The New Financial Wizards

The stereotypical and "quintessential 1980s business character" was the financier or investment banker who attempted to shake off the shackles of 1970s restraint through heavy debt and restructuring.[1] Risk-prone investment firms like Kohlberg Kravis Roberts (KKR) and Drexel Burnham Lambert pushed leverage to new limits, creating a wave of massive, debt-laden takeovers. Henry R. Kravis, along with his partners, Jerome Kohlberg and George Roberts, was particularly instrumental in legitimizing the use of leveraged buyouts (LBOs) for underperforming organizations. KKR did not just specialize in orchestrating LBOs; it perfected the practice, which culminated in the unprecedented $25 billion buyout of RJR Nabisco in 1988. By making LBOs part of the financial mainstream of American business, Kravis reshaped the perception of debt as a motivating factor for corporate performance.[2]

Similarly, Michael Milken of Drexel Burnham Lambert pioneered the use of junk bonds to acquire companies. These high-yield, high-risk bonds were designed for companies that did not qualify for investment-grade bonds. In addition, junk bonds became the tool of choice for leveraged buyouts, for which the assets of the target company were pledged to repay the debt of the acquiring entity. With this risky but effective leverage tool, a corporate raiding frenzy ensued. In an effort to protect their independence, many targets of takeover attempts bought back their shares from raiders at a premium. Under this practice, which became known as *greenmail*, the raider pocketed enormous sums of money while the corporate entity, though independent, was often left with crippling debt. In the glory days of the 1980s, heavy leverage became a marker of success; it signified a willingness and an appetite to take bold risks.

A consummate risk-taker, Reginald F. Lewis was a significant contributor to this leverage-based reshaping of American business. He not only broke through the conventional molds of financing, but also broke through the barriers for African Americans on Wall Street. Though he was loath to be

The floor of the New York Stock Exchange during the "go-go" 1980s. (Source: Bettmann/CORBIS)

characterized as a role model for aspiring African American business executives, he was nonetheless catapulted to the center stage when, in 1987, he orchestrated the largest offshore leveraged buyout in history. His fierce determination and drive enabled him to overcome the explicit and implicit barriers to success for those born outside the gilded walls of privilege.

Reginald F. Lewis (1942–1993), The TLC Group

Reginald Lewis lived in the segregated city of Baltimore with his mother and maternal grandparents for four years (between the ages of five and nine) after his parents divorced. Since his mother worked long hours as a postal worker and a waitress, Lewis's grandparents became very influential in guiding his early development. His mother and grandparents instilled in him what he called the "very American values" of honesty, hard work, and determination. When Lewis was nine years old, his mother remarried and the family moved to West Baltimore, where the newly married couple soon had children of their own.

Not wanting to be a burden to the growing family, Lewis secured his first weekly paying job when he was just ten. He began delivering the *Baltimore Afro-American* newspaper to ten homes and soon had built his route into a hundred-home delivery business. Lewis juggled his entrepreneurial activities with his studies and his athletic pursuits. During high school, he was the captain of the baseball, football, and basketball teams, and he dreamed of one day becoming a professional athlete. Upon graduating from high school in 1961, Lewis secured an athletic scholarship to Virginia State College, but his hoped-for shot at professional athletics was soon derailed after he suffered a shoulder injury. His relatively small stature (five feet ten), early injury, and limited success on the field resulted in his being named third-string quarterback. Believing that his professional dream was out of reach, Lewis walked away from football and his funding. Losing his athletic scholarship, Lewis was forced to secure a number of employment opportunities to fund his education. His jobs included managing the night shift at a bowling alley and working as a salesman for a photography studio.

Just before his senior year, Lewis learned of an experimental summer program offered by Harvard Law School to introduce minority students to the study and practice of law. Lewis secured from Virginia State the last nomination to the summer program and made the most of his exposure to Harvard

Law School and its key decision makers. Though the program explicitly stated that it was not a feeder for Harvard Law School, Lewis treated it as such. He distinguished himself in the classroom and sought out professors and administrators in an effort to display his intense interest. The combination of Lewis's classroom work and persistence was enough for Harvard to bend its stated policy. Without completing the formal application process, Lewis not only received admission to Harvard Law School, but also was awarded a scholarship from the Rockefeller Foundation.

When he graduated in 1968, Lewis joined the New York law firm of Paul, Weiss, Rifkind, Wharton, & Garrison. In this position, he acquired the initial skills he needed to establish corporations, prepare joint venture and merger agreements, and create the legal groundwork for initial public offerings. Lewis left the firm in 1970 to become a partner with a fellow Harvard classmate, Fred Wallace, in the firm of Wallace, Murphy, Thorpe and Lewis, one of the first black-run law firms on Wall Street. Within three years, two of the partners left the firm and Lewis bought out the rest of his colleagues' portfolios.

He soon hired a corporate attorney, Charles Clarkson, and the new firm, christened Lewis & Clarkson, specialized in the legal services associated with venture capital transactions. In the year that he began his new firm, Lewis became a frequent columnist for the Business and the Law section of *Black Enterprise* magazine. In a portent of things to come, Lewis covered topics ranging from business acquisitions to venture capital to initial public offerings (IPOs). For the next ten years, Lewis & Clarkson helped a number of companies, including Aetna, Equitable, Norton Simon, and General Foods, lend money to minority-owned firms. The law firm's work with minority-owned business enterprises expanded quickly, and it began to specialize in supporting MESBICs (Minority Enterprise Small Business Investment Companies), "venture capital firms formed by corporations which operate under the supervision of the US Small Business Administration."[3] Lewis's reputation continued to grow, and he soon became the leading MESBIC transaction lawyer in the country.

Helping to secure funds and preparing the legal foundation for new enterprises ignited a desire in Lewis to move from business adviser to owner-acquirer. He was clear about how he was going to get there: "When I decided to shift my career from law to active investment, I wanted to build on my strengths, and they were in the area of acquisitions and finance. For me to go out and start my own business was not something I was prepared to do."[4] In the late 1970s and early 1980s, Lewis tried unsuccessfully to acquire several business operations. His secured his first acquisition in 1982: a small radio station on the island of St. Thomas. Lewis had hoped to use this tiny station as the basis of a Caribbean Basin Broadcasting Network, but the station foundered and never turned a profit. Undeterred by this failure, Lewis looked for additional opportunities. In 1983, he was given a tip that the McCall Pattern Company was ripe for acquisition. The 113-year-old producer of sewing patterns was struggling from a shrinking market and declining profitability. In the midst of this otherwise dismal outlook, Lewis saw untapped potential and decided to put together a bid for the company.

Having learned from several failed acquisition attempts, Lewis made the offer not under his individual name but under the name The TLC Group. Though *TLC* stood for "The Lewis Company," he did not reveal its meaning and believed that attaching the word *Group* would signify a much more substantial enterprise than the reality of Lewis as an individual. Nor did he dissuade those who believed the so-called group that he represented consisted of white men. Competing against some of what he called "the bastions of white power on Wall Street," Lewis made every effort to ensure that race was not a factor in the bidding process.[5] Lewis's winning bid for McCall amounted to $22.5 million, of which only $1 million came from his own personal commitments; the bulk of the financing came from a $19 million loan from Bankers' Trust. A key factor in The TLC Group's winning the McCall business was Lewis himself. As soon as he decided to bid on the company, he spent countless hours learning the sewing pattern business and considerable time with the company's principal officers.

After he bought McCall, Lewis demonstrated the same level of focus and determination in helping to reverse the declining trends in the business. He oversaw a significant streamlining process, reduced rebates to retailers, raised prices, recruited new senior management talent from key competitors, and even devised a new product line for the company: greeting cards. The paper presses used to make the company's flagship paper sewing patterns were easily repurposed for producing a new line of greeting cards. His dedicated focus in turning around the business paid off handsomely. By 1986, the company was financially strong and had posted profitability levels that set all-time records for McCall. In fact, the company's profit of $14 million in 1986 was two times more than it had ever earned in any other single year in its 115-year history.

Lewis orchestrated a significant recapitalization program (bringing in $19 million) in late 1986 and hoped to take the company public. With funds from a public offering, Lewis was going to use McCall as a base for additional acquisitions, but the planned IPO never took off. The market was reluctant to back a company in a declining industry. Failing to build a liquid equity base, Lewis decided instead to auction the company. In June 1987, McCall was sold to the British textile giant, John Crowther Group, for $86 million. The deal included $63 million in cash and the absorption of $23 million in long-term debt. The $1 million that Lewis had personally invested in McCall in 1984 resulted in a 60-to-1 return, as The TLC Group pocketed close to $60 million. As was the fate with many debt-laden acquisitions in the 1980s, McCall slid into bankruptcy two years after the sale was completed. CEO Earle Angstadt reflected on the quick sale of the company: "McCall was a means to an end for Reg. He didn't give a damn about the pattern business. He wanted to use it for one purpose only, which was to make a lot of money quickly."[6] Crowthers and Travelers, both of which had assumed the long-term bonds of McCall, sued Lewis for misrepresenting the financial condition of the company. The court ruled against the plaintiffs, arguing that Lewis could not be held responsible for the company's declining performance after he was no longer part of its management team or board of directors.

Meanwhile, Lewis's incredible success in turning around McCall dramatically enhanced his reputation on Wall Street, and he was ready for a much larger opportunity. While many would have settled for a deal five or ten times the size of McCall, Lewis was interested in something much bigger and seemingly unfathomable. His next deal was forty-four times larger than his initial purchase of McCall. Lewis set his sights on the $2.5 billion international division of Beatrice, which was being auctioned by Kohlberg Kravis Roberts. Beatrice's international division consisted of sixty-four properties operating in thirty-one countries. His preliminary bid of $950 million was submitted to Salomon Brothers, the investment firm charged with orchestrating the sale for KKR. The Salomon executive running the deal demanded a face-to-face meeting with Lewis, declaring, "quite frankly, no one knows who the hell you are."[7] Lewis knew that he had to enhance the credibility of The TLC Group to compete with the hordes of analysts working for Citibank, Shearson Lehman Brothers, Pillsbury, and others. He turned to Michael Milken, who had recently contacted him after being impressed with the return that

Reginald Lewis (1952–1993) orchestrated the largest offshore leveraged buyout in 1987, when he took control of Beatrice.
(Source: The Reginald F. Lewis Foundation, Incorporated)

Lewis had generated from the sale of McCall. Milken agreed to help finance The TLC's bid: "My philosophy is that human capital is a scarce resource, not money. With the McCall deal, Reg showed that he had the scarce resources of management talent, a vision of the future and the ability to motivate people and get them to work together."[8]

Bringing Drexel to the table to support The TLC bid was just the first step for Lewis. He summarized his plans in his unfinished autobiography: "We would bid the entire deal, but between contract and closing we would take advantage of the fact that there had been an auction. Not only for the whole company, but for different pieces of the company. And we would effectuate sales during contract closing, while we had nothing at risk. We would then use those proceeds to reduce our debt, effectively selling assets at a higher multiple than we were buying them. This would enable us to reduce our leverage, making what looked like a $1 billion deal really a $400 million or $500 million deal. Then we would focus on a core group of operations, which we would then refinance and grow."[9] Lewis executed the plan almost flawlessly. The little-known The TLC Group produced the winning bid of $985 million for Beatrice's international division. In true LBO fashion, Lewis had to commit only $15 million of his own funds to consummate the deal and receive 55 percent equity in the $2.5 billion operation. For its willingness to back the almost $1 billion deal, Drexel, in contrast, received the remainder of equity.

According to plan, Lewis sold various Beatrice properties, including 80 percent of the Canadian subsidiary for $235 million, the Australian operation for $101 million, and the Spanish meat-processing investment for $90 million. Some of these businesses were sold on the actual day of the LBO. The Latin American operation and the Far East businesses were sold in 1988 for an additional $200 million. Shortly after gaining control of the far-flung enterprise, Lewis had consolidated it into a European core of businesses and had paid down all but $100 million of the company's $700 million in debt. Lewis attempted to pay down the remainder of the debt through an IPO, but again, his plans to cash out a portion of his investments were curtailed. The offering was canceled after negative media coverage made potential investors skittish. The media were centered on the ongoing suit from the McCall sale and the likelihood that Lewis, personally as the largest shareholder, was to be the single greatest beneficiary of the IPO.

Though disappointed again, Lewis threw himself into the operations of Beatrice, paring down unprofitable product lines, slashing costs, and focusing on high-margin performance. Lewis had an uncanny knack for understanding European culture and tastes. He immersed himself in the company's operations, walked the factory floors, taught himself French, and divided his time between U.S. headquarters and Beatrice's European offices. The success of Beatrice and The TLC Group did not come easily. By all accounts, Lewis was a brutal taskmaster who did not tolerate mistakes. During his five-year tenure as head of TLC Beatrice, a slew of executives came and went. An intense perfectionist, Lewis drove others as hard as he drove himself. His unforgiving, hot-tempered, fiery personality left many casualties in his wake. Despite his irascible moods, Lewis produced results, as a food analyst for Merrill Lynch noted in 1991: "There is no question that the company has delivered on what was thought to be some pretty aggressive goals."[10]

For Lewis and many other LBO specialists, the results warranted significant pay and perks. He had no reservations asking the board to approve a $3 million salary in 1990, retroactive to 1988, despite his salary being fifteen times larger than the highest-paid operational executive in Beatrice. For him, the risks that he had taken to orchestrate the unprecedented LBO justified the compensation. He made no apologies for his success.[11] For Lewis and other financial manipulators, success was not always about the long-term value of the enterprise as much as it was about short-term financial gain. And for some, the personal financial gain was phenomenal. In one year, Milken declared earnings of over $0.5 billion.[12]

The government's willingness to take a largely hands-off policy with financial manipulators enabled them to proceed with minimal oversight and little fear of antitrust legislation. The get-rich-quick excitement of the investment world was alluring. Investment banking became the career path of choice for business-school students throughout the country. The epitome of success

TABLE 9-1

Business events that shaped the 1980s

Date	Event
1980	Banking industry deregulated
1980	Supreme Court rules that new life forms created in labs can be patented; supports biotechnology
1980	Cable News Network debuts—first 24-hour-a-day news programming
1980	Prime interest rate for banks reaches high of 21.5 percent
1980	Business management becomes most popular college major
1981	Economic Recovery Tax Act passed, reduces personal tax rates
1981	Columbia Space Shuttle launched for first time
1981	President Reagan breaks PATCO strike
1981	Chrysler reports $1.7 billion loss, largest in U.S. business history
1981	MTV debuts
1981	IBM enters personal computer market
1981	MS-DOS introduced
1982	AT&T agrees to break up business
1982	Congress deregulates savings and loans institutions
1982	*USA Today* introduced
1983	Compact disc player introduced
1984	Women outnumber men in workforce for the first time
1984	United States becomes debtor nation, with $107.4 billion deficit
1984	Apple introduces first computer mouse
1985	Supreme Court rules local banks can form regional networks to compete with big banks
1985	Home Shopping Network goes nationwide
1985	Windows program introduced by Microsoft
1986	*Challenger* space shuttle explodes
1986	Senate approves most complete tax reform since World War II
1987	Dow Jones hits record 2,700 before October crash, drops 508 points ($500 billion in value)
1987	Baldridge Quality Award introduced
1988	Savings and loan crisis peaks
1988	Kohlberg Kravis Roberts engineers record $25.07 billion leveraged buyout of RJR Nabisco
1988	Compact discs outsell vinyl records for first time
1988	Initial funding for Human Genome Project commences
1989	*Exxon Valdez* spills 11 million gallons of oil in Alaska
1989	Communism falls throughout Eastern Europe
1989	Berlin Wall falls
1989	Apartheid begins to dismantle in South Africa

was no longer managing a company, but buying it, selling it, and securing commissions along the way.[13] Eventually, the allure became too bright for traders like Milken and Ivan Bosky. Their high-profile arrests for insider trading tarnished Wall Street, but businesses, in general, did not experience a major backlash. On the contrary, they operated with a free rein through much of the 1980s.

Another Friend in the White House

When he took office, President Ronald Reagan cited "Silent Cal" Coolidge as his favorite chief executive "because he had been so silent, keeping the hand of the federal government out of the conduct of society and allowing business to prosper throughout the twenties."[14] Like Coolidge, Reagan was generally indifferent to details and saw the world not through shades of gray, but in black and white. Both sought simplicity in policies, in statements, and in actions, and both looked to business to jump-start the economy. Reagan's economic recovery plan, labeled Reaganomics, encompassed a healthy dose of military spending combined with significant tax-relief policies. Reagan characterized "godless communism" and "big government" as the two primary obstacles to American recovery.[15] The most far-reaching expenditure designed to demonstrate the superiority of the U.S. military arsenal was the Strategic Defense Initiative. Dubbed Star Wars, the initiative "would use laser-beam technology, à la Buck Rogers, to build an umbrella of protection that would destroy any incoming missile."[16] Though Star Wars was more science fiction than reality, the president's vocal and pressing support for the initiative did much to bolster the military armament programs of the United States and USSR.

The second pillar of Reaganomics was manifested in the 1981 Economic Recovery Tax Act, which for Reagan marked the end of the "era of the government solution."[17] Under the provisions of the act, personal income tax was reduced by 25 percent over a thirty-three-month period, the maximum tax rate was lowered from 70 percent to 50 percent, and the capital gains tax was decreased from 28 percent to 20 percent.[18] According to Reagan's plan, keeping more income in the economic stream would spur investment and unleash a strong entrepreneurial spirit in the country. The initial reduction in federal revenues was accompanied by a series of budget cuts designed to dismantle the welfare state created by the Great Society. Budget cuts included reductions in funding for educational programs, food stamps, Medicaid, Social Security disability benefits, the National Endowment for the Arts, public television, and school lunches. All told, between 1980 and 1984, government spending for social programs was reduced by $140 billion. During the same period, defense spending increased by $181 billion.[19]

As defense spending far outstripped the cuts in social programs, the federal deficit spiraled to record levels. The intense defense spending, however, helped curtail unemployment, and as monetary restraint took hold, the country experienced an economic recovery. The recovery was given a gigantic and fortuitous boost by OPEC's loss of clout. The gradual reduction in oil prices that began in 1983 did much to energize both the lives of Americans and business investment. The oil price decrease also resulted in a reduction in funding for non-oil-based energy sources (solar power, wind, etc.) that had grown in popularity in the 1970s. Business and consumer spending surged through the remainder of the decade. Debt was no longer considered risky or imprudent; it took on a whole new level of prominence, even in the typically conservative banking community.

In 1980, the banking industry was deregulated, a step that provided higher interest rates for small investors and interest payments on checking accounts. The industry had been severely hampered by being forced to pay double-digit interest rates on deposits (upward of 18 percent) while only collecting an average of 8 percent from mortgage holdings.[20] As a result, between 1980 and 1983, five hundred savings and loan institutions (S&Ls) went bankrupt.[21] The U.S. Congress repealed the restrictive investing policies that S&Ls were required to follow and allowed the institutions to invest at first 40 percent and then their entire asset base in nonreal-estate holdings. The government also agreed to federally insure deposits in S&Ls. In an effort to recoup significant losses from the mismatch between interest and mortgage rates, S&Ls invested in riskier ventures, including more speculative real estate and junk bonds. The collapse of the market in 1987, combined with extremely imprudent investing and outright fraud, forced many more S&Ls into bankruptcy and triggered panic. In 1987, more than one-third of the nation's S&Ls lost money or were on the verge of bankruptcy.[22] With its promise to insure S&L transactions, the government was left with a bail-out crisis that reached more than $300 billion.[23]

The experience with S&Ls did not weaken the government's resolve to allow businesses to operate largely unimpeded. Business deregulation that

Charles Keating (right) awaits jury selection in his trial. He was accused of bank fraud in the collapse of the Lincoln Savings and Loan.
(Source: Reuters/CORBIS)

opened opportunities for S&Ls had already changed the competitive land-scape for airlines. While airlines experienced a surge of new competitors (most notably People's Express), the flooded market eventually gave way to massive industry consolidation. Deregulation followed in the utilities sector, with the opening up of markets for electricity, other energy sources, and telecommunications. The outcome for these industry sectors was not too different from banking and airlines. The limited government appetite for regulation and oversight paved the way for the merger activity and consolidation that ensued for the rest of the century. Many Americans celebrated the lack of regulation. After almost two decades of having to adjust to fundamental changes in social, fiscal, and global policies, Americans sought comfort in a return to laissez-faire government and nationalistic pride.

A Turning Point in World Affairs

Reagan's passionate embrace of all things American and his heartfelt conviction against communism resonated with a country trying to reassert its place in the world. Many Americans believed that the country had allowed its global positioning to languish for far too long. The lack of closure from the Vietnam War and the humiliation of being held hostage, both literally and symbolically, by the Middle East were incredibly troubling. Americans were ready to move outside the gray zones of foreign diplomacy. Reagan understood this mind-set and did much to reinforce it. His characterization of the Soviet Union as the "evil empire" in a speech at the National Association of Evangelicals Convention in 1983 established a welcoming and comforting tone for many Americans. He framed the military arms build-up between the Soviet Union and the United States as a "struggle between right and wrong and good and evil."[24]

Mikhail Gorbachev's rise to prominence as the Soviet premier in 1985 marked a turning point in relations between the United States and USSR. When Reagan and Gorbachev met for the first time, they had hoped to lay the foundation for arms control. Despite reaching consensus on a number of cultural and scientific exchanges, they failed to secure an arms treaty. Two years after their initial talks had stalled, Gorbachev and Reagan did reach an agreement to eliminate intermediate-range nuclear force (INF) missiles with a range capacity of 300 to 3,000 miles. Though the treaty resulted in an elimination of just 5 percent of the total nuclear arsenal of the two nations, it had far-reaching implications.[25]

The Soviet policies that helped facilitate the arms-control agreement were, in essence, an extension of the path that Gorbachev took in the early days of his administration. His calls for *glasnost* (openness) and *perestroika* (restructuring) were initially designed to restore faith in the communist state. Instead, they provided the foundation for a quiet, yet immensely powerful revolution. Gorbachev rejected the historically imperialistic efforts of the Soviet Union. He authorized the withdrawal of troops from Afghanistan in early 1989 after nine years of civil strife, and as simmering revolutions percolated throughout the Eastern Bloc of the Soviet Union, the rebellions were not summarily put down. One after another, a series of mostly "bloodless revolutions" ensued in Poland, Hungary, Czechoslovakia, and Bulgaria.[26] The most dramatic and symbolic representation of the collapse of the old world order occurred in November 1989, when Germans from east and west began to chisel away at the Berlin Wall that had separated a city, a country, and a world.

As the former bulwark of communism began to fall, so too did an oppressive political structure in South Africa—apartheid. Overriding a Reagan veto, the U.S. Congress in 1986 endorsed a series of economic sanctions against South Africa. The aim was to pressure the ruling party to enact sweeping changes in both human rights and government structure.[27] Just as Gorbachev became the catalyst for unprecedented change in the Soviet Union,

One of the most haunting symbols of the Cold War begins to crumble—the Berlin Wall falls in 1989. (Source: Jacques Langevin/CORBIS SYGMA)

F. W. de Klerk played a similar role in South Africa. Becoming state president in 1989, he called for a nonracist South Africa, laid the foundation for a new constitution, and paved the way for the release of Nelson Mandela. Most of the sweeping world changes occurred as Americans watched and celebrated from the sidelines. The long, dark days of the Cold War came to an end, and though it was entirely unclear what the future held, it looked bright for Americans. In the end, many believed that good had triumphed over evil.

A Turn to the Right

The silent majority that had gone underground in the wake of the Watergate scandal reemerged in the 1980s as the Moral Majority, a loose, though vastly influential coalition of evangelical Christians and conservative Republicans and Democrats. During the late 1970s and early 1980s, the religious right gained tremendous prominence, especially with its adept use of television. The number of Christian ministries on television increased from 25 in 1978 to 336 by 1989.[28] Though many ministries would experience high-profile falls from grace, these religious groups nonetheless captured a deep and entrenched sentiment in the country. During the Reagan administration, the Moral Majority fully embraced and eventually influenced conservative doctrine, including efforts to reinstate school prayer, weaken abortion legislation, strengthen the death penalty, and censor classroom literature.

Despite Reagan's best efforts to the contrary, America became a less inclusive, more self-indulgent society. Whereas the 1960s and 1970s were all about *them* (the underserved and underrepresented), the 1980s were all about *me*. In the age of glamour and glitz, it was expected that "if you have it [money, looks, or power], you should flaunt it." For some, the manifestation of the self-indulgent society was the continuation of the nation's obsession with health and appearance. Books on dieting and exercise—for example, *The Beverly Hills Diet, Richard Simmons' Never-Say-Diet Book, Jane Fonda's Workout Book,* and *Weight Watchers 365-Menu Cookbook*—became best sellers. The sporting-goods industry also received a tremendous boost in the fitness conscious decade. Between 1980 and 1991, the market for sports clothing increased fourfold, from $3.1 billion to $11.9 billion, and the overall sporting-goods industry grew from $16.7 billion to $45.1 billion.[29]

The generous tax reductions, wild stock market speculation, and huge investment returns brought untold wealth to a small, yet highly visible segment of the population. Between 1980 and 1989, the earnings of CEOs of major U.S. companies jumped from forty times to ninety-three times the salary of the average factory worker.[30] During the decade, over 100,000 new millionaires were minted each year, creating a need to distinguish the merely wealthy from the ultrarich (billionaires).[31] While young urban professionals (yuppies) tried to emulate the lives of the rich and famous, a vast segment of the population was struggling for survival. The other side of massive consumption and gaudy, uninhibited displays of wealth was abject poverty. Despite the efforts of many to build fortresses between the two communities with gated subdivisions and walled-off residences, there was no escaping the severe bifurcation in society. The inequality in opportunity and economic status was especially pronounced for black males. By 1991, nearly 30 percent of black males were likely to be incarcerated, while only 15 percent were expected to complete college.[32]

The decade that reenergized the conspicuous display of greed and consumption simultaneously showcased massive poverty, severe crime and drug abuse, and a frightening health epidemic. The elimination of funding for many social programs and the de-institutionalization of psychiatric wards and other mental-health facilities created a massive surge in the number of homeless Americans. By 1987, one out of every five Americans (including over 12 million children) lived in poverty, an increase of 24 percent since 1979.[33]

While cocaine was the drug of choice for the elite segment of the population in the 1980s, its lower-brow derivative, crack, became widely popular with the urban poor. The high incidence of drug use across all social sectors fueled an increase in violent crime and inspired the ubiquitous "Just Say No" campaign of Nancy Reagan. The same phrase was hurled at homosexuals and intravenous drug users, both of which groups had been linked to a deadly disease—acquired immune deficiency syndrome (AIDS). The initial discovery of AIDS cases in the early 1980s (an estimated 1,300 by 1983) elicited deep concern from health professionals. This concern turned into more generalized public panic by the mid-1980s.[34] It also fueled and reinforced the conservative backlash against the previous decades' sexual revolution and societal permissiveness. Misinformation about AIDS proliferated, hate crimes intensified, and social boundaries fractured. As the death toll reached close to ninety thousand and spread beyond a small segment of the population, the calls for medical research overwhelmed the voices of condemnation.[35]

For all its focus on conservative traditional values, the 1980s witnessed a continued decline in the nuclear family. The proportion of married persons among adults declined from 67 percent in 1960 to 57 percent by 1990 while the proportion of individuals who had never married increased from 22 percent to 27 percent of the population.[36] In addition, the number of households with unmarried couples living together tripled during the decade.[37] The age of men and women when they first married increased, and the overall population of the country aged.[38] During the 1980s, the first wave of the baby-boom generation began to hit middle age, and as these individuals progressed through the life cycle, their numbers and clout influenced the types of issues and businesses that gained prominence.

Immigration Soars

The impact of the aging demography of the country was matched by another fundamental shift in the population—immigration growth. The 1980s was the third decade in a row that witnessed a sharp increase in the number of immigrants coming to the United States. The number grew from 4.5 million in the 1970s to 7.3 million in the 1980s, contributing over 30 percent of the total population growth of 23 million. This 63 percent increase from the 1970s was significant on a number of levels.[39] It was the largest total growth in immigration since

TABLE 9-2

Social and demographic facts about the 1980s

- U.S. population grows from 227 million to 249 million
- National debt reaches $2 trillion by 1986
- United States visited by more tourists (20 million per year) than Americans touring other countries
- AIDS epidemic in United States identified; AIDS quilt unveiled in 1987
- Tabloid TV thrives
- Sandra Day O'Connor becomes first woman member of U.S. Supreme Court
- Sally Ride becomes the first American woman in space
- Fads: preppy clothes, aerobics, Valley girls, tanning salons
- Games: Trivial Pursuit, Pictionary, Cabbage Patch dolls, Smurf, Pac Man, Teenage Mutant Ninja Turtles
- New words: *yuppie, nanosecond, telecommuter, totally awesome, greenmail, wannabe*
- Minimum wage (1980): $3.10 per hour
- Average annual earnings (1980): $15,757 per year
- Life expectancy (1980): 78.2 years for females, 71.1 years for males

the first decade of the twentieth century, and it marked a turning point in the origin of the immigrants.[40] There were eight times as many immigrants from Asia and the Americas than from all of Europe. With these massive increases, the overall composition of the nation changed fundamentally. By 1990, 12 percent of the country's 250 million inhabitants were black, 9 percent Hispanic, 3 percent Asian, and almost 1 percent Native American. Although the percentage of blacks and Native Americans was consistent with the 1970s, the percentage of Asians in the U.S. population doubled and the percentage of Hispanics grew by 40 percent.[41] As large as the numbers of immigrants were, these figures were considered vastly understated, as the country's porous borders allowed easy access for those who sought to circumvent official channels. The growth in illegal immigration led to the passage of the Immigration Reform and Control Act of 1986. This act sought to curtail illegal immigration by enforcing stricter border checks and imposing sanctions on businesses hiring illegal aliens.[42]

As seen in the past, the waves of immigration created significant opportunities for future business executives—ethnic markets opened up, new pools of labor developed, and new challenges in managing and leveraging diversity emerged. During the 1980s, however, the explosive growth in non-English-speaking immigrants ignited resentment in certain communities where tax dollars were earmarked for bilingual education and training programs. Battle lines were drawn between proponents of immersion programs and supporters of gradual assimilation.[43] There was a corresponding battle waging within the struggling labor movement. The decades-old argument raged between those who considered immigrants detrimental to labor's bargaining positions and those who saw opportunities in increasing their dues-paying membership base. Regardless of labor's position on immigration, the stark reality for the labor movement was quite clear: it was in trouble.

Labor's Deep Descent

Reagan delivered a severe blow to the labor movement almost as soon as he was elected to office. In 1981, the Professional Air Traffic Controllers Organization (PATCO) defied federal law and staged a strike, essentially placing the nation's airways in a perilous position. Given the inherent stress associated with their position, PATCO members believed that they were entitled to a raise in their base salary, a shorter work week, and better retirement benefits. Believing that the public would stand behind them, 13,000 of the 17,000 air traffic controllers walked off the job in 1981.[44] The public support that they sought did not materialize; it had turned into outrage and condemnation. Reagan skillfully portrayed the striking PATCO workers as dishonest; they had taken an oath not to strike and had reneged on their word. He gave the striking workers an ultimatum: return to work in forty-eight hours, or lose your job permanently. The majority of striking workers stayed out of work and consequently lost their jobs. Many of the open positions were filled with abundant management resources while a high-profile new hiring campaign ensued. Within three days of the firings, the nation's air traffic was running at 75 percent of capacity. While the cost of training new, nonunion air-traffic controllers was more than PATCO's initial settlement demands, the moral and symbolic victory of a tough president willing to make tough choices was invaluable.[45] Unable to recover from the broken strike, PATCO declared bankruptcy at the end of 1981, and so began a "dismal decade for labor."[46]

Although unions represented 25.2 percent of the nation's workforce in 1980, they only represented 17 percent by 1987, and their numbers continued to fall for the rest of the century.[47] Besides being stymied by an adversarial government administration, the union effort was also deeply impacted by the loss of manufacturing jobs. As businesses began to move manufacturing facilities offshore, the "once mighty economic axis stretching from Detroit to Pittsburgh took on a new appellation: 'The Rust Belt.'"[48] The merger mania and consolidation efforts that swept through the country also resulted in a severe streamlining of manufacturing opportunities. Empty factories resulted in high unemployment in the manufacturing sector and a corresponding loss of bargaining clout. The only area of job growth was in the service sector. Between 1979 and 1987, 98 percent of all new jobs were created in the service sector.[49]

The growth in the service sector and the explosion of productivity tools fundamentally changed the playing field for labor, whose future organizing efforts would shift from the manufacturing shop floor to the office desk. The new technologies that had been introduced in the workplace in earlier decades began to show significant promise, especially in the area of office productivity. Facsimile machines, laser printers, and cellular phones became both more affordable and more accessible as the decade progressed. The initial wave of cellular phones, permanently installed in cars, never reached more than 200,000 customers, but the new version of truly portable phones had a much different fate.[50] After ten years of testing and after spending more than $150 million in research, Motorola introduced the first portable cellular phone in 1983. The introductory package cost $3,000 for the phone and $150 per month for service.[51] Despite the steep fees, portable phones were a must-have for the wheelers and dealers in the explosive 1980s. Although cell phones were initially a status symbol for business professionals, the breakup of AT&T and the opening of satellite transmission lines provided the means and impetus for cost reductions, essentially placing the new telephony within the reach of the masses. The availability of this full compliment of office productivity tools provided the conditions for a new type of employee—the telecommuter.

Productive Technology

IBM's entry in the personal computer (PC) market in 1981 did much to bring a level of legitimacy and credibility to the burgeoning industry. Within two years of the PC's introduction, IBM captured 75 percent of the PC market, and the market kept growing.[52] By 1984, there were 19 million PCs in use in the United States, with usage split evenly between homes and businesses.[53] Though IBM quickly eclipsed Apple in sales, Apple continued to build a loyal following and introduced new innovations designed to simplify the operation of a PC. For instance, Apple's introduction of "a handheld device called a mouse" was touted by the *New York Times* as a major selling point in reducing the skill level of a PC user.[54]

By the end of the decade, the number of PCs in use had tripled to over 60 million.[55] Moreover, almost 40 percent of employees were using a computer at work.[56] Although IBM dominated the early years of the PC explosion, the company soon lost ground, failing to grasp several pivotal opportunities. With the clarity that comes from hindsight, IBM would have benefited tremendously from taking a much larger stake in two of its primary suppliers—Microsoft and Intel. IBM's endorsement of both companies and its willingness to refrain from exclusive contracts fundamentally leveled the playing field. IBM also failed to focus on the changing consumer demands and did not sustain its technological investment. These oversights paved the way for more agile manufacturers and marketers, such as Dell, Gateway, and Compaq.[57]

The technological computer revolution sweeping through the nation's businesses and homes was molded and shaped by venturous entrepreneurs who were able to see far beyond present-day applications. Envisioning a fully interconnected world where communication and data transfer were seamless, the entrepreneurs built businesses to harness the outer limits of this technological innovation. For them, a futuristic world of interconnection did not signify a loss of freedom or privacy, but an unparalleled ability to connect with others in a multitude of ways. Technology became a bridge to communication, a vehicle for productivity, and a significant opportunity for business growth.

In 1982, Scott G. McNealy created Sun Microsystems, one of the most powerful and influential computer manufacturers in the world. Through the development of the interconnected, networked computer model, his company harnessed the technological computing power that functioned as the fundamental infrastructure for a host of business processes, including logistical tracking, operational management, and customer interaction systems. The development of the networked computer model was followed by the design and development of the Java programming language. The combination of a networked infrastructure and online coding language enabled companies to meet the large-scale, real-time data-processing needs warranted by the Internet, and as a result, both Sun and its customers were able to tap into the Internet's vast potential.[58]

While McNealy focused on the infrastructure requirements of an interconnected world, Stephen M. Case concerned himself with the means of one-to-one communication. As a marketing executive at Pizza Hut in the early 1980s, Case spent many nights on the road. To stay in touch with the developments in the home office, Case purchased a Kaypro portable computer and subscribed to one of the earliest online services, called The Source. Case noted: "I remember it being frustrating, but actually magical when you first got into the system and got access to information and were able to talk to people all over the world."[59] Case was so enthralled with this magic that, in 1983, he left his position with Pizza Hut to join Control Video, an online service for users of Atari computer games. Though Case joined Control Video just as the gaming industry was reaching saturation and Atari was imploding, he saw tremendous potential in Control's online offering. With Jim Kimsey, he created the successor to Control Video in 1985. Called Quantum Computer Services, the company offered "the Q-link online service targeted to the general computer user, rather than the computer game enthusiast."[60] Though slow to gain acceptance at first, the Q-link service, renamed America Online (AOL) in 1989, began to generate nationwide interest and excitement. Case's marketing background was an essential element of pushing AOL to the forefront in personal e-mail usage and acceptance. His focus on ease of use, relationship building (chat rooms), one-stop shopping, and seamless interconnectivity became key elements of AOL's marketing programs and helped to establish it as the world's largest online service provider by the early 1990s.[61]

As McNealy and Case were breaking the mold of technology usage, one of their contemporaries was breaking molds in business processes and customer management. Beginning his business in his University of Texas dorm room when he was only nineteen years old, Michael Dell fundamentally transformed the purchasing process for PCs. Recognizing that the explosive growth of PCs had accelerated the computer's fate as a commodity product, Dell embarked on a revolutionary direct-retail system called mass customization. Through Dell's offering, an individual could configure a PC that met his or her unique specifications and requirements, and Dell would subsequently build it to order within two or three days. Dell provided both on-site and remote customer service to ensure that the transaction and setup were as easy and smooth as possible. In 1992, Dell, at twenty-seven years of age, became the youngest CEO of a *Fortune* 500 company. He continued revolutionizing the PC retail market space by being the first to offer, sell, and service PCs over the Internet.[62]

In addition to enhancing office productivity functions, computers were being employed more regularly in all areas of business. In the product design and manufacturing arenas, sophisticated computer-aided design (CAD) and computer-aided manufacturing (CAM) applications helped improve drafting efficiency, eliminated several intense manual labor processes, and enhanced overall productivity levels. The widespread use of CAD/CAM helped contribute to the quality-improvement efforts that became so prevalent and necessary as America attempted to regain some of its lost global competitiveness.[63]

The enthusiasm for technology also spread to a renewed interest in the nation's space program. The maiden voyage of the Columbia space shuttle in 1981 symbolized a resurgent pride and revival in the U.S. space program. The early and significant success of the first few launches helped escalate both funding for and interest in space exploration. The shuttle program also benefited from Reagan's efforts to showcase American superiority in the lingering years of the Cold War, but it did not take long before shuttle launches became almost routine affairs. In an effort to continue to capture the imaginations of Americans of all ages, the twenty-fifth space shuttle flight (Challenger), which was scheduled in 1986, included a pubic-school science teacher as a passenger-astronaut. A major publicity campaign was unleashed, and television monitors were placed in classrooms throughout the country on the day of the launch. When the Challenger exploded one minute and thirteen seconds after takeoff, disbelief and anguish engulfed the nation. A series of high-profile investigations and finger-pointing ensued between NASA administrators, scientists, and contractors. The mighty $1.2 billion spacecraft "had been felled by the malfunction of a $900 synthetic O-Ring."[64] As the space shuttle program went on hiatus for over a year, NASA attempted to redesign its quality-control processes and overall management procedures. NASA's intense quality efforts were being replicated in businesses of all shapes and sizes in the 1980s. After years as a secondary concern, quality had reached the center stage of management attention.

Leaders: Wizardry Through
Restructuring and Realignment

America's waning global competitiveness was in part linked to consumer frustration with having to pay more for relatively lower-quality goods. In the 1980s, U.S. manufacturing concerns adopted Japanese management techniques such as the minimization of line setups, the utilization of just-in-time inventory processes, and the incorporation of supply-chain management in a major drive to bring quality and efficiency to their operations. Less was more—less staff, fewer setups, and less work in progress. Leveraging the 1950s pioneering work of W. Edward Deming and Joseph M. Juran, Philip Crosby Associates was formed specifically to support the quality-control efforts of American businesses. By 1986, some thirty-five thousand business executives had graduated from Crosby's Quality College.[65]

The U.S. automobile manufacturing industry essentially had no choice but to change its processes and procedures. By 1980, Japan had become the world's largest automobile producer, and in that same year, all four major U.S. automobile companies lost money. American Motors lost $156 million, General Motors lost $762 million, and Ford lost $1.5 billion.[66] The biggest money loser was Chrysler. Having posted a record loss of $1.7 billion in 1980, Chrysler was on the brink of bankruptcy when Lee Iacocca, Chrysler's CEO, orchestrated an unprecedented government bailout program. Iacocca essentially convinced the government that it was in the best interests of the country to avoid the massive bankruptcy of an American icon. Considering that Chrysler then employed over 130,000 individuals, the prospect of all those job losses in combination with Iacocca's commitment to enforce strict cost-containment measures was enough to convince the government to authorize a financial rescue plan using taxpayers' dollars. The $1.5 billion government loan guarantees were predicated on Chrysler's ability to secure wage and benefit concessions of $142.5 million from union members and $125 million from nonunion members.[67] With the loan guarantee in place and the endorsement of the major unions, Iacocca embarked on a massive restructuring and realignment of Chrysler.

Over the course of three years, Iacocca discontinued certain car lines, cut inventory levels by $1 billion, invested in promising new models (most notably the minivan), and reduced the number of Chrysler employees.[68] By

1983, the employee count was down to seventy-four thousand, and the net loss of $1.7 billion in 1980 had become a profit of $900 million.[69] With $1.5 billion in cash reserves, Chrysler was in a position to repay its loan to the government. In turning around a company that was considered a national institution, Iacocca was vaulted to celebrity status, and he capitalized on his exposure by penning his autobiography in 1984. It became the leading nonfiction best seller for two years running, ousting the top spot from fellow management gurus Thomas J. Peters and Robert H. Waterman Jr.

Lee Iacocca's turnaround of Chrysler became the embodiment of the CEO as leader and celebrity. (Source: Time Life Pictures/ Getty Images)

At the top of the best-selling list in 1983, Peters and Waterman's influential work, *In Search of Excellence: Lessons from America's Best-Run Companies*, provided advice and other insight for hungry business leaders searching for new ideas and best practices. The authors advocated flexibility and innovation, prudent risk taking, and employee and customer focus. Though the advice was commonsensical, businesses did not have an easy time enacting it. The advice was nevertheless revolutionary in its impact and potential. In many ways, successful leaders had to embrace a back-to-basics approach to managing their operations. For some business leaders, this approach came in the form of streamlining extraneous product lines or whole business segments. For others, it meant severe cost containment and corporate restructuring à la Iacocca. The pruning of business operations often provided short-term, yet painful financial relief, whereas long-term success depended on prudent investment strategies.

When Reuben Mark took over Colgate-Palmolive in 1984, the consumer goods giant was in the midst of reinventing itself. The company had grown tremendously in the seventies through a series of less than stellar acquisitions, and one of Mark's first tasks was to sell off those subsidiaries that were not performing well. Restructuring continued with several rounds of layoffs, plant closings, and reconfigurations. Finally satisfied, Mark began investing again and engineered Colgate's acquisition of Mennen in 1992. Other international purchases followed and these acquisitions, coupled with increased marketing efforts behind its core brands, helped Colgate achieve record profitability levels.[70]

In many ways, the epitome of the 1980s leader who maximized the potential of restructuring, realignment, and focus was Jack Welch. Though not a classical "raider," Welch adopted an inside-raider's approach to confronting the challenges faced by General Electric. His first few years as CEO consisted of extensive cost cutting. He eliminated underperforming operations such as air-conditioning, consumer electronics, and coal mining and concentrated on high-value-added manufacturing businesses (aircraft engines, turbines, medical equipment, etc.), financial services, and entertainment. In total, Welch eliminated 200 businesses (25 percent of the total sales of the company) between 1981 and 1990, which freed up more than $11 billion in capital.[71] During the same time frame, he acquired 370 entities, including Employers Reinsurance, Westinghouse's lighting business, and Kidder, Peabody.

The restructuring of GE in the 1980s resulted in the elimination of over 120,000 positions, even when one factors in the employees who were added through acquisitions. Through this process, Welch transformed GE into one of the most efficient conglomerates of its time. The conglomerate was an industry leader in everything, from aircraft engines to television (NBC) to credit. In fact, Welch asserted that he was not interested in any business that was not, or could not become, the number one or number two competitor in its industry. Beyond his streamlining efforts, Welch refashioned GE by discontinuing corporate planning and moving more decisions closer to individual business units. GE's decentralized management approach, which Welch reformulated, along with central resources and support, provided the foundation for training a slew of great business executives. As a result, the disciplined structure and culture of GE has been adopted by businesses throughout the world.[72]

Managers: Growth Through Innovation

The corporate restructuring and realignment efforts of the 1980s were important strategies for reshaping many devalued and deflated industries. For many of the decade's managers who ran large-scale, historically entrenched businesses, restructuring was not enough; they often had to be far more innovative in their approaches. Some managers bought innovation by leaping on the merger bandwagon to diversify their organizations. Others turned to non-traditional forms of employment practices and embraced wide-scale productivity improvements. For all managers, the promise of extended value and opportunity from quality consciousness was tightly intertwined in their efforts to service their consumers. The demands of consumers had been percolating since the 1960s, and though their concerns waned in the recession of the 1970s, these considerations were back in full force in the 1980s.

Managers who adopted the principles of quality management and embraced the consumer were evident in a host of industries, from soft drinks to financial services to diversified manufacturing. D. Wayne Calloway is credited with streamlining PepsiCo's organization, empowering its employees at all levels and generating substantial growth. Under his leadership, Calloway organized PepsiCo into three major business units: soft drinks, snack foods, and fast-food restaurant operations. By divesting noncore businesses and encouraging risk taking throughout the organization, Calloway posted a four-fold increase in revenues, from $8 billion to $32 billion, and grew PepsiCo's market capitalization from $7 billion to $46 billion between 1986 and 1998.[73]

In the banking arena, John Reed is credited with building Citibank into one of the most powerful and significant financial institutions in the United States. His command of the operational aspects of the business enabled him to create a lean and efficient organization. Having fundamentally streamlined the bank's operational procedures, Reed turned his attention as CEO to investing in its technological infrastructure. Through a heavy focus on automation and technology (especially in the proliferation of ATMs) and through shrewd cost management, Reed posted stellar financial returns that set the stage for the firm's eventual merger with The Travelers Group.[74]

Not only did Paul H. O'Neill lead Alcoa to become the world's largest aluminum conglomerate, but he also gave the company a solid image of integrity, emphasizing life-long learning by all employees and making occupational safety and environmental concerns synonymous with good business. The first outsider to run Alcoa, O'Neill initially focused on one major concern—safety. He rightly believed that improving the company's already strong safety record would lead to greater efficiency and productivity. In many ways, O'Neill's approach created a culture of empowerment and teamwork. O'Neill also turned the hierarchical notions of management upside down, even moving his CEO office into a nine-by-nine-foot cubicle. Though the move was highly symbolic, O'Neill was certainly not considered a touchy-feely manager. For him, the office design provided a means for greater efficiency and communication, which, in turn, would lead to improved operational performance.[75]

O'Neill's notions of office design would certainly have resonated with Max O. De Pree. No doubt, some of Alcoa's furniture requirements were sourced from De Pree's business, Herman Miller. The third family member to run Herman Miller, De Pree grew the business into the second-largest office-furniture maker in the world. Under his direction, Herman Miller stood for much more than high-quality, innovative furniture; it stood for a fundamentally new approach to managing employees. Employees were treated as partners in the growth of the company, sharing in its success as it quintupled in size from $230 million to $743 million. Throughout this dramatic growth, De Pree continued to nurture and develop Herman Miller's unique corporate culture, which consistently placed the company among *Fortune*'s most-admired, most-innovative, and best-managed companies.

Max O. De Pree (1924–), Herman Miller, Incorporated

The path that Max O. De Pree followed to vault Herman Miller to most-admired and most-innovative status was, in many ways, the road less traveled in the 1980s. De Pree rejected the avarice, greed, and spotlight seeking of his fellow CEOs. In his highly acclaimed 1989 book, *Leadership Is an Art*, De Pree expressed his contrarian convictions: "to be at the leading edge of consumption, affluence, and instant gratification is to be at the dying edge."[76] While others measured the totality of their success in financial terms and often-personal financial gain, De Pree and Herman Miller measured success by employee and customer satisfaction metrics.

As one of seven children, De Pree had no plans to enter the family business. Though he worked for the company throughout high school as a janitor, an upholsterer, and a general manufacturing hand, De Pree set his sights on a career as a physician. He moved toward that goal by enrolling in Wheaton College after high school, but when his second year of studies began in 1943, he did not travel to Illinois. He ventured much farther. He headed to the home front, having enlisted in the Army Medical Corps to support the U.S. effort in World War II. When his tour of duty ended, he was ready to get on with life, not go back to school. He reflected: "I didn't have any stomach for more school. I wanted to get married and go to work."[77] That's just what he did. De Pree married his high school sweetheart, and over the objections of his father, he joined Herman Miller full-time in 1947. There he stayed for almost fifty years. He did finish his degree a few years later, graduating from Hope College.

Between 1947 and 1968, De Pree held a variety of management positions within Herman Miller's domestic operations, serving in the company's headquarters in his hometown of Zeeland, Michigan, and in various subsidiary facilities. Shortly after organizing the company's marketing and sales efforts in the late 1950s, he was asked by his older brother, Hugh, who had taken over the company from their father, to reorganize and lead Herman Miller's European operation. The company had entered into a number of licensing agreements as a first, relatively risk-free step in targeting the European continent. After several years of making inroads into the market, Herman Miller was ready to take its international operation to the next level. Named executive vice president of international operations, De Pree relocated his family to Europe to close down the licensing program and establish a joint venture with one of the company's successful licensees.

De Pree returned to Zeeland in the early 1970s to help take the company public. Under his brother's leadership, the company pioneered several furniture design innovations for the open-office concept that gained prominence in the 1970s and flourished in the last two decades of the twentieth century. Hugh maintained his father's practice of reaching out to some of the nation's foremost designers, enabling Herman Miller to sustain its reputation as an elegant, high-quality, innovative furniture designer as it moved from a concentration on the home to the office. Max was instrumental in supporting this transition, and when the company became a public entity, he was charged with organizing a board of directors and advisory team to support the company's transition. In addition, he oversaw the rapid expansion of the company's manufacturing facilities and, in the process, sought to design manufacturing, warehouse, and office space that conveyed the innovative design structure at the core of the company's furniture offerings.

When Hugh retired in 1980, Max was named CEO. He inherited a close-knit company that had been built on a foundation of deep-seated values. Max's father and brother, who ran the company for the preceding fifty-seven years, had created an employee-centric culture in which the employees were encouraged to contribute ideas for improvement and all the employees shared in the profits of the company. The De Prees were firm believers in treating employees not as a means to an end, but as an integral part of the company's fabric and purpose. Max was faced with the challenge of nurturing and sustaining this culture as the company grew in size and scope. As a growing public concern, the company faced skeptics who wondered if it could retain the characteristics that made it so unique and so successful.

Max did not shrink at the challenge. Remarkably, he extended the employee-centric culture in many ways while increasing the sales base of the company by a factor of five. De Pree enhanced the company's commitment to participatory management by instituting what he called roving leadership. With roving leadership, he empowered employees at all levels of the organization to institute change and suggest improvements in productivity or design, or both. He explained his reasoning: "It's no mystery that organizations stand a better chance of reaching their potential when we bring the gifts of everyone to bear on reality than when an organization limits itself to the gifts of a few people at the top."[78] In its hiring practices, the company sought character and chemistry over traditional capabilities, believing that fit was far more important than functional expertise. For De Pree, participatory management was a natural outcome from a fundamental trust in people and their potential. Ongoing communication was also a key component in nurturing an open and participatory environment, and to that end, De Pree willingly shared detailed financial and market information with all employees. With a viable stake in the performance of the company, employees welcomed the monthly information-sharing sessions.

De Pree modified the company's bonus and profit-sharing programs, allowing all employees to share in the financial gains from the suggestions for productivity improvement. He also instituted an innovative employee protection program, which was dubbed the silver parachute plan. While golden parachutes protected the fortunes of a select few individuals within a company, De Pree's silver parachute was designed to protect all employees. Under the provisions of the silver parachute, all 3,500 employees were entitled to generous severance payments. Those with one to five years of completed service were entitled to a full year of severance pay if Herman Miller was acquired and they lost their jobs or quit voluntarily within two years of the acquisition. Those with more than five years of service were entitled to even larger severance provisions. Finally, De Pree championed fairness across the ranks by instituting a CEO compensation plan that capped the pay of the CEO at no more than twenty times the pay of an average factory worker.

The international outreach plans that he began in the previous decade were expanded on a large scale in the 1980s, as new manufacturing operations were built in England and France and dealerships were established in Korea, Malaysia, and Australia. Several additional facilities were built in the United States, and De Pree also embarked on an acquisition strategy, acquiring several innovative furniture-design operations. These companies included Vaughan Walls, manufacturer of movable walls; Tradex, maker of work stations; and Miltech, producer of computer support furniture. As he expanded the company's product lines, De Pree invested heavily in new product development, devoting up to 3 percent of revenue to research efforts. Through acquisitions, strategic partnerships, and targeted research, De Pree extended Herman Miller's offerings from furniture to full office systems.

Although the acquisitions and international expansion of Herman Miller vaulted it to the ranks of the *Fortune* 500 in 1986, De Pree's convictions did not waver as the company doubled in size every few years. The benefits of the participatory management approach were evident in the cost savings derived from employees' suggestions for improving manufacturing operations and product designs. The benefits also extended to the company's absenteeism rate, which, at 1–2 percent, was well below the industry average of 6 percent. In addition, the employee turnover rate of 7 percent was less than half the industry norm of 15–20 percent. De Pree's focus on the employee did much to ward off union organizing efforts, which further enhanced the company's competitive cost position, yet he did not hesitate to enact severe cost-cutting measures, even laying off employees, when the office construction industry suffered downfalls. One shift manager described the Herman Miller culture as "participative, not permissive."[79]

When De Pree retired from the CEO post at the board-mandated age of sixty-five, he was the last family member to run the company. In keeping with their focus on participatory management, Hugh and Max did not want to limit the potential of any employee by supporting nepotism. As such, no De Pree offspring could assume the CEO post. De Pree wanted Herman Miller to be a place where people could realize their fullest potential. By all accounts, that's just what happened.[80]

Business Glory Reaches New Excess

The business boom unleashed by Reagan's business-friendly policies during the 1980s fueled the rise in the Dow Jones Industrial Average, which climbed ever higher until October 19, 1987. On that day, the market suffered a massive course correction, losing 508 points. The total market loss was $500 billion, including market value declines of $20 billion for IBM, $8 billion for General Electric, $6 billion for AT&T, and $4 billion for Procter & Gamble.[81] The market correction was precipitated in part by computer trading models that were scheduled to unleash stock sales based on anticipated or actual drops in index levels. These huge program-based sell orders collided on October 19. As the market dropped by 22.6 percent in one day, panic-stricken investors couldn't help but think back to the 1929 stock market crash. Those fears, however, soon dissipated as no depression followed. Within two years, the market had regained its value.

The readjustment of the market was, in many ways, just another in a series of realignments and readjustments that occurred in the 1980s. To be successful, business executives had to be extremely agile in their ability to adjust to new market realities. While many sought to invest in quality efforts to ensure long-term competitiveness and sustainability, they had no choice but to also pay attention to short-term market conditions. The threat of eroding global competitiveness was matched by the threat of a corporate raider. Under these threats, business executives faced three requirements. First, they needed to be flexible yet focused in their business operations. Second, they needed to be innovative, but prudent in their use of investment dollars. And finally, they needed to ensure quality while adhering to intense measures of productivity and throughput. As businesses continued to thrive, many CEOs embraced their celebrity status. Some became the new super-heroes of America, known as much for their media savvy and skills as for their business acumen.

TABLE 9-3

Entrepreneurs, managers, and leaders of the 1980s

Entrepreneurs

Gordon M. Binder, Amgen
Michael R. Bloomberg, Bloomberg, L. P.
Donald C. Burr, People's Express
Stephen M. Case, America Online
James H. Clark, Silicon Graphics
Scott D. Cook, Intuit
Robert L. Crandall, American Airlines
Michael Dell, Dell Computer Corporation
David Duffield, PeopleSoft
David L. Geffen, Geffen Records
Fred M. Gibbons, Software Publishing
 Company
Andrew S. Grove, Intel
William Guthy, Guthy-Renker Corporation
H. Wayne Huizenga, Blockbuster
Irwin M. Jacobs, QUALCOMM
Robert L. Johnson, Black Entertainment
 Television
Henry R. Kravis, Kohlberg Kravis Roberts
Reginald F. Lewis, TLC Group
John P. Mackey, Whole Foods Market
Scott G. McNealy, Sun Microsystems
Howard Schultz, Starbucks
Joseph M. Segel, QVC
Russell Simmons, Def Jam Records
Steven Spielberg, Amblin Entertainment/
 DreamWorks
Thomas G. Stemberg, Staples
Theodore W. Waitt, Gateway
Oprah G. Winfrey, Harpo Productions

Managers

Lester M. Alberthal Jr., Electronic Data Systems
H. Brewster Atwater Jr., General Mills
Don H. Barden, Barden Communications
James L. Broadhead, FPL Group
Vincent A. Calarco, Crompton Corporation
D. Wayne Calloway, PepsiCo
Lodwrick M. Cook, Atlantic Richfield Company
John W. Culligan, American Home Products
Max De Pree, Herman Miller
Michael D. Eisner, Walt Disney Company
David D. Glass, Wal-Mart
Roberto C. Goizueta, Coca-Cola Company
Eugene P. Grisanti, International Flavors &
 Fragrances
Harold V. Haverty, Deluxe Corporation
Allen F. Jacobson, 3M
Bruce E. Karatz, KB Home
James R. Kuse, Georgia Gulf Corporation
Ralph S. Larsen, Johnson & Johnson Company

Leonard A. Lauder, Estée Lauder
J. Bruce Llewellyn, Philadelphia Coca-Cola
 Bottling
Robert P. Luciano, Schering-Plough Corporation
Kenneth A. Macke, Dayton Hudson Corporation
Clayton L. Mathile, The Iams Company
Hugh L. McColl Jr., NationsBank/Bank of
 America
James R. Moffett, Freeport-McMoRan
Charles W. Moritz, Dun & Bradstreet
J. Richard Munro, Time Warner
J. Larry Nichols, Devon Energy Corporation
John D. Nichols, Illinois Tool Works
Paul H. O'Neill, Alcoa
C. William Pollard, ServiceMaster Company
James E. Preston, Avon Products
Larry L. Prince, Genuine Parts Company
William B. Rayburn, Snap-on Incorporated
John S. Reed, Citibank/Citicorp
Walter V. Shipley, Chase Manhattan/Chemical
 Bank
James D. Sinegal, Costco Wholesale
 Corporation
Herbert A. Sklenar, Vulcan Materials Company
John G. Smale, Procter & Gamble
P. Roy Vagelos, Merck & Company, Inc.
Sanford I. Weill, Travelers Group/CitiGroup
Henry Wendt, SmithKline Beecham
Joseph D. Williams, Warner-Lambert
 Corporation
Edgar S. Woolard Jr., DuPont Corporation

Leaders

Vaughn L. Beals Jr., Harley-Davidson
Hans W. Becherer, Deere & Company
Stanley C. Gault, Rubbermaid
Stanley P. Goldstein, Melville Corporation
Christine A. Hefner, Playboy Enterprises
Edward G. Jefferson, DuPont Corporation
Lewis W. Lehr, 3M
Reuben Mark, Colgate-Palmolive Company
Hamish Maxwell, Philip Morris Companies
Raymond J. Noorda, Novell
Donald E. Petersen, Ford Motor Company
George A. Schaefer, Caterpillar Tractor Company
John R. Sculley, Apple Computer
Roger B. Smith, General Motors Corporation
John R. Stafford, American Home Products
David J. Stern, National Basketball Association
William P. Stiritz, Ralston Purina Company
Linda J. Wachner, Warnaco
John F. (Jack) Welch Jr., General Electric
 Company

TEN

1990–1999

Reengineering, Restructuring,

and Reality Check

The world is poised on the cusp of an economic and cultural shift as dramatic as
that of the Industrial Revolution. (OK, it doesn't take a genius,
or even a politician, to figure out that big changes are afoot when we have a
medium that lets someone throw up a virtual storefront on the
Web and instantly gain access to the global market.)

—Steven Levy, "Random Access," *Newsweek,* July 7, 1997

IN THE WANING HOURS of the century, America seemed to be on the verge of delivering on the promises of its long-held dreams of prosperity for all. In every year of the 1990s, the Dow Jones Industrial Average hit record highs.[1] Between November 1995 and March 1999, the Dow more than doubled, increasing from 5,000 to an unprecedented 10,000.[2] Declining interest rates, increased productivity, and low inflation fueled the incredible performance. American business thrived, and capitalism was showcased as a symbol of prosperity and inclusion. More Americans got swept up in the euphoria of the times than in any preceding decade, with 25 percent of U.S. household wealth invested in the stock market compared with just 10 percent in the 1980s.[3]

The conspicuous consumption of the 1980s continued unabated throughout much of the 1990s as the average savings rate for Americans dipped to a fifty-eight-year low in 1998—a mere 3.8 percent.[4] There was no shortage of

With its indoor roller coaster and theme park, the Mall of America brought consumerism to new heights. (Source: Owen Franken/ CORBIS)

available new products for the consumption-hungry population. By the end of the century, over twenty thousand brand-new products were launched each year, not counting the multitude of "improved" items that were constantly reintroduced.[5] The epitome of consumption was the opening of the 4.2-million-square-foot Mall of America in Bloomington, Minnesota, with a fully enclosed roller coaster, a 1.2-million-gallon walk-through aquarium, and five hundred retail outlets spread over 4.3 miles of store frontage.[6] Called a consumption theme park, the Mall of America employed over ten thousand people and generated over a billion dollars in economic activity.[7]

Though prosperity abounded for many, the concentration of real wealth accumulation was very narrow. While the income and wealth of the richest 5 percent of Americans increased by 20 percent during the decade, the income of the poor and middle class stayed relatively flat or declined.[8] By 1995, the richest 1 percent of Americans held 40 percent of the nation's wealth and had an average net worth of $8 million. In comparison, the bottom 40 percent of Americans had an average net worth of just $1,000.[9] The splintering of the society was evident in the massive proliferation of private security forces to guard the wealthy. By the end of the 1990s, the number of private security forces employed for the rich exceeded the total of all publicly funded police departments.[10]

While long employed by media celebrities, private security even became a status marker for the newly created celebrities of the 1990s: the high-profile CEOs. The celebrity status of CEOs contributed to celebrity-like pay with little correlation to company performance.[11] The typical CEO of a *Fortune* 500 business who in 1990 earned 84 times the pay of an average company worker was in 1999 making 475 times the average company worker's salary.[12] Thomas McCraw aptly describes the phenomenon: "Company lawyers behaving like agents for athletes, drafted stock option and other 'incentive' plans that often ensured that executives would come out ahead no matter what happened to the firm."[13]

The 1990s CEO was part showman, part gambler, part magician, and part businessperson. There were often no counterbalancing forces to prevent the excesses that ensued, and for the most part, no one was challenging the status quo. When companies like Yahoo!, with 637 employees, minimal sales, and negative margins in 1998, had the same market capitalization as Boeing, with 230,000 employees, deciphering between rational and irrational economic behavior became increasingly problematic.[14] In the euphoria of the times, hardcore financial analysis took a backseat to the speed of launching high-tech IPOs. There was no time for reflection; speed was the new mantra of the times.

Globalization Takes Center Stage

Speed was not just the domain of business. It applied to all things, even war, in the 1990s. In the opening year of the decade, Saddam Hussein's attack on Kuwait initiated a war like no other that Americans had seen or experienced. The advent of twenty-four-hour satellite news coverage, most notably from Ted Turner's Cable News Network (CNN), set a new standard of real-time war reporting. In addition, the use of smart bombs, or precision-guided missiles designed by companies like Raytheon, were widely touted as part of a new "surgical" military strike force designed to minimize civilian casualties while delivering a powerful blow to strategic enemy caches. The six-week war resulted in fewer than 150 American casualties, but tens of thousands of Iraqi dead.[15] The unofficial counts of 100,000 or more Iraqi dead bore witness that much more intelligence was required for truly "smart" bombs, yet the swiftness of the victory was wildly heralded. Though Saddam Hussein remained in power for another thirteen years, CNN's and other television networks' broadcasting of both the physical destruction of Baghdad and the images of Iraqi soldiers surrendering in droves reassured a public long grown weary of military intervention. When Soviet foreign minister, Eduard Shevardnadze, and U.S. secretary of state, James Baker, issued a joint statement of condemnation of

CNN's broadcast of the Persian Gulf War marked a turning point in war coverage. (Sources: top, Zen Icknow/ CORBIS; bottom, Ricki Rosen/CORBIS)

Iraqi aggression, it marked the first time since World War II that the two superpowers had acted in concert. With this convergence of opinion, the tectonic plates of communism and capitalism began an irrevocable shift.[16]

The market reforms that Mikhail Gorbachev initiated at the close of the 1980s continued in the 1990s with the Soviet state's formal approval of private ownership of businesses; it was a privilege that had been denied for almost six decades. The initial taste of freedom unleashed an almost unquenchable thirst. The momentum was swift and incredibly forceful. By 1991, fifteen republics had declared independence from the Soviet Union, and Gorbachev, though popular on the world stage, had lost domestic support. Gorbachev survived a coup attempt in 1991, but the price of survival was high. He was forced to resign as head of the Communist Party and eventually from the presidency of a dismantling Soviet state. He could do little but watch as nation after nation broke its allegiance to the Soviet Union.[17]

Though fueled by euphoria and excitement, the hard and bitter struggle of reformation for many of these burgeoning economies had just begun. Moving from a centrally controlled state to private-enterprise- and market-based economies proved difficult especially when privatization efforts resulted in inflation and monetary devaluation. The euphoria of freedom lasted a few months; the austerity of reform lasted for years. As former communist nations flirted with capitalism, they soon realized that even gradual market-based movements often produced harsh initial results. For many years after the declarations of independence, the standard of living for the majority of citizens actually declined.[18] For those in formerly communist controlled Yugoslavia, the result was far worse. The dismantling of the communist state exposed the fragility of the peaceful coexistence of diverse ethnic allegiances. Civil wars erupted throughout the country, resulting in the reprehensible practice of ethnic cleansing.[19]

The barbarism of an imploding Yugoslavia was matched by civil war in Somalia, ethnic strife in Rwanda, coups in Haiti, and constant tension between Israelis and Palestinians. Although the so-called Empire of Evil had been subdued, regional conflicts with a wide variety of ideological, political, and historical causes arose to take its place. For U.S. foreign policy, the end of the Cold War brought an end to a sense of clarity if not moral righteousness and an easily defined enemy. George H. W. Bush and his successor, William J. Clinton, struggled as presidents to define a consistent agenda for the United States in the post–Cold War world, as U.S. foreign policies were almost always fraught with strife and ambiguity. The role of the U.S. military also changed from conventional warfare and preparedness to peacekeeping and stabilization.[20] With that shift, defense spending was markedly curtailed, and many businesses like Boeing had to cope with a significant loss of government contracts.

Even as ethnic conflicts dominated the global landscape and threatened the stability of many nations, the Asian financial crisis threatened to cripple a large portion of the world economy. Thailand's currency, the baht, was the first to falter in 1997, and it was quickly followed by collapses in South Korea, Indonesia, Malaysia, and the Philippines. All these nations sought economic relief from the International Monetary Fund, which granted the relief in exchange for strict fiscal management policies. By 1998, the faltering Asian crisis had spread to the economic crown jewel of the region, Japan. Japan's Nikkei 225 stock index lost two-thirds of its peak value in 1998, and its once red-hot real-estate market became tepid and lackluster.[21] The government of Japan tried to prop up the Japanese economy through the strength of the country's historical trade surpluses, but the relief was temporary. Continued efforts to sustain employment levels took a tremendous toll on the economy.

As Asia struggled to regain some of its former glory, eleven European nations were on the verge of uniting. Under the Single Europe Act, England, France, a newly united Germany, and eight other nations agreed to abide by a single currency by 1999 and to establish a European Central Bank. Their efforts to join forces were designed to provide greater economic clout on the world stage and improve intercountry trading on the continent. The initial creation of the European Union resulted in a market containing an estimated 340 million people, a size that put it on par with the North American marketplace.[22]

For its part, North America created a free-trade zone through the adoption of the North American Free Trade Agreement (NAFTA). NAFTA, which went into effect on January 1, 1994, was designed to gradually eliminate tariffs on goods between Mexico and the United States. A similar free-trade policy already existed between the United States and Canada. When the agreement

The two sides of the North American Free Trade Agreement, which ultimately passed in 1994. (Sources: left, DAEMMRICH BOB/CORBIS; right, Matthew Mcvay/CORBIS)

was enacted, Mexican tariffs on American imports averaged 13 percent.[23] NAFTA was designed to lessen trade barriers and "to demonstrate once and for all free trade's vast power to turn a developing nation into a modern economy."[24] The results during the first ten years have borne out some of the promises outlined when the agreement was initially enacted. By 2004, Mexican exports increased from $52 billion to $161 billion, per-capita income increased 24 percent to $4,000, and exports as a percentage of gross domestic product increased from 15 percent to 30 percent.[25] As expected, foreign investment in Mexico rose tremendously, and many American businesses sought cheap manufacturing labor to compete with the flood of imports to the United States.

Labor Struggles with Globalization and Reengineering

It was just this fear of job loss from the United States that sparked labor's deep opposition to NAFTA. Broader globalization brought fears of massive outsourcing and displacement. While many manufacturing jobs did go south and elsewhere, the reality of massive unemployment and dislocation did not fully materialize. When NAFTA was enacted in 1994, the U.S. unemployment rate stood at 6.1 percent. The unemployment rate fell in every subsequent year of the decade, reaching a low of 4.2 percent by 1999.[26]

Though the unemployment figures told a positive story for labor, the reality of prosperity was very different. The falling unemployment rate did not address the underemployed, the multiple jobholders, the move toward replacing full-time employees with part-time ones to limit benefits, or the loss of bargaining clout by the union movement, which by 1990 represented less than 20 percent of the U.S. workforce.[27] When the 1990s began, the country was in the midst of a recession, and with the downturn came a massive effort to streamline and reengineer companies. In 1991, Xerox and IBM cut more than 30,000 salaried employees from their payrolls; General Motors announced 74,000 cuts on the heels of 200,000 lost jobs in the 1980s.[28] The primary victims of the reengineering efforts were middle and upper management, which were twice as likely to be laid off as their blue-collar colleagues. Between October and December 1991, some 2,600 white-collar workers were losing their jobs *every day*.[29] Their ability to reestablish themselves in equivalent positions was extremely difficult; a 1996 *New York Times* article reported that only 35 percent of laid-off white-collar workers found jobs of equivalent pay and level.[30]

Having and keeping a job in the 1990s often did result in greater overall wages but generally much longer working hours. The number of hours worked per year increased from 1,600 in 1990 to 1,950 by 2000, which was the highest amount of any industrialized nation.[31] Part of the increase resulted from displaced employees who had to work multiple jobs to maintain a comparable living wage, part came from the intensity of having to work at companies with fewer employees, and a final part came from the frenzy to capitalize on the promises of accelerating technology. As work hours increased, so too did real wages. Between 1991 and the end of the decade, real-wage gains for all private-sector workers increased by 1.3 percent a year, compared with a 0.2 percent overall gain per year in the 1980s. Many economists point to the increase in real wages as one factor continuing to fuel the massive consumption desires of the decade. The wage increase was overshadowed by big gains in productivity, which rose at a 2.2 percent annual rate during the same period.[32]

As in the previous two decades, job growth was concentrated in the service sector. By 1998, government and service sectors accounted for 75 percent of the U.S. gross domestic product.[33] The shift to service-sector opportunities was again accelerated by the adoption of technology. Though technology helped standardize a cadre of lower-level functions, it also fundamentally realigned the role of the manager. Advances in office technology facilitated a "self-service" approach to clerical duties. Managers now wrote their own reports, prepared their own presentations, maintained their own calendars, and reabsorbed "many of those activities that were carved out, routinized, and precipitated by lower level clerical work."[34]

Beyond realigning the office landscape, technology transformed the nature and value of certain positions. Technology facilitated a "shift into a fundamentally different sort of economy in which knowledge and human resources represented the only sources of sustainable advantage."[35] The incredible thrust to find technology-savvy employees in the dot-com frenzy of the 1990s stood as a testament to the new values. Though businesses were derided for their waning loyalty to employees, technology-savvy individuals thought little of jumping from job to job in their effort to find the new oil well of the 1990s— the high-flying tech IPO.

Technology's Internet Boom

Often called the backbone of the information revolution, the information superhighway was—like the computer before it—a "child of the cold war."[36] The superhighway began its life as the Advanced Research Projects Agency Network (ARPANET), designed as an internal networking vehicle for fostering collaboration within various Department of Defense groups in the 1960s. Through the use of satellite communications, telephone lines, and, later, fiber-optic cables, ARPANET was a decentralized network of linked computers. For two decades the network remained in the domain of officials in the U.S. government and scientists throughout the nation's universities. The National Science Foundation assumed control of the network in the 1980s and for a short time attempted to prohibit its commercial use. The network might have remained the playground for scientists and under the tight control of government officials if not for the work of Tim Berners-Lee, who in 1989 conceived and developed the World Wide Web while employed at CERN (now called the European Laboratory for Particle Physics).

Though e-mail had long existed and many companies were using electronic data-interchange services to connect with upstream suppliers and downstream buyers, the development of hypertext markup language (HTML) paved the way for a fundamental shift in how individuals communicated and businesses interacted. Berners-Lee developed a universal document identifier, later called universal resource locator (URL), which linked documents to specific computers and locations. He wrote a program that he called World Wide Web, using a point-and-click hypertext editor (http, for hypertext transfer protocol). In 1991, Berners-Lee released the first Web server, on which he published the specifications for URLs, HTML, and http to "promote wide adoption and discussion."[37] One of the sites to gain access to the new Web server was the National Center for Computing Applications at the University of Illinois.

It was there in 1992 that undergraduate student Marc Andreesen participated in a team effort to develop a more enhanced version of a Web browser that could run on the popular UNIX-based computer networks and could be accessible by most personal computers. The team called the browser Mosaic, and it accommodated both text and color graphics. In 1994, Andreesen licensed the rights to Mosaic from the University of Illinois, and with the help of Jim Clark, founder of Silicon Graphics, launched Mosaic Communications. The University of Illinois had licensed Mosaic to several other companies and soon threatened Andreesen with a lawsuit to cease and desist in operating under the name Mosaic Communications. In late 1994, Andreesen and Clark reorganized the company as Netscape Communications and launched a much-enhanced version of Mosaic using the name Navigator.

Deciding to gamble with a relatively uncertain revenue model, Netscape chose to distribute Navigator for free. With this move, Navigator quickly became the dominant Web browser.[38] Its ease of use and portability thrust the World Wide Web on an unprecedented growth path. One year after the release of Netscape Navigator, 100,000 Web sites were online.[39] In 1996, Netscape went public and garnered a first-day market capitalization of $2.3 billion.[40] With its twenty-four-year-old billionaire founder, Netscape set a precedent for achieving an incredible valuation with virtually no track record of sales and profits. Internet-based companies, Internet-related companies, and even Internet wannabes circumvented traditional financial analysis and valuation protocols as part of the dot-com hysteria in the late 1990s.

The popularity of the Web was largely unprecedented, gaining acceptance "into the mainstream of American life" faster than any other technology.[41] In 1993, ninety thousand Americans had access to the Internet. By the end of the decade, that number had increased a hundredfold.[42] In 1998, the number of e-mails transferred between computer users exceeded 600 billion, 500 billion more "pieces of mail" than were delivered by the U.S. Postal Service.[43] Fiber-optic networks, digital cable lines, and wireless technology all contributed to an acceleration of Internet enhancements and user acceptance. What once seemed like science fiction—an interconnected world with billions of bits of data flying across hidden communication lines—had entered the mainstream.

Unfathomable advances in medical science matched the speed with which Internet technology developed and made the unreal, real. The fervor that was elicited with the first test-tube baby in 1978 was considered mild when a sheep named Dolly was cloned in 1997. A *Time* magazine cover story appearing a week after the cloning announcement read: "A line has been crossed, and reproductive biology will never be the same for people or for sheep."[44] If cloning sheep could be done, what was next? The seemingly impossible became possible in the late 1990s, especially in the field of fertility, as a sixty-three-year-old woman gave birth to a baby, as another woman gave birth to seven, and as a middle-aged mother became a surrogate womb for her infertile daughter. The advances in medical science unleashed a flurry of social, moral, and political debates that have continued to rage on. The acceleration of change challenged the government to define boundaries for research and exploration—boundaries that often defied consensus.

Government's Missed Opportunities and Broken Promises

Government consensus on any issue in the 1990s was difficult at best. Both presidents served with congressional bodies that were at times outright hostile and at times merely bipartisan. Though President Bush's popularity soared after the Gulf War and exceeded approval ratings of 90 percent, he stumbled badly in addressing the economic recession that gripped the country in the years following the war. By election year 1992, the unemployment rate hit an eight-year high of 7.5 percent.[45] Although he had declared a war on the government's spiraling deficit and heeded calls for greater protectionism, Bush could do little to bolster confidence in the overall economy and in his presidency.

Challenging Bush from the right in the 1992 presidential race were Patrick Buchanan, an archconservative, and H. Ross Perot, a staunch protectionist. From the left, the Democrats, under candidate Bill Clinton, moved their issues to the center. In so doing, the Democrats captured the White House. Perot's ability to garner almost 19 percent of the vote essentially denied a second term for Bush.[46]

Clinton entered the presidency full of promise and hope, yet he left the White House eight years later considerably disgraced and dishonored. His difficulties began even before he assumed the presidency. Clinton and the first lady, Hillary Rodham, were accused of financial and legal misconduct in land development activities while he was governor of Arkansas. Although the charges, under what became known as the Whitewater Affair, did not produce evidence of wrongdoing by the Clintons, the independent-counsel investigation that initiated the inquiry later resulted in far more damaging personal revelations that consumed the nation.

Though he had the advantage of Democratic majorities in the House and Senate during his first two years in office, Clinton struggled with the passage of broad-reaching legislation. Angering key constituents, Clinton backed away from campaign pledges to enact a middle-class tax cut and to provide a safe haven for gays in the military. A hotly contested package including spending cuts and tax hikes on corporations and high-income individuals passed by a very slim margin. Clinton, however, did succeed in passing two important pieces of legislation—the Family and Medical Leave Act and the Brady Bill—in his first term. The Family and Medical Leave Act enabled employees to take extended job leaves to care for a new child, a family member, or themselves without the fear of losing their jobs.[47] The Brady Bill, named for Reagan's press secretary, who was shot in an attempted assassination of the president in 1981, called for background checks and a five-day waiting period for the purchase of a handgun.[48]

Though lauded for these two bills, Clinton was less successful in pushing forth his most important initiative, health-care reform. With almost $700 billion spent on medical care in 1990 and an estimated 38 million Americans without adequate insurance, health care seemed ripe for reform.[49] Chaired by the first lady, the health-care reform task force was charged with developing an affordable plan of universal health coverage, but pharmaceutical manufacturers, insurance providers, small-business owners, and others who feared the financial repercussions of the potential legislation soon thwarted the task force's efforts. Unable to bridge a bipartisan gap, Clinton had to abandon universal health coverage by the time congressional elections were under way in the fall of 1994.[50]

The 1994 congressional elections reversed the majority numbers in the House and Senate for the first time in fifty-two years and thrust House speaker, Newton Gingrich, into the national spotlight with his "Contract with America." Believing that the Republican victories in the elections signaled a mandate for change, Gingrich's "contract" sought to limit the size of government, reduce regulation, balance the federal budget, enact welfare reform, reduce conservation efforts, set term limits, and provide the president with a line-item veto on budget proposals.[51] During the next year, the Republicans in Congress proposed a plethora of bills to "fulfill the terms of the contract," yet only four relatively low-profile bills of the twenty-six proposed were officially enacted.

By the 1996 election year, the "Contract with America" unceremoniously expired as the economy improved. The election year also brought with it a short window of opportunity for consensus between Democrats and Republicans. The minimum wage of $4.25 per hour was increased by ninety cents over thirteen months; significant tax cuts, to be phased in over a ten-year period, were enacted for small businesses; and most importantly, the Personal Responsibility and Work Opportunity Reconciliation Act was passed. The act, which included the most significant changes to welfare since 1935, turned over the responsibility for welfare management to the states. Another goal of the legislation was to reduce Aid to Families with Dependent Children, food stamps, and other welfare programs by $56 billion over the course of six years.[52]

On the wings of welfare reform and a booming economy, Clinton easily won reelection. Ironically, from a fiscal perspective, Clinton's actions and accomplishments delivered on many of the mandates from the Republican "contract." During his administration, the number of government employees was significantly reduced, the budget was balanced, the trade deficit became a surplus, the national debt was reduced, welfare was reformed, and the economy thrived with low unemployment, low inflation, and massive capital investment.[53] The limited government appetite for regulation continued and paved the way for the unprecedented $37 billion merger of WorldCom and MCI in the telecommunications sector. This merger was then dwarfed by the $70 billion merger of Citicorp and Travelers in the financial services

sector. The resulting entity, Citigroup, shattered many provisions of the Glass-Steagall Act of 1933, which was designed to fundamentally separate specific financial-service offerings between operating entities.[54]

While generally pro-business, the government kept a watchful eye on the growing importance and ubiquity of some forms of commerce—most notably, the dissemination of software and Internet access. With its Windows operating system controlling 85 percent of the market and its constant practice of buying upstart competitors or driving them out of business, Bill Gates's Microsoft was accused of predatory pricing and monopolistic behavior. A widely publicized antitrust attack against

Microsoft chairman, Bill Gates, testifies before Senate Joint Economics Committee to defend his company against antitrust allegations. (Source: Reuters/CORBIS)

Microsoft was reminiscent of the breakup of Rockefeller's Standard Oil some eighty-eight years earlier. Though Microsoft withstood most of the attacks, it remained under close scrutiny, a target of its own success and excess.[55]

Though Clinton presided over the country during one of its most dramatic and far-reaching periods of growth, he was constantly embroiled in scandals, which tainted both his reputation and the office of the president. Clinton showed the same weakness that Nixon suffered, an inability to admit a mistake in the face of irrefutable evidence, and both men suffered more from their attempts to cover up scandals than from the scandals themselves. After being the first president to testify before a grand jury and after seven months of vehement denials, Clinton admitted to an inappropriate relationship with a White House intern. The act of contrition was too late to salvage his reputation, and calls for his resignation intensified. Though he held off an impeachment attempt late in his presidency, Clinton could not hold back public discontentment. Many of his actions fueled the fires of an already-growing conservative movement in the country.[56]

A Fractious Society

The U.S. Supreme Court nomination and subsequent appointment of Clarence Thomas became a lightning rod for the clash between conservatives and liberals. Bush nominated Thomas in 1991 to replace Thurgood Marshall, the first African American member of the U.S. Supreme Court. A black federal judge, Thomas held staunchly conservative views; he took issue with the idea of a minimum wage, desegregation through school busing, and affirmative action.[57] His hotly contested views notwithstanding, it was the allegations of sexual harassment and abuse brought forth by Anita Hill that captivated the attention of the American public. A black law professor, Hill had worked for Thomas when they were both employed at the Equal Employment Opportunity Commission from 1982 to 1990. Hill's forceful and tempered accusations of inappropriate language and behavior were passionately denied by Thomas, and the testimony surrounding Thomas's nomination became embroiled in an essentially unresolvable "he said, she said." Though Hill suffered a blow to her own personal reputation, she had brought the specter of workplace sexual harassment to the national consciousness. With a 52-to-48 vote in the Senate, Thomas was narrowly confirmed as a Supreme Court justice. With a conservative majority on the court, decisions were made to limit affirmative action, limit the legal remedies for segregated public schools, and limit the use of election districts drawn to create black or Hispanic majorities.[58]

The conservative court ignited simmering racial tension in the United States. The simmering burst into a raging flame in 1992, when white Los Angeles police officers accused of brutally beating a black man during an arrest were acquitted. The incident would certainly not have consumed national media attention without the existence of a videotaped recording of the arrest and beating. The tape showed clear evidence of at least fifty-six blows over eighty-one seconds to Rodney King and galvanized blacks, who had long believed that they were targeted for much harsher police treatment than other suspects.[59] When the acquittal was announced, riots raged throughout South Central Los Angeles. The three-day mayhem, which involved mostly black-on-black violence, resulted in the deaths of fifty-four people and property damage approaching $1 billion.[60]

The strained racial relations that were exposed in the King trial were only a warm-up to the case that riveted and shocked the nation. From the white Bronco chase on the Los Angeles freeways to the police standoff in the driveway to the infamous glove demonstration, the trial against Orenthal James "O. J." Simpson became a national obsession for close to a year. Every detail, every facet of the case, and every conceivable expert was paraded on national television, all day, every day. When his "dream defense team" helped secure Simpson's televised acquittal, his victory, heralded by blacks as vindication and condemned by whites as unjust, symbolized the deep divide in the country.[61]

The splintering of society so evident during the Simpson trial was, unfortunately, not an isolated instance. During the 1990s, the militia movement mustered a strong resurgence. These antigovernment groups believed that an increasingly overreaching congressional force was jeopardizing civil liberties, especially after the passage of the Brady Bill.[62] The militia's distrust of the government also greatly intensified after the fateful fire that killed almost ninety members of the Branch Davidian apocalyptic religious sect in Waco, Texas. When the Federal Bureau of Alcohol, Tobacco, and Firearms responded to allegations of child abuse and fears of a potential mass suicide, the bureau called in the national guard. After a fifty-day standoff, the guard thrust flammable tear gas into the buildings, hoping to facilitate a mass exit, but the result was far different.[63] The buildings were incinerated almost beyond recognition, and the national guard's actions were heavily scrutinized. For the militia movement, the actions of the government were further evidence of the slow disintegration of individual rights.[64]

On the second anniversary of the Waco incident, a bomb burst through the Alfred P. Murrah federal building in Oklahoma City, killing 168. What at first was thought to be the act of a foreign terrorist was soon discovered to be the work of a veteran U.S. soldier. The arrest of Timothy McVeigh shortly after the explosion created an aftershock that mirrored the wide-scale hysteria that was evident on the day of the bombing. It was hard for many Americans to believe that one of their own citizens could conceive and execute such a heinous act.[65] Unfortunately, it was all too easy for Americans to believe that the bombing could come from the hands of foreign terrorists. The witch hunts that occurred after the bombing, especially aimed at Arabs, showcased some of the worse aspects of the fractured country and its evolving melting pot. The huge waves of immigrants to the United States in the 1990s continued to change the mix of the country's population and provided fodder for antigovernment rhetoric.

TABLE 10-1

Social and demographic facts about the 1990s

- U.S. population grows from 249 to 281 million
- 25 percent of Americans live in Sun Belt
- 2 percent of Americans are farmers
- 25 percent of Americans are college graduates
- 58.9 percent of women are in the workforce
- O. J. Simpson trial captivates nation
- 1995 bombing of federal building in Oklahoma City shakes nation
- Massive proliferation of casinos
- U.S. Army adopts "don't ask, don't tell" policy on homosexuals
- Fads: feng shui, Martha Stewart home crafts, grunge, hip-hop, casual Fridays, beanie babies, WWJD
- Games: Furby, Tickle Me Elmo, in-line skating
- New words: *cybercafé, Generation X, page views, stickiness, Ebonics, millennium bug, Y2K*
- Minimum wage (1990): $3.80 per hour
- Average annual earnings (1990): $25,889
- Life expectancy (1990): 79.0 years for females, 72.4 years for males

A New Melting Pot

Almost one-third of the population growth in the 1990s stemmed from immigration as the number of immigrants topped 9 million, the largest surge in the twentieth century. The last time the number of immigrants had approached 9 million was during the first decade of the twentieth century, when 8.7 million came to America's shores. Though comparable in terms of sheer size, the immigrant pools had vastly different compositions. At the turn of the century, 90 percent of immigrants hailed from Europe. At the close of the century, only 15 percent came from Europe. Fifty percent came from the Americas (Mexico, Central America, the Caribbean, and South America), and 31 percent came from Asia (most notably China, India, and the Philippines).[66]

The growth of immigration from Mexico and other Latin American countries resulted in a shift in the largest minority group in the country. Between 1980 and 2000, the U.S. Hispanic population more than doubled, reaching 35.3 million, and by the end of the decade, the U.S. census confirmed that persons of Hispanic or Latin origin, representing 12.5 percent of the population, outpaced the 12.3 percent of the population classified as black, or African American.[67] Also by the end of the decade, at least 18 percent of the U.S. population spoke a language other than English in their homes.[68] This was especially the case in California and Texas, where the vast majority of immigrants (both legal and illegal) from the Americas settled. Though the official estimates of immigration were set at 9 million, the number of undocumented immigrants crossing the border was estimated to be significantly greater.

While immigration was dramatically transforming the melting pot, the overall demographic composition of the country was also experiencing a fundamental shift. As the country stepped on the precipice of the twenty-first century, U.S. households with married couples comprised just over 50 percent of the population, down from 78.1 percent in 1950.[69] More individuals were either not marrying or delaying the date of marriage. As the population continued to grow older, the country's median age hit a record 35.3 years in 2000; its previous high was 30.2 years prior to the baby boom.[70] The aging population, the changing mix of immigrants, and the growth in nontraditional family types all contributed to the explosion of diversity in the country.

Businesses sought to capitalize on this diversity in a number of ways—by targeting products to specific constituents, by expanding their employee talent pool, and by tapping into innovative new ways of managing.

Managers: Standardizing Innovation

One individual who sought to capitalize on global diversity on a grand scale was Alfred M. Zeien of the Gillette Company. Already considered one of the most successful multinational corporations in the world, Gillette became, in the words of Zeien, a "truly global company" in the 1990s when it developed the capabilities to simultaneously release new products in multiple countries with minimal or no customization. Zeien believed that Gillette should not be in any business in which it could not be the world leader. He explained that his focus on world dominance was reflected in the company's unique and extensive research and product-development focus: "we have never launched a major new product without having its successor in development. Leadership can only be achieved if you are in command of your business. And command of your business means being in command of your product development."[71] In many ways, Gillette took product cannibalization to a new level, a level that infused a sense of aggressiveness and drive in the product development efforts of the century-old institution.

Alfred M. Zeien (1930–), Gillette Company

Alfred Zeien was raised in Jackson Heights, a New York City neighborhood rich in cultural diversity and ethnic flavor. His father was a skilled craftsman who specialized in cabinet making and spoke four languages. Being multilingual and having practical skills in carpentry, plumbing, and wiring were requirements in the Zeien household. Alfred mastered these skills and translated this focus on self-sufficiency to excellence in his studies, graduating at the top of his elementary and high school classes. Though he had his pick of colleges, including scholarships to Harvard University and the Massachusetts Institute of Technology, Zeien set his sights on the Webb Institute of Naval Architecture. From an initial applicant pool of eight hundred, Zeien was one of only sixteen who were admitted to the prestigious institute and one of only nine who completed the rigorous program to become a naval architect.

TABLE 10-2

Business events that shaped the 1990s

Date	Event
1990	Soviet Union allows private ownership of business
1990	Clean Air Act signed into law, enforces stricter fuel emission standards
1990	Americans with Disabilities Act signed into law
1991	HTTP and HTML introduced by Tim Berners-Lee
1991	Operation Desert Storm commences in Persian Gulf
1991	Soviet Union dismantles into independent states
1992	Mall of America opens in Minnesota
1992	Single Europe Act begins process of building European Union
1992	World Wide Web emerges on public scale
1992	Mosaic (precursor to Netscape Navigator) created as first successful Web browser
1993	Family and Medical Leave Act signed into law
1993	Brady Bill (handgun control) passed
1993	World Trade Center struck by terrorist bomb
1993	Pentium processor introduced
1993	Sears catalog ends publication after 97 years
1994	U.S. sanctions lifted in South Africa as apartheid falls; Nelson Mandela elected president
1994	North American Free Trade Agreement begins
1995	Java programming language introduced
1995	DVD invented
1996	Personal Responsibility and Work Opportunity Reconciliation Act reforms welfare
1997	Asian financial crisis
1997	Sheep named "Dolly" cloned
1997	Andrew S. Grove of Intel named *Time*'s Man of the Year
1997	China resumes control of Hong Kong
1998	Unemployment hits lowest point in almost 25 years
1998	AOL and Netscape merge
1998	Microsoft accused of antitrust activity
1998	Citicorp and Travelers merge in $70 billion transaction
1999	European Union adopts common currency
1999	Dow Jones Industrial Average tops 10,000 (up from 2,800 in 1990)
1999	United States returns control of Panama Canal zone to Panama

Graduating in 1952, Zeien and a few others started their own firm to design yachts and other boating components for various shipping yards throughout the East Coast. When the Korean War changed the nature of boat building, Zeien sought to diversify his skill set and enrolled in the MBA program at Harvard Business School. As it had done during World War II, the MBA program offered a series of courses on military leadership and strategy. The school's nuclear submarine programs particularly fascinated Zeien, and on completing the MBA program in 1956, he joined the General Dynamics shipyard as a chief estimator in Groton, Connecticut. Within five years, he was in charge of overseeing the company's merger and acquisition efforts, including the purchase of a large shipbuilding yard in Quincy, Massachusetts.

Zeien was soon asked to take over operational responsibility for General Dynamics' eight-thousand-person operation in Quincy, but after four years at the shipyard, he had accurately assessed that the glory days of shipbuilding were coming to an end, and he looked for his next career opportunity. He didn't have to look very far. Just a few miles north, in the city of Boston, were the headquarters of the Gillette Company. Zeien joined Gillette in 1968, shortly after it had acquired Braun AG, a German manufacturer of personal-care products and small appliances. Sent to Frankfurt as a general manager for the new international division, Zeien was charged with streamlining the business and ensuring that the company's electric-shaver operation was successful throughout Europe. He oversaw the divestiture of noncore business lines, consolidated Braun's key product offerings into a single Gillette international division, and instilled a stronger commitment to globalization.

Having succeeded in his first assignment, Zeien was called back to Boston in 1973 to become the group vice president in the Diversified Companies operation. His time at the headquarters office was short-lived, however. In 1974, though Braun was functioning well in the international marketplace, it was foundering in its home country of Germany after government-sponsored pricing-support programs were eliminated. Despite widespread calls to divest, Zeien decided instead to retool and restructure the German operation through the deployment of a matrix management operation. In matrix management, all key decisions were shared by at least two responsible managers. This reorganization effort produced what Zeien called "dynamic conflict."[72] That conflict resulted in reversing the company's failing fortunes and ultimately led to Zeien's promotion to chairman of the board of Braun.

In 1978, Zeien headed back to Boston, where he would remain for the rest of his career. He was appointed senior vice president of the company's technical operations, in which capacity Zeien developed a zealous drive to ensure that Gillette's product offerings and research capabilities were at the cutting edge. Though Gillette's flagship product, its razor-and-blade shaving system, was under constant competitive pressure from disposable razors, Zeien was an ardent supporter of the company's tradition. While it may have been easier to devote the company's resources to less expensive and easier-to-produce disposable products, Zeien wasted no expense in advancing traditional shaving technology.

As head of the company's technical operations, Zeien consolidated the company's research and development, engineering, and manufacturing operations into one unit. The result was an opening of communication lines that enabled Gillette to double its output of traditional razors and blades with the same number of employees. Zeien's restructuring approach was deployed throughout the company's various divisions and was a key factor in enhancing overall product development efforts. In 1981, Zeien's scope of responsibilities was dramatically increased when he was named vice chairman of technical operations and new business development. In that capacity, he oversaw the expansion of the company through a broadening of its international operations, orchestrated a series of key acquisitions, and sold off twenty-two companies that did not have the potential to achieve world market dominance.

Though Gillette was building a very strong international organization and had some breakthrough new products in development during the 1980s, its annual revenue growth rate slowed to roughly 3 percent, making it susceptible to hostile raiders. Between 1986 and 1990, Gillette had to fend off three hostile takeover bids from Ronald Perelman, famous for his unfriendly acquisition of Revlon. Zeien, who was overseeing the product development efforts of the company's core business, was also charged with defending Gillette's independence. He and other senior managers constantly stressed that Gillette was sitting on a tremendous amount of potential that would be effectively eliminated if the company were forced to merge with Revlon. Gillette's fight for independence was aided by some fortuitous circumstances, such as the 1987 stock market crash and Perelman's tangential links to individuals embroiled in insider-trading scandals. Gillette prevailed in defending its independence, but the victory came at a tremendous cost. The company agreed to pay a premium for the stock held by Perelman. Though it believed that it had weathered the worst, Gillette's most difficult test came at the end of the 1980s, when it became embroiled in a proxy fight with the hostile Coniston Group. Coniston sought to gain a majority representation on the company board, including the seat of the then CEO and chairman, Colman Mockler.

Management won by a slim margin, gaining all but a handful of votes from small shareholders, mostly employees or retirees, while Coniston received the bulk of votes from institutional investors.

The 51-to-49 victory for management was, in the words of Zeien, a "very sobering influence on the company."[73] The wake-up call for Gillette had begun with the first hostile raid, when the company embarked on a series of efforts to realign its growth prospects with a specific focus on new product development. The company's introduction of the Sensor razor system in 1990 could not have come at a better time. Its tremendous success greatly enhanced Gillette's reputation and more than delivered on the executives' promises of a strong, independent company. Zeien was one of the first proponents of the movable, or floating-blade, concept that was at the core of the Sensor razor. In development for almost a decade and at a cost of $200 million, the Sensor razor would never have come to market without his ongoing support and commitment. Sensor sold 24 million razors and 350 million blades in its first year, exceeding expectations by 6 million and 150 million, respectively.[74] The successor to Sensor was in product development at the time of the launch. With the 1998 introduction of the Mach-3 shaving system, the phenomenal success of Sensor was repeated.

On the heels of the Sensor success, Zeien was promoted to president and chief operating officer, and when Colman Mockler succumbed to a fatal heart attack in early 1991, Zeien was named CEO. Having fended off the hostile raiders and overseen the development of an expanded international operation and new product development effort, Zeien could easily have become a caretaker CEO, and many believed he would follow this easier path. His aspirations were completely different. He outlined a plan that would ensure the company would be less susceptible to corporate raiders and articulated it in a mission statement: "Our mission is to achieve or enhance clear leadership, worldwide, in the existing or new core consumer product categories in which we choose to compete."[75] Zeien's commitment to the new mission statement was soon tested when Joel P. Davis, the president of Gillette's Stationery Products Group, sought corporate approval to purchase the Parker Pen Company, the world's second-largest pen company. Zeien did not flinch; he approved the acquisition and, in so doing, helped Gillette make significant strides in achieving its global goal for the stationery operation.

As CEO of Gillette, Zeien redoubled his commitment to new product development. To that end, the company annually introduced over twenty new products that worked well with the company's entrenched international distribution network. The products included Sensor for Women, Oral-B Indicator toothbrushes, and the Gillette Series Cool Wave line of male grooming products. Zeien explained this shotgun approach: "We are a technology-driven company, and we figure it takes about fifteen products in research for every three that go into development. And for every three that go into development, we only get one to market. And that one has to be great."[76] To achieve twenty breakthrough products per year, Gillette therefore had to have at least three hundred products in development each year at one of its eleven research centers. The results of the new product introductions were impressive. Revenues from products introduced in the preceding five years increased from 35 percent in 1992 to over 50 percent by the end of the decade.[77] Although research and development were central to achieving Gillette's goals of new product introductions, the company also benefited from key acquisitions, including the $7 billion stock purchase of Duracell International. The company fit the strict guidelines that Zeien had outlined for acquisitions—it was a market leader, it had an international presence, it could leverage the Gillette distribution network, and it had untapped growth potential.

Globalization and new product development were two of the three primary pillars of Zeien's approach to the CEO role. The third pillar was focused on employee development. To that end, Zeien spent an inordinate amount of time on the road helping to identify and cultivate leadership potential within the company. On average, he visited and provided feedback for approximately eight hundred employees in any given year. He was an ardent supporter of the company's policy that encouraged diagonal promotions—that is, promotions that were not vertical within the same business unit but across business unit lines. In fact, he declared that no more than 10 percent of promotions each year could be vertical.

Gillette's commitment to successor product development, human resources, and globalization were key factors in its ability to grow a business that had essentially reached maturity in the 1960s. Zeien once noted: "About 20 billion blades are sold around the world every year. Thirty years ago, twenty years ago, ten years ago—it has not increased more than a billion up or down in that period of time."[78] Despite the maturity of the market, Gillette's world-wide share, under Zeien's tenure, rose from 30 percent to 50 percent.[79] In a *Forbes* magazine article, Zeien described what he considered an important measure of success: "The best measure of a company is not what it's accomplished, but how well it's improved the prospects for the future."[80] Zeien certainly improved the prospects for Gillette.[81]

Like Zeien's Gillette, successful companies in the 1990s were able to deliver on the promises of being customer focused and streamlined in their operations. Many enterprises, also like Gillette, invested in technology, not for technology's sake, but for enhanced productivity and innovation. They turned to technology providers for answers and poured millions into systems-related projects and hoped-for solutions. During the decade, businesses spent $3.4 trillion on information technology equipment and software.[82] In many ways, the long-term impact of these technology investments dwarfed the hypothetical, though wildly touted, promises of the Internet age. Managers took advantage of the surge in the technology sector across the spectrum, from the mundane world of component distribution to the complex world of network infrastructures to the intensity of data storage.

Personal-computer sales that blossomed in the 1980s continued to grow at an even more accelerated pace in the 1990s, and companies like Ingram Industries, led by Martha R. Ingram, built successful businesses around the warehousing and distribution of computer parts and components. As Ingram Industries expanded through the massive explosion in the PC marketplace, John T. Chambers was reaping enormous benefits from the proliferation of the Internet. Taking the helm of Cisco Systems in 1994, Chambers wasted no time building a large sales and distribution network for the company's routers and switchers, which "direct the flow of data on the Net and [over] corporate networks."[83] As Web hosting expanded by geometric proportions, the need for Cisco's backbone infrastructure (often referred to as the plumbing of the Internet) became increasingly important. A salesman by training, Chambers filled the sales pipeline with a vast product-development operation. What he didn't or couldn't build through internal product-development investments, he bought. At an unbelievably dizzying pace, Cisco acquired seventy-three companies—virtually any company that had any promise of delivering some new product enhancement—between 1993 and 2000. The massive sales growth of Cisco from $1.2 billion in 1994 to $19 billion in 2000, combined with its rocketlike stock price increases (growing from $2.27 per share to $82.00 during the same period), helped fuel the funding of the company's acquisition frenzy.[84]

Cisco's massive upward trajectory was matched by the growth of storage-systems provider EMC Corporation. When Michael C. Ruettgers came to EMC in 1988, two years after it had gone public, he was charged with rectifying severe quality problems with the company's disk drives. After attacking and resolving those problems, Ruettgers set his sights on growth, believing that there was a strong need for storage-device systems that could house data across disparate mainframe platforms for easy retrieval and analysis. He targeted companies that owned old-line mainframes and were frustrated with the expense and inefficiency of their memory components. EMC's answer was an interconnected collection of smaller hard-disk drives, which had the power of the large-memory devices but were priced at a fraction of their cost. His gamble paid off as customers flocked to the cheaper, more efficient EMC product line. Ruettgers went on to capitalize on the vast requirements for data storage as Web sites proliferated. Businesses across a broad spectrum of industries sought to capture a host of customer or prospect interactions, including Web clicks, transactions, and information requests. During his tenure, EMC grew from under $500 million in sales to over $7 billion, and its stock price grew from under $3 per share to over $100 per share.[85] The success enjoyed by Ruettgers at EMC often came at the expense of an American business icon—IBM. In fact, Ruettgers specifically targeted IBM customers, believing that they were hungry to work with more nimble and cost-effective technology partners.

Leaders: Reformulation and Revitalization

At the height of the technology surge in the country, IBM, the once-dominant trendsetter and powerhouse, was on the brink of disaster after having lost billions of dollars in the early 1990s. As speculation grew that the company might be split into pieces, investment bankers and analysts hovered like vultures waiting to dismember the former mighty symbol of corporate America. Recruited in the midst of this feeding frenzy, Louis V. Gerstner Jr. was charged with the seemingly impossible: to reverse the fate of a $64 billion mammoth. When James Burke, former Johnson & Johnson head who spearheaded IBM's

CEO recruitment process, met with Gerstner, he framed the position not just as a great business opportunity but as a once-in-a-lifetime chance to save an American legacy. For many, IBM had "changed the face of Corporate America," and its potential extinction was unthinkable.[86]

Louis V. Gerstner Jr. (1942–), IBM Corporation

When the announcement of Louis Gerstner's appointment to the CEO position of IBM was revealed in 1993, *Newsweek* covered the story under the headline "Can He Make an Elephant Dance?" The $64 billion elephant had just posted flat sales figures and a $4.9 billion loss for 1992, almost double the loss in 1991. Turning around the elephant was deemed an impossible task, but making it dance as a technology leader again was considered ludicrous. Ten years after the *Newsweek* article, Gerstner published his account of the IBM turnaround under the title *Who Says Elephants Can't Dance?* By the end of the decade, IBM was dancing its way back into its familiar lead position as a top-flight technology provider.

The quintessential path that Gerstner took as the business world's leading turnaround specialist was, in many ways, a tried-and-true one, from preparatory school to ivy-league college to business school to management consulting. Gerstner was born in 1942 into a devoutly Catholic family in the lower-middle-class town of Mineola, New York. His father worked as a milk-truck driver and later as superintendent for the F&M Schaefer Brewing Company, and his mother worked in the registrar's office for a local community college and also as a real estate agent. While neither parent attended college, this was simply not an option for Gerstner and his three brothers. All the Gerstner boys attended strict Catholic preparatory schools as a stepping-stone to college.

Gerstner graduated second in his class at Chaminade High School and received an academic scholarship to Dartmouth College. Though he had set his sights on Notre Dame, Gerstner accepted the scholarship. He realized that it would be a great financial relief to his parents, who had worked constantly to fund both the high school and the college educational expenses for the family. Gerstner was as serious a student at Dartmouth as he was in high school, always trying to excel in his academic work. His college roommate remarked: "Lou was the guy who got up before everyone else in the morning to go study and came back after everybody was asleep."[87] An engineering major, Gerstner was named an Alfred P. Sloan National Scholar and graduated magna cum laude in 1963.

From Dartmouth, Gerstner immediately enrolled in the MBA program at Harvard Business School. Graduating in 1965, Gerstner joined the management-consulting firm McKinsey & Company, where he quickly emerged as a strong and ambitious force. One colleague described Gerstner's focus: "He goes for the jugular in any problem-solving exercise. He really has a finely honed analytical ability to spot the logical flaws."[88] Gerstner's rather brash and confrontational style did not impede his success as he progressed up the partner track in nearly record time. He was tasked with building and leading the Finance Practice Group in New York City, and in this capacity he laid the foundation for his next career move. McKinsey's principal officers asked Gerstner to take on the American Express account and build a fruitful relationship with the company's new chairman and CEO, James Robinson III. The relationship proved to be extremely beneficial for Gerstner and American Express. In 1978, Robinson offered Gerstner an opportunity to join American Express as an executive vice president in the Travel Related Services division, which, among other activities, was responsible for the issuance of American Express credit cards and traveler's checks. After thirteen years in consulting, Gerstner was ready for a change: "I no longer wanted to be the guy putting slides on the machine; I wanted to be making the decisions."[89]

Gerstner had plenty of opportunity to exercise his decision-making capabilities at American Express. Over the course of his eleven years with the company, Gerstner's push for performance and ambitious drive to succeed, both personally and professionally, resulted in a series of promotions, culminating in his being named the CEO of the Travel Related Services division. Under his leadership, the division's earnings grew at a compounded rate of 17 percent, and the number of card members grew from 8 million to over 30 million. Gerstner presided over the rapid expansion of the corporate card program, the successful launch of the "Do You Know Me?" and the "Don't Leave Home Without It" advertising campaigns, and the company's highly visible, cause-related marketing programs. Also in this role, Gerstner developed what he called "a sense of the strategic value of information technology."[90] Along with CEO Robinson, Gerstner helped initiate Project Genesis in 1988, a five-year $250 million global initiative to upgrade and integrate the company's disparate technological infrastructure. As he climbed the corporate ladder, Gerstner made no secret of his ambition to become the heir apparent to Robinson, but just when he was on the cusp of realizing that potential, he made his next career move.

Gerstner left American Express in 1989 at the urging of Henry Kravis of Kohlberg Kravis Roberts. Kravis believed that Gerstner could help transform the company's prized leveraged-buyout property, RJR Nabisco. Having bought RJR Nabisco for a staggering $25 billion, the company was saddled with debt. Gerstner's role quickly became focused on matters of fiscal management and streamlining, especially in light of the company's commitment to pay $3 billion in annual interest payments. Over the course of four years, he sold off several assets, discontinued plans to develop new factories, eliminated a plethora of corporate excesses such as a fleet of corporate jets and lavish real estate holdings, and decreased the company's overall debt level by 50 percent. The $1.1 billion net loss that he inherited in 1989 became a profit of $299 million by 1992.[91] The debt burdens were so high that Gerstner had little time or ability to expand operations; the task was clearly one of consolidation and contraction. After four years of breaking up a company, Gerstner was mildly intrigued about the possibilities of rebuilding a company like IBM, but he also had some serious reservations.

When Gerstner was initially approached for the IBM position in the fall of 1992, he was apprehensive about his ability to step into the hot seat of a technology company. With no experience in technology, except as a customer, he believed that he lacked the proper credentials to take the position. It didn't help when fellow CEO contender, Larry Bossidy, publicly stated that what IBM needed was someone "who is thirty-five years old, knows computers, and can clone himself twenty-five times."[92] What IBM got instead was a fifty-one-year-old strategist and generalist.

The long-dominant player in the technology sector was on life support when Gerstner came aboard as the first outsider to run IBM. Though it had entered the PC domain with a bang, the company failed to sustain its early lead and ceded much of the growth opportunity to Microsoft and Intel. In addition, as the company grew in size and bureaucracy, it failed to keep pace with the broader-scale advances in back-office computing, especially succumbing to more nimble and cost-effective competitors in its heretofore bread-and-butter arena—the IBM mainframe. As one former IBM staffer noted, the company was "very much in denial around client/server computing" and the movement away from proprietary technology to "plug compatible open systems."[93] The company was late to market with new products and failed to consistently deliver the high levels of customer service that in the past had enabled IBM to garner a premium price.

Though IBM suffered on numerous fronts, the speed with which its fortunes shifted was unprecedented. In 1990, just three years prior to Gerstner's arrival, IBM posted revenues of $69 billion and net income of $6 billion, making it the most profitable *Fortune* 500 company in the United States. In the following two years, sales fell by $5 billion and profits fell by over $11 billion, marking the worst two years in the company's history. In 1992, the company abandoned its unstated, though implicit, policy of lifetime employment, as over 117,000 employees accepted early retirement or faced termination. That same year, the company absorbed $11.6 billion in restructuring charges.

Taking the helm of IBM in April, Gerstner soon realized that the company was on track to post an even greater loss in fiscal year 1993. Showing an uncanny and somewhat uncharacteristic level of restraint, however, he made no knee-jerk decisions. In some ways, he hearkened back to his management consulting days and treated the company as his most important analytical assignment. He did quickly dispense with some of the rigidity and formality that was so entrenched in the company's culture by disbanding the powerful, yet mostly ceremonial management committee, the top fifty or so managers in the company. In the committee's place, he created a smaller, more nimble advisory board composed of both long-term IBM personnel and colleagues he brought with him from American Express and RJR Nabisco. In addition, he quickly changed the senior-management compensation system to provide some significant upside for critical resources that might otherwise be inclined to disembark a potentially sinking ship.

Gerstner's most important decision in his first six months was to refrain from breaking up the company. He called off the investment bankers and walked away from a strategy that had been percolating at the company for almost a year. His experience as a customer convinced him that what businesses needed and valued from IBM was its ability to integrate and service a wide variety of technologies. Though IBM had suffered badly as customer-purchasing decisions became more decentralized, Gerstner foresaw a shift in the buying patterns and power positions within corporate information technology. IBM had long been a partner of corporate Management Information Systems (MIS) directors, yet it had let smaller rivals chip away at that relationship. At the same time, the power of corporate MIS departments to control their organizations' information technology requirements was slowly eroding. The decentralization of technology decision making within large corporations had led to the proliferation of disparate, unconnected systems, yet despite this new

Lou Gerstner is credited with keeping IBM together and repositioning it as a major player in the new economy. (Source: Najlah Feanny/CORBIS SABA)

landscape, the process of integration often fell back on the corporate MIS function. Gerstner believed that these MIS directors would greatly value IBM's role and experience as a technology integrator.

After deciding to keep the company together, Gerstner spent six months visiting IBM operations around the globe and analyzed every business sector of the company. He then outlined his initial plan. It called for an additional thirty-five thousand terminations, massive price reductions combined with technological reconfigurations on its mainframe computers to keep abreast of severe competitive pressures, the sell-off of noncore operations, and the realignment of the company under customer-focused versus product-focused teams. In addition, Gerstner embarked on a streamlining process of internal operations; IBM had 125 separate data centers, 128 chief information officers, 31 separate networks, and data-processing costs that were three times more than the industry average.[94] Though the plan called for a considerable amount of restructuring and cost containment, Gerstner did retain and even increased funding for critical research and development initiatives. At the end of 1993, the company took an additional restructuring charge of $8.6 billion and posted an $8.1 billion net loss, but the seeds had been sown for the company's turnaround.

Gerstner's early belief that customers would value IBM's integration experience was soon justified in his discussions with customers. One of his early decisions was to initiate what he called "Operation Bear Hug," whereby each senior manager would be responsible for reaching out to at least five IBM customers each month, and his or her direct reports would reach out to an additional level of customers, and so on. One customer noted: "We don't need one more disk drive company, we don't need one more database company, we don't need one more UNIX server company. The one thing that you guys do that no one else can do is help us integrate and create solutions."[95] Recognizing a huge growth opportunity for IBM, Gerstner made the decision to dramatically expand the company's small-services and solutions group, Integrated Systems Solution Corporation, which had been formed in 1991. Gerstner's gamble paid off; IBM's service business was its fastest-growing entity and accounted for 80 percent of its revenue growth during the late 1990s.

By 1994, the company was producing positive net income and the reputation of IBM was beginning to regain some of its former luster. During this time, Gerstner decided to centralize the company's software development activities. Though it was the world's largest producer of software, mostly operating software for IBM machines, the company was not leveraging its expertise in this area. As he brought the various software units together he charged them with a "massive multi-year effort to rewrite all of [IBM's] critical software, not only to be networked-enabled, but to run on Sun, HP, Microsoft, and other platforms."[96] He was doing the unthinkable, moving away from proprietary IBM solutions to open systems. Although his decision created both tension and excitement, Gerstner believed that if IBM was going to deliver on the promises of being a true solutions provider, it had little choice. It was also during this effort that Gerstner orchestrated the successful acquisition of Lotus Development Corporation for $3.2 billion to expand the company's middleware portfolio. The speed with which IBM pursued and consummated the deal with Lotus signaled that IBM was fundamentally changing its ways.

In opening up its software development efforts, IBM also initiated a gargantuan project to convert its hardware to open-systems formats and to make its components and research available to others in the industry. Though some saw this transformation as a major threat to IBM, Gerstner and others believed that it would open formerly closed markets. Gerstner added to the growing marketplace buzz surrounding IBM by revamping the company's branding and advertising activities. He recruited a former American Express colleague, under whose direction IBM consolidated its advertising (which had been split between thirty-five agencies) into one global agency. IBM's initial branding effort, "Solutions for a Small Planet," gained widespread acclaim and reinforced the company's key differentiating factor. Market branding was also pivotal in positioning the company as a solutions provider in the e-business arena.

Gerstner had unveiled IBM's vision for "network-centric computing" at a major trade show in 1995, and though it generated relatively little coverage at the time, it became the backbone of the company's e-business strategy. In line with its efforts to be a solutions provider and systems integrator, IBM's initial $300 million investment in its e-business strategy was focused on the practical requirements to connect disparate data sources. In many ways, the back-office computing requirements, though far less sexy than the high-flying Internet IPOs, became a surprisingly new revenue source for IBM mainframes. As the hype of the Internet went from the "wow" of interconnection to the "so what do we do with this information?" IBM was well poised to step into this critical role.

By focusing on the solutions to interconnection, IBM not only survived the Internet bubble, but also prospered as companies scrambled to identify their real assets. In the process, IBM regained its reputation as a technology leader. IBM biographer Doug Garr sums up Gerstner's achievement: "He's changed the culture, turned around the battleship so it was headed toward open water and got the wind behind IBM's back again."[97] When Gerstner stepped down from the CEO post, the elephant was dancing to the tune of $86 billion in sales and $8 billion in net income.[98]

Like Gerstner, his counterparts were also faced with the challenge of turning around the fortunes of their companies, but often in the absence of some breakthrough approach, technology, or innovation. When Gordon M. Bethune took over Continental Airlines in 1994, the company was nearly out of cash, had barely survived two crippling bankruptcy reorganizations, was embroiled in severe conflict between employees and management, and was ranked last in customer satisfaction. Bethune initiated a market research campaign to determine what frequent flyers wanted and were willing to pay for in an airline. He also infused a spirit of cooperation and no-nonsense communication in the company, quickly building a reputation for honesty and integrity in his interactions with employees. His efforts to embrace both employees and customers paved the way for an incredible turnaround.

Within a few years, labor relations and customer satisfaction, both of which had been at the bottom in the industry, were among the best of any U.S. company. By the end of the decade, the near-bankrupt company was turning a profit ($484.7 million in 1999 versus a net loss of $613.3 million in 1994) and was ranked as the sixth largest airline in the country.[99] Though the airline's fate has been drastically altered by the massive decline in air travel after the September 11, 2001, terrorist attacks on the United States, Bethune has maintained the airline's focus on customer service and has retained strong relations with employees despite some severe reductions and cost-containment measures.[100]

In similar fashion, Lawrence A. Bossidy wasted no time applying the lessons that he learned from his thirty-one years as a disciple and veteran of General Electric to the fate of AlliedSignal. In 1991, AlliedSignal had a declining revenue base and had posted a net loss of $273 million. Through a number of sweeping initiatives, including the introduction of Six Sigma, a total-quality management program designed to increase productivity while reducing defects; the disposal of noncore businesses; and the reduction of the workforce by 20 percent, Bossidy turned AlliedSignal around. Bossidy was so relentless in his pursuit of cost containment and growth that he maintained a list of underperforming divisions, which he monitored with laserlike precision. Appearing on that list for two consecutive quarters resulted in the termination of the division's senior leader.[101] The results under Bossidy's tenure were impressive and included consistent, double-digit growth in earnings per share and rapid stock-price appreciation. He capped off his turnaround of AlliedSignal by orchestrating its merger with Honeywell International in 1999, catapulting the company's revenue base from $12 billion when he arrived in 1991 to almost $25 billion.[102] High-profile turnarounds like those at AlliedSignal and others captivated the nation. They seemed to exemplify the unlimited prospects for the new millennium.

Entrepreneurs of the New Millennium

Given the relative newness of breakthrough business models and approaches in the 1990s—and hence the limited amount of time to assess their impact—our study of great business executives only includes a handful of entrepreneurs, whom we included with much trepidation. As we have seen in our

Company founder, Pierre Omidyar, with CEO, Meg Whitman, have made eBay's online auction site one of the few shining stars of the Internet. (Source: Getty Images)

analysis of previous decades, the full impact of an entrepreneur's work is often not visible for many years; these businesspeople often push the limits of what is possible and even what is conceivable. By their nature, entrepreneurs and their businesses are ahead of the curve, and it is relatively dangerous to assess performance and impact as it is unfolding. For instance, when we began this research project in 2001, we would have certainly included Martha Stewart among prospective entrepreneurs. As the years have progressed, however, her legacy has unraveled, and she has been removed from the study.*

Nevertheless, we believe that a few individuals will be considered entrepreneurs when elapsed time permits a full analysis. One individual who did not qualify for the list, because her tenure did not begin until 1998 (an individual had to be CEO or founder for at least five years before 2000), but has all the markings of an entrepreneur is Meg Whitman of eBay. Whitman's ability to take the company public and build the fledgling retail model into a vibrant and dedicated community of passionately loyal customers and small-business proprietors sets her apart from her peers. The cybercommunity of eBay is one of the few Internet-based enterprises to produce solid results. The early prognosis for this modern version of auctioning looks very promising, and Whit-

*Individuals who have been tried and convicted of federal crimes have been excluded from our study. We chose not to exclude individuals solely on the basis of accusation, though we are well aware that many individuals on our list are far from exemplary citizens.

man's ability to blend traditional customer relationship building with the speed and reach of the Internet has, thus far, produced a winning formula. If this performance is sustained, she will undoubtedly become a heralded entrepreneur of the new millennium.

The New Century

In 1998, Federal Reserve Board chairman, Alan Greenspan, spoke enthusiastically: "The current economic performance, with its combination of strong growth and low inflation, is as impressive as any I have witnessed in my near half-century of daily observation of the American economy."[103] His effusive praise of the economic performance of the country seemed to capture the spirit of America in the last half of the last decade of the twentieth century. For many, the personal sacrifices of the 1970s, the business investments in the 1980s, and the restructuring and reengineering in the early 1990s had borne fruit and deserved rich praise and celebration. The country had emerged from the dismantled Cold War as the world's sole superpower, it had reasserted its military might in the Persian Gulf, it had balanced its national budget after years of deficits, and it had spent its way out of a potentially crippling Asian monetary crisis. In addition, the nation had recaptured the quality and productivity in its manufacturing infrastructure while reducing unemployment below 5 percent. Success seemed unstoppable.

At the end of his speech, however, Greenspan included a cautionary note: "This set of circumstances [continued high growth, low inflation, and low unemployment] is not what historical relationships would have led us to expect at this point in the business expansion, and while it is possible that we have, in a sense, moved 'beyond history,' we also have to be alert to the possibility that less favorable historical relationships will eventually reassert themselves."[104] Those historical forces reasserted themselves with a fury in the ensuing years as dot-coms imploded, the economy faltered in the aftermath of terrorism, global instability intensified, and trust in business executives eroded with high-profile exposures of corporate corruption, misdeeds, and other scandals. Although the end of the century brought forth largely unfounded fears of Y2K catastrophes and witnessed a resurgence in predictions of Armageddon, the real threats were lurking just around the corner.

TABLE 10-3

Entrepreneurs, managers, and leaders of the 1990s

Entrepreneurs

Jeffrey P. Bezos, Amazon.com
Thomas M. Siebel, Siebel Systems
Jerry Yang, Yahoo!

Managers

C. Michael Armstrong, American Telephone &
  Telegraph
Carol Bartz, Autodesk
Duane L. Burnham, Abbott Laboratories
John T. Chambers, Cisco Systems
Ronald W. Dollens, Guidant Corporation
Robert J. Eaton, Chrysler Corporation
William W. George, Medtronic
Vincent A. Gierer Jr., UST
Raymond V. Gilmartin, Merck & Company, Inc.
Melvin R. Goodes, Warner-Lambert
  Corporation
Charles A. Heimbold Jr., Bristol-Myers Squibb
  Company
Martha R. Ingram, Ingram Industries
William T. Kerr, Meredith Corporation
Richard J. Kogan, Schering-Plough
  Corporation
Rochelle Lazarus, Ogilvy and Mather
John Pepper, Procter & Gamble
Laurence F. Probst III, Electronic Arts
Lee R. Raymond, Exxon Mobil Corporation
Richard M. Rosenberg, BankAmerica
  Corporation

Michael C. Ruettgers, EMC Corporation
Stephen W. Sanger, General Mills
Charles R. Shoemate, CPC International
  (BestFoods)
William Steere Jr., Pfizer
Alex Trotman, Ford Motor Company
Daniel P. Tully, Merrill Lynch & Company, Inc.
Alfred M. Zeien, Gillette Company

Leaders

Gordon M. Bethune, Continental Airlines
Lawrence A. Bossidy, AlliedSignal, Inc.
Owsley Brown II, Brown-Forman Corporation
Steven A. Burd, Safeway
Robert N. Burt, FMC Corporation
Peter H. Coors, Adolph Coors Brewing
  Company
Millard S. Drexler, Gap
Roger A. Enrico, PepsiCo
Donald V. Fites, Caterpillar Tractor Company
Richard S. Fuld Jr., Lehman Brothers
Louis V. Gerstner Jr., IBM
Harvey Golub, American Express Company
David W. Johnson, Campbell Soup Company
Lucio A. Noto, Mobil Corporation
Leonard D. Schaeffer, Wellpoint Health
  Networks
Robert L. Tillman, Lowe's Companies, Inc.
Randall L. Tobias, Eli Lilly and Company
Michael A. Volkema, Herman Miller
Walter R. Young Jr., Champion Enterprises

Epilogue

THROUGHOUT THIS BOOK, we have attempted to illustrate how great business executives succeeded by capitalizing on the opportunities presented by the context of their time. Within each decade, business executives faced essentially the same contextual forces, but how they seized the zeitgeist of their times and how they approached the consumer varied greatly. Their level of sensitivity to and understanding of their context was pivotal to their overall success. Some saw new possibilities, some saw tremendous growth potential, and others saw opportunities for reinvention and rebirth. In essence, the context of their time provided the milieu for individuals to assess and explore opportunities and to hone their own leadership skills and approaches as entrepreneurs, managers, and leaders.

Entrepreneurs uncovered new business opportunities and were energized by the process of creation and innovation. Some entrepreneurs were ahead of their times; their visionary mind-sets allowed them to grasp a fledgling opportunity or promising technology and through perseverance and determination build a successful new enterprise. Dee Ward Hock of Visa International is emblematic of this type of entrepreneur. Long before the technology was a viable reality, he foresaw an interconnected world of electronic interchange. Bill Gates of Microsoft and Steve Jobs of Apple Computer had similar abilities. A few decades earlier, Edward DeBartolo also possessed this capability. He rightly predicted that there would be vast opportunities for serving the suburbanized population of the United States after World War II. His development of strip malls and shopping centers shifted the center of economic activity from the urban downtown to its suburban counterpart. Entrepreneurs became key players in shaping the evolving contextual and competitive landscape for business. This was especially true for someone like Clarence

Saunders, who revolutionized the way Americans shopped. Though the idea was initially the target of ridicule, his self-service grocery store concept became the cornerstone of the supermarket industry. As we have seen over and over in this book, the businesses and services first created by entrepreneurs often formed the basis of growth opportunities for managers in subsequent decades.

Managers derived personal and professional value less from creation than from expansion. The managers we studied were extremely adept at leveraging scale and scope, aligning resources, and maximizing market potential. Howard Morgens of Procter & Gamble was an example of a great manager. He continuously tinkered with P&G's brand-management structure to develop a thriving, well-researched product pipeline. For managers like Morgens, seizing the zeitgeist meant capitalizing on growth prospects and market potential. Across the sweep of the twentieth century, successful managers knew how to apply the right levers to an organization to reap the greatest possible value. Consider Louis Neumiller, who helped Caterpillar derive enormous benefits from its military mobilization efforts in the 1940s. By focusing on its own core product line, Caterpillar supplied vital machinery to the war front and was ready to thrive in the postwar construction boom in the United States and abroad.

The managers we analyzed were not all CEOs of companies on an upward growth trajectory. Some founded enterprises to capitalize on the successful efforts of trailblazing entrepreneurs, and some were second-generation family members who discovered ways to turn their forebears' ideas into vital, long-term business successes. For example, as the third family member to take the helm of Herman Miller, Max De Pree capitalized on the company's design strengths and quality focus to ensure its continued growth through a consistent and vibrant product pipeline.

The third approach to context-based leadership was embraced by individuals who confronted change and identified latent potential in businesses that others considered stagnant, mature, moribund, or in decline. *Leaders* transformed businesses, often tackling some of the most difficult and intractable challenges. It is hard to imagine a more daunting situation than the one faced by Lee Iacocca at Chrysler. His ability to work with the government to orchestrate a massive level of assistance was unprecedented. In many ways, it was Iacocca's success in the face of seemingly insurmountable obstacles that brought popularity and acclaim to business leaders in the last few decades of the twentieth century. For them, the glory was in the reinvention and rebirth of an enterprise.

Although the leader archetype has been more heralded in the past few decades, these individuals have been present throughout the century and have always been vital to the country's evolving business landscape. The work of William Fairburn at Diamond Match Company is a case in point. His tireless efforts to revolutionize a dangerous and stagnant industry in the 1910s had positive repercussions for consumers, employees, and the overall industry. Though he could have easily monopolized the marketplace with his discovery of a safety match, Fairburn instead made the patented process available to the entire industry at no cost. His generosity sent the match industry on a reinvigorated growth path.

Though we have classified one thousand business executives into one of these three primary leadership archetypes—entrepreneurs, managers, or leaders—some executives have moved from one type to another throughout their careers. We based our archetype classifications on the decade in which a business executive founded his or her company or assumed the role of CEO. As contexts changed during the course of an individual's tenure, his or her approach to business sometimes changed with it. Malcom McLean of SeaLand Industries is an example. McLean was both an entrepreneur and a leader. He not only transformed the centuries-old shipping industry, but also pioneered designs that made containerized cargo a viable and cost-effective option for transporting goods. Many individuals who maintained long-term success possessed what Warren Bennis and Robert Thomas have called *adaptive capacity*—the ability to be flexible and adapt to new situations and contexts.[1] Bennis and Thomas call these individuals *first-class noticers*: "being a first class noticer allows you to recognize talent, identify opportunities, and avoid pitfalls."[2] First-class noticers are individuals who have built and continue to build a strong level of contextual intelligence. As we have seen through the stories in this book, building an appreciation of context is an ongoing process that requires constant vigilance.

Lessons Learned

The vibrancy of the American economy in the twentieth century relied on the work of entrepreneurs, managers, and leaders. All three were important players in the regenerative cycle of business. Though there has been a shift in the distribution of these archetypes over the course of the twentieth century—more entrepreneurs in the early decades and more leaders in the later decades—the cycle of business creation, maturity, and regeneration always provides ample opportunity for all three executive types. As is evident in table E-1, the opportunities uncovered by early entrepreneurs sometimes became the major focal points for managers and leaders in subsequent decades. For instance, the primary focus of entrepreneurs in the first decade of the twentieth century was on national marketing and branding. This was the first time that nationally branded products were considered viable, given the expanded railway system and the broad reach of newspapers and magazines. Twenty years later, this focus on national reach and consumer marketing had become part of the mainstream of American business. It was now the focus of the managers of the 1920s. In essence, the burgeoning consumer growth of those years was the result of the early entrepreneurial focus on the innovative idea of national marketing and branding.

Similarly, the conglomerate movement of the 1960s gave way to a massive divestment effort in the 1970s. Although managers built large-scale conglomerates in the 1960s to take advantage of the booming stock market and the antitrust loophole that allowed unrelated business acquisitions, many businesspeople were unprepared for the shift in the contextual landscape in the 1970s. During the stagnation of the 1970s, the real potential of conglomerates shifted from pure growth to a focus on cost management and streamlining. While some managers were able to make the transition, the context seemed tailor-made for leaders who thrived on business transformation and reinvention.

As we analyzed the interaction between context and great business executives over the course of the twentieth century, a number of key lessons emerged.

1. *Context matters—moving beyond the "great man" theory*: Our review of the American business landscape has taught us that long-term success is not derived from the sheer force of an individual's personality and character. Without a sensitivity to context, long-term success is unlikely and an individual risks being surpassed by competitors or falling victim to hubris. Companies do not succeed or fail in a vacuum. It is important to understand the contextual framework in which success or fail-

ure occurred. Without this understanding, too much emphasis (good and bad) is placed on the role of the individual.

2. *Different paths to greatness*: Though business executives often face the same contextual factors, there are multiple ways to succeed. Understanding the context of a particular time and one's role in that context is important to determining which approach is appropriately aligned with one's strengths and capabilities. Some individuals may find success as entrepreneurs, others as managers, and yet others as leaders. All three paths are always available and if properly pursued can leave a lasting legacy. It is also important to ascertain which approach is best suited to the life-cycle stage of the company or its industry. Is the company building, maturing, or contracting? Aligning the individual with the life-cycle stage of the business is critical.

3. *Great leadership is a function of context plus personal characteristics plus adaptive capacity*: To sustain growth and maximize potential over a long period, an individual must possess the flexibility and courage to change direction when the environment changes. This requires both an awareness of the changing landscape and the ability to adapt with it. Juan Trippe, whom we profiled in our discussion of the 1920s, is an example of an individual whose adaptive capacity was less developed. Though Pan American Airways thrived during the early decades of his tenure, it was ill-prepared to handle the onslaught of competition in the 1960s and 1970s. Always enamored of the latest technology, Trippe overinvested in larger, more advanced aircraft even in the face of strong external pressures not to do so. Over time, his success had bred a level of arrogance that essentially prevented him from accepting change.

4. *Betting on the right person for the right time*: As boards and other corporate entities look to fill key leadership positions, their focus should not be exclusively on an individual's past record of success. Success in one time and in one place does not necessarily translate to success in another time and in another context. Rather, the focus should center on the individual's unique ability to identify, understand, and adapt to different situational contexts. In considering transitions of leadership, it is important to address the contextual environment in which the candidate will operate.

TABLE E-1

The convergence of context and leadership approaches across the twentieth century

Context		Entrepreneurs	Managers	Leaders
1900s Growing demography, vast market expansion, minimal labor impact, initial government intervention but strong big business power	Focus	National marketing and consumer value	Consolidation, size, scale and leverage	Reinvestment and product line adaptation
	Industries	Packaged foods, consumer products	Heavy manufacturing	Manufacturing, utilities
	Case	Cyrus Curtis, Curtis Publishing Company	Clarence Woolley, American Radiator Company	Frank Ball, Ball Brothers Company
1910s Heavy regulation, World War I, business conversions, explosive technology, minimal labor power	Focus	Expand national branding and advertising	Frontier expansion, commercialize technology	Business reinvention
	Industries	Retail, advertising, distribution	Oil, automobiles	Manufacturing
	Case	Clarence Saunders, Piggly Wiggly Company	Frank Phillips, Phillips Petroleum	William Fairburn, Diamond Match Company
1920s Government retrenchment, isolationist views, bifurcated society, broad technology expansion, anti-immigration, massive consumer credit	Focus	Technological innovation	Value of customer, advertising	From business-to-business to business-to-consumer
	Industries	Radio, movie production, aviation	Automobiles, consumer products, advertising	Commercial manufacturing, textiles
	Case	Juan Trippe, Pan American Airways	Robert Woodruff, Coca-Cola	Gerard Swope, General Electric
1930s Heavy government influence, Great Depression, broad social programs, union progress, technology adaptation, migration	Focus	Escapism, niche marketing and positioning	Capitalize on government programs	Navigating government regulation
	Industries	Cosmetics and other small luxury items	Railroads, mining, construction	Banking, financial management, services
	Case	Margaret Rudkin, Pepperidge Farm	Martin Clement, Pennsylvania Railroad	Harold Stanley, Morgan Stanley & Company
1940s World War II mobilization, cooperation (business, labor, and government), postwar baby boom, pent-up consumer demand	Focus	Distribution and market reach	War mobilization and conversion	Re-tooling and conversion
	Industries	Retail distribution, consumer products	Heavy machinery	Heavy machinery
	Case	Edward DeBartolo, Edward J. DeBartolo Corporation	Louis Neumiller, Caterpillar	E. Morehead Patterson, American Machine and Foundry

Decade		Column 1	Column 2	Column 3
1950s Baby boom, unfettered business focus, conservative social norms, labor progress, technology commercialization, Korean War, Cold War	**Focus**	Distribution and market reach	Consumer focus, exploit television medium	Reinvention and expansion
	Industries	Franchised enterprises	Consumer goods	Transportation
	Case	Ray Kroc, McDonald's	Howard Morgens, Procter & Gamble	Malcom McLean, SeaLand Industries
1960s Social discord (civil rights, Vietnam, experimentation), antitrust legislation, conglomerates, bulging population, technology focus, booming economy	**Focus**	Cost-conscious, customer and service	Unrelated diversification and expansion	Business reformulation
	Industries	Communications, retail, services	Conglomerates	Steel, consumer products
	Case	Sam Walton, Wal-Mart	Henry Singleton, Teledyne, Incorporated	Kenneth Iverson, Nucor Corporation
1970s Oil embargo, stagflation, value of computer technology, weakening labor, moderate government intervention, massive international competition	**Focus**	Technological commercialization	Scientific investments, multinational reach	Diversification and realignment
	Industries	Technology, services, processing	Pharmaceuticals	Food
	Case	Dee Ward Hock, Visa International	Edmund Pratt, Pfizer	C. Michael Harper, ConAgra
1980s Competition, deregulation, quality focus, debt, social conservatism, decline of labor, service focus, streamlining	**Focus**	Leverage and debt as motivators	Capitalizing on innovation, quality	Restructuring and retrenchment
	Industries	Investment banking	Consumer goods, industrial products	Former conglomerates, automobile
	Case	Reginald Lewis, The TLC Group	Max De Pree, Herman Miller	Lee Iacocca, Chrysler
1990s Globalization, diversity, reengineering, booming economy, massive immigration, Internet opportunities	**Focus**	Capitalizing on the Internet	Product development and enhancement	Streamlining, reengineering, and convergence
	Industries	Distribution, online enterprises, consumer goods	Consumer goods, communication	Technology, "brick and mortar"
	Case	Meg Whitman, eBay	Alfred Zeien, Gillette	Lou Gerstner, IBM

When evaluating the company context, boards should consider the following questions: What has the success/failure of the company been based on in the past? What were the contextual factors that contributed to this success or failure? What is the global competitive landscape of the company? and, How will the company be impacted by impending regulations or consumer shifts? Boards should place greater value on candidates who have demonstrated the flexibility to adapt to changing contexts. If the business is attempting to maximize growth, a *manager* may be the best choice of CEO. In times of crisis or decline, a *leader* may be needed. Boards should refrain from recruiting the next "celebrity CEO" or ultimate charismatic leader if that individual's strengths are not properly aligned with where the company is going or needs to go. Instead, they should consider the following questions when evaluating candidates for senior-level positions: In what type of environment did the individual lead? Does the individual possess an openness and willingness to see beyond his or her own experiences? Is the business life-cycle stage aligned with the individual's key strengths? and, Has the individual demonstrated the capacity to adapt and change over time?

5. *Betting on the right company at the right time*: Both providers of capital and providers of labor (employees) can greatly benefit from understanding the context of the companies to which they commit themselves. Venture capitalists, bankers, and other funding sources should pay particular attention to the context in which the businesses they plan to invest in will operate. These investors must understand the environmental landscape at a sophisticated level in order to maximize returns and mitigate risks. Venture capitalists, for example, will be better positioned to provide proper advice and counsel and will be better prepared to identify when CEOs should adjust to a changing business climate. The importance of context is not only vital to the funding of start-ups. Businesses at all stages require funding, and the providers of equity, debt, or investment capital would be better positioned to evaluate their funding decisions if they understood the evolving contextual landscape in which the businesses they invest in operate.

Just as investors need to bet on the right company at the right time, so too do individuals. As individuals consider career choices, they would be better prepared to succeed if they aligned their personal strengths and preferences with the life-cycle stage and context of their potential employer. Do they thrive in growth environments, start-ups, or turnarounds? The same sensing capacity that has brought success to the CEOs and founders that we discuss in this book can and should be developed by individuals as they select potential employers. The context of a business or industry reveals a lot about the opportunities that exist for personal development and professional growth.

6. *The importance of business history:* Too many business schools relegate the study of business history to the periphery. While it is important to focus on "the next new thing" and the best ideas and frameworks for becoming a more effective manager, it is equally important to understand what has worked and what has not worked in the past. There is often a tendency to overlook the *context* of an individual's success and simply glorify the individual. The environment in which an executive succeeded is as important as the characteristics that this individual possessed. We believe that it is important for business schools to reconnect with history and its role in shaping the landscape for business.

7. *Enhancing your contextual intelligence, becoming a "first-class noticer":* There are a number of steps that individuals can take to develop contextual intelligence. First, an interest in and appreciation for history is critically important. Willingness to learn from the past will help individuals better understand the present opportunities and challenges that confront them. Second, while it is often difficult to take the time to read, individuals would have a better sense of context if they stayed abreast of trends in regulations, geopolitics, and technology. Third, it is vitally important to break out of one's own world. Traveling to new market geographies and interacting with customers and employees are far more beneficial to leaders than staying behind a desk. It is very difficult to understand the real impact of global affairs if one's experience is only derived from prepared reports. Consider what's happening in China and India today. Those individuals who take the time to understand these market economies firsthand will be better prepared to address the opportunities and challenges that emerge. In addition, individuals can

further develop their contextual intelligence through participation in conferences and industry associations, especially those that focus on new competitive landscapes and opportunities. Fourth, contextual intelligence can be enhanced through engaging in disciplined processes for imagining the future including scenario assessment, strategic planning, and contingency modeling. Regardless of the approach, individuals and companies can be better positioned for the future if they engage in some specific forms of thinking to help the company prepare for new opportunities and to consider its response to potential threats. Finally, the development of contextual intelligence is an ongoing process that requires constant attention. Individuals must not only develop an awareness of context, but also possess the ability and desire to act on that awareness.

A Look Forward: A New Century

As we look toward the new century, there are clear signs that business contexts have changed and continue to change. How will business leadership emerge in the new millennium? What can history teach us about what to expect? Though it is too soon to fully appreciate the overall contextual landscape of this first decade of the twenty-first century, the years 2000 to 2005 have provided some insight into the complexities, challenges, and opportunities for emerging entrepreneurs, managers, and leaders.

Though it may have seemed briefly in the 1990s that business had moved into a new, untouchable realm (in essence, beyond history), the pendulum of history swung back to realign the contextual landscape.[3] The contextual factors that made businesses so successful in the 1990s have changed dramatically. Not surprisingly, the sweeping shift in the contextual framework necessitates a new form of business leadership. Celebrity has been replaced with competence and judgment. Results have trumped hype. Execution has dethroned vision. And consumer skepticism has overshadowed awe and unfiltered acceptance.

The business scandals that rocked the corporate world at the beginning of the decade have many politicians and academics (and a very few practitioners) calling for more stringent oversight and regulation of business. Though the government has refrained from tightening the reins on many businesses, senior company officials are under much heavier personal scrutiny, and businesses themselves have been forced to play a broader role in their own self-regulation. In a *BusinessWeek* cover story, columnist John A. Byrne noted that "in the anything goes 1990s, greed overwhelmed the system because there were no countervailing forces to keep it in check. Instead, there were accounting firms, which were bent on drumming up lucrative consulting fees; outside lawyers intent on maintaining their flow of business from corporations; and directors, who failed to exercise oversight as the fiduciary representatives of the shareholders."[4]

In the post-1990s, board governance, CEO compensation, reported financial results, and stock option grants have received a much greater degree of evaluation, assessment, and focus. Business schools are also reevaluating their own curricula and adding new courses on corporate accountability, ethical decision making, law, and board governance. Despite the greatest scrutiny on business executives since the Depression of the 1930s and the "greed scandals" of the 1980s, the government has thus far refrained from taking a heavy-handed, interventionist role in corporate affairs. The pro-business polices of the George W. Bush administration have generally resisted the urge to introduce and enforce greater levels of regulation and oversight, leaving it to the business community to self-regulate and deal with its own mess. Given this latitude, business executives have a small window of opportunity to rise to the occasion and, in essence, heal themselves. In the absence of any tangible and meaningful action taken voluntarily by individuals, history has demonstrated that the forces of regulation are always waiting in the wings. They can descend with a thunderous force and dramatically alter the opportunity structure for business. The Sarbanes-Oxley regulations provide an example of just how onerous the law can be.

While the U.S. government has taken a moderate line with business in terms of intervention, the country has been anything but reticent on the world stage. Global events, already very intense in the 1990s, have grown increasingly more complex. The attacks on the United States in September 2001, followed by the U.S. invasions of Afghanistan and Iraq, the proliferation of nuclear armaments in developing countries, and the festering civil conflicts throughout the Middle East and Africa, have heightened the already sensitive and precarious position of the United States in the world. Executives trying to operate on the global stage are faced with increasing levels of uncertainty and instability. For those who can help create a sense of security in these uncertain times, business opportunities abound. Though unrest has gripped many parts of the world, the long-anticipated opening of the Chinese and Indian markets might very well provide a new base for business growth and prosperity. Capitalizing on these rapidly emerging economies could hold vast potential.

The rising intensity of geopolitics in the new century is matched by the rapid pace of technological change. Computer technology, the basis for much of the innovation since the 1980s, will undoubtedly continue to be refined, particularly as advances in wireless communications, data integration, and graphic transfer come to market. Though investments in technology have fallen off precipitously since the Internet implosion, there has been a renewed focus on productive technology—technology not for technology's sake, but with a purpose, focus, and bottom-line rationale. Information technology in the new millennium will most likely become the domain of managers and leaders whose ability to harness its power and to capitalize on the latent opportunity of the Internet will set them apart from their peers.

Scientific breakthroughs in medicine, which have paralleled the growth trajectory of innovations in information technology, are poised for even more rapid expansion in the new millennium. As the baby boom generation moves into its golden years and faces the prospects of debilitating health, even greater emphasis will be placed on medicine. New drug therapies and over-the-counter medications to stem the lifestyle impact of aging have already become ubiquitous. Biotechnology, which has yet to deliver on its oft-heralded promises, also appears to be on the cusp of new breakthroughs, and medical research using controversial stem-cell technology is yielding treatments for diseases and conditions that were previously thought to be chronic or fatal. The social controversy surrounding medical research has by no means dissipated. In fact, the new century has already borne witness to the contentious debates regarding using stem cells, frozen embryos, and cloning. Navigating this political landscape will be necessary for businesses to succeed in the health-care sector.

The scandal-ridden days of the final Clinton term opened the door for the "compassionate conservatism" of George W. Bush and a corresponding movement toward greater traditionalism. In a decade that began with an unsettling and divisive U.S. Supreme Court verdict on the most contentious presidential race in history, the country united as Americans in the aftermath of the events on September 11, 2001. This united front lasted through the attack on Afghanistan, and to a much lesser degree into the full-blown "war on terrorism" and its associated color-coded warning systems, which culminated in the attack on Saddam Hussein in Iraq. In many ways, Bush's conservative approach to the presidency, to social issues, and to global affairs is very reminiscent of the 1980s. Challenges to affirmative action, abortion, and voting districts have again gained prominence. Not since the 1980s have the lines been drawn so vehemently between "right and wrong," between "black and white," and between "good and evil."

The bifurcation of society has continued to widen as the new government's early fiscal policies have tended to favor the wealthy. Labor has also continued to struggle as companies try to grapple with the recession that followed the collapse of the Internet bubble and the devastation brought forth in the post–9/11 world. The airline, travel, and hospitality industries have suffered considerably, the effect of which has rippled through a host of other businesses and corresponding employment opportunities, especially in the manufacturing sector. The low unemployment rate that was emblematic of the economic surge in the 1990s is now but a faint memory. The incidences of multiple-job holders and underemployed individuals have only proliferated. Reengineering and realignment strategies have been even stronger forces in the new century as companies grapple with the downsized economy. Outsourcing, which has displaced thousands of jobs, has become the new strategic mantra for companies attempting to retain or regain their competitiveness on the global stage.

Though prosperity has become more uncertain in the United States during the new century, the country is still a beacon for immigrants searching for the American dream. That search, however, has been somewhat thwarted in the cautious and controlled climate of the post–9/11 world. Immigration, which had soared to record levels in the 1990s, has fallen off in the wake of stricter individual scrutiny and tighter regulations. Even so, the changing ethnic and cultural diversity of the country's melting pot has become a reality that cannot be ignored by business executives, especially those who want to succeed on a global scale.

The entrepreneurs, managers, and leaders of the new millennium face the potential of increased regulation, heightened global uncertainty, a vastly changed demography, conservative social mores, and reticent consumers.

The euphoria and delirium of the 1990s has been replaced with caution, pragmatism, and conservatism. While no decade is exactly like another, the exploration of historical context can provide us with clues to what it takes to be successful in our present environment. By understanding the path taken by our predecessors, we can better assess the road ahead and make the most of the times in which we live and work.

{ APPENDIX }

Methodology

The candidates included in our pool of one thousand business executives had to have been a founder or chief executive officer (CEO) of a U.S.-based company for at least five years, between 1900 and 2000. As such, any CEO whose tenure began after 1996 was automatically excluded from this survey. At the other end of the century, we included individuals whose tenures began before 1900 if they held the CEO or top company official position for at least five years in the first decade. For the earlier decades of the twentieth century, we drew on the work of Richard S. Tedlow, Courtney Purrington, and Kim Eric Bettcher. In their working paper, *The American CEO in the Twentieth Century: Demography and Career Path*, they chronicle the evolution of the CEO title, citing its first official use in business in 1917 by the U.S. Steel Corporation. In accordance with their research findings, we have chosen to designate an individual as CEO, regardless of specific title, if he or she was regarded as the primary and, in some cases, sole individual setting the company's direction, allocating resources, and monitoring its progress.[1] Prior to the common usage of the CEO title, the top company business official may have been labeled president, partner, managing director, or chairman. Several candidates on our list, especially those whose tenures occurred before 1920, held one of these titles. Whenever a company used the CEO title (typically after 1917), this individual was always chosen for our study.

We used a minimum five-year-tenure screen to ensure that we captured a relevant time frame in which a CEO or founder could make an impact on an organization. The five-year tenure was adapted from a research study conducted by John J. Gabarro, who evaluated the timing of an executive's impact on an organization. Through his research on the process of taking charge, Gabarro determined that a new executive's full impact on a company was not felt immediately, but over the course of several months in office. Further, it typically took two years to fully assimilate all the executive-level decisions of the previous administration. The first few years also provided an opportunity for a business official to set his or her strategic course of direction and to determine its initial impact on the organization. According to Gabarro's study, new executives orchestrated their most significant structural changes during their third year within the organization. Although his study examined the actions of senior executives, not necessarily CEOs, we believe that his findings are applicable to CEOs.[2] In fact, the taking-charge process for CEOs is often considerably shorter and scrutinized even more closely. By using a minimum five-year-tenure threshold, we believed that we provided a conservative time frame in which CEOs could impact the performance of their company in meaningful and lasting ways. As a point of reference, the average CEO tenures for our pool of business executives ranges from a high of thirty years in the beginning part of the century to just under eight years today. Beyond this five-year-tenure requirement, business executives had to have achieved either, or both, of two specific accomplishments: demonstrate at least four consecutive years of top financial performance, or lead a business or service that changed the way Americans lived, worked, or interacted in the twentieth century.

The financial performance criteria were demonstrated through three primary metrics: (1) Tobin's Q performance (market to book value), (2) return-on-assets ratios, and (3) market-value appreciation. Given the sparse availability of easily accessible and complete financial information across the twentieth century (especially before 1925), we used a multitiered financial-analysis approach. Through a combination of manual research in Moody's and Standard and Poor's references, we captured asset performance for the two hundred largest U.S. corporations (defined by gross sales or revenues) between 1900 and 1925; this initial set of companies was drawn from research on the largest industrial corporations in the United States in 1917.[3] Using the CRSP (Center for Research in Security Prices) Database of the University of Pennsylvania's Wharton School, we evaluated market value appreciation data between 1925 and 1950 for the 1,250 largest companies in the United States.

Finally, we used the Compustat Database to obtain performance metrics for all three variables (Tobin's Q, return on assets, and market-value appreciation) between 1950 and 2000 for the largest 1,250 companies in the United

States (ranked by gross sales or revenue). CEOs who produced at least four consecutive years of top-level performance on at least one of these metrics were included. Top-level performance was defined as having achieved a financial metric (Tobin's Q score, return-on-assets ratio, or market-value-appreciation growth index) within the top 10 percent of all businesses for a given year. Being a part of the top 10 percent of any one of these metrics for four consecutive years earned the CEO a spot on our list. The financial screening process yielded approximately 260 candidates.

Measuring a leader's impact on society, on business, or on both is admittedly a subjective task. Approximately three-quarters of the individuals included in our candidate pool of one thousand did not qualify when we applied our financial thresholds. The bulk of these individuals were culled from an extensive review of historical biographical references and business rankings. The rankings included historical lists by *Fortune, Forbes, Time,* the *Wall Street Journal,* the *New York Times,* business encyclopedias, and other sources. A list of references is included at the end of this appendix. In many cases, these individuals were cited for the advances that they made in American business—opening new markets, creating industries, instituting modern management practices, or advancing technology. We were particularly interested in the impact that a CEO or founder had within the context of his or her time. Though dominated by *Fortune* 100–type CEOs, the list is much broader. It endeavors to capture impact beyond simply size, and it seeks to capture individuals outside the normal or traditional business realm. As a result, the list includes heads of many smaller enterprises whose business legacies have endured the test of time, or that have opened up new opportunities for others, or that have done both. This was often the case for many women and minorities on our list. These individuals broke through barriers to establish themselves in business, thereby forging a path for future generations.

Given the thousands and thousands of individuals who served as the head of both large public and small private enterprises during the last hundred years, we have sought to capture only the small fraction who sit at the pinnacle of success—individuals whose legacies have truly stood the test of time. Though we tried to be vigilant in the selection process, our personal judgments and interpretations of historical information played a significant role. As a result, there is certainly room to argue with some of our selections. Through this book, we have only been able to profile a few dozen individuals in depth.

Information on all one thousand business legends is included on our Web sites, at http://www.hbs.edu/leadership/ and http://www.intheirtime.com.

Having identified our pool of great business legends, we organized the data by the decades in which these individuals initially came into the CEO position or founded their company. We chose to evaluate candidates on the beginning of their CEO tenure in an effort to understand the contextual elements and influences that they faced at the outset. By analyzing executives by decade, certain leadership patterns emerged. These patterns, in conjunction with our analysis of the historical contextual factors at play, formed the basis of the leadership archetypes—entrepreneurs, managers, and leaders—that we discuss in this book. To us, these entrepreneurs, managers, and leaders became much more than company heads who met a financial threshold or left some social mark. Essentially, they became our guides for understanding how context shapes individuals and how individuals shape context.

The following are some sources we used to classify and evaluate business executives:

B. C. Forbes, *America's Fifty Foremost Business Leaders* (New York: B. C. Forbes & Sons Publishing Company, 1948)

This book chronicles the lives of fifty CEOs from 1917 to 1947 in celebration of Forbes's thirtieth anniversary. The CEOs were selected by a nationwide survey of business executives. Forbes conducted a similar survey in 1917.

News Front Editors, *The 50 Great Pioneers of American Industry* (Maplewood, NJ: C. S. Hammond & Company, 1964)

This book includes a compilation of reprints of *News Front Magazine* stories about business pioneers in the early decades of the twentieth century.

Junior Achievement National Business Hall of Fame, 1975–2003, http://www.ja.org/gbhf/past_laureates.shtml

Created in conjunction with *Fortune* magazine, the Junior Achievement Hall of Fame includes 205 business titans who have "made legendary contributions to the free enterprise system."

John N. Ingham, *Biographical Dictionary*
of American Business Leaders
(Westport, CT: Greenwood Press, 1983)

This four-part anthology includes biographical profiles of 1,100 business officials since the beginning of the American economy. The profiles selected for Ingham's work were derived from consultation with eleven business historians at major universities and colleges.

Judith A. Leavitt, *American Women Managers and Administrators:*
A Selective Biographical Dictionary of Twentieth-Century
Leaders in Business, Education, and Government
(Westport, CT: Greenwood Press, 1985)

This book includes biographical portraits of 226 women who excelled in business, education, or government. It includes women who were the firsts in their respective fields, women who were founders of major companies, and women who held senior executive positions within large corporations.

Joseph J. Fucini and Suzy Fucini, *Entrepreneurs: The Men and Women*
Behind Famous Brand Names and How They Made It (Boston: G. K. Hall
& Co., 1985)

This book profiles the lives and contributions of 225 individuals who founded companies that have become enduring brand names.

John N. Ingham and Lynne B. Feldman, *Contemporary American*
Business Leaders: A Biographical Dictionary
(Westport, CT: Greenwood Press, 1990)

This source includes biographical profiles of forty-two business officials whose tenures occurred between 1945 (after World War II) and 1985. The list includes individuals who were credited with the introduction or advancement of a significant business trend in the development of the American business system during the forty years following World War II.

Richard Robinson, *U.S. Business History, 1602–1988: A Chronology*
(Westport, CT: Greenwood Press, 1990)

The author chronicles the most significant business events for each year between 1602 and 1988.

Kenneth M. Morris, Marc Robinson, and Richard Kroll,
American Dreams: One Hundred Years of Business Ideas
and Innovation from the "Wall Street Journal"
(New York: Lightbulb Press, 1992)

This source chronicles achievements in twentieth-century business by decade, as reported by the *Wall Street Journal*.

John N. Ingham and Lynne B. Feldman,
African-American Business Leaders
(Westport, CT: Greenwood Press, 1994)

This source includes biographies on 123 African American business officials from colonial times to the 1990s, with the bulk of entries focused on individuals who emerged after 1880. The authors concentrated their research on major urban centers in the United States.

Frank N. Magill, ed., *Great Events from History II:*
***Business and Commerce*, 4 vols.**
(Pasadena, CA: Salem Press, 1994)

This four-volume series includes detailed descriptions of events in business and government that shaped the legacy of capitalism over the twentieth century.

"Time 100: Builders and Titans," *Time*, December 7, 1998

Chosen by the editors of *Time* magazine, this list showcases twenty individuals believed to have shaped capitalism in the twentieth century.

"People Who Most Influenced Business This Century: The 50,"
Los Angeles Times, October 25, 1999

The article includes information on fifty people who most influenced business in the twentieth century, as determined by the business editorial staff of the *Los Angeles Times.* Individuals had to have made a significant global impact as well as an impact on the lives of Southern Californians. Business editors in consultation with academics made the final determination of the top fifty.

Neil A. Hamilton, *American Business Leaders,*
from Colonial Times to the Present
(Santa Barbara, CA: ABC-CLIO, 1999)

This encyclopedia source includes four hundred entries of American business professionals with a concentration on the most prominent founders within specific industry sectors, including finance, food processing, communications, heavy industry, computers, and entertainment.

Thomas J. Neff and James M. Citrin, *Lessons from the Top:*
The Search for America's Best Business Leaders
(New York: Doubleday, 1999)

The authors (executive recruiters from Spencer Stuart) used a three-pronged approach to define the list of the top fifty business leaders: (1) Gallup Poll survey of 575 business leaders and educators; (2) ranking of top one thousand companies' total return to shareholders and growth in cash flow relative to the company's market value; and (3) subjective evaluation by industry practice leaders of Spencer Stuart.

Floyd Norris and Christine Bockelmann,
The New York Times Century of Business
(New York: McGraw-Hill, 2000)

This book includes a compilation of major business news stories covered by the *New York Times* during the twentieth century.

Virginia G. Drachman, *Enterprising Women:*
250 Years of American Business
(Chapel Hill: University of North Carolina Press, 2002)

Enterprising Women is the companion publication to the national traveling exhibition organized by the Schlesinger Library of the Radcliffe Institute for Advanced Study at Harvard University and the National Heritage Museum of Lexington, Massachusetts. It chronicles the untold stories of women in building and shaping industry over the last 250 years.

We extensively used the following three sources to identify CEOs through financial screening:

- *Moody's Industrial Manual* (New York: published annually by Moody's Investor Service)

- *Standard and Poor's Register of Corporations, Directors and Executives* (New York: published annually by Standard and Poor's Corp.)

- *Who Was Who in America* (Chicago: various volumes published by Marquis).

Introduction

1. Our use of the term *contextual intelligence* applies to the manner in which business executives are sensitive to macro-level contextual factors (specifically, government intervention, global affairs, demography, social mores, technology, and labor) in the creation, growth, or transformation of businesses. The term *contextual intelligence* was identified by Robert J. Sternberg, *The Triarchic Mind: A New Theory of Human Intelligence* (New York: Viking, 1988), as "the ability to adapt well to one's environment but also to modify this environment in order to increase the fit between the environment and one's adaptive skills."

2. Pearl S. Buck, *My Several Worlds* (New York: J. Day Company, 1954).

3. Carle C. Conway, "Business Must Go Ahead; It Is Time We Lifted Up Our Heads," speech to Real Estate Board of Kansas City, Kansas City, MO, 24 October 1941.

4. Ibid.

5. Noam Wasserman, Bharat Anand, and Nitin Nohria, "When Does Leadership Matter?" working paper 01-063, Harvard Business School, Boston, 2001; also see S. Lieberson & J. O'Connor, "Leadership and organization performance: A study of large corporations" *American Sociological Review* 37: 117–130.

6. Carol Loomis, "Warren Buffett on the Stock Market," *Fortune*, 10 December 2001.

7. For a review of past classifications of business executives, see Blaine McCormick and Burton W. Folsom Jr., "A Survey of Business Historians on America's Greatest Entrepreneurs," *Business History Review*, winter 2003.

8. Joseph A. Schumpeter, *The Theory of Economic Development* (Cambridge, MA: Harvard University Press, 1961), 74.

9. Ibid., 92.

10. Joseph A. Schumpeter, *Capitalism, Socialism and Democracy* (New York: Harper & Row, 1950), 132.

11. Ibid.

12. Alfred D. Chandler Jr., *The Visible Hand* (Cambridge, MA: Harvard University Press, 1977), 7.

13. Ibid., 484.

14. Nitin Nohria, Davis Dyer, and Frederick Dalzell, *Changing Fortunes: Remaking the Industrial Corporation* (New York: John Wiley & Sons, 2002), 17–22.

15. Warren Bennis and Burt Nanus, *Leaders: The Strategies for Taking Charge* (New York: Harper & Row, 1985), 17–18.

16. The process of classifying each of the one thousand business executives into one of the three archetypes (entrepreneur, manager, or leader) involved a review of biographical

data from a number of sources, including historical biographies, company documents, press coverage, and other archival material. The classifications were all based on secondary source material and archival research. In reviewing these sources, we focused specifically on how business executives approached their organization at the time of its formation or when the individual became CEO. We were particularly focused on how the individuals approached their business situation—did they forge something new? Did they derive maximum potential from a defined business opportunity? Or did they transform a business? As in any classification process, a considerable amount of subjective judgment takes place. While we have tried to minimize this subjectivity, we recognize that some of the classifications are based on our personal judgments and our interpretation and analysis of the available secondary source information.

17. Thomas K. McCraw, *American Business, 1920–2000: How It Worked* (Wheeling, IL: Harlan Davidson, 2000).

18. Nancy F. Koehn, *Brand New: How Entrepreneurs Earned Consumers' Trust from Wedgwood to Dell* (Boston: Harvard Business School Press, 2001).

19. Orrin E. Klapp, "Heroes, Villains and Fools, as Agents of Social Control," *American Sociological Review* (February 1954): 59.

20. Martin Luther King Jr., *Strength to Love* (New York: Harper & Row, 1963).

Chapter One

1. U.S. Bureau of the Census, *Historical Statistics of the United States, Colonial Times to 1970*, bicentennial ed. (Washington, DC: U.S. Bureau of the Census, 1975), part 1, 105.

2. Ibid.

3. Ibid., part 1, 8.

4. For population figures for most of these cities in 1870, see *U.S. Census, 1880*, vol. 1, *Population* (Washington, DC: Government Printing Office, 1883), 108, 132, 268. For the 1870 figures for Seattle, see *U.S. Census, 1870*, vol. 1, *Population* (Washington, DC: Government Printing Office, 1873), 283. For Denver's population of 1870, consult figures available at www.denvergov.org. For population figures of 1900, see *U.S. Census, 1900*, vol. 1, *Population* (Washington, DC: U.S. Census Office, 1901), 438, 439, 440, 443, 465, 478.

5. U.S. Bureau of the Census, *Historical Statistics of the United States*, part 1, 154–155; and Albert Rees, *Real Wages in Manufacturing, 1890–1914* (Princeton, NJ: Princeton University Press, 1961), tables 10 and 13.

6. On the political motivations of the Progressives, Sidney Milkis writes: "Progressives sought to dissolve the concentration of wealth, specifically the power of giant trusts, which, according to reformers, constituted uncontrolled and irresponsible units of power in American society . . . This threat, in turn, focused attention on the decentralized polity of the nineteenth century, as reformers came to believe that the great business interests . . . had captured and corrupted state legislatures and local officials for their own profit. Party leaders—Democrats and Republicans alike—were viewed as irresponsible 'bosses' who did the bidding of these 'special interests.'" Sidney M. Milkis, introduction to *Progressivism and the New Democracy*, ed. Sidney M. Milkis and Jerome M. Mileur (Amherst: University of Massachusetts Press, 1999), 6.

7. Teddy Roosevelt delivered this speech on 14 April 1906 at an address during the laying of the cornerstone of the House Office Building in Washington, DC. See *Bartlett's Familiar Quotations*, ed. Justin Kaplan, 16th ed. (Boston: Little, Brown, 1992), 576.

8. Roosevelt made this statement during his First Annual Message to Congress, 3 December 1901. See Mario R. DiNunzio, *Theodore Roosevelt*, American Presidents Reference Series (Washington, DC: CQPress, 2003), 132.

9. Bruce Andre Beaubouef, "The Supreme Court Rules Against Northern Securities," in *Great Events from History II: Business and Commerce*, ed. Frank N. Magill (Pasadena, CA: Salem Press, 1994), 92.

10. "Disaster and Ruin in Falling Market," *New York Times*, 10 May 1901.

11. Clifton K. Yearley, "The Supreme Court Upholds the Beef Trust," in *Great Events from History*, 108.

12. Elisabeth A. Cawthon, "Congress Passes the Pure Food and Drug Act," in *Great Events from History*, 129.

13. Gregory P. Marchildon, "A Financial Panic Results from a Run on the Knickerbocker Trust," in *Great Events from History*, 134–138.

14. Beaubouef, "The Supreme Court Rules Against Northern Securities," 94.

15. Francis L. Broderick, *Progressivism at Risk: Electing a President in 1912*, Contributions in American History, no. 134 (New York: Greenwood Press, 1989), 35.

16. Paul A. Shoemaker, "The Tariff Act of 1909," in *Great Events from History*, 168.

17. U.S. Bureau of the Census, *Historical Statistics of the United States*, part 1, 126.

18. Jack McDonogh, *Fire Down Below: The Great Anthracite Strike of 1902* (Scranton, PA: Avocado Productions, 2002). See also Floyd Norris and Christine Bockelmann, *New York Times Century of Business* (New York: McGraw-Hill, 2000), 16.

19. U.S. Bureau of the Census, *Historical Statistics of the United States*, part 1, 178.

20. Beaubouef, "The U.S. Government Creates the Department of Commerce and Labor," in *Great Events from History*, 86.

21. "New York 10-Hour Law Is Unconstitutional," *New York Times*, 18 April 1905.

22. For information on Madam C. J. Walker, see A'Lelia Perry Bundles, *On Her Own Ground: The Life and Times of Madam C. J. Walker* (New York: Scribner, 2001); and John N. Ingham and Lynne B. Feldman, *African-American Business Leaders: A Biographical Dictionary* (Westport, CT: Greenwood Press, 1994), 680–693.

23. Jerry Keenan, *The Encyclopedia of the Spanish-American and Philippine-American Wars* (Santa Barbara: ABC Clio, 2001), 68–69, writes: "The Spanish American War was the briefest war in U.S. history, and combat casualties were correspondingly low. Army casualties amounted to 281 killed and 1,577 wounded; Navy losses totaled 16 killed and 68 wounded . . . Spanish losses are more difficult to determine. Army casualties reportedly amounted to 500 to 600 killed and 300 to 400 wounded."

24. For a thorough discussion of the United States as an emerging world power around 1900, see Thomas G. Paterson and Stephen G. Rabe, eds., *Imperial Surge: The U.S. Abroad, The 1890s–Early 1900s* (Lexington, MA: D.C. Heath and Co., 1992).

25. Louis Auchincloss, *Theodore Roosevelt*, The American Presidents Series (New York: New York Times Books, 2001), 59.

26. "Hoover's Company Profiles: United States Steel Corporation," *Hoover's Online*, 6 August 2002, available from Factiva, http://www.factiva.com (accessed 28 August 2002).

27. Timothy E. Sullivan, "International Harvester Company Is Founded," in *Great Events from History*, 52–56; and Clifton K. Yearley, "Tobacco Companies Unite to Split World Markets," in *Great Events from History*, 57–61.

28. American Standard Company, "Company History," American Standard Company Web site, http://americanstandard.com/CompanyHistory.asp?Section=AboutUs (accessed 17 December 2002).

29. John N. Ingham, *Biographical Dictionary of American Business Leaders* (Westport, CT: Greenwood Press, 1983), 1675–1677.

30. Daniel J. Boorstin, *The Americans: The Democratic Experience* (New York: Random House, 1973), 354–355.

31. Ingham, *Biographical Dictionary*, 1675–1677.

32. Mira Wilkins, "An American Enterprise Abroad: American Radiator Company in Europe, 1895–1914," *Business History Review* 43 (1969): 326–346.

33. Bernard Nagengast, "An Early History of Comfort Heating," *The Air Conditioning, Heating and Refrigeration News*, 6 November 2001, http://www.achrnews.com (accessed 17 December 2002).

34. For information on Clarence M. Woolley, see American Standard Company, "Company History"; Ingham, *Biographical Dictionary*, 1675–1677; Milton Moskowitz, Robert Levering, and Michael Katz, *Everybody's Business: A Field Guide to the 400 Leading Companies in America* (New York: Doubleday/Currency, 1990), 124–126; Nagengast, "Early History of Comfort Heating"; Ben Wattenberg (Host/Essayist), "The First Measured Century, Living Arrangements," PBS Web site, http://www.pbs.org/fmc/book/5living4.html (accessed 17 December 2002); and Wilkins, "American Enterprise Abroad," 326–346.

35. Mary Ellen Waller-Zuckerman, "Creating America: George Horace Lorimer and the Saturday Evening Post. Review," *Business History Review* 63 (1989): 670.

36. Mary Ellen Waller-Zuckerman, "Old Homes, in a City of Perpetual Change: Women's Magazines, 1890–1916," *Business History Review* 63 (1989): 715.

37. Ibid.

38. Ibid.

39. Ingham, *Biographical Dictionary*, 230–234.

40. Ibid.

41. Helen Damon-Moore, *Magazines for the Millions, Gender and Commerce in the Ladies' Home Journal and Saturday Evening Post 1880–1910* (Albany: State University of New York Press, 1994), 117, 149–150.

42. For information on Cyrus H. K. Curtis, see Lynn Hayes Bromfield, "The Ways We Were, Celebrating 250 Years of Magazine Publishing," *Folio* 20 (1 March 1991); Steve Campbell, "Mainers of the Century: Twenty Who Made the Greatest Mark on Maine Politics, Commerce and Culture," *Portland Press Herald*, 12 December 1999; Damon-Moore, *Magazines for the Millions*; Ingham, *Biographical Dictionary*, 230–234; Waller-Zuckerman, "Creating America": 670; and Waller-Zuckerman, "Old Homes, In a City of Perpetual Change," 715.

43. Ingham, *Biographical Dictionary*, 194–195.

44. Ball Corporation, "The History of Ball Corporation," Ball Corporation Web site, http://www.ball.com/bhome/history.html (accessed 16 December 2001).

45. Robert S. Lynd and Helen Merrell Lynd, *Middletown in Transition: A Study in Cultural Conflicts* (New York: Harcourt, Brace and Company, 1937), 75.

46. Ibid., 76.

47. For information on Frank C. Ball, see Ball Corporation, "History of Ball Corporation"; "Ball Corporation Profile," December 2002, available from OneSource Information Services, http://www.onesource.com (accessed 18 December 2002); Ingham, *Biographical Dictionary*, 42–43; and Lynd and Lynd, *Middletown in Transition*, 74–101.

Chapter Two

1. Frederick Winslow Taylor, *The Principles of Scientific Management* (New York: Harper, 1911).

2. Ibid.

3. Kenneth M. Morris, Marc Robinson, and Richard Kroll, *American Dreams: One Hundred Years of Business Ideas and Innovation from the Wall Street Journal* (New York: Lightbulb Press, 1992), 53.

4. Bill Underwood, "Mid-Continent Tower: City's First Skyscraper Combines Old, New," *Tulsa World*, 19 March 1997.

5. Richard Austin Smith, "Phillips Petroleum: Youngest of the Giants," *Fortune 50* (August 1954): 72–81.

6. Michael Wallis, *Oil Man: The Story of Frank Phillips and the Birth of Phillips Petroleum* (New York: Doubleday, 1988), 127.

7. For information on Frank Phillips, see Neil A. Hamilton, *American Business Leaders, from Colonial Times to the Present* (Santa Barbara, CA: ABC-CLIO, 1999), 548–550; John N. Ingham, *Biographical Dictionary of American Business Leaders* (Westport, CT: Greenwood Press, 1983), 1088–1090; Milton Moskowitz, Robert Levering, and Michael Katz, *Everybody's Business: A Field Guide to the 400 Leading Companies in America* (New York: Doubleday/Currency, 1990), 484–485; Phillips Petroleum Company, "About Phillips, History," Phillips Petroleum Company Web site, http://www.phillips66.com/about/history.html (accessed 15 March 2002); "Phillips Petroleum Company Profile," January 2003, available from OneSource Information Services, http://www.onesource.com (accessed 16 January 2003); Smith, "Phillips Petroleum: Youngest of the Giants"; "US Top Eleven Gasoline Companies in 2001 Ranked by Gross Sales in Gallons and Market Share in Percent" (2002), available from OneSource Information Services, http://www.onesource.com (accessed 16 January 2003); and Wallis, *Oil Man*.

8. Jim Lee, "The Supreme Court Breaks Up the American Tobacco Company," in *Great Events from History II: Business and Commerce*, ed. Frank N. Magill (Pasadena, CA: Salem Press, 1994), 212.

9. Bruce Andre Beaubouef, "The Supreme Court Rules Against Northern Securities," in *Great Events from History*, 278.

10. Eugene Garaventa, "The Federal Trade Commission Is Organized," in *Great Events from History*, 269.

11. Kendrick A. Clements and Eric A. Cheezum, *Woodrow Wilson*, American Presidents Reference Series (Washington, DC: CQ Press, 2003), 106–114.

12. Steven R. Weisman, *The Great Tax Wars, Lincoln to Wilson: The Fierce Battles Over Money and Power That Transformed the Nation* (New York: Simon and Schuster, 2002), 281.

13. Ibid.

14. Norris and Bockelmann, *New York Times Century of Business*, 45. As it turned out, the exact number of tax returns for 1913 was 357,598. See U.S. Bureau of the Census, *Historical Statistics of the United States, Colonial Times to 1970*, bicentennial ed. (Washington, DC: U.S. Bureau of the Census, 1975), part 2, 1110.

15. U.S. Bureau of the Census, *Historical Statistics of the United States*, part 1, 166.

16. Wilson made this statement to his Princeton colleague, the biologist Edward Grant Conklin. See David D. Anderson, *Woodrow Wilson* (Boston: Twayne, 1978), 120. For Wilson turning his attention from domestic to foreign policy, see ibid., 127, 133.

17. "Governors Close Stock Exchange," *New York Times*, 1 August 1914.

18. Clements and Cheezum, *Woodrow Wilson*, 74.

19. Byron Farwell, *Over There: The United States in the Great War, 1917–1918* (New York: W. W. Norton, 1999), 38, reports: "On 1 April 1917 the regular army consisted of only 5,791 officers and 121,797 enlisted men. There were 66,594 National Guardsmen in federal service (most serving on the Mexican border) and 101,174 National Guardsmen still under state control, but none of these troops was organized or equipped for service in Europe."

20. Ibid., 190. Farwell describes the American air force at this moment: "In May 1917 the French had 1,700 planes at the front; the United States army possessed only fifty-five, of which fifty-one were obsolete and four were obsolescent; none was fit for combat." See also Peter Jennings and Todd Brewster, *The Century* (New York: Doubleday, 1998), 87.

21. John S. D. Eisenhower with Joanne Thompson Eisenhower, *Yanks: The Epic Story of the American Army in World War I* (New York: Free Press, 2001), 25, 305n23.

22. Srinivasan Ragothaman, "The U.S. Government Begins Using Cost-Plus Contracts," in *Great Events from History*, 246–251.

23. Ingham, *Biographical Dictionary*, 1525–1526.

24. Ibid., 483.

25. Ibid., 317.

26. Ibid., 358.

27. Robert E. Rosacker, "Wartime Tax Laws Impose an Excess Profits Tax," in *Great Events from History*, 319.

28. Hanson W. Baldwin, *World War I: An Outline History* (New York: Harper and Row, 1962), passim.

29. Ibid., 130, 151, 153.

30. This total number combines two data sets gathered in the U.S. Census: (1) "Native Population of Foreign or Mixed Parentage" and (2) "Foreign-Born Population." In 1910, the former amounted to 18.9 million; the latter to 13.5 million. See U.S. Bureau of the Census, *Historical Statistics of the United States*, part 1, 116–117.

31. During the campaign, Republicans hoped to win over the vote of German Americans who felt that Wilson had betrayed his claims of neutrality by promoting foreign policies favorable to the English over the Germans during World War I. See John Higham, *Strangers in the Land: Patterns of American Nativism, 1860–1925* (New Brunswick, NJ: Rutgers University Press, 1955; fourth paperback printing, 1998), 199. When Wilson received a hot-headed telegram from the pro-German Irish American political figure

Jeremiah O'Leary (who was associated with a German-Irish pacifist group called the Friends of Peace), he deliberately gathered the press together at a special conference. Wilson's terse reply was hailed by Democratic newspapers everywhere: "I would feel deeply mortified to have you or anybody like you vote for me. Since you have access to many disloyal Americans and I have not, I will ask you to convey this message to them." See Clifton James Child, *The German-Americans in Politics, 1914–1917* (Madison: University of Wisconsin Press, 1939), 143–149; and Frederick L. Paxson, *American Democracy and the World War: Pre-War Years, 1913–1917* (Boston: Houghton Mifflin, 1936), 335, 348–350.

32. For an excellent and influential discussion of the growth of anti-immigration feeling in the United States around 1916, see Higham, *Strangers*, 194–201.

33. Ibid., 109.

34. Dale T. Knobel, *America for the Americans: The Nativist Movement in the United States* (New York: Twayne, 1996), 246. See also Higham, *Strangers*, 202–204.

35. *Statistical Abstract of the United States: 1917* (Washington, DC: Government Printing Office, 1918), 105.

36. One of the earliest and most influential statements concerning this loss of innocence in the 1910s can be found in Henry F. May, *The End of American Innocence: The First Year of Our Own Time, 1912–1917* (Oxford: Oxford University Press, 1956). See pages 393 to 396 for May's summary statement: "This was the end of American innocence. Innocence, the absence of guilt and doubt and the complexity that goes with them, had been the common characteristic of the older culture . . . The most obvious aspect of change was the complete disintegration of the old order, the set of ideas which had dominated the American mind so effectively from the mid-nineteenth century until 1912." These ideals were morality, "the old moral idealism [that] had become a caricature of Woodrow Wilson"; progress, "the prewar *kind* of progressivism with its supreme confidence"; and culture, "the old culture [symbolized] by [William Dean] Howells," who was rejected by younger intellectuals who thought nineteenth-century writers were too timid and genteel.

37. According to James Marone, *Hellfire Nation: The Politics of Sin in American History* (New Haven: Yale University Press, 2003), 476–477, "sinners lie at the heart of our prohibition [throughout American history]—that's why race and ethnic fears play such crucial roles . . . the collapse of liquor prohibition played the preceding factors in reverse. The dangerous characters faded from political view. New immigrants stopped arriving, and the second generation moved into the middle class. The dangerous industry—breweries and the saloons—had vanished. Interestingly, local prohibition lingered longest precisely where the dangerous other remained in place."

38. Athan G. Theoharis and John Stuart Cox, *The Boss: J. Edgar Hoover and the Great American Inquisition* (Philadelphia: Temple University Press, 1988), 56, 60.

39. Knobel, *America for the Americans*, 249, notes that around World War I, many "'new' immigrants ran afoul of the anxieties Americanizers felt about Russia's Bolshevik revolution and the emergence of a Soviet Union which promoted itself as the herald of worldwide socialism. There was already a long tradition in the United States of labeling socialism and communism 'foreign' ideas, represented in America only by virtue of immigration." According to Stanley Coben, *A. Mitchell Palmer: Politician* (New York: Da Capo Press, 1972), 187, Wilson's infamous attorney general (A. Mitchell Palmer) did everything

he could to encourage this association in the minds of the American people by "combining these groups into one gigantic enemy."

40. Harold Evans, *The American Century* (New York: Alfred A. Knopf, 1998), 106.

41. U.S. Bureau of the Census, *Historical Statistics of the United States*, part 1, 105.

42. Ibid.

43. Bruce Andre Beaubouef, "The U.S. Government Creates the Department of Commerce and Labor," in *Great Events from History*, 88–89.

44. Clements, *Woodrow Wilson*, 115–116.

45. "Henry Ford Explains Why He Gives Away $10 Million," *New York Times Magazine*, 11 January 1914, 1.

46. Ibid.

47. Peter Joshua Freeman et al., eds., *Who Built America? Working People and the Nation's Economy, Politics, Culture, and Society* (New York: Pantheon Books, 1992), 2: 227.

48. U.S. Bureau of the Census, *Historical Statistics of the United States*, part 1, 177.

49. Ibid., 172.

50. This is ironic because, at first, the War Industries Board had the opposite effect. Along with other wartime labor measures taken by Wilson, the board "dealt with and legitimized organized labor in a fashion unprecedented in American history, facilitating a large growth in union membership and a pattern of generous wage settlements for workers." See Alonzo L. Hamby, "Progressivism: A Century of Change and Rebirth," in *Progressivism and the New Democracy*, ed. Sidney M. Milkis and Jerome M. Mileur (Amherst: University of Massachusetts Press, 1999), 51.

51. Morris, Robinson, and Kroll, *American Dreams*, 61.

52. Thomas K. McCraw, *American Business, 1920–2000: How It Worked* (Wheeling, IL: Harlan Davidson, 2000), 12.

53. Lorring Emery, "Ford Implements Assembly Line Production," in *Great Events from History*, 234–238.

54. Morris, Robinson, and Kroll, *American Dreams*, 52.

55. Donald R. Hoke, *Ingenious Yankees: The Rise of the American System of Manufactures in the Private Sector* (New York: Columbia University Press, 1990), 133.

56. Smith Corona Company, "Smith Corona History," Smith Corona Web site, http://www.smithcorona.com/About_Smith_Corona/Mission.cfm?.cfi (accessed 13 January 2003).

57. Seth Thomas Clock Company, "Timeline," Seth Thomas Clock Company Web site, http://www.seththomas.com/timeline.html (accessed 17 January 2003).

58. Herbert Manchester, *William Armstrong Fairburn: A Factor in Human Progress* (New York: Blanchard Press, 1940), 22.

59. For information on William Fairburn, see Ingham, *Biographical Dictionary*, 361–363; Herbert Manchester, *The Diamond Match Company: A Century of Service, of Progress, and of Growth 1835–1935* (New York: Diamond Match Company, 1935); Manchester, *William Armstrong Fairburn*; "The Diamond Match Company," *Fortune* 19 (May 1939): 89–94; and "W. A. Fairburn Dies, Match Firm Head," *New York Times*, 3 October 1947.

60. Susan Strasser, *Satisfaction Guaranteed: The Making of the American Mass Market* (New York: Pantheon Books, 1989), 231; and Richard S. Tedlow, *New and Improved: The Story of Mass Marketing in America* (Boston: Harvard Business School Press, 1996), 182.

61. The background information on A&P was derived from: Tedlow, *New and Improved*.

62. Piggly Wiggly Company, "About Us," Piggly Wiggly Company Web site, http://www.pigglywiggly.com/cgi-bin/customize?acoutus.html (accessed 18 March 2002).

63. Laurel Campbell, "Inventors Struggled, and Some Succeeded Big Time," *Commercial Appeal*, 4 July 1999.

64. Ingham, *Biographical Dictionary*, 1246

65. "Piggly Wiggly, Inc., Inquiry Started," *New York Times*, 14 March 1923.

66. "Saunders Now Out of Piggly Wiggly; Spectacular Financier Turns Over Assets Which He Values at $9,000,000," special to *New York Times*, 14 August 1923, 25.

67. The background information on the Clarence Saunders fight with Wall Street was derived from various accounts within the *New York Times* and the *Wall Street Journal* between December 1922 and February 1924. Additional information was provided from John S. Wright and Parks B. Dimsdale Jr., eds., *Pioneers in Marketing* (Atlanta: Georgia State University Publishing Services Division, 1974).

68. Campbell, "Inventors Struggled."

69. "Fortune-Maker Left $2,000," *New York Times*, 22 October 1953.

70. For information on Clarence Saunders, see *Dictionary of American Biography*, supplement 5 (New York: Charles Scribner's Sons, 1977), 603–604; Edward J. Davies II, "Clarence Saunders Introduces Self-Service Grocery," in *Great Events from History*, 302–307; Ingham, *Biographical Dictionary*, 1245–1247; Piggly Wiggly Company, "About Us"; Wright and Dimsdale, *Pioneers in Marketing*; and M. M. Zimmerman, *The Super Market, A Revolution in Distribution* (New York: Mass Distribution Publications, 1955).

Chapter Three

The epigraph is from President Calvin Coolidge's speech before the American Society of Newspaper Editors (January 1925). In this speech, Coolidge uttered the more famous phrase that "the chief business of the American people is business. They are profoundly concerned with producing, buying, selling, investing and prospering in the world." Though his speech was intended to highlight areas that newspaper editors and journalists should focus on in their reporting, it captured the essence of the prevailing attitudes in the country.

1. Thomas K. McCraw, *American Business, 1920–2000: How It Worked* (Wheeling, IL: Harlan Davidson, 2000), 13–14.

2. Peter Jennings and Todd Brewster, *The Century* (New York: Doubleday, 1998), 109.

3. Susan Strasser, "Consumption," in *Encyclopedia of the United States in the Twentieth Century*, ed. Stanley I. Kutler et al. (New York: Charles Scribner's Sons, 1996), 1021–1022.

4. McCraw, *American Business*, 20.

5. Ibid., 21.

6. For additional comparative analysis on the approach to the automobile industry by Henry Ford and Alfred Sloan, see Thomas K. McCraw, *American Business, 1920–2000: How It Worked* (Wheeling, IL: Harlan Davidson, 2000), 10–27.

7. Kenneth M. Morris, Marc Robinson, and Richard Kroll, *American Dreams: One Hundred Years of Business Ideas and Innovation from the Wall Street Journal* (New York: Lightbulb Press, 1992), 72.

8. Julapa Jagtiani, "The Number of U.S. Automakers Falls to Forty-Four," in *Great Events from History II: Business and Commerce*, ed. Frank N. Magill (Pasadena, CA: Salem Press, 1994), 533.

9. Strasser, "Consumption," 1022.

10. Daniel Pope, *The Making of Modern Advertising* (New York: Basic Books, 1983), 25–29.

11. Jennings and Brewster, *The Century*, 113.

12. Allan Metcalf and David K. Barnhart, *America in So Many Words: Words That Have Shaped America* (Boston: Houghton Mifflin Company, 1997), 218.

13. Luke 12: 48.

14. Frederick Allen, *Secret Formula: How Brilliant Marketing and Relentless Salesmanship Made Coca-Cola the Best-Known Product in the World* (New York: HarperCollins, 1994), 146.

15. Mark Pendergrast, *For God, Country and Coca-Cola: The Unauthorized History of the Great American Soft Drink and the Company That Makes It* (New York: Charles Scribner's Sons, 1993), 161.

16. Pat Watters, *Coca-Cola: An Illustrated History* (Garden City, NY: Doubleday, 1978), 153.

17. Pendergrast, *For God, Country and Coca-Cola*, 177.

18. For information on Robert W. Woodruff, see Allen, *Secret Formula*; H. W. Brands, *Masters of Enterprise: Giants of American Business from John Jacob Astor and J. P. Morgan to Bill Gates and Oprah Winfrey* (New York: Free Press, 1999); Roger Enrico, *The Other Guy Blinked and Other Dispatches from the Cola Wars* (New York: Bantam Books, 1986); B. C. Forbes, *America's Fifty Foremost Business Leaders* (New York: B. C. Forbes & Sons, 1948); Neil A. Hamilton, *American Business Leaders, from Colonial Times to the Present* (Santa Barbara, CA: ABC-CLIO, 1999), 751–752; John N. Ingham, *Biographical Dictionary of American Business Leaders* (Westport, CT: Greenwood Press, 1983), 1670–1672; E. J. Kahn, *The Big Drink* (New York: Random House, 1950); Peter Krass, "Leaders and Success: Coca-Cola's Robert Woodruff," *Investor's Business Daily*, 4 June 1998; Thomas Oliver, *The Real Coke, The Real Story* (New York: Random House, 1986); Pendergrast, *For God, Country and Coca-Cola*; "Robert Woodruff: The Man Behind The Real Thing," *Houston Chronicle*, 14 April 1985; and Watters, *Coca-Cola: An Illustrated History*.

19. John W. Coogan, "Wilsonian Diplomacy in War and Peace," in *American Foreign Relations Reconsidered, 1890–1993* (New York: Routledge, 1994), 83.

20. For a thorough description of American foreign policy under Calvin Coolidge, see L. Ethan Ellis, *Frank B. Kellogg and American Foreign Relations* (New Brunswick, NJ: Rutgers University Press, 1961).

21. Robert K. Murray, *The Harding Era: Warren G. Harding and His Administration* (Minneapolis: University of Minnesota Press, 1969), 153–154.

22. Alfred E. Eckes Jr. and Thomas W. Zeiler, *Globalization and the American Century* (Cambridge: Cambridge University Press, 2003), 44.

23. For a discussion of protectionism during the Harding administration, see Murray, *The Harding Era*, 265–293.

24. Ibid., 276–280.

25. Ingham, *Biographical Dictionary*, 1579.

26. On the connection between Germany's postwar debt and the rise of nationalism, see Peter Pulzer, *Germany, 1870–1945: Politics, State Formation, and War* (Oxford: Oxford University Press, 1997), 117–118, 121–122.

27. Andrew Sinclair, *The Available Man: The Life Behind the Masks of Warren Gamaliel Harding* (New York: MacMillan, 1965), 198–199, notes that one contemporary commentator defined "the nostalgia in people for normalcy . . . as the desire that everything remain as it never was."

28. Jim Lee, "The Supreme Court Rules in the U.S. Steel Antitrust Case," in *Great Events from History*, 348.

29. Floyd Norris and Christine Bockelmann, *New York Times Century of Business* (New York: McGraw-Hill, 2000), 65.

30. Jim Lee, "The U.S. Government Loses Its Suit Against Alcoa," in *Great Events from History*, 434.

31. Robert H. Ferrell, *The Presidency of Calvin Coolidge* (Lawrence: University Press of Kansas, 1998), 43–48.

32. Bruce Andre Beaubouef, "The Teapot Dome Scandal Prompts Reforms in the Oil Industry," in *Great Events from History*, 464.

33. Ferrell, *The Presidency of Calvin Coolidge*, 207.

34. Geoffrey Perret, *America in the Twenties: A History* (New York: Simon and Schuster, 1982), 231.

35. Gene Smiley and Richard H. Keehn, "Federal Income Tax Policy in the 1920s," *Journal of Economic History* 55 (1995): 285; and James D. Savage, *Balanced Budgets and American Politics* (Ithaca: Cornell University Press, 1988), 147, 290.

36. Harold Evans, *The American Century* (New York: Alfred A. Knopf, 1998), 182.

37. For a detailed history of anti-Catholic bigotry in the 1928 election, see Edmund A. Moore, *A Catholic Runs for President: The Campaign of 1928* (New York: Rowld Press, 1956).

38. On prohibition's effect on alcohol consumption, see Thomas R. Pegram, *Battling Demon Rum* (Chicago: Ivan R. Dee, 1998), 163–165. For its allure as a forbidden substance, see Michael Woodiwiss, *Crime, Crusades and Corruption: Prohibitions in the U.S., 1900–1987* (Totowo, NJ: Barns and Noble Books, 1988), 1.

39. On prohibition's providing opportunities for organized crime, see Pegram, *Battling Demon Rum*, 173–174. On crime figures like Al Capone, see Laurence Bergreen, *Capone: The Man and His Era* (New York: Touchstone, 1994), passim, esp. 211–212, 220–221.

40. Woodiwiss, *Crimes, Crusades and Corruption*, 11.

41. Ibid., 28. The total number of speakeasies in the United States during the prohibition era amounted to an estimated 219,000. See Pegram, *Battling Demon Rum*, 173.

42. U.S. Bureau of the Census, *Historical Statistics of the United States, Colonial Times to 1970*, bicentennial ed., (Washington, DC: U.S. Bureau of the Census, 1975), part 2, 131.

43. Morris, Robinson, and Kroll, *American Dreams*, 68.

44. For a colorful description of media accounts of the crime and corruption of Chicago during the prohibition era, see Bergreen, *Capone*, 210–212.

45. Historian Blake McKelvey, *The Emergence of Metropolitan America* (New Brunswick, NJ: Rutgers University Press, 1968), 64, writes that "rural and highly moralistic America"

attempted "to impose prohibition on the cities." Paul A. Carter, *The Twenties in America* (London: Routledge, 1968), 71–72, notes that "the editor of the Anti-Saloon League's *Yearbook* . . . warned in 1931 that great city domination is the rock upon which past civilizations have been wrecked."

46. Ann Douglas, *Terrible Honesty: Mongrel Manhattan in the 1920s* (New York: Noonday Press, 1995), 73.

47. For the most thorough discussion of the Harlem Renaissance, see ibid., passim.

48. U.S. Citizenship and Immigration Services, "Immigration to the United States: Fiscal Years 1820–2000," table 1, available at http://uscis.gov/graphics/shared/aboutus/statistics/IMM99tables.pdf (accessed 24 September 2004).

49. Philip Taylor, *The Distant Magnet: European Emigration to the U.S.A.* (London: Eyret Spottiswoode, 1971), 48–65. A contemporary analyst of Mexican emigration to the United States in the 1920s stated: "Mexican immigration has thus reached astonishing proportions, and has rightly become a subject of concern to both governments, arousing discussion as to how best to deal with the situation." Manuel Gamio, *Mexican Immigration to the United States: A Study of Human Migration and Adjustment* (Chicago: University of Chicago Press, 1930; reprint, New York: Arno Press, 1969), 1.

50. Neil A. Hamilton, *Rebels and Renegades: A Chronology of Social and Political Dissent in the United States* (New York: Routledge, 2002), 173.

51. John Higham, *Strangers in the Land: Patterns of American Nativism, 1860–1925* (New Brunswick, NJ: Rutgers University Press, 1959; fourth paperback printing, 1998), 309–311, 324. See also Sean Cashman, *America in the Twenties and Thirties: The Olympian Age of FDR* (New York: New York University Press, 1989), 46–47.

52. Evans, *The American Century*, 185.

53. R. Douglas Hurt, *Problems of Plenty: The American Farmer in the Twentieth Century* (Chicago: Ivan R. Dee, 2002), 46.

54. Ferrell, *The Presidency of Calvin Coolidge*, 207.

55. George Vaseik, "Labor Unions Win Exemption from Antitrust Laws," in *Great Events from History*, 284.

56. Timothy E. Smith, "The Supreme Court Rules Against Minimum Wage Laws," in *Great Events from History*, 426–429.

57. Eli Ginzberg and Hyman Berman, *The American Worker in the Twentieth Century: A History Through Autobiographies* (New York: Free Press of Glencoe, 1963), 254.

58. Ibid., 154.

59. Jennings and Brewster, *The Century*, 112.

60. William J. Wallace, "Station KDKA Introduces Commercial Radio Broadcasting," in *Great Events from History*, 364.

61. Ray Barfield, *Listening to Radio, 1920–1950* (Westport, CT: Praeger, 1996), 3–5.

62. William L. Hagerman, "WEAF Airs the First Paid Radio Commercial," in *Great Events from History*, 396.

63. Morris, Robinson, and Kroll, *American Dreams*, 67.

64. S. A. Marino, "The National Broadcasting Company Is Founded," in *Great Events from History*, 522–525.

65. Ibid., 525.

66. James S. Olson, *Historical Dictionary of the 1920s: From WWI to the New Deal, 1919–1933* (Westport, CT: Greenwood Press, 1988), 273.

67. Steven J. Ross, *Working-Class Hollywood: Silent Films and the Shaping of Class in America* (Princeton, NJ: Princeton University Press, 1998), 185.

68. Robert Sklar, *Movie-Made America: A Social History of American Movies* (New York: Random House, 1975), 100. See also Garth Jewett, *Film: The Democratic Art* (Boston: Little, Brown, 1976), 154–156.

69. Cashman, *America in the Twenties and Thirties*, 352–353, 356.

70. McCraw, *American Business*, 1.

71. Morris, Robinson, and Kroll, *American Dreams*, 74.

72. Theodore O. Wallin, "The Air Commerce Act Creates a Federal Airways System," in *Great Events from History*, 499.

73. Morris, Robinson, and Kroll, *American Dreams*, 74.

74. James D. Matthews, "The Post Office Begins Transcontinental Airmail Delivery," in *Great Events from History*, 360.

75. Ibid., 361.

76. Richard Branson, "Pilot of the Jet Age: Juan Trippe," *Time*, 7 December 1998.

77. Marilyn Bender and Selig Altschul, *The Chosen Instrument: Pan Am, Juan Trippe, The Rise and Fall of an American Entrepreneur* (New York: Simon and Schuster, 1982), 59.

78. R. E. G. Davies, *A History of the World's Airlines* (London: Oxford University Press, 1964), 486.

79. For information on Juan Trippe, see Bender and Altschul, *The Chosen Instrument*; Branson, "Pilot of the Jet Age"; Robert Daley, *An American Saga: Juan Trippe and His Pan Am Empire* (New York: Random House, 1980); Davies, *History of the World's Airlines*; Ingham, *Biographical Dictionary*, 1477–1479; Hamilton, *American Business Leaders*, 681–683; and "Obituary: Juan Trippe," *New York Times*, 4 April 1981.

80. John N. Ingham and Lynne B. Feldman, *Contemporary American Business Leaders: A Biographical Dictionary* (Westport, CT: Greenwood Press, 1990): 660–669.

81. Ingham, *Biographical Dictionary*, 243–244.

82. Ibid., 1419–1421.

83. Evans, *The American Century*, 231.

84. Robert Sobel, *Herbert Hoover at the Onset of the Great Depression, 1929–1930* (New York: Lippincott, 1975), 86.

85. Morris, Robinson, and Kroll, *American Dreams*, 82.

86. Norris and Bockelmann, *New York Times Century of Business*, 77.

Chapter Four

1. David M. Kennedy, *Freedom from Fear: The American People in Depression and War, 1929–1945* (New York: Oxford University Press, 1999), 38. For a brief discussion of the many theories concerning the cause of the Great Crash, see Robert F. Himmelberg, *The Great Depression and the New Deal*, Greenwood Press Guides to Historic Events of the Twentieth Century (Westport, CT: Greenwood Press, 2001), 22–31.

2. Peter Jennings and Todd Brewster, *The Century* (New York: Doubleday, 1998), 149.

3. Kenneth M. Morris, Marc Robinson, and Richard Kroll, *American Dreams: One Hundred Years of Business Ideas and Innovation from the Wall Street Journal* (New York: Lightbulb Press, 1992), 83.

4. Thomas K. McCraw, *American Business, 1920–2000: How It Worked* (Wheeling, IL: Harlan Davidson, 2000).

5. Kennedy, *Freedom from Fear*, 163; Michael E. Parrish, *Anxious Decades: America in Prosperity and Depression, 1920–1941* (New York: Norton, 1992), 20.

6. AmericanPresident.org, "Herbert Hoover," http://www.americanpresident.org/history/herberthoover/biography/AmericanFranchise.common.shtml (accessed 20 February 2004).

7. Parrish, *Anxious Decades*, 247–248.

8. Anthony Patrick O'Brien, "Hoover Signs Smoot-Hawley Tariff," in *Great Events from History II: Business and Commerce*, ed. Frank N. Magill (Pasadena, CA: Salem Press, 1994), 591.

9. Douglas R. Hurt, *Problems of Plenty: The American Farmer in the Twentieth Century* (Chicago: Ivan R. Dee, 2002), 65–66; Harold Evans, *The American Century* (New York: Alfred A. Knopf, 1998), 218.

10. O'Brien, "Hoover Signs Smoot-Hawley Tariff," 595.

11. Clifton K. Yearley, "The United States Establishes a Permanent Tariff Commission," in *Great Events from History*, 300.

12. U.S. Bureau of the Census, *Historical Statistics of the United States, Colonial Times to 1970*, bicentennial ed. (Washington, D.C.: U.S. Bureau of the Census, 1975), part 1, 224.

13. Douglas Knerr, "The Reconstruction Finance Corporation Is Created," in *Great Events from History*, 630.

14. Joan Hoff Wilson, *Herbert Hoover: Forgotten Progressive* (Boston: Little, Brown, 1975), 162–164.

15. Parrish, *Anxious Decades*, 289–294; Jennings and Brewster, *The Century*, 157.

16. Kennedy, *Freedom from Fear*, 135–137, 139.

17. Jennings and Brewster, *The Century*, 159.

18. Himmelberg, *The Great Depression*, 39.

19. Ibid.; and Parrish, *Anxious Decades*, 291.

20. Himmelberg, *The Great Depression*, 39–44.

21. Benjamin K. Klebaner, "The Banking Act of 1933 Reorganizes the American Banking System," in *Great Events from History*, 656.

22. Alonzo Hamby, *For the Survival of Democracy: Franklin Roosevelt and the World Crisis of the 1930s* (New York: Free Press, 2004), 126–129; and Parrish, *Anxious Decades*, 295.

23. Jon R. Carpenter, "The Securities Exchange Act Establishes the SEC," in *Great Events from History*, 679–684; Floyd Norris and Christine Bockelmann, *New York Times Century of Business* (New York: McGraw-Hill, 2000), 94; and William E. Leuchtenburg, *Franklin D. Roosevelt and the New Deal, 1932–1940* (New York: Harper and Row, 1963), 90–91.

24. Siva Balasubramanian, "Congress Requires Premarket Clearance for Products," in *Great Events from History*, 788.

25. Richard Robinson, *U.S. Business History: A Chronology 1602–1988* (Westport, CT: Greenwood Publishing, 1990), 227.

26. Richard O'Connor, *The Oil Barons: Men of Greed and Grandeur* (Boston: Little, Brown, 1971), 143–145. For a comprehensive study of Standard Oil of New Jersey during the 1930s, see Henrietta M. Larson, Evelyn H. Knowlton, and Charles S. Popple, *New Horizons, 1927–1950: History of the Standard Oil Company* (New Jersey) (New York: Harper and Row, 1972).

27. Parrish, *Anxious Decades*, 286, 340, 377–379; Evans, *The American Century*, 226.

28. Kennedy, *Freedom from Fear*, 354–359.

29. Ibid.; Parrish, *Anxious Decades*, 378.

30. U.S. Bureau of the Census, *Historical Statistics of the United States*, part 1, 126.

31. Jack Blicksilver, "The Social Security Act Provides Benefits for Workers," in *Great Events from History*, 711.

32. Kennedy, *Freedom from Fear*, 147, 354–358.

33. Parrish, *Anxious Decades*, 315; and Hamby, *For the Survival of Democracy*, 275–277.

34. Hamby, *For the Survival of Democracy*, 280; Parrish, *Anxious Decades*, 347–348; and Kennedy, *Freedom from Fear*, 252, 285. Kennedy reports that in 1936 the WPA employed 7 percent of the U.S. workforce.

35. Kennedy, *Freedom from Fear*, 151–153; and Himmelberg, *The Great Depression*, 13.

36. Anthony Patrick O'Brien, "The National Industrial Recovery Act Is Passed," in *Great Events from History*, 662.

37. Hamby, *For the Survival of Democracy*, 161–174, 289–290; and Parrish, *Anxious Decades*, 310–316.

38. Clifton K. Yearley, "The Wagner Act Promotes Union Organization," in *Great Events from History*, 707–708.

39. Jennings and Brewster, *The Century*, 195.

40. Joshua Freeman et al., eds., *Who Built America? Working People and the Nation's Economy, Politics, Culture, and Society* (New York: Pantheon Books, 1992), 2: 129.

41. Clifton K. Yearley, "The CIO Begins Unionizing Unskilled Workers," in *Great Events from History*, 731.

42. Morris, Robinson, and Kroll, *American Dreams*, 93.

43. Evans, *The American Century*, 281.

44. Kennedy, *Freedom from Fear*, 308–315, 317; Freeman et al., *Who Built America?* 384–394; and Parrish, *Anxious Decades*, 357.

45. Clifton K. Yearley, "Roosevelt Signs the Fair Labor Standards Act," in *Great Events from History*, 792.

46. Paul B. Trescott, "The Norris-LaGuardia Act Adds Strength to Labor Organizations," in *Great Events from History*, 638.

47. B. C. Forbes, *America's Fifty Foremost Business Leaders* (New York: B. C. Forbes & Sons, 1948), 215–220.

48. Jennings and Brewster, *The Century*, 149.

49. Kennedy, *Freedom from Fear*, 387, remarks that many historians from the 1930s contended that World War I had not "been fought . . . to make the world safe for democracy but to make it safe for Wall Street bankers and grasping manufacturers . . . The only winners were the 'merchants of death'—financiers and munitions-makers who harvested obscene profits from the war . . . The indictment was grossly overdrawn, but it fell on receptive ears, especially in the antibusiness atmosphere of the Great Depression."

50. Parrish, *Anxious Decades*, 441, 445–447.

51. Jennings and Brewster, *The Century*, 206.

52. Kennedy, *Freedom from Fear*, 426–434.

53. U.S. Bureau of the Census, *Historical Statistics of the United States*, part 1, 105–106.

54. Parrish, *Anxious Decades*, 245–247. Hurt, *Problems of Plenty*, 63, provides these sobering statistics for the agriculture of the 1930s: "Between 1929 and 1932 agricultural commodity prices declined from an index of 93 to 58, a 37 percent drop. Gross farm income declined from $13.8 to $6.5 billion, or by 52 percent. Per capita farm income fell from $945 to $304 annually. Rural income averaged only 70 percent of that of manufacturing workers while land values declined by half during those years. Wheat exports decreased from 354 million to 143 million bushels, while cotton exports fell in value from approximately $2.5 billion to $1 billion, and meat exports declined from $246 million to $81 million. Domestic food and fiber consumption also plunged."

55. Evans, *The American Century*, 232.

56. Ibid., 233. For an excellent extended study of this phenomenon, see R. Douglas Hurt, *The Dust Bowl: An Agricultural and Social History* (Chicago: Nelson Hall, 1982).

57. Historian Michael Parrish, in *Anxious Decades*, 414, notes: "In 1931, for the first time in the country's history, more people left the United States than entered."

58. Kennedy, *Freedom from Fear*, 165, adds: "The Depression's gloom seeped even into the nation's bedrooms, as married couples had fewer children—15 percent fewer in 1933 than 1929." Parrish, *Anxious Decades*, 78, provides another insight into the effect of depression on family life: "Joe Rudiak played in a band that made the wedding circuit [in the early 1930s], and he found that 'even the weddings had slowed up. The churches were falling apart, the social activities and everything. So we went hungry with the rest of them.' He and his fellow musicians had counted on the food at the weddings to supplement their diet. Those who had children had fewer of them. In 1915 the birth rate per 1,000 Americans was 25; in 1933 it was 6.5."

59. Kennedy, *Freedom from Fear*, 165.

60. William H. Young with Nancy K. Young, *The 1930s, American Popular Culture Through History*, ed. Ray B. Browne (Westport, CT: Greenwood Press, 2002), 128, 133–135, 140–142, 148, 211–214; and David E. Kyvig, *Daily Life in the United States, 1920–1939: Decades of Promise and Pain*, Daily Life Through History Series (Wesport, CT: Greenwood Press, 2002), 71–72.

61. McCraw, *American Business*, 41. On escapism in the movies, see David E. Kyvig, *Daily Life in the United States, 1920–1939: Decades of Promise and Pain*, Daily Life Through History Series (Wesport, CT: Greenwood Press, 2002), 85–86. On movie attendance, see Kyvig, *Daily Life in the United States*, 83, 87; and Colin Shindler, *Hollywood in Crisis: Cinema and American Society, 1929–1939* (London: Routledge, 1996), 43. A *Business Week* article from 1936 commented: "Though attendance in 1936 will not pop to an all time high, it ought to average not less than 88 million persons weekly, which would be 10% higher than 1935 and not far removed from the 1930's record 110 million." *Business Week*, quoted in Shindler, *Hollywood in Crisis*, 43.

62. Norris and Bockelmann, *New York Times Century of Business*, 101.

63. John N. Ingham, *Biographical Dictionary of American Business Leaders* (Westport, CT: Greenwood Press, 1983), 140–142.

64. Sue Bailey, "Du Pont Announces the Discovery of Nylon 66," in *Great Events from History*, 798–802.

65. Owens Corning, "Harold Boeschenstein: The Business Perspective," http://pressroom.owenscorning.com/boeschenstein.html (accessed 24 January 2003).

66. James D. Matthews, "The DC-3 Opens a New Era of Commercial Air Travel," in *Great Events from History*, 754.

67. Ibid., 756.

68. McCraw, *American Business*, 41.

69. John N. Ingham and Lynne B. Feldman, *Contemporary American Business Leaders: A Biographical Dictionary* (Westport, CT: Greenwood Press, 1990), 544–549; and Richard S. Tedlow, *Giants of Enterprise* (New York: HarperCollins, 2001), 247–305.

70. Joseph J. Fucini and Suzy Fucini, *Entrepreneurs: The Men and Women Behind Famous Brand Names and How They Made It* (Boston: G. K. Hall; 1985), 130–133; and Jodi Wilgoren and Henry Weinstein, "Max Factor, Jr., Cosmetic Company Legend, Dies," *Los Angeles Times*, 9 June 1996.

71. Julie M. Fenster, *In the Words of Great Business Leaders* (New York: John Wiley & Sons, 2000), 350.

72. Ibid, 345.

73. Margaret Rudkin, *The Margaret Rudkin Pepperidge Farm Cookbook* (New York: Margaret Rudkin, 1963), 14.

74. "Pepperidge Farm Celebrates 50th Anniversary," *PR Newswire*, 17 September 1987, available from Dow Jones Interactive, http://ptg.djnr.com (accessed 9 April 2002).

75. Fenster, *In the Words of Great Business Leaders*, 351.

76. Ibid., 342.

77. "High Performance Urged in 3 Fields," *New York Times*, 5 October 1949, 44.

78. Fenster, *In the Words of Great Business Leaders*, 349.

79. For information on Margaret Rudkin see ibid.; Ingham and Feldman, *Contemporary American Business Leaders*, 561–565; "Mrs. Margaret Rudkin Is Dead, Founder of Pepperidge Farm," *New York Times*, 2 June 1967, 41; "Pepperidge Farm Celebrates 50th Anniversary," *PR Newswire*, 17 September 1987, available from Dow Jones Interactive, http://ptg.djnr.com (accessed 9 April 2002); and Rudkin, *Margaret Rudkin Pepperidge Farm Cookbook*.

80. Ingham, *Biographical Dictionary*, 626–628.

81. Ingham and Feldman, *Contemporary American Business Leaders*, 677–688.

82. Ingham, *Biographical Dictionary*, 1483–1488.

83. "Obituary: Harold Stanley," *New York Times*, 15 May 1963.

84. Vincent P. Carosso, *Investment Banking in America: A History* (Cambridge, MA: Harvard University Press, 1970), 300.

85. "Morgan Aides Form Investment House," *New York Times*, 6 September 1935.

86. Morgan Stanley & Company: A Summary of Financing 1935–1965 (internal company publication).

87. "Morgan Stanley: Hoover's Company Profiles," *Hoover's Online*, 3 July 2002, available from Factiva, http://global.factiva.com (accessed 26 July 2002).

88. Harold Stanley, *Competitive Bidding for New Issues of Corporate Securities* (New York: Morgan Stanley & Company, 1939), 2.

89. John H. Crider, "Harold Stanley Before the TNEC," *New York Times*, 20 December 1939, 39.

90. Stanley, *Competitive Bidding*, 3.

91. Ingham, *Biographical Dictionary*, 1345.

92. For information on Harold Stanley, see Carosso, *Investment Banking in America*; Ingham, *Biographical Dictionary*, 1344–1346; "Morgan Stanley: Hoover's Company Profiles"; "Obituary: Harold Stanley"; and Stanley, *Competitive Bidding*.

93. Ingham, *Biographical Dictionary*, 1688–1693.

94. Forbes, *America's Fifty Foremost Business Leaders*, 351–358; and "South Server," *Time*, 1 November 1937.

95. "Matthew S. Sloan, Head of M-K-T Since 1934, Dies," *Wall Street Journal*, 15 June 1945; "M. S. Sloan Dead; Utilities Official," *New York Times*, 15 June 1945; and Missouri-Kansas-Texas Lines, "1946 Annual Report" (St. Louis, MO: Missouri-Kansas-Texas Railroad Company, 1947).

96. "Pennsylvania Railroad Spent Four Billions During Past Decade," *Wall Street Journal*, 28 February 1940, 11.

97. Allan Metcalf and David K. Barnhart, *America in So Many Words: Words That Have Shaped America* (Boston: Houghton Mifflin Company, 1997), 231–232.

98. George H. Burgess and Miles C. Kennedy, *Centennial History of the Pennsylvania Railroad Company, 1846–1946* (Philadelphia: Pennsylvania Railroad Company, 1949), 658.

99. Ibid., 652.

100. Ibid.

101. Pennsylvania Railroad Company, "One Hundred Years, 1846–1946: Ninety Ninth Annual Report for Year Ended December 31, 1945" (Philadelphia: Pennsylvania Railroad Company, 1945).

102. Burgess and Kennedy, *Centennial History of the Pennsylvania Railroad Company*, 692.

103. For information on Martin Clement, see ibid.; Forbes, *America's Fifty Foremost Business Leaders*, 53–60; Ingham, *Biographical Dictionary*, 170–171; "Martin Clement of Pennsy Is Dead," *New York Times*, 31 August 1966, 43; Pennsylvania Railroad Company, "One Hundred Years"; and Robert Sobel, *The Fallen Colossus* (New York: Weybright and Talley, 1977).

Chapter Five

1. Thomas K. McCraw, *American Business, 1920–2000: How It Worked* (Wheeling, IL: Harlan Davidson, 2000), 73.

2. Peter Jennings and Todd Brewster, *The Century* (New York: Doubleday, 1998), 245.

3. McCraw, *American Business*, 76.

4. Eric C. Orlemann, *Caterpillar Chronicle: The History of the World's Greatest Earthmovers* (St. Paul, MN: Motorbooks International, 2000), 13.

5. Gilbert Cross, "The Gentle Bulldozers of Peoria," *Fortune*, July 1963, 171.

6. For sales figures, see Caterpillar Tractor Company, "1941 Annual Report" (Peoria, IL: Caterpillar Tractor Company, 1941). For employment numbers, see Caterpillar Tractor Company, *Fifty Years on Tracks* (Peoria, IL: Caterpillar Tractor Company, 1954), 51.

7. John N. Ingham and Lynne B. Feldman, *Contemporary American Business Leaders: A Biographical Dictionary* (Westport, CT: Greenwood Press, 1990), 76.

8. Cross, "The Gentle Bulldozers of Peoria."

9. For Caterpillar's profit numbers, see Urmila Sheshagiri, "Influential Residents Who Built Peoria: Some Are Unfamiliar but They Changed the History of Peoria," *Peoria Journal Star*, 23 September 1991. For comparison of Caterpillar with other companies, see Cross, "The Gentle Bulldozers of Peoria," 166.

10. Caterpillar Tractor Company, *Fifty Years on Tracks*, 79.

11. For information on Louis B. Neumiller, see "Caterpillar Diversifies," *Business Week*, 2 August 1947, 36–39; Caterpillar Tractor Company, "1941 Annual Report"; Caterpillar Tractor Company, *Fifty Years on Tracks*; "Corporations: Big Cat," *Time*, 7 February 1949, 77–79; Cross, "The Gentle Bulldozers of Peoria"; "Eberhard of Caterpillar," *Fortune*, August 1954; Ingham and Feldman, *Contemporary American Business Leaders*, 72–85; "The Machines That Are Changing the Face of the Earth," *Forbes*, 15 April 1965; William L. Naumann, *The Story of Caterpillar Tractor Co.* (New York: Newcomen Society in North America, 1977); Walter A. Payne, ed., *Benjamin Holt: The Story of the Caterpillar Tractor* (Stockton, CA: University of the Pacific, 1982); Sheshagiri, "Influential Residents Who Built Peoria"; "The Wages of Virtue," *Forbes*, 15 December 1971; and Charles Woolfson, *Track Record: The Story of the Caterpillar Occupation* (London: Verso, 1988).

12. William H. Chafe, *The Unfinished Journey: America Since World War II*, 3rd ed. (New York: Oxford University Press, 1995), 7; and David M. Kennedy, *Freedom from Fear: The American People in Depression and War, 1929–1945* (New York: Oxford University Press, 1999), 427.

13. McCraw, *American Business*, 75.

14. James T. Patterson, *Grand Expectations: The United States, 1945–1974* (New York: Oxford University Press, 1996), 13.

15. Kennedy, *Freedom from Fear*, 473–475.

16. Harold Evans, *The American Century* (New York: Alfred A. Knopf, 1998), 304.

17. McCraw, *American Business*, 91, adds: "The manufacture of home refrigerators, the most prized of all household appliances, dropped by 99.7 percent between 1941 and 1943. Most significantly, no civilian cars were produced. The last one rolled off the assembly line in 1942."

18. Jennings and Brewster, *The Century*, 245.

19. McCraw, *American Business*, 94.

20. Ibid., 79.

21. Ibid., 94.

22. Robert F. Himmelberg, *The Great Depression and the New Deal*, Guides to Historic Events of the Twentieth Century (Westport, CT: Greenwood Press, 2001), 27. For a detailed comparative study, see Mark Harrison, "Resource Mobilization for World War II: The U.S.A., U.K., U.S.S.R., and Germany, 1938–1945," *Economic History Review* 41 (1988): 171–192.

23. John Braeman, "Roosevelt Signs the Emergency Price Control Act," in *Great Events from History II: Business and Commerce*, ed. Frank N. Magill (Pasadena, CA: Salem Press, 1994), 833.

24. McCraw, *American Business*, 87.

25. Ibid., 88.

26. Evans, *The American Century*, 314; Kennedy, *Freedom from Fear*, 617, 619; and Himmelberg, *Great Depression*, 27.

27. John Braeman, "Roosevelt Signs the Emergency Price Control Act," in *Great Events from History*, 833.

28. Kenneth M. Morris, Marc Robinson, and Richard Kroll, *American Dreams: One Hundred Years of Business Ideas and Innovation from the Wall Street Journal* (New York: Lightbulb Press, 1992), 110.

29. Kennedy, *Freedom from Fear*, 620–621, 640.

30. Robert Sobel, "NBC Is Ordered to Divest Itself of a Radio Network," in *Great Events from History*, 827–831.

31. Paul B. Trescott, "Alcoa Is Found in Violation of Sherman Antitrust Act," in *Great Events from History*, 869.

32. Ibid., 869–873.

33. Richard Robinson, *U.S. Business History: A Chronology, 1602–1988* (Westport, CT: Greenwood Publishing, 1990), 299.

34. Jennings and Brewster, *The Century*, 247.

35. Ibid., 285.

36. Patterson, *Grand Expectations*, 4.

37. Chafe, *Unfinished Journey*, 49; and James Gilbert, *Another Chance: Postwar America 1945–1985* (Chicago: Dorsey Press, 1986), 41–42.

38. Paul B. Trescott, "The General Agreement on Tariffs and Trade Is Signed," in *Great Events from History*, 916.

39. Patterson, *Grand Expectations*, 129–133, 135, 147.

40. President Truman, quoted in ibid., 128.

41. Morris, Robinson, and Kroll, *American Dreams*, 122.

42. Evans, *The American Century*, 410.

43. Patterson, *Grand Expectations*, 107, 114–115. The influential career diplomat George Kennan penned an anonymous article that greatly shaped the policy of containment. See Anonymous, "The Sources of Conduct," *Foreign Affairs* 25 (July 1947): 566–582. For one of the most influential analyses of containment, see John Lewis Gaddis, *Strategies of Containment: A Critical Appraisal of Postwar American National Security Policy* (New York: Oxford University Press, 1982).

44. Thiokol Corporation, 1947 Annual Report (Trenton, NJ: Thiokol Corporation, 1947); and Thiokol Corporation, 1963 Annual Report (Trenton, NJ: Thiokol Corporation, 1963).

45. For a concise yet detailed history of the origins of the Joint Chiefs of Staff, see John C. Ries, "Congressman Vinson and the 'Deputy' to the JCS Chairman," *Military Affairs* 30 (1966): 16–24. See also Patterson, *Grand Expectations*, 133–134.

46. Evans, *The American Century*, 314.

47. Ibid.

48. Morris, Robinson, and Kroll, *American Dreams*, 112.

49. Norris and Bockelmann, *New York Times Century of Business*, 119; and Evans, *The American Century*, 346.

50. Morris, Robinson, and Kroll, *American Dreams*, 104.

51. Ibid.

52. Evans, *The American Century*, 347.

53. McCraw, *American Business*, 99.

54. Ibid., 77.

55. Robinson, *U.S. Business History, A Chronology*, 290; and Norris and Bockelmann, *New York Times Century of Business*, 127.

56. Morris, Robinson, and Kroll, *American Dreams*, 108.

57. U.S. Bureau of the Census, *Historical Statistics of the United States, Colonial Times to 1970*, bicentennial ed. (Washington, DC: U.S. Bureau of the Census, 1975), part 1, 126, 135.

58. Eli Ginzberg and Hyman Berman, *The American Worker in the Twentieth Century: A History Through Autobiographies* (New York: Free Press of Glencoe, 1963), 267.

59. "Detroit's Plants Taking On Women," *New York Times*, 19 February 1942.

60. Eugenia Kaledin, *Daily Life in the United States, 1940–1959: Shifting Worlds* (Westport, CT: Greenwood Press, 2000), 21, 35; and Kennedy, *Freedom from Fear*, 776, 778.

61. Evans, *The American Century*, 348.

62. On black migration, see Kennedy, *Freedom from Fear*, 768–769; and Patterson, *Grand Expectations*, 19. On the growth of the NAACP, see Chafe, *Unfinished Journey*, 86.

63. Clifton K. Yearley, "Truman Orders the Seizure of Railways," in *Great Events from History*, 880.

64. Clifton K. Yearley, "The Taft-Hartley Act Passes over Truman's Veto," in *Great Events from History*, 908–913.

65. William S. White, "Bill Curbing Labor Becomes Law As Senate Overrides Veto, 68–25," *New York Times*, 24 June 1947.

66. Yearley, "Taft-Hartley Act Passes," 910.

67. Ginzberg and Berman, *American Worker in the Twentieth Century*, 267.

68. Patrick D. Reagan, "Roosevelt Signs the G.I. Bill," in *Great Events from History*, 848.

69. On the U.S. population, see U.S. Bureau of the Census, *Historical Statistics of the United States*, part 1, 8. On the baby boom, see Kaledin, *Daily Life in the United States*, 111. On overall trends in the numbers of immigrants in the 1930s and 1940s, see Patterson, *Grand Expectations*, 62.

70. For official estimates, see Charles Zelden, "The United States Begins Bracero Program," in *Great Events from History*, 842.

71. McCraw, *American Business*, 90.

72. Ibid., 112.

73. Kaledin, *Daily Life in the United States*, 128.

74. Jon Teaford, *The Twentieth-Century American City: Problems, Promise, and Reality* (Baltimore: Johns Hopkins University Press, 1986), 100–101.

75. Morris, Robinson, and Kroll, *American Dreams*, 115.

76. Ibid.

77. Kaledin, *Daily Life in the United States*, 25–26.

78. Gene Bylinsky, "Industrial Management and Technology/Elite Plants," *Fortune*, 14 August 2000.

79. John N. Ingham, *Biographical Dictionary of American Business Leaders* (Westport, CT: Greenwood Press, 1983), 778–780.

80. Ingham and Feldman, *Contemporary American Business Leaders*, 557–561.

81. Ingham, *Biographical Dictionary*, 17–20.

82. John N. Ingham and Lynne B. Feldman, *African-American Business Leaders: A Biographical Dictionary* (Westport, CT: Greenwood Press, 1994), 371–372.

83. Ingham and Feldman, *Contemporary American Business Leaders*, 277–283, 594–599.

84. Gary W. Diedrichs, "Edward J. DeBartolo: The Pharaoh from Youngstown," *Cleveland Magazine*, July 1976.

85. Ingham and Feldman, *Contemporary American Business Leaders*, 116.

86. "$33 Million for Notre Dame from Developer and His Son," *New York Times*, 5 May 1989, A20.

87. William Severini Kowinski, *The Malling of America: An Inside Look at the Great Consumer Paradise* (New York: William Morrow, 1985), 103.

88. Ibid., 115–121.

89. Homer Hoyt, *A Re-Examination of the Shopping Center Market*, Technical Bulletin 33 (Washington, DC: Urban Land Institute, 1958).

90. Diedrichs, "Edward J. DeBartolo."

91. Ingham and Feldman, *Contemporary American Business Leaders*, 118.

92. Diedrichs, "Edward J. DeBartolo."

93. Ibid.

94. Ibid.

95. Ingham and Feldman, *Contemporary American Business Leaders*, 117.

96. For more information on Edward J. DeBartolo, see Isadore Barmash, "Shopping Centers, Showing Age, Seek a New Look," *New York Times*, 12 September 1981, F9; Jeffrey H. Birnbaum, "New-Store Slowdown; Building of Shopping Centers Is Curbed by Mortgage Problems, Scarcity of Sites," *Wall Street Journal*, 13 August 1980, 50; Adam Bryant, "Edward J. DeBartolo, Developer, 85, Is Dead; A Belief That the Shopping Mall Was the True Downtown," *New York Times*, 20 December 1994, B9; James F. Clarity, "DeBartolo: A Man in Search of Approval," *New York Times*, 11 December 1980, B15; Diedrichs, "Edward J. DeBartolo"; Neil A. Hamilton, *American Business Leaders, from Colonial Times to the Present* (Santa Barbara, CA: ABC-CLIO, 1999), 126–127; Hoyt, *Re-Examination of the Shopping Center Market*; Ingham and Feldman, *Contemporary American Business Leaders*, 115–119; C. T. Jonassen, *The Shopping Center Versus Downtown* (Columbus: Ohio State University, 1955); Kowinski, *The Malling of America*; "Obituary of Edward J. DeBartolo, Chairman of the Edward J. DeBartolo Corporation, Vice Chairman of DeBartolo Realty Corporation," *PR Newswire*, 19 December 1994, available from Lexis-Nexis (accessed 11 March 2002); and Mark C. Peyko, "A Brief History of Downtown Youngstown, Ohio," http://www.youngstowndrc.com/downtown_history.html (accessed 22 May 2003).

97. Junior Achievement, National Business Hall of Fame, "William M. Allen: The Boeing Company" (2002), available at http://www.ja.org/gbhf/viewLaureate.asp?id=1& alpha=A (accessed 29 November 2004).

98. McCraw, *American Business*, 100.

99. Ingham, *Biographical Dictionary*, 406–408.

100. "AMF Wins $29,300,000 Contract to Design Titan Launching System," *Wall Street Journal*, 26 November 1958.

101. For information on Eugene Morehead Patterson, see Robert E. Bedingfield, "Personality: Silver Spoon Was Not Enough; Morehead Patterson Greatly Widened A.M.F.'s Scope," *New York Times*, 17 January 1960, F3; Ingham, *Biographical Dictionary*, 1060–1062; Stacy V. Jones, "A New Pinsetter That Eliminates Unnecessary Motion Is Patented," *New York Times*, 15 December 1956, 39; "Morehead Patterson, 64, Dies; Chairman of American Machine," *New York Times*, 6 August 1962, 25; and Wayne Raguse, "Pinspotters Celebrate 50 Years," *Peoria Journal Star*, 31 March 1996.

Chapter Six

1. Harold Evans, *The American Century* (New York: Alfred A. Knopf, 1998), 435.

2. On the bomb-shelter craze, see Bruce Watson, "We Couldn't Run, So We Thought We Could Hide," *Smithsonian* 25 (1994): 46–58. On McCarthyism, see the useful and concise discussion in James T. Patterson, *Grand Expectations: The United States, 1945–1974* (New York: Oxford University Press, 1996), 196–205.

3. U.S. Senate Committee on Armed Services, *Confirmation Hearing on the Nomination of Charles E. Wilson*, 83d Congress, 1st sess., 15 January 1953, 26.

4. U.S. Bureau of the Census, "Population, Housing Unites, Area Measurements, and Density: 1790 to 1990," available at http://www.census.gov/population/censusdata/table-2.pdf (accessed 24 September 2004).

5. U.S. Citizenship and Immigration Services, "Immigration to the United States: Fiscal Years 1820–2000," table 1, available at http://uscis.gov/graphics/shared/aboutus/statistics/IMM99tables.pdf (accessed 24 September 2004).

6. Hawaiian Kingdom, "Focus on Hawaiian History," Hawaiian Kingdom.Org Web site, http://www.HawaiianKingdom.org (accessed 27 June 2003); and J. Gregory Williams, "Alaska Population Overview, 1999 Estimates," Alaska Department of Labor and Workforce Development, May 2000.

7. William H. Chafe, *The Unfinished Journey: America Since World War II* (New York: Oxford University Press, 1995), 123; Peter Jennings and Todd Brewster, *The Century* (New York: Doubleday, 1998), 339, 685; and William L. O'Neil, *American High: The Years of Confidence, 1945–1960* (New York: Free Press, 1986), 40.

8. For a history of the development of the polio vaccine, see Jane S. Smith, *Patenting the Sun: Polio and the Salk Vaccine* (New York: Morrow, 1990). For a description of the anxiety caused by the polio virus in the United States before the Salk vaccine, see Daniel J. Wilson, "Crippling Fear: Experiencing Polio in the Era of FDR," *Bulletin of the History of Medicine* 72 (1998): 464–495. For an insider's view of the discovery of DNA, see James D. Watson, *The Double Helix: A Personal Account of the Discovery of the Structure of DNA* (London: Weidenfeld and Nicolson, 1997).

9. Chafe, *Unfinished Journey*, 118.

10. Douglas R. Hurt, *Problems of Plenty: The American Farmer in the Twentieth Century* (Chicago: Ivan R. Dee, 2002), 120–122.

11. James T. Patterson, *Grand Expectations: The United States, 1945–1974* (New York: Oxford University Press, 1996), 333.

12. On the tendency of black Americans to move to urban centers in the 1950s and 1960s, see James Gilbert, *Another Chance: Postwar America, 1945–1985*, 2nd ed. (Chicago: Dorsey Press, 1985), 105–107.

13. U.S. Census Bureau, "Historical Census of Housing Graphs, Ownership Rates," http://www.census.gov/hhes/www/housing/census/historic/orgraph.html (accessed 28 September 2004).

14. Bill Delaney, "The First Homeowner's Insurance Policies Are Offered," in *Great Events from History II: Business and Commerce*, ed. Frank N. Magill (Pasadena, CA: Salem Press, 1994), 965.

15. Chafe, *Unfinished Journey*, 249.

16. Ibid., 248–256; and Gilbert, *Another Chance*, 142–143.

17. Gilbert, *Another Chance*, 143–147.

18. For a thorough discussion of Eisenhower's determination to keep defense spending down in the wake of the Korean War, see Douglas Kinnard, "President Eisenhower and the Defense Budget," *Journal of Politics* 39 (1977): 596–623.

19. Marsha Huber, "U.S. Tax Laws Allow Accelerated Depreciation," in *Great Events from History*, 1030–1034.

20. For a history of the Small Business Administration, see U.S. Small Business Administration, "Overview and History of the SBA," http://www.sba.gov/aboutsba/history.html (accessed 17 November 2004). For reducing subsidies to farmers, see Hurt, *Problems of Plenty*, 110–112. For Eisenhower's health-care and public-works policies, see Chester J. Pach Jr. and Elmo Richardson, *The Presidency of Dwight D. Eisenhower*, American Presidency Series, revised ed. (Lawrence: University Press of Kansas), 56–58. For the expansion of highways under Eisenhower, see Patterson, *Grand Expectations*, 274. See also Robert Griffith, "Dwight D. Eisenhower and the Corporate Commonwealth," *American Historical Review* 87 (1982): 106; and Pach and Richardson, *Dwight D. Eisenhower*, 122–124.

21. Jonathan Bean, "The Celler-Kefauver Act Amends Antitrust Legislation," in *Great Events from History*, 970–974.

22. Siva Balasubramanian, "Congress Sets Standards for Chemical Additives in Foods," in *Great Events from History*, 1097–1101.

23. On Eisenhower's cautious domestic policy, see Chafe, *Unfinished Journey*, 139–140. Chafe attributes at least part of Eisenhower's leadership style to his experiences in the military: "There, he had risen through the command structure, not by sticking his neck out or becoming involved in bitter internecine fights, but by playing it safe, waiting for all the evidence of his lieutenants to come in, and then issuing a command decision."

24. Eugenia Kaledin, *Daily Life in the United States, 1940–1959: Shifting Worlds* (Westport, CT: Greenwood Press, 2000), 111. For a comprehensive history behind the insertion of the phrase "one nation under God" in the Pledge of Allegiance, see Matthew W. Cloud, "'One Nation, Under God': Tolerable Acknowledgment of Religion or Unconstitutional Cold War Propaganda Cloaked in American Civil Religion?" *Journal of Church and State* 46 (2004): 311–340.

25. U.S. Bureau of the Census, *Historical Statistics of the United States*, Colonial Times to *1970*, bicentennial ed. (Washington, DC: U.S. Bureau of the Census, 1975), part 1, 391. See also Chafe, *Unfinished Journey*, 120; and O'Neil, *American High*, 212. Kaledin, *Daily Life in the United States*, 111, adds: "by 1959, an all-time high of 69% of polled Americans acknowledged church membership."

26. Michael Korda, *Making the List: A Cultural History of the American Bestseller 1900–1999* (New York: Barnes & Noble Publishing, 2001).

27. Ibid.

28. On popular culture in the 1950s, with an emphasis on the influence of television, see Kaledin, *Daily Life in the United States*, 133–147.

29. For a brief history of the company and its expansion beginning in the 1950s, see Peggy Robbins, "Levi Strauss," *American History Illustrated* 6, no. 5 (1971): 33–35.

30. James T. Patterson, *"Brown v. Board of Education": A Civil Rights Milestone and Its Troubled Legacy* (New York: Oxford University Press, 2001), 11 and passim. For another excellent discussion of the *Brown* case, see *"Brown v. Board of Education* at 40: A Commemorative Issue Dedicated to the Late Thurgood Marshall," *Journal of Negro Education* 63, no. 3 (summer 1994).

31. Harvard Sitkoff, *The Struggle for Black Equality, 1954–1992*, rev. ed. (New York: Hill and Wang, 1993), 37–56; and Janet Stevenson, "Rosa Parks Wouldn't Budge," *American Heritage* 23, no. 2 (1972): 56–64, 85.

32. Jennings and Brewster, *The Century*, 331. See also Patterson, *Grand Expectations*, 348–349.

33. "TV Dinners," Food Reference Web site, http://www.foodreference.com/html/arttvdinners.html (accessed 29 September 2004).

34. Jennings and Brewster, *The Century*, 331. See also Sterling Kittross, *Stay Tuned: A Concise History of American Broadcasting* (Belmont, CA: Wadsworth Publishing, 1978), 290–294; and Douglas T. Miller and Marion Nowak, *The Fifties: The Way We Really Were* (Garden City, NJ: Doubleday, 1977), 344.

35. Kittross, *Stay Tuned*, 291, 535.

36. The section on color television draws heavily from Thomas K. McCraw, *American Business, 1920–2000: How It Worked* (Wheeling, IL: Harlan Davidson, 2000), 129–131.

37. John N. Ingham, *Biographical Dictionary of American Business Leaders* (Westport, CT: Greenwood Press, 1983), 524–526, 683–685; J. Erik Jonsson, "Memorial Tribute: Patrick Eugene Haggerty, 1914–1980," *National Academy of Engineering* 2 (1984), 101–105; Adam Nossiter, "J. E. Jonsson, Ninety-Three, Industrialist and Ex–Dallas Mayor, Dies," *New York Times*, 4 September 1995.

38. Kenneth Morris, Marc Robinson, and Richard Kroll, *American Dreams: One Hundred Years of Business Ideas and Innovation from the Wall Street Journal* (New York: Lightbulb Press, 1990), 148.

39. Richard Robinson, *U.S. Business History: A Chronology 1602–1988* (Westport, CT: Greenwood Publishing, 1990), 313, 328.

40. Evans, *The American Century*, 476. For an extended discussion on Sputnik, see Robert A. Divine, *The Sputnik Challenge* (New York: New York University Press, 1993).

41. Fred Reed, "The Day the Rocket Died," *Air & Space/Smithsonian* 2, no. 4 (1987): 46–52.

42. Patterson, *Grand Expectations*, 420–421.

43. U.S. Bureau of the Census, *Historical Statistics of the United States*, part 1, 948; Chafe, *Unfinished Journey*, 113, makes this illustration: "It took 310 labor hours to make a car at the end of the war, only half of that fifteen years later."

44. Floyd Norris and Christine Bockelmann, *New York Times Century of Business* (New York: McGraw-Hill, 2000), 140–142.

45. Clifton K. Yearley, "The AFL and CIO Merge," in *Great Events from History*, 1064–1069.

46. Ibid.

47. Mitchell Langbert, "The Landrum-Griffin Act Targets Union Corruption," in *Great Events from History*, 1122–1127.

48. Chafe, *Unfinished Journey*, 114.

49. Robert E. Bedingfield, "Avery Overcomes Drive by Wolfson to Control Ward," *New York Times*, 23 April 1955.

50. "Eckerd History Is a Microcosm of Industry," *Chain Drug Review*, 16 November 1992; "Founder of Eckerd Drug Chain Dies at Ninety-One," *Knight Ridder Tribune Business News*, 20 May 2004; "Jack Eckerd Made the Right Decision," *Chain Drug Review*, 14 September 1998; and "Jack Eckerd Still Has No Time for Idleness," *Drug Topics*, 20 May 1991.

51. For quote on packaging of Marlboro cigarettes, see Ingham, *Biographical Dictionary*, 228–230.

52. Ibid., 228–230, 492–492.

53. Arthur M. Louis, "The Hall of Fame for U.S. Business Leadership," *Fortune*, 22 March 1982, 104.

54. Oscar Schisgall, *Eyes on Tomorrow: The Evolution of Procter & Gamble* (Chicago: J. G. Ferguson Publishing, 1981), 128–129.

55. Advertising Age, ed., *Procter & Gamble: The House That Ivory Built* (Lincolnwood, IL: NTC Business Books, 1988), 185.

56. McCraw, *American Business*, 53.

57. Schisgall, *Eyes on Tomorrow*, 193.

58. Alfred Lief, *"It Floats": The Story of Procter & Gamble* (New York: Rinehart & Company, 1958), 272.

59. Louis, "Hall of Fame," 104.

60. Advertising Age, *The House That Ivory Built*, 24.

61. Ibid., 27.

62. Lief, *"It Floats,"* 277.

63. Alfred Lief, *The Moon and Stars: The Story of Procter & Gamble and Its People* (Cincinnati: Procter & Gamble Company, 1963), 30–31.

64. Henry R. Bernstein, "P&G's Marketing Philosophy No Secret, Morgens Testifies," *Advertising Age*, 30 June 1975.

65. For information on Howard J. Morgens, see Advertising Age, *The House That Ivory Built*; Bernstein, "P&G's Marketing Philosophy No Secret"; Fred Danzig, "Top 100 Ad-

vertising People," *Advertising Age*, 29 March 1999; Charles L. Decker, *Winning with the P&G 99: 99 Principles and Practices of Procter & Gamble's Success* (New York: Pocket Books, 1998); "He Began Selling Soap to Indians," *New York Times*, 8 September 1957; Howard J. Morgens, "War and Peace," *Advertising Age*, 18 June 1990; Lief, *"It Floats"*; Lief, *The Moon and Stars*; Louis, "Hall of Fame"; McCraw, *American Business*, 42–58; "Morgens Turned P&G Global," *Cincinnati Post*, 29 January 2000; Jack Neff, "Creating a Brand Management System Was Only the Start of a Legacy Devoted to Nurturing Brands By Leaders Who Understood Consumers," *Advertising Age*, 13 December 1999; Procter & Gamble Company, "P&G History: 1946–1979," Procter & Gamble Web site, http://www.pg.com/about_pg/overview_facts/history.jhtml (accessed 2 July 2003); Schisgall, *Eyes on Tomorrow*; Oscar Schisgall, "P&G: Past Is Prolog," *Advertising Age*, 11 January 1982; Alecia Swasy, *Soap Opera: The Inside Story of Procter & Gamble* (New York: Times Books, 1993); and Randy Tucker, "Former P&G President Dies; Howard Morgens Led Explosive Growth," *Cincinnati Enquirer*, 29 January 2000.

66. H&R Block, "H&R Block Company Information," H&R Block Web site. http://www.hrblock.com/about/company_info/hbloch.html (accessed 7 March 2002); and John N. Ingham and Lynne B. Feldman, *Contemporary American Business Leaders: A Biographical Dictionary* (Westport, CT: Greenwood Press, 1990), 27–32.

67. Ingham, *Biographical Dictionary*, 1652–1653; and Louis, "Hall of Fame," 105.

68. Ray Kroc with Robert Anderson, *Grinding It Out: The Making of McDonald's* (New York: St. Martin's Press, 1977), 13.

69. John F. Love, *McDonald's: Behind the Arches* (New York: Bantam Books, 1986), 7.

70. For information on Raymond A. Kroc, see Jeffrey L. Bradach, *Franchise Organizations* (Boston: Harvard Business School Press, 1998), 4; Ingham, *Biographical Dictionary*, 741–743; Kroc with Anderson, *Grinding It Out*; Love, *Behind the Arches*; and McCraw, *American Business*, 156–192.

71. Ingham and Feldman, *Contemporary American Business Leaders*, 283–293.

72. Ingham, *Biographical Dictionary*, 1117–1121.

73. Robert Mottley, "The Early Years: Malcolm McLean," *American Shipper*, 1 May 1996.

74. Ibid.

75. "McLean Buys All Stock in Two Subsidiaries of Waterman Steamship," *Wall Street Journal*, 24 January 1955, 17.

76. Marvin A. Chatinover, "'Fishy-Back': Coastal Operators Seek Economic Rescue; Haul Trucks, Trains," *Wall Street Journal*, 8 February 1955, 1.

77. "Railroads Assail Sea-Trailer Plan," *New York Times,* 13 February 1955, 187.

78. "ICC to Investigate Ship, Truck Holdings of Malcolm P. McLean," *Wall Street Journal*, 18 May 1955, 15.

79. Sean Kilcarr, "The Passing of a Pioneer," *Drivers Magazine*, 1 June 2001.

80. Michael Bohlman, "Tribute to Malcolm McLean, Founding Father of the Freight Container," International Organization for Standardization, http://www.iso.ch/iso/en/commcentre/news/malcolmmclean.html (accessed 25 July 2003).

81. "R.J. Reynolds, McLean Holders Approve Merger," *Wall Street Journal*, 14 May 1969, 40.

82. For information on Malcolm P. McLean, see Bohlman, "Tribute to Malcolm McLean"; Wally Bock, "A Man Who Changed the World," *Monday Memo*, 11 June 2001, available from: http://www.mondaymemo.net/010611feature.htm (accessed 24 July 2003); "Centennial Journal: 100 Years in Business—McLean Makes Containers Shipshape, 1956," *Wall Street Journal*, 10 August 1989; Chatinover, "'Fishy-Back,'" 1; "Containerization Marks 40th Anniversary on April 26, 1996: A New Jersey Innovation," *Business Wire*, 17 April 1996, available from Factiva, http://www.factiva.com (accessed 24 July 2003); Kilcarr, "Passing of a Pioneer"; Louis, "Hall of Fame," 103; Maersk Sealand Company, "The Evolution of the Revolution in Containers," Maersk Sealand Web site, http://www2.maersksealand.com/maersksealand/evolution.htm (accessed 24 July 2003); "Malcolm Purcell McLean, Pioneer of Container Ships, Died on May 25th, Aged 87," *Economist*, 2 June 2001; Joseph G. Mattingly Jr., "Containerization," editorial in *Defense Transportation Journal*, 1 June 2001; Mottley, "The Early Years: Malcolm McLean"; Richard Pearson, "Malcolm McLean Dies; Revolutionized Shipping," *Washington Post*, 27 May 2001; Wolfgang Saxon, "M. P. McLean, 87, Container Shipping Pioneer," *New York Times*, 29 May 2001, 13; James Surowiecki, "The Financial Page: The Box That Launched a Thousand Ships," *New Yorker*, 11 December 2000, 46; and Wayne K. Talley, "Ocean Container Shipping: Impacts of a Technological Improvement," *Journal of Economic Issues*, 1 December 2000.

83. Patterson, *Grand Expectations*, 315.

84. "Americans Owe $607 Billion," *U.S. News & World Report*, 4 February 1955.

Chapter Seven

1. Floyd Norris and Christine Bockelmann, *New York Times Century of Business* (New York: McGraw-Hill, 2000), 195.

2. Kenneth M. Morris, Marc Robinson, and Richard Kroll, *American Dreams: One Hundred Years of Business Ideas and Innovation from the Wall Street Journal* (New York: Lightbulb Press, 1992), 132.

3. Shoshana Zuboff, "Work," in *Encyclopedia of the United States in the Twentieth Century*, ed. Stanley I. Kutler (New York: Charles Scribner's Sons, 1996), 1106.

4. Jonathan Bean, "The Celler-Kefauver Act Amends Antitrust Legislation," in *Great Events from History II: Business and Commerce*, ed. Frank N. Magill (Pasadena, CA: Salem Press, 1994), 970–974.

5. Robert Sobel, *The Rise and Fall of the Conglomerate Kings* (New York: Stein and Day, 1984), 11.

6. Norris and Bockelmann, *New York Times Century of Business*, 195.

7. John F. Winslow, *Conglomerates Unlimited: The Failure of Regulation* (Bloomington, IN: Indiana University Press, 1973), 9.

8. Stanley E. Boyle and Philip W. Jaynes, *Conglomerate Merger Performance: An Empirical Analysis of Nine Corporations*, staff report to Federal Trade Commission (Washington, DC: Federal Trade Bureau, National Technical Information Service, 1972), 16.

9. Norris and Bockelmann, *New York Times Century of Business*, 202.

10. "Making Big Waves with Small Fish," *Business Week*, 30 December 1967, 36.

11. "Infant with a Giant Appetite," *BusinessWeek*, 11 January 1964, 66.

12. Ibid., 68.

13. John N. Ingham and Lynne B. Feldman, *Contemporary American Business Leaders: A Biographical Dictionary* (Westport, CT: Greenwood Press, 1990), 621.

14. "The Rocket-Like Pace at Teledyne," *Forbes*, 15 January 1968, 22.

15. Ibid.

16. "Two PhDs Turn Teledyne into a Cash Machine," *BusinessWeek*, 22 November 1976, 133.

17. Ingham and Feldman, *Contemporary American Business Leaders*, 623.

18. Roy J. Harris Jr., "Quiet Growth: Teledyne, a Giant Now, Is Still Just Tele-Who to a Lot of Investors," *Wall Street Journal*, 16 January 1978, 1.

19. "Making Big Waves," 37.

20. Robert J. Flaherty, "The Singular Henry Singleton," *Forbes*, 9 July 1979, 48.

21. Ibid., 46.

22. Singleton, quoted in ibid., 50. For other sources on Henry E. Singleton, see Robert J. Flaherty, "The Sphinx Speaks," *Forbes*, 20 February 1978; Harris, "Quiet Growth"; "Henry Singleton of Teledyne: A Strategy Hooked to Cash Is Faltering," *BusinessWeek*, 31 May 1982; "Henry Singleton's Singular Conglomerate," *Forbes*, 1 May 1976; "Infant with a Giant Appetite" ; Ingham and Feldman, *Contemporary American Business Leaders*, 619–624; Harry H. Lynch, *Financial Performance of Conglomerates* (Boston: Harvard University, 1971); "Making Big Waves"; Andrew Pollack, "Henry E. Singleton, a Founder of Teledyne, Is Dead at 82," *New York Times*, 3 September 1999; "Rocket-Like Pace at Teledyne"; Barry Stavro, "Waiting for Henry," *Financial World*, 16 June 1987; A. David Silver, *Entrepreneurial Megabucks: The 100 Greatest Entrepreneurs of the Last 25 Years and How They Did It* (New York: Wiley, 1985); and "Two PhDs Turn Teledyne into a Cash Machine."

23. Howard Zinn, *The Twentieth Century* (New York: HarperCollins, 2003), 191.

24. William H. Chafe, *The Unfinished Journey: America Since World War II*, 3rd ed. (New York: Oxford University Press, 1995), 147, 171–173.

25. Zinn, *The Twentieth Century*, 199.

26. For long-term trends in the black population, see "Population of the Coterminous United States by Race, Residence, and Region: 1870 to 1960," in Daniel O. Price, in cooperation with the Social Science Research Council, *Changing Characteristics of the Negro Population*, 1960s Census Monograph series (Washington, DC: U.S. Bureau of the Census, 1969), 245–247. On the lack of prosperity in the black population, see Chafe, *Unfinished Journey*, 215–216. See also Karl Tauber and Alma Tauber, *Negroes in Cities: Residential Segregation and Neighborhood Change* (Chicago: Aldine Publishing, 1965), 1–10.

27. For unemployment rates, see U.S. Bureau of the Census, *Historical Statistics of the United States, Colonial Times to 1970*, bicentennial ed. (Washington, DC: U.S. Bureau of the Census, 1975), part 1, 135. For poverty rates, see Zinn, *The Twentieth Century*, 201.

28. Chafe, *Unfinished Journey*, 366–367.

29. Harold Evans, *The American Century* (New York: Alfred A. Knopf, 1998), 596–597.

30. James Gilbert, *Another Chance: Postwar America 1945–1985* (Chicago: Dorsey Press, 1986), 64, 277–278. See also Judith Hennessee, *Betty Friedan: Her Life* (New York: Random House, 1999).

31. For a brief history of early birth control (often referred to as the pill), see Kenneth Davis, "The Story of the Pill," *American Heritage* 29 (1978): 80–91.

32. For the effect of the antiestablishment culture on fashion, see Edward J. Reilly, *The 1960s*, American Popular Culture Through History series (Westport, CT: Greenwood Press, 2003), 84–89.

33. Ingham and Feldman, *Contemporary American Business Leaders*, 300–307, 334–340.

34. Peter Jennings and Todd Brewster, *The Century* (New York: Doubleday, 1998), 369. For a discussion of youth culture in the 1960s, see Reilly, *The 1960s*, 23–36.

35. Evans, *The American Century*, 542. See also Edward P. Morgan, *The 60s Experience: Hard Lessons about Modern America* (Philadelphia: Temple University Press, 1991), 162–163.

36. Zinn, *The Twentieth Century*, 242.

37. Jennings and Brewster, *The Century*, 359. See also Kurt Lang and Gladys Lang, *Politics and Television* (Chicago: Quadrangle Books, 1968), 213.

38. Jennings and Brewster, *The Century*, 360. See also Lang and Lang, *Politics and Television*, 213; and Theodore H. White, *The Making of the President, 1960* (New York: Atheneum Publishers, 1961), 294.

39. Evans, *The American Century*, 516. See also Chafe, *Unfinished Journey*, 235. For an extended discussion of Johnson's legislative achievements during this time, see Robert Dallek, *Flawed Giant: Lyndon Johnson and His Times, 1961–1973* (New York: Oxford University Press, 1998), 189–237.

40. James Reston, "That Kennedy Remark Berated Steel Men, Not All in Business," *New York Times*, 10 May 1962.

41. For a detailed account of Kennedy's economic policies, see Bruce Miroff, *Pragmatic Illusions: The Presidential Politics of John F. Kennedy* (New York: David McKay, 1976), 167–222.

42. Alene Staley, "The Kennedy-Johnson Tax Cuts Stimulate the U.S. Economy," in *Great Events from History*, 1218–1223.

43. U.S. Bureau of the Census, *Historical Statistics of the United States*, part 1, 135.

44. Morris, Robinson, and Kroll, *American Dreams*, 162.

45. Ibid.

46. Martin J. Lecker, "Nader's Unsafe at Any Speed Launches a Consumer Movement," in *Great Events from History*, 1270–1275.

47. Morris, Robinson, and Kroll, *American Dreams*, 158.

48. Gilbert, *Another Chance*, 232–233, 292–293.

49. Jennings and Brewster, *The Century*, 371. See also Elizabeth Cobbs Hoffman, *All You Need Is Love: The Peace Corps and the Spirit of the 1960s* (Cambridge, MA: Harvard University Press, 1999), 91–94.

50. Zinn, *The Twentieth Century*, 178.

51. Gilbert, *Another Chance*, 157–158, 202, 204.

52. Chafe, *Unfinished Journey*, 197–205; and Gilbert, *Another Chance*, 202–203.

53. David L. Anderson, *The Columbia Guide to the Vietnam War*, Columbia Guides to American History and Cultures (New York: Columbia University Press, 2002), 22–36.

54. Ibid., 37–45.

55. Ibid., 45–46 and 122–123. See also Chafe, *Unfinished Journey*, 278–280.

56. Anderson, *Vietnam War*, 63–69; Chafe, *Unfinished Journey*, 278–290; and Morgan, *The 60s Experience*, xxii. For a look at the debates within the Johnson administration about Vietnam policy in the middle 1960s, see Dallek, *Flawed Giant*, 340–351.

57. For a succinct overview of the Vietnam strategy of the Johnson administration, see Anderson, *Vietnam War*, 43–69.

58. James Schefter, *The Race: The Definitive Story of America's Battle to Beat Russia to the Moon* (London: Century, 1999), 130–136, 143–144.

59. Between 1961 and 1969, NASA spent a total of $33 billion. See Gilbert, *Another Chance*, 165–167.

60. Evans, *The American Century*, 555.

61. Morris, Robinson, and Kroll, *American Dreams*, 148–149.

62. Thomas K. McCraw, *American Business, 1920–2000: How It Worked* (Wheeling, IL: Harlan Davidson, 2000), 132.

63. Ibid.

64. Morris, Robinson, and Kroll, *American Dreams*, 163, 167.

65. Mark D. Hannah, "Firms Begin Replacing Skilled Laborers with Automatic Tools," in *Great Events from History*, 1128–1132.

66. Clifton K. Yearley, "The AFL and CIO Merge," in *Great Events from History*, 1064–1069.

67. For an informative contemporary assessment of the Equal Pay Act and Title VII of the 1964 Civil Rights Act, see Robert D. Mann, "Reducing Discrimination: Role of the Equal Pay Act," *Monthly Labor Review* 93 (1970): 30–34.

68. Zuboff, "Work," 1107.

69. For statistics on farm labor, see U.S. Bureau of the Census, *Historical Statistics of the United States*, part 1, 127.

70. Elisabeth A. Cawthon, "Congress Restricts Immigration with 1924 Legislation," in *Great Events from History*, 459–463.

71. U.S. Bureau of the Census, *Historical Statistics of the United States*, part 1, 105.

72. Katrina Brooker, "Can Anyone Replace Herb?" *Fortune*, 8 April 2000: 186; and Thomas Neff, *Lessons From the Top: The Search for America's Best Business Leaders* (New York: Currency, 1999), 187–192.

73. Ingham and Feldman, *Contemporary American Business Leaders*, 727–733; Nitin Nohria, Davis Dyer, and Frederick Dalzell, *Changing Fortunes: Remaking the Industrial Corporation* (New York: John Wiley & Sons, 2002), 226–226; and Richard S. Tedlow, *Giants of Enterprise: Seven Business Innovators and the Empires They Built* (New York: HarperBusiness, 2001), 315–360.

74. "United Telecommunications Announces Henson Retires," *Business Wire*, 17 April 1990. Available at http://www.lexisnexis.com/universe (accessed 6 November 2001).

75. Discovery Channel, "Inventions Inspired by Apollo 11, July 6, 1999," Discovery Channel Web site, http://www.exn.ca/apollo/science/products.cfm (accessed 18 September 2002).

76. "Alonzo Decker, Home Power Tool Pioneer, Retires from Black & Decker," *Associated Press Newswire*, 3 January 2001.

77. "Stockholder Meeting Briefs," *Wall Street Journal*, 27 January 1970.

78. "Black & Decker Sees Net Rising 20% in Year," *Wall Street Journal*, 25 August 1972. For other sources on Alonzo G. Decker Jr., see "Alonzo G. Decker, Obituary: The Register," *Times* (London), 20 March 2002; June Arney, "Decker Retires from B&D; Son of Power Tool Firm's Co-founder; a Director 60 Years," *Baltimore Sun*, 3 January 2001; Lawrence Freeny, "End of an Era at Black & Decker," *New York Times*, 29 April 1979; Sean Somerville, "He's Still a Company Man; Alonzo G. Decker, Jr., Son of One of the Founders of Black & Decker," *Baltimore Sun*, 5 January 1997; and Thomas Walton, "The Black & Decker Corporation: Compact Power—Innovation in the Cordless Professional Drill and Driver Market," *Design Management Journal*, October 1997.

79. Jerry Jasinowski and Robert Hamrin, *Making It in America: Proven Paths to Success from Fifty Top Companies* (New York: Simon and Schuster, 1995), 122.

80. Jeffrey L. Rodengen, *The Legend of Nucor Corporation* (Fort Lauderdale, FL: Write Stuff Enterprises, 1997), 24.

81. Ken Iverson with Tom Varian, *Plain Talk: Lessons from a Business Maverick* (New York: John Wiley & Sons, 1998), 125–126.

82. Ibid., 53.

83. Martin Donsky, "Man of Steel Talks Nuts and Bolts," *Business*, North Carolina, May 1989.

84. Ibid.

85. Iverson with Varian, *Plain Talk*, 75–76.

86. For information on F. Kenneth Iverson, see Tom Balcerek, "The Man Who Broke the Mould of US Steel," *Metal Bulletin Monthly*, July 2002; Len Boselovic, "Nucor, at Middle Age, Seeks to Re-energize Itself," *Pittsburgh Post-Gazette*, 1 October 1995; Tom Brown, "The Art of Keeping Management Simple: An Interview with Ken Iverson of Nucor Steel," *Harvard Management Update*, May 1998; Jim Collins, *Good to Great* (New York: HarperCollins, 2001); Donsky, "Man of Steel"; Jonathan P. Hicks, "Innovative Steel Mill Is Off to a Slow Start," *New York Times*, 2 December 1989; Ingham and Feldman, *Contemporary American Business Leaders*, 257–261; F. Kenneth Iverson, "Changing the Rules of the Game," *Planning Review*, September/October 1993; Ken Iverson, "Now Nucor Works," *Iron Age New Steel*, November 1997; Iverson with Varian, *Plain Talk*; Jasinowski and Hamrin, *Making It in America*; Richard I. Kirkland Jr., "Pilgrims' Profits at Nucor," *Fortune*, 6 April 1981; Farrell Kramer, "At F. Kenneth Iverson's Steel Company, Everyone Wears the Same Colored Hard Hat," *Investor's Business Daily*, 8 March 1993; Rodengen, *Legend of Nucor Corporation*; Michael Schroeder and Walecia Konrad, "Nucor: Rolling Right into Steel's Big Time," *BusinessWeek*, 19 November 1990; Irwin Speizer, "The Crucible," *Business, North Carolina*, 1 October 1999; and "Steel Man: Ken Iverson," *Inc.*, April 1986.

87. Nohria, Dyer, and Dalzell, *Changing Fortunes*, 27.

Chapter Eight

1. Peter Jennings and Todd Brewster, *The Century* (New York: Doubleday, 1998), 433.

2. Dorothea H. El Mallakh, "The Private Consumer and Energy Conservation," *Current History* 74 (1978): 198–201, 226–227.

3. "The Return of Stagflation," 30 December 2000, available from Blanchard Economic Research, http://www.blanchardonline.com (accessed 6 October 2003).

4. Thomas K. McCraw, *American Business, 1920–2000: How It Worked* (Wheeling, IL: Harlan Davidson, 2000), 157.

5. George Thomas Kurian, *Datapedia of the United States: American History in Numbers*, 3rd ed. (Lanham, MD: Bernan Press, 2004), 114.

6. Richard Robinson, *U.S. Business History: A Chronology 1602–1988* (Westport, CT: Greenwood Publishing, 1990), 393.

7. From 1966 to 1972, the U.S. military dropped more than 6.4 million tons of munitions. See David L. Anderson, *The Columbia Guide to the Vietnam War*, Columbia Guides to American History and Cultures (New York: Columbia University Press, 2002), 59–60, 128, 291.

8. On the Kent State tragedy, see William H. Chafe, *The Unfinished Journey: America Since World War II*, 3rd edition (New York: Oxford University Press, 1995), 406–407.

9. On Nixon's approach to withdrawing from Vietnam, see James Gilbert, *Another Chance: Postwar America, 1945–1985* (Chicago: Dorsey Press, 1986), 297–300; and Anderson, *Columbia Guide to the Vietnam War*, 72–77.

10. Chafe, *Unfinished Journey*, 401–404; and Gilbert, *Another Chance*, 300.

11. John N. Ingham, *Biographical Dictionary of American Business Leaders* (Westport, CT: Greenwood Press, 1983), 533–536.

12. Bruce Andre Beaubouef, "The United States Plans to Cut Dependence on Foreign Oil," in *Great Events from History II: Business and Commerce*, ed. Frank N. Magill (Pasadena, CA: Salem Press, 1994), 1555–1560.

13. Joseph R. Rudolph Jr., "Arab Oil Producers Curtail Oil Shipments to Industrial States," in *Great Events from History*, 1547.

14. Harold Evans, *The American Century* (New York: Alfred A. Knopf, 1998), 604.

15. Jennings and Brewster, *The Century*, 431. For statistics on commuting, see U.S. Bureau of the Census, "Means of Transportation to Work for the U.S.: 1980 Census," http://www.census.gov/population/socdemo/journey/mode6790.txt (accessed 25 October 2004).

16. "Energy, 1945–1980: From John F. Kennedy to Jimmy Carter," *Wilson Quarterly* 5 (1981): 70–90. See also Gilbert, *Another Chance*, 308–309.

17. Joseph R. Rudolph Jr., "Carter Orders Deregulation of Oil Prices," in *Great Events from History*, 1700.

18. For Nixon's economic policies, see Paul W. McCracken, "Economic Policy in the Nixon Years," *Presidential Studies Quarterly* 26 (1996): 65–77. See also Richard Reeves, *Richard Nixon: Alone in the White House* (New York: Simon and Schuster, 2001), 350–357. For Nixon's funding of NASA, see T. A. Heppenheimer, "Lost in Space: What Went Wrong with NASA?" *American Heritage* 43 (1992): 60–72. For the election of 1972, see Chafe, *Unfinished Journey*, 381–387 and 417–419.

19. Chafe, *Unfinished Journey*, 420–427.

20. Ibid., 450–451. See also Richard A. Watson, "The President's Veto Power," *Annals of the American Academy of Political and Social Science* 499 (1988): 41.

21. International Institute for Democracy and Electoral Assistance, "North America and the Caribbean: Voter Turnout from 1945 to Date," http://www.idea.int/voter_turnout/northamerica/usa.html (accessed 27 October 2004).

22. Chafe, *Unfinished Journey*, 451–452.

23. Ibid., 454.

24. Sharon C. Wagner, "Nixon Signs the Consumer Product Safety Act," in *Great Events from History*, 1522.

25. Ibid., 1522–1523.

26. For data on the proliferation of airlines, see Kenneth M. Morris, Marc Robinson, and Richard Kroll, *American Dreams: One Hundred Years of Business Ideas and Innovation from the Wall Street Journal* (New York: Lightbulb Press, 1992), 184.

27. Richard T. Seldon, "An Economist Looks at the 80's," *Virginia Quarterly Review* 56 (1980): 216–233.

28. Michael E. Kraft, "U.S. Environmental Policy and Politics: From the 1960s to the 1990s," *Journal of Policy History* 12 (2000): 22–26.

29. Kurian, *Datapedia of the United States*, 114.

30. Bureau of Labor Statistics, "Household Data Annual Averages," http://stats.bls.gov/cps/cpsaat1.pdf (accessed 28 October 2004). See also Bureau of Labor Statistics, "The American Workforce, 1992 to 2005: Historical Trends, 1950–92, and Current Uncertainties," http://www.bls.gov/opub/mlr/1993/11/art1abs.htm (accessed 27 October 2004).

31. According to the U.S. Census, productivity experienced a steady decline between 1972 and 1980, with a particularly steep loss of 4 percent in 1974. See chart and index in U.S. Bureau of the Census, *Statistical Abstract of the United States: 1980*, 101st ed. (Washington, DC, 1980), 416, also available at http://www2.census.gov/prod2/statcomp/documents/1980-01.pdf (accessed 26 October 2004).

32. On Yablonski, see Kenneth C. Wolensky, "Living for Reform," 27 (2001): 13–23. On Nixon and Hoffa, see Reeves, *President Nixon*, 394, 413.

33. Evans, *The American Century*, 563. See also Meta Mendel-Reyes, "Remembering Cesar," *Radical History Review* 58 (1994): 142–150.

34. John F. O'Connell, "Nixon Signs the Occupational Safety and Health Act," in *Great Events from History*, 1466.

35. Ibid., 1470.

36. Robert McClenaghan, "The Supreme Court Orders the End of Discrimination in Hiring," in *Great Events from History*, 1495.

37. John N. Ingham and Lynne B. Feldman, *African-American Business Leaders: A Biographical Dictionary* (Westport, CT: Greenwood Press, 1994), 181–198.

38. Ibid., 58–75, 120–129, 287–293.

39. Gilbert, *Another Chance*, 303.

40. Ibid., 278–281.

41. For an informative discussion of *Roe v. Wade* and its ramifications, see Johanna Schoen, "Reconceiving Abortion: Medical Practice, Women's Access, and Feminist Politics Before and After *Roe v. Wade*," *Feminist Studies* 26 (2000): 349–377.

42. Howard Zinn, *The Twentieth Century* (New York: HarperCollins, 2003), 268–297.

43. For a concise discussion of the 1970s self-help phenomenon, see Kim Shienbaum, "Popular Culture and Political Consciousness Ideologies of Self-Help, Old and New," *Journal of Popular Culture* 14 (1980): 10–19. For Jim Jones's cult, see Ernest J. Green, "Jonestown," *Utopian Studies* 4 (1993): 162–165; and John R. Hall, "Apocalypse at Jonestown," *Society* 16 (1979): 52–61.

44. Jennings and Brewster, *The Century*, 426.

45. For the most authoritative book on Nike, see Donald Katz, *Just Do It: The Nike Spirit in the Corporate World* (New York: Random House, 1994). See also, Phil Knight, "High-Performance Marketing: An Interview with Nike's Phil Knight," *Harvard Business Review*, 1 July 1992.

46. McCraw, *American Business*, 157.

47. U.S. Bureau of the Census, "Population, Housing Units, Area Measurements, and Density: 1790 to 1990," http://www.census.gov/population/censusdata/table-2.pdf (accessed 27 October 2004).

48. U.S. Bureau of the Census, "Population: 1790 to 1990," http://www.census.gov/population/censusdata/table-2.pdf (accessed 28 October 2004).

49. U.S. Bureau of the Census, "Nativity of the Population and Place of Birth of the Native Population: 1850 to 1990," table 1, available at http://www.census.gov/population/www/documentation/twps0029/tab01.html (accessed 27 October 2004).

50. Kamala Arogyaswamy, "Genentech Is Founded," in *Great Events from History*, 1616–1620.

51. Jennings and Brewster, *The Century*, 452.

52. McCraw, *American Business*, 200.

53. Richard Barrett, "The Pocket Calculator Is Marketed," in *Great Events from History*, 1518.

54. Ibid., 1517–1521.

55. Patrick Bridgemon, "Visicalc Spreadsheet Software Is Marketed," in *Great Events from History*, 1687–1691.

56. Nitin Nohria, Davis Dyer, and Frederick Dalzell, *Changing Fortunes: Remaking the Industrial Corporation* (New York: John Wiley & Sons, 2002), 29.

57. Ibid.

58. Zinn, *The Twentieth Century*, 300.

59. Paul Gibson, "Being Good Isn't Enough Anymore," *Forbes*, 26 November 1979; and Michael Waldholz, "Merck Picks Vagelos, Its Top Scientist, to Be Chief Executive and President," *Wall Street Journal*, 24 April 1985.

60. Lawrence Van Gelder, "Corporate Chief Ponders 'Drug Lag'," *New York Times*, 1 April 1984.

61. David Finn, "CEO: The Whole Man. Fame Versus The Family/Edmund T. Pratt Jr. of Pfizer Inc.," *Across the Board*, December 1985: 37.

62. Jeffrey L. Rodengen, *The Legend of Pfizer* (Fort Lauderdale, FL: Write Stuff Syndicate, 1999), 103.

63. Ibid., 107.

64. Anthony Baldo, "One Quarter Doesn't Matter," *Financial World*, 11 July 1989.

65. Suzanne L. Oliver, "Sticking with It: Pfizer's Boss Ignored Wall Street's Impatience with His R&D," *Forbes*, 13 May 1991.

66. Edmund T. Pratt Jr., "Keeping an Eye on America's Future," *Directors & Boards*, winter 1993.

67. Michael A. Santoro and Lynn Sharp Paine, "Pfizer: Global Protection of Intellectual Property," Case 9-392-073 (Boston: Harvard Business School, 1992), 6.

68. Oliver, "Sticking with It."

69. For information on Edmund T. Pratt Jr., see Baldo, "One Quarter Doesn't Matter"; "Distinguished Alumnus," *Duke Magazine*, September–October 2001; Bruce R. Ellig, "My Years with the Pfizer Board," *Directors & Boards*, summer 1997; Finn, "Edmund T. Pratt Jr."; Thomas Jaffe with Jon Schriber, "Miracle on 42nd Street?" *Forbes*, 27 April 1981; Andrew A. Leckey, *The 20 Hottest Investments for the 21st Century* (Chicago: Contemporary Books, 1994); Oliver, "Sticking with It"; Jeffrey A. Perlman, "Pfizer Names E. Pratt Chairman and Chief. G. Laubach President," *Wall Street Journal*, 20 December 1972; Edmund T. Pratt Jr., "Intellectual Property: Tales of Piracy and Retaliation," *Directors & Boards*, summer 1989; Pratt, "Keeping an Eye on America's Future"; Edmund T. Pratt, Jr., *Pfizer: Bringing Science to Life* (New York: Necomen Society of America, 1985); Rodengen, *The Legend of Pfizer*; Monica Roman, "The Corporation: Pfizer Finally Sees Its Payoff," *BusinessWeek*, 1 July 1991; Wolfgang Saxon, "Edmund Taylor Pratt Jr., 75, a Former Chairman of Pfizer," *New York Times*, 7 September 2002; and United Press International, "A Chief Executive's Charmed Life, Pfizer Chief Also Did Government Stint," *Northern New Jersey Record*, 28 September 1984.

70. Nohria, Dyer, and Dalzell, *Changing Fortunes*, 241.

71. Ibid., 241–242.

72. Ibid., 244–245.

73. John N. Ingham and Lynne B. Feldman, *Contemporary American Business Leaders: A Biographical Dictionary* (Westport, CT: Greenwood Press, 1990), 162–166.

74. Ibid., 625–635.

75. Dee Hock, *Birth of the Chaordic Age* (San Francisco: Berrett-Koehler Publishers, 1999), 59.

76. Bonnie Durrance, "The Evolutionary Vision of Dee Hock: From Chaos to Chaords," *Training & Development*, April 1997.

77. Hock, *Birth of the Chaordic Age*, 64.

78. Ibid., 80.

79. Paul Chutkow, *VISA: The Power of an Idea* (Chicago: Harcourt, 2001), 82.

80. Ibid.

81. Ibid., 93.

82. Ibid., 98.

83. M. Mitchell Waldrop, "The Trillion-Dollar Vision of Dee Hock," *Fast Company*, October/November 1996.

84. Chutkow, *VISA*, 117.

85. "Otherwise Dee Hock, the Birth of the Chaordic Century: Out of Control and Into Order," Paradigm Shift International Web site, http://www.parshift.com/speakers/speak009.htm (accessed 9 July 2003).

86. Chutkow, *VISA*, 158.

87. Ibid.

88. For information on Dee W. Hock, see Roslan Ali, "Visa 'Chameleon' in the Business World," *Business Times*, 24 March 1993; Warren Bennis and Robert Thomas, *Geeks and Geezers: How Era, Values, and Defining Moments Shape Leaders* (Boston: Harvard Business School Press, 2002); Chutkow, *VISA*; Durrance, "Evolutionary Vision of Dee Hock"; Hock, *Birth of the Chaordic Age*; "The Iconoclast Who Made Visa No. 1," *BusinessWeek*,

22 December 1980; Jeffrey Kutler, "Looking Beyond Cards, Visa's First Chief Has Found a Wider World to Conquer," *American Banker*, 16 April 1998; Arthur M. Louis, "Visa Stirs Up the Big Banks—Again," *Fortune*, 3 October 1983; "The National Business Hall of Fame," *Fortune*, 11 March 1991; "Otherwise Dee Hock"; and Waldrop, "Trillion-Dollar Vision of Dee Hock."

89. John P. Kotter, *A Force for Change: How Leadership Differs from Management* (New York: Free Press, 1990), 131.

90. Jeff Bailey, "Plains Giant: What Makes ConAgra, Once on Brink of Ruin, a Wall Street Favorite?" *Wall Street Journal*, 13 June 1990.

91. Mark Ivey, "The Corporation: How ConAgra Grew Big—and Now Beefy: Acquisition Whiz Mike Harper Just Bought a Huge Meatpacker," *Business Week*, 18 May 1987.

92. Ibid.

93. Jane E. Limprecht, *ConAgra Who? $15 Billion and Growing* (Omaha: ConAgra, 1989), 114.

94. For information on Charles M. Harper, see Bailey, "Plains Giant"; Jeff Blyskal, "The Best Damn Food Company in the U.S.," *Forbes*, 24 October 1983; "ConAgra: Buying a Frozen-Food Maker to Get at Its Chickens," *Business Week*, 1 December 1980; Ingham and Feldman, *Contemporary American Business Leaders*, 207–211; Ivey, "How ConAgra Grew Big"; Limprecht, *ConAgra Who?*; Julie Liesse, "Harper: ConAgra's Healthy Choice," *Advertising Age*, 7 January 1991; and Seth Lubove, "I Hope My Luck Holds Out," *Forbes*, 20 July 1992.

Chapter Nine

1. Peter Jennings and Todd Brewster, *The Century* (New York: Doubleday, 1998), 484.

2. John N. Ingham and Lynne B. Feldman, *Contemporary American Business Leaders: A Biographical Dictionary* (Westport, CT: Greenwood Press, 1990), 316–322.

3. Martin K. Hunt and Jacqueline Hunt, *History of Black Business: The Coming of America's Largest Black-Owned Businesses* (Chicago: Knowledge Express Company, 1998), 111.

4. Alfred Edmond Jr., "Reginald Lewis Cuts the Big Deal," *Black Enterprise*, November 1987.

5. Thayer C. Taylor, "Living the Dream *Why Should White Guys Have All the Fun?* by Reginald F. Lewis and Blair S. Walker," *Sales and Marketing Management*, January 1995.

6. Reginald F. Lewis and Blair S. Walker, *Why Should White Guys Have All the Fun? How Reginald Lewis Created a Billion-Dollar Business Empire* (New York: John Wiley & Sons, 1995), 165.

7. George Anders and Constance Mitchell, "Self-Made Man: How Reginald Lewis Has Elbowed His Way into an LBO Fortune," *Wall Street Journal*, 15 October 1992.

8. Edmond, "Reginald Lewis Cuts the Big Deal."

9. Lewis and Walker, *Why Should White Guys Have All the Fun?* 198.

10. Jonathan P. Hicks, "The Wall Streeter Who Runs TLC Beatrice," *New York Times*, 9 June 1991.

11. For information on Reginald F. Lewis, see Anders and Mitchell, "Self-Made Man"; Erik Calonius, "For Reg Lewis: Mean Streets Still," *Fortune*, 15 January 1990;

Thomas N. Cochran, "Beatrice International's IPO," *Barron's*, 4 December 1989; Daniel F. Cuff, "90-to-1 Return for Investor," *New York Times*, 10 July 1987; Derek T. Dingle, "TLC's Final Act," *Black Enterprise*, September 1999; Alfred Edmond Jr., "Dealing at the Speed of Light," *Black Enterprise*, June 1988; Edmond, "Reginald Lewis Cuts the Big Deal"; Arthur S. Hayes, "Crowthers McCall Sues Investor Lewis, Charging Buy-Out Triggered Its Slide," *Wall Street Journal*, 11 September 1989; Jonathan P. Hicks, "Beatrice Unit Brings $985 Million," *New York Times*, 10 August 1987; Jonathan P. Hicks, "Reginald F. Lewis, 50, Is Dead: Financier Led Beatrice Takeover," *New York Times*, 20 January 1993; Hicks, "Wall Streeter"; Hunt and Hunt, *History of Black Business*; John N. Ingham and Lynne B. Feldman, *African-American Business Leaders: A Biographical Dictionary* (Westport, CT: Greenwood Press, 1994), 434–440; Andrew Kupfer, "Reginald Lewis: The Newest Member of the LBO Club," *Fortune*, 4 January 1988; Lewis and Walker, *Why Should White Guys Have All the Fun?*; Jay Matthews and Brett Fromson, "Reginald Lewis' Restless Vision: Beatrice Chairman's Drive Built Largest Black-Owned Company," *Washington Post*, 20 January 1993; Judy Temes, "McCall's Unravels; Who's to Blame?" *Crain's New York Business*, 11 June 1990; Kevin D. Thompson, "TLC Deal Signals New Era for Black Business," *Black Enterprise*, October 1987; "Travelers Drops Appeal Involving Reginald Lewis," *Wall Street Journal*, 17 July 1991; Blair S. Walker, "Beatrice CEO Dies: Brain Cancer Just Disclosed a Day Before," *USA Today*, 20 January 1993; and Juliet E. K. Walker, *The History of Black Business in America: Capitalism, Race, Entrepreneurship* (New York: Twayne Publishers, 1998).

12. Larry Schweikart, "Insider Trading Scandals Mar the Emerging Junk Bond Market," in *Great Events from History II: Business and Commerce*, ed. Frank N. Magill (Pasadena, CA: Salem Press, 1994), 1922.

13. Ibid.

14. Jennings and Brewster, *The Century*, 474.

15. Harold Evans, *The American Century* (New York: Alfred A. Knopf, 1998), 617.

16. William H. Chafe, *The Unfinished Journey: America Since World War II*, 3rd ed. (New York: Oxford University Press, 1995), 491.

17. Jennings and Brewster, *The Century*, 470.

18. Thomas B. Edsall, "The Tax Bill: The Effect on Business and Investment," *Washington Post*, 6 August 1981.

19. Howard Zinn, *The Twentieth Century* (New York: HarperCollins, 2003), 346.

20. Evans, *American Century*, 642.

21. Nathaniel C. Nash, "Who to Thank for the Thrift Crisis," *New York Times*, 12 June 1988.

22. Ibid.

23. Davita Glasberg and Dan Skidmore, "The Dialectics of State Economic Intervention: Bank Deregulation and the Savings and Loan Bailout," *Sociological Quarterly* 38 (1997): 67–93.

24. Ronald Reagan, speech to the National Association of Evangelicals, Orlando, FL, 8 March 1983.

25. George L. Rueckert, *Global Double Zero: The INF Treaty from Its Origins to Implementation*, Contributions in Military Studies, no. 135 (Westport, CT: Greenwood Press, 1993), 178–179.

26. Chafe, *Unfinished Journey*, 500–501.

27. Constantine C. Menges, "Sanctions '86: How the State Department Prevailed," *National Interest* 13 (1988): 65–77.

28. Evans, *American Century*, 629.

29. Corinne Elliott, "Health Consciousness Creates Huge New Markets," in *Great Events from History*, 1419.

30. Zinn, *The Twentieth Century*, 351.

31. Jennings and Brewster, *The Century*, 480.

32. U.S. Department of Justice, "Bureau of Justice Statistics Special Report: Prevalence of Imprisonment in the U.S. Population, 1974–2001," http://www.ojp.usdoj.gov/bjs/pub/pdf/piuspo1.pdf (accessed 12 October 2004).

33. Zinn, *The Twentieth Century*, 346; and Jennings and Brewster, *The Century*, 488.

34. Eric K. Lerner and Mary Ellen Hombs, *Aids Crisis in America*, 2nd ed. (Santa Barbara, CA: ABC-CLIO, 1988), 3, 40–44; and Kenneth J. Doka, *Aids, Fear, and Society: Challenging the Dreaded Disease* (Washington: Taylor & Francis, 1997), 68–71.

35. By the end of 1989, the Centers for Disease Control reported a total of 86,614 deaths from AIDS since 1981 (with 70,000 from 1987 to 1989 alone). See the Centers for Disease Control, *HIV/AIDS Surveillance Reports*, 1987 and 1990 year-end editions (Washington, DC: Department of Health and Human Services) http://www.cdc.gov/hiv/stats/hasrlink.htm (accessed 9 November 2004).

36. U.S. Bureau of the Census, "Census Questionnaire Content, 1990 CQC-6: Marital Status" (Washington, DC: U.S. Department of Congress, 1993).

37. Richard Robinson, *U.S. Business History: A Chronology, 1602–1988* (Westport, CT: Greenwood Publishing, 1990), 448.

38. U.S. Bureau of the Census, Current Population Reports, P23-180, *Marriage, Divorce, and Remarriage in the 1990's* (Washington, DC: U.S. Government Printing Office, 1992), http://www.census.gov/population/socdemo/marr-div/p23-180/p23-180.pdf (accessed 18 November 2004); AgingStats.Gov (Web site of the Federal Interagency Forum on Aging-Related Statistics), "Older Americans 2000: Key Indicators of Well-Being," appendix A, "Detailed Tables," http://www.agingstats.gov/chartbook2000/tables-population.html# Indicator %201 (accessed 9 November 2004).

39. U.S. Citizenship and Immigration Services, "U.S. Immigration Statistics," table 2, "Immigration by Region and Selected Country of Last Residence: Fiscal Years 1820–1997," available at http://uscis.gov/graphics/shared/aboutus/statistics/97immtbls.htm (accessed 8 November 2004).

40. U.S. Citizenship and Immigration Services, "U.S. Immigration Statistics," table 3, "Immigrants Admitted by Region and Country of Birth: Fiscal Years 1987–97," available at http://uscis.gov/graphics/shared/aboutus/statistics/97immtbls.htm (accessed 8 November 2004).

41. U.S. Bureau of the Census, "Race and Hispanic Origin of the Population by Nativity: 1850 to 1990," table 8, http://www.census.gov/population/www/documentation/twps0029/tab08.html (accessed 25 November 2003).

42. D. G. Papademetriou, "The Immigration Reform and Control Act of 1986: America Amends Its Immigration Law," *International Migration* 25 (1987): 325–334.

43. Jack Citrin, Beth Reingold, and Donald Green, "American Identity and the Politics of Ethnic Change," *Journal of Politics* 52 (1990): 1124–1154.

44. Evans, *The American Century*, 626.

45. Ibid.

46. Jennings and Brewster, *The Century*, 473; and Herbert R. Northrup, "The Rise and Demise of PATCO," *Industrial and Labor Relations Review* 37 (1984): 167–184.

47. George Thomas Kurian, *Datapedia of the United States: American History in Numbers*, 3rd ed. (Lanham, MD: Bernan Press, 2004), 123.

48. Nitin Nohria, Davis Dyer, and Frederick Dalzell, *Changing Fortunes: Remaking the Industrial Corporation* (New York: John Wiley & Sons, 2002), 49.

49. Shoshana Zuboff, "Work," in *Encyclopedia of the United States in the Twentieth Century*, ed. Stanley I. Kutler (New York: Charles Scribner's Sons, 1996), 1117.

50. Kenneth M. Morris, Marc Robinson, and Richard Kroll, *American Dreams: One Hundred Years of Business Ideas and Innovation from the Wall Street Journal* (New York: Lightbulb Press, 1992), 201.

51. Ibid.

52. Robert Sobel, "IBM Introduces Its Personal Computer," in *Great Events from History*, 1811.

53. Susan Strasser, "Consumption," in *Encyclopedia of the United States in the Twentieth Century*, ed. Stanley I. Kutler (New York: Charles Scribner's Sons, 1996), 1031.

54. David E. Sanger, "For Apple, a Risky Assault on I.B.M.," *New York Times*, 23 January 1984.

55. Strasser, "Consumption," 1031.

56. Zuboff, "Work," 1120.

57. Sobel, "IBM Introduces Its Personal Computer," 1809–1814.

58. Jim Kerstetter and Peter Burrows, "A CEO's Last Stand," *BusinessWeek*, 26 July 2004; and Michael J. Miller, "Interview with Scott McNealy," *PC Magazine*, 4 September 2001.

59. "Steve Case." *Newsmakers 1996*, Issue 4. Gale Research, 1996.

60. Nohria, Dyer, and Dalzell, *Changing Fortunes*, 237.

61. "Case Study Steve Case," *Newsweek*, 24 January 2000; Michael Krantz, "AOL, You've Got Netscape," *Time*, 7 December 1998; "Steve Case." *Newsmakers 1996*; and Nohria, Dyer, and Dalzell, *Changing Fortunes*, 237–240.

62. Brian Dumaine, "Self-Made Millionaires," *Fortune*, 23 September 2002; Nohria, Dyer, and Dalzell, *Changing Fortunes*, 242–243; and Andrew Park and Peter Burrows, "Dell, The Conqueror," *BusinessWeek*, 24 September 2001.

63. Jay Nathan, "CAD/CAM Revolutionizes Engineering and Manufacturing," in *Great Events from History*, 1721–1725.

64. Jennings and Brewster, *The Century*, 493.

65. Robinson, *U.S. Business History: A Chronology*, 439.

66. Robert Sobel, "Japan Becomes the World's Largest Automobile Producer," in *Great Events from History*, 1754.

67. Judith Miller, "Congress Approves a Compromise Plan on Aid to Chrysler," *New York Times*, 21 December 1979.

68. Patricia C. Matthews, "The Loan Guarantee Act Saves Chrysler," in *Great Events from History*, 1764.

69. John Holusha, "Chrysler's Sharp Turnaround," *New York Times*, 15 July 1983.

70. Tina Grant, ed., *International Directory of Company Histories* (Farmington Hills, MI: St. James Press, 2001), 110–115; Nelson D. Schwartz, "Colgate Cleans Up," *Fortune*, 6 April 2001; and H. John Steinbreder, "The Man Brushing Up Colgate's Image," *Fortune*, 11 May 1987.

71. Christopher A. Bartlett and Meg Wozny, "GE's Two-Decade Transformation: Jack Welch's Leadership," Case 399-150 (Boston: Harvard Business School, 2004), 2.

72. Ibid.; Carol Hymowitz and Matt Murray, "Raises and Praises or Out the Door," *Wall Street Journal*, 21 June 1999; Thomas J. Neff and James M. Citrin, *Lessons from the Top: The Search for America's Best Business Leaders* (New York: Doubleday, 1999), 339–346; and Allan Sloan, "Judging GE's Jack Welch," *Newsweek*, 15 November 1999.

73. Bloomberg Business News, "Pepsico's Top Executive Is Set to Resign," *New York Times*, 23 February 1996; Constance L. Hays, "Wayne Calloway Dies at 62," *New York Times*, 10 July 1998; Andrea Rothman, "Can Wayne Calloway Handle the Pepsi Challenge?" *BusinessWeek*, 27 January 1992; and "Was Chief at Pepsico 10 Years"; *New York Times*, 10 July 1998.

74. Charles Gasparino and Jathon Sapsford, "Sanford Weill to Be Sole Citigroup CEO After John Reed's Retirement in April," *Asian Wall Street Journal*, 1 March 2000; Noelle Knox, "John Reed to Retire from Citigroup in April," *Associated Press*, 28 February 2000; and Leslie Scism, Anita Raghavan, and Stephen E. Frank, "Can Titans' Egos Fit Under One Umbrella?" *Asian Wall Street Journal*, 8 April 1998.

75. Neff and Citrin, *Lessons from the Top*, 241–246; Michael Arndt, "How O'Neill Got Alcoa Shining," *BusinessWeek*, 5 February 2001; and "No Corner Office for Paul O'Neill," *Industry Week*, 15 April 1996.

76. Max De Pree, *Leadership Is an Art* (New York: Dell, 1989), 22.

77. Susan Ager, "Lessons on Leadership," *Nation's Business*, March 1986.

78. Max De Pree, "The Leadership Quest: Three Things Necessary," *Business Strategy Review*, spring 1993.

79. Kenneth Labich, "Hot Company, Warm Culture," *Fortune*, 27 February 1989.

80. For information on Max O. De Pree, see Ager, "Lessons on Leadership"; Warren Bennis, "Four Pioneers Reflect on Leadership," *Training & Development*, July 1998; Jeffrey L. Cruikshank and Clark Malcolm, *Herman Miller, Inc.: Buildings and Beliefs* (Washington, DC: American Institute of Architects Press, 1994); Hugh De Pree, *Business As Unusual: The People and Principles at Herman Miller* (Zeeland, MI: Herman Miller, 1986); Max De Pree, *Leadership Is an Art*; "De Pree Receives Business Enterprise Lifetime Achievement Award," *Facilities Design & Management*, April 1997; Herman Miller, "Where We've Been: Company Timeline," Herman Miller Web site, http://www.hermanmiller.com (accessed 16 December 2003); Jerry Jasinowski and Robert Hamrin, *Making It in America: Proven Paths to Success from Fifty Top Companies* (New York: Simon and Schuster, 1995); Labich, "Hot Company, Warm Culture"; Joani Nelson-Horchler, "A Catchall Parachute," *Industry Week*, 9 February 1987; Nelson-Horchler, "The Magic of Herman Miller," *Industry Week*, 18 February 1991; Peter Nulty, "The National Business Hall of Fame," *Fortune*, 23 March 1992; Mary Radigan, "Herman Miller Chairman Elected to Hall of Fame," *Grand Rapids Press*, 5 March 1992; and Tedd Saunders and Loretta McGovern, *The Bottom Line of Green Is Black: Strategies for Creating Profitable and Environmentally Sound Businesses* (San Francisco: Harper San Francisco, 1993).

81. Morris, Robinson, and Kroll, *American Dreams*, 210.

Chapter Ten

1. Edward Wyatt, "Share of Wealth in Stock Holdings Hits 50-Year High," *New York Times*, 11 February 1998.

2. Gretchen Morgenson, "Dow Finishes Day over 10,000 Mark for the First Time," *New York Times*, 30 March 1999.

3. Thomas K. McCraw, *American Business, 1920–2000: How It Worked* (Wheeling, IL: Harlan Davidson, 2000), 36.

4. Wyatt, "Share of Wealth in Stock Holdings."

5. McCraw, *American Business*, 10.

6. Mall of America, "Media: Mall Facts," Mall of America Web site, http://www .mallofamerica.com/about_the_mall/mallfacts.aspx (accessed 6 January 2004).

7. Susan Strasser, "Consumption," in *Encyclopedia of the United States in the Twentieth Century*, ed. Stanley I. Kutler (New York: Charles Scribner's Sons, 1996), 1034.

8. Howard Zinn, *The Twentieth Century* (New York: HarperCollins, 2003), 457.

9. McCraw, *American Business*, 163.

10. Ibid., 164.

11. Rakesh Khurana, *Searching for a Corporate Savior: The Irrational Quest for Charismatic CEOs* (Princeton, NJ: Princeton University Press, 2002).

12. Zinn, *The Twentieth Century*, 457.

13. McCraw, *American Business*, 165.

14. Ibid., 206.

15. Alberto Bin, Richard Hill, and Archer Jones, *Desert Storm: A Forgotten War* (Westport, CT: Praeger, 1999), 237, 241; and Alan Brinkley and Ellen Fitzpatrick, *America in Modern Times—Since 1890* (New York: McGraw-Hill, 1997), 581–582.

16. Ibid., 37.

17. Brinkley and Fitzpatrick, *America in Modern Times*, 576–577.

18. For an analysis of East German wages after the fall of communism (an analysis that could be applicable to all of post-Soviet Eastern Europe), see Edward Bire, Johannes Schwarze, and Gert G. Wagner, "Wage Effects of the Move Toward Free Markets in East Germany," *Industrial and Labor Relations Review* 47 (1994): 390–400. The authors contend that the key factor in the decline of wages for many older workers was a lack of work experience during East Germany's transition to capitalism between 1989 and 1991.

19. For an overview of recently published memoirs about the civil war in Yugoslavia, see Sabrina Ramet, "Views from Inside: Memoirs Concerning the Yugoslav Breakup and War," *Slavic Review* 61 (2002): 558–580.

20. For a description of the military's adjustment to President Clinton's policy of small-scale military intervention tied to peacekeeping efforts, see Robert Worth, "Clinton's Warriors: The Interventionists," *World Policy Journal* 15 (1998): 43–48.

21. Floyd Norris and Christine Bockelmann, *New York Times Century of Business* (New York: McGraw-Hill, 2000), 295.

22. Joseph R. Rudolph Jr., "The European Market Unifies," in *Great Events from History II: Business and Commerce*, ed. Frank N. Magill (Pasadena, CA: Salem Press, 1994), 2053.

23. Patricia Matthews, "The North American Free Trade Agreement Goes into Effect," in *Great Events from History*, 2072.

24. Geri Smith and Cristina Lindbald, "A Tale of What Free Trade Can and Cannot Do," *BusinessWeek*, 22 December 2003.

25. Ibid.

26. U.S. Department of Labor, "Employment Status of the Civilian Non-Institutional Population 16 Years and Over, 1969 to Date" 2003, http://www.bls.gov/rofod/3110.pdf (accessed 22 May 2004).

27. Clifton K. Yearley, "The AFL and CIO Merge," in *Great Events from History*, 1068.

28. Albert R. Karr, "A Special Report on People and Their Jobs in Offices, Fields and Factories," *Wall Street Journal*, 19 March 1992; John Jordon, "IBM Downsizing Has Little Impact on Workforce in Fairfield County," *Fairfield County Business Journal*, 2 November 1992; and John N. Ingham and Lynne B. Feldman, *Contemporary American Business Leaders: A Biographical Dictionary* (Westport, CT: Greenwood Press, 1990), 642.

29. Louis Uchitelle and N. R. Kleinfield, "On the Battlefields of Business, Millions of Casualties," *New York Times*, 3 March 1999; and Alan Murray and David Wessel, "Swept Away: Torrent of Job Cuts Shows Human Toll of Recession Goes On," *Wall Street Journal*, 12 December 1991.

30. Uchitelle and Kleinfield, "On the Battlefields of Business."

31. McCraw, *American Business*, 166.

32. Michael J. Mandel, "Restating the '90's," *BusinessWeek*, 1 April 2002.

33. Nitin Nohria, Davis Dyer, and Frederick Dalzell, *Changing Fortunes: Remaking the Industrial Corporation* (New York: John Wiley & Sons, 2002), 37.

34. Shoshana Zuboff, "Work," in *Encyclopedia of the United States in the Twentieth Century*, ed. Stanley I. Kutler (New York: Charles Scribner's Sons, 1996), 1124.

35. Nohria, Dyer, and Dalzell, *Changing Fortunes*, 59.

36. McCraw, *American Business*, 203.

37. Matt Loney, "Web Creator Berners-Lee Knighted," CNET News.com, http://adnet.com.com/2100-1104-5134229.html, 31 December 2003 (accessed 8 January 2004).

38. Nohria, Dyer, and Dalzell, *Changing Fortunes*, 238–239.

39. John Markoff, "If the Medium Is the Message, the Message Is the Web," *New York Times*, 20 November 1995.

40. Nohria, Dyer, and Dalzell, *Changing Fortunes*, 239.

41. Peter Jennings and Todd Brewster, *The Century* (New York: Doubleday, 1998), 555.

42. McCraw, *American Business*, 204.

43. Ibid.

44. J. Madeleine Nash, "The Age of Cloning," *Time*, 20 March 1997.

45. U.S. Department of Labor, "Employment Status of the Civilian Non-Institutional Population 16 Years and Over, 1969 to Date," 2002, http://uscis.gov/graphics/shared/aboutus/statistics/IMM02yrbk/IMM2002list.htm (accessed 2 May 2004).

46. Brinkley and Fitzpatrick, *America in Modern Times*, 582–583.

47. Peter B. Levy, *Encyclopedia of the Clinton Presidency* (Westport, CT: Greenwood Press, 2002), 128–129. For a historical perspective on the act of 1993, see Steven K. Wisensale, "The White House and Congress on Child Care and Family Leave Policy: From Carter to Clinton," *Policy Studies Journal* 25 (1997): 75–86.

48. Levy, *Encyclopedia of the Clinton Presidency*, 32–33. For an analysis of the Brady Bill, placed in the context of a quarter century of federal gun control efforts, see Carol J.

DeFrances and Steven K. Smith, "Federal-State Relations in Gun Control: The 1993 Brady Handgun Violence Prevention Act," *Publius* 24 (1994): 69–82.

49. Elizabeth Drew, *On the Edge: The Clinton Presidency* (New York: Simon and Schuster, 1994), 190; and National Center for Health Statistics, *Health: United States, 2003* (Washington, DC, 2003), 309–311, http://www.cdc.gov/nchs/data/hus/hus03.pdf (accessed 12 November 2004). This report also shows that between 1980 and 1990, per-capita spending on health care rose from $931 to $2,398.

50. Levy, *Encyclopedia of the Clinton Presidency*, 175–177. For a detailed account of President Clinton's efforts to pass a universal health-care program, see Jacob S. Hacker, *The Road to Nowhere: The Genesis of President Clinton's Plan for Health Security*, Princeton Studies in American Politics: Historical, International, and Comparative Perspectives (Princeton, NJ: Princeton University Press, 1997).

51. Levy, *Encyclopedia of the Clinton Presidency*, 78.

52. Douglas J. Besharov and Peter Germanis, "Welfare Reform: Four Years Later," *Public Interest* 140 (2000): 17–35; and National Alliance to End Homelessness, "Changes in Laws Relating to Immigration: Impact on Homeless Assistance Providers," http://www.endhomelessness.org/pub/immigration/imig2.htm (accessed 12 May 2004).

53. M. Stephen Weatherford and Lorraine McDonnell, "Clinton and the Economy: The Paradox of Policy Success and Political Mishap," *Political Science Quarterly* 111 (1996): 403.

54. Norris and Bockelman, *New York Times Century of Business*, 309.

55. Steve Lohr, "Gates, on Capitol Hill, Presents Case for an Unfettered Microsoft," *New York Times*, 4 March 1998.

56. For an informative discussion on the American public's perception of government, see Joseph P. Nye Jr., Philip D. Zelikow, and David C. King, eds., *Why People Don't Trust Government* (Cambridge, MA: Harvard University Press, 1997).

57. For a comparison between Thomas's views on hot-button racial issues and the views of the black community at large in 1992, see Lee Sigelman and James S. Todd, "Clarence Thomas, Black Pluralism, and Civil Rights Policy," *Political Science Quarterly* 107 (1992): 231–248.

58. For a detailed chronology of the events leading to Thomas's confirmation by the U.S. Senate, see "The Clarence Thomas Confirmation," *Black Scholar*, 22 (1992): 1–3.

59. Peter Jennings and Todd Brewster, *The Century* (New York: Doubleday, 1998), 537.

60. Ibid., 539.

61. Brinkley and Fitzpatrick, *America in Modern Times*, 598.

62. Levy, *Encyclopedia of the Clinton Presidency*, 32–33.

63. One scholar argues that the FBI unwittingly conformed to "David Koresh's millenarian worldview." See Michael Barkun, "Millenarian Groups and Law Enforcement Agencies: The Lessons of Waco," *Terrorism and Political Violence* 6 (1994): 75–95.

64. Robert L. Snow, *The Militia Threat: Terrorists Among Us* (New York: Plenum Trade, 1999), 172, passim.

65. Ibid., 93–99.

66. U.S. Citizenship and Immigration Services, "U.S. Immigration Statistics," table 2, "Immigration by Region and Selected Country of Last Residence: Fiscal Years 1820–2000,"

available at http://uscis.gov/graphics/shared/aboutus/statistics/IMMo2yrbk/IMM2002
list.htm (accessed 29 May 2004).

67. U.S. Bureau of the Census, "USA Quick Facts," http://quickfacts.census.gov/
qfd/states/00000.html (accessed 12 January 2004).

68. Ibid.

69. Ibid.

70. Frank Hobbs and Nicole Stoops, "Demographic Trends in the Twentieth Century" (Washington, DC: U.S. Bureau of the Census, 2002), http://www.census.gov/
prod/2002pubs/censr-4.pdf (accessed 24 July 2004).

71. William H. Miller, "Gillette's Secret to Sharpness," *Industry Week*, 3 January 1994.

72. Gordon C. McKibben, *Cutting Edge: Gillette's Journey to Global Leadership* (Boston:
Harvard Business School Press, 1998), 381.

73. Alfred M. Zeien, *The Gillette Company* (New York: Newcomen Society of the
United States, 1999), 14.

74. McKibben, *Cutting Edge*, 252.

75. Ibid., 262.

76. Charles M. Farkas, *Maximum Leadership: The World's Leading CEOs Share Their Five
Strategies for Success* (New York: H. Holt, 1996), 68.

77. Jim Huguet, *Great Companies, Great Returns* (New York: Broadway Books, 1999),
174.

78. Zeien, *The Gillette Company*, 18.

79. Ibid.

80. Rita Koselka, "It's My Favorite Statistic," *Forbes*, 12 September 1994.

81. For information on Alfred M. Zeien, see "Business: Taking It on the Chin," *Economist*, 18 April 1998; J. P. Donlon, "An Iconoclast in a Cutthroat World," *Chief Executive*,
March 1996; Farkas, *Maximum Leadership*; Huguet, *Great Companies, Great Returns*; Laura
Johannes and William M. Bulkeley, "Gillette's Zeien Is Retiring from Helm After Eight
Years; Hawley Is Successor," *Wall Street Journal*, 19 February 1999; Koselka, "It's My Favorite Statistic"; McKibben, *Cutting Edge*, 252; William H. Miller, "Gillette's Secret to
Sharpness," *Industry Week*, 3 January 1994; Thomas J. Neff and James M. Citrin, *Lessons
from the Top* (New York: Doubleday, 1999), 347–352; Michel Robert, *Product Innovation
Strategy Pure and Simple* (New York: McGraw-Hill, 1995); William C. Symonds, "Gillette's
Edge," *BusinessWeek*, 19 January 1998; Steven Syre and Charles Stein, "Gillette's Former
Chief Zeien Did No Favor for His Successor," *Boston Globe*, 25 June 1999; Sharon Walsh,
"The Razor's Edge, Gillette's Alfred Zeien, Retires," *Washington Post*, 19 February 1999;
and Zeien, *The Gillette Company*.

82. Michael J. Mandel, "Restating the '90's," *BusinessWeek*, 1 April 2002.

83. Peter Burrows, "Cisco's Comeback," *BusinessWeek*, 24 November 2003.

84. "Cisco Systems, Incorporated Profile," available from Hoover's Online Services,
http://www.hoovers.com (accessed 14 January 2004); Andy Reinhardt, "Mr. Internet:
Cisco Systems CEO John Chambers Has a Vision of a New World Order with Cisco As
Its No. 1 Supplier," *BusinessWeek*, 13 September 1999; and Andy Serwer, "There's Something About Cisco," *Fortune*, 15 May 2000.

85. Steven Burke, "Michael Ruettgers: Storage High Roller," *CRN*, 18 November
2002; "EMC Corporation Profile," available from Hoover's Online Services, http://

www.hoovers.com (accessed 15 January 2004); Paul C. Judge, "High Techstar: The Insider Story of How Mike Ruettgers Turned EMC Into a Highflier," *Business Week*, 15 March 1999; and Chin Wong, "Q&A: Michael Ruettgers, EMC Chairman: 'Keep Watching So You Won't Be Surprised,'" *Computerworld*, 28 May 2001.

86. Robert Slater, *Saving Big Blue: Leadership Lessons and Turnaround Tactics* (New York: McGraw Hill, 1999), 5.

87. Doug Garr, *IBM Redux: Lou Gerstner and the Business Turnaround of the Decade* (New York: HarperCollins, 1999), 85.

88. Ibid., 89.

89. Ibid., 94.

90. Louis V. Gerstner Jr., *Who Says Elephants Can't Dance?* (New York: HarperCollins, 2002), 3.

91. Slater, *Saving Big Blue*, 48.

92. Garr, *IBM Redux*, 22.

93. Robert D. Austin and Richard L. Nolan, "IBM Corporation Turnaround," Case 600-098 (Boston: Harvard Business School, 2000), 4.

94. Ibid., 5.

95. Ibid., 8.

96. Gerstner, *Who Says Elephants Can't Dance?* 142.

97. Riva Richmond and Marcelo Prince, "Gerstner Retirement Ends Career That Transformed Big Blue," *Dow Jones News Service*, 29 January 2002.

98. For information on Louis V. Gerstner Jr., see Austin and Nolan, "IBM Corporation Turnaround"; James W. Cortada and Thomas S. Hargraves, *Into the Networked Age: How IBM and Other Firms Are Getting There Now* (New York: Oxford University Press, 1999); Frank Dzubeck, "Assessing the Gerstner Era," *Network World*, 11 February 2002; Garr, *IBM Redux*; Gerstner, *Who Says Elephants Can't Dance?*; David Kirkpatrick, "The Future of IBM," *Fortune*, 18 February 2002; Jeffrey A. Krames, *What the Best CEOs Know* (New York: McGraw-Hill, 2003); Steve Lohr, "IBM's New Leader," *New York Times*, 27 March 1993; "Louis V. Gerstner Jr.: IBM," *Business Week*, 14 January 2002; Neff and Citrin, *Lessons from the Top*, 137–141; Slater, *Saving Big Blue*; and Richmond and Prince, "Gerstner Retirement."

99. "Continental Airlines, Incorporated Profile," available from Hoover's Online Services, http://www.hoovers.com (accessed 19 January 2004).

100. Andrew Clark, "Interview: Sex, Scotch and Speed—Gordon Bethune, Chairman and Chief Executive, Continental Airlines," *Guardian* (London), 21 September 2002; Lisa Fingeret and Jeff Pruzan, "Concorde Suit Could Cloud Bethune's Clear Skies," *Financial Times*, 27 September 2000; Scott McCartney, "Flight of Fancy: Continental Airlines Keeps Little Things, and It Pays Off Big," *Wall Street Journal*, 4 February 2002; and Neff and Citrin, *Lessons from the Top*, 55–60.

101. Linda A. Johnson, "Retired CEO Returns to Take Reins at Honeywell," *Buffalo News*, 6 July 2001.

102. Ibid.; Neff and Citrin, *Lessons from the Top*, 61–66; and Joseph R. Perone, "AlliedSignal's Retiring CEO Caps His Career with a Coup," *Knight-Ridder Tribune Business News*, 13 June 1999.

103. Alan Greenspan, "Testimony of Chairman Alan Greenspan," update on the economic condition of the United States before the Joint Economic Committee of the U.S. Congress, 10 June 1998, Washington, DC, http://www.federalreserve.gov/boarddocs/testimony/1998/19980610.htm (accessed 1 July 2004).

104. Ibid.

Epilogue

1. Warren G. Bennis and Robert J. Thomas, *Geeks & Geezers: How Era, Values, and Defining Moments Shape Leaders* (Boston: Harvard Business School Publishing, 2002), 19.

2. Ibid.

3. Alan Greenspan, "Testimony of Chairman Alan Greenspan," update on the economic condition of the United States before the Joint Economic Committee of the U.S. Congress, 10 June 1998, Washington, DC, http://www.federalreserve.gov/boarddocs/testimony/1998/19980610.htm (accessed 1 July 2004).

4. John A. Byrne, "Restoring Trust in Corporate America," *BusinessWeek*, 24 June 2002.

Appendix

1. Richard S. Tedlow, Courtney Purrington, and Kim Eric Bettcher, "The American CEO in the Twentieth Century: Demography and Career Path," working paper 03-097, Harvard Business School, Boston, 2003, 7–10.

2. John J. Gabarro, *The Dynamics of Taking Charge* (Boston: Harvard Business School Press, 1987).

3. Tedlow, Purrington, and Bettcher, "American CEO in the Twentieth Century."

Merck, 264, 268

mergers and acquisitions. *See also* conglomerates

AFL-CIO, 190

antitrust interventions, 212

Citicorp/Travelers, 327

Coast Metals, 239

Colgate/Mennen, 306–307

early industry consolidations, 17, 19

Gulf and Western auto parts, 182

Herman Miller's, 312

hostile takeovers, 335

IBM/Lotus Development Corporation, 345

junk bonds for leveraged buyouts, 284

Lewis's, 287

Mason Fruit Jar & Bottle Company, 30

Phillips Petroleum/Conoco, 41

Procter & Gamble's, 197–198

radiator manufacturers, 20

Rust Belt, 301

Singleton's, 216, 218

Welch's, 307

WorldCom/MCI, 327

Merrill, Charles, 58

MESBICS (Minority Enterprise Small Business Investment Companies), 286

methodology for choosing business executives, 365–372

Mexico, 44–45, 161

Michigan Radiator and Iron Company, 21

Microsoft, 327–328

microwave ovens, 230

Middle East peace talks, 252

migrant farm workers, 115–116. *See also* immigration

military

bases on U.S. territories, 15

business reassignment to military production, 148–154

first peacetime conscription, 146

integration of, 164

World War I, 45–49

military production, 189

Milken, Michael, 284, 288–289, 292

milk industry, 19

millionaires, 14, 297

Mills, C. Wright, *White Collar Society*, 189

minimum wage, 87, 113. *See also* wages

Missouri-Kansas-Texas Railroad, 133

Mockler, Colman, 335–336

monopolies, 80–81, 132, 150, 327

moon race, 228–230

Moore, Gordon, 188, 270

Moral Majority, 296

Morgan, J. P., 8, 10, 17, 21–22, 129

Morgan, Stanley & Company, 129–132

Morgens, Howard J., 194–198, 352

Folgers, 197–198

Oxydol, 195

Procter & Gamble, 194–198

Mosaic Communications, 323–324

Motown Records, 256

movies, 90–91, 118

muckrakers, 6–7

Nader, Ralph, *Unsafe at Any Speed*, 225

NAFTA (North American Free Trade Agreement), 320–321

Nanus, Burt, *Leaders: The Strategies for Taking Charge* (Bennis and Burt), xxv

NASA (National Aeronautics and Space Agency [later Administration]), 189, 236, 304

National Association for the Advancement of Colored People (NAACP), 158

National Bank-Americard Incorporated (NBI), 275–278

National Broadcasting Company (NBC), 89, 149, 307

National Center for Computing Applications (University of Illinois), 323

National Commission on Public Safety, 252

National Endowment for the Arts, 224

National Housing Act of 1949, 164

National Industrial Recovery Act (NIRA), 111

National Labor Relations Act (Wagner Act), 112–113, 159

Tony Mayo is a Lecturer in the Organizational Behavior Unit and is the Director of the Leadership Initiative at Harvard Business School. The Leadership Initiative is an inter-disciplinary center that strives to serve as a catalyst for cutting-edge leadership research and course development (see http://www.hbs.edu/leadership).

As Director of the Leadership Initiative, Tony oversees several comprehensive research projects on emerging, global, and legacy leadership and manages a number of executive education programs on leadership development. He was a co-creator of Harvard Business School's High Potentials Leadership and Leadership Best Practices programs and has been a principal contributor to the design of a number of custom leadership development programs.

Prior to his current role, Tony pursued a career in database marketing where he held senior general management positions at the advertising agency, Hill Holliday; the database management firm, Epsilon; and the full-service direct marketing company, DIMAC Marketing Corporation. Previously, Tony served as the Director of MBA Program Administration at Harvard Business School.

Tony has served as an advisory board member for Target Software and SmartGiving. He completed his MBA at Harvard Business School and received his BA, *summa cum laude*, from Boston College. He lives in Needham, Massachusetts, with his wife Denise and three children, Hannah, Alex, and Jacob.

Nitin Nohria is the Richard P. Chapman Professor of Business Administration and Director of Research at the Harvard Business School. His research centers on leadership and organizational change.

His most recent previous book, *What Really Works: The 4+2 Formula for Sustained Business Success*, coauthored with William Joyce and Bruce Roberson, is the culmination of a systematic and large-scale study of management practices that create business winners. Professor Nohria has written or edited several other critically acclaimed books including, *Changing Fortunes: Remaking the Industrial Corporation*, *Driven*, *The Arc of Ambition*, *Master Passions*, *Breaking the Code of Change*, *Beyond the Hype*, *Building the Information Age Organization*, *Fast Forward*, and *The Differentiated Network*, which won the 1998 George R. Terry Book Award given annually by the Academy of Management for the best book. He is also the author of more than 50 articles and cases that have appeared in journals such as *Harvard Business Review*, *Sloan Management Review*, and *Strategic Management Journal*.

Professor Nohria lectures to corporate audiences around the globe and serves on the advisory boards of several small and large firms. He has been interviewed by ABC, CNN, and NPR, and cited frequently in *BusinessWeek*, *The Economist*, *Financial Times*, *Fortune*, *New York Times*, and *The Wall Street Journal*.

In addition to teaching courses in Harvard's MBA and Executive Education programs, Professor Nohria is an adviser to PhD students in the school's Organizational Behavior program. He has also been a visiting faculty member of the London Business School.

Prior to joining the Harvard Business School faculty in July 1988, Professor Nohria received his PhD in Management from the Sloan School of Management, Massachusetts Institute of Technology, and a BTech in Chemical Engineering from the Indian Institute of Technology, Bombay.